THE MYSTICAL ORIGINS OF HASIDISM

THE LITTMAN LIBRARY OF
JEWISH CIVILIZATION

The Littman Library of Jewish Civilization is a registered UK charity
Registered charity no. 1000784

THE
MYSTICAL
ORIGINS OF
HASIDISM

◆

RACHEL ELIOR

The Littman Library of Jewish Civilization
in association with Liverpool University Press

The Littman Library of Jewish Civilization
in association with Liverpool University Press
4 Cambridge Street, Liverpool L69 7ZU, UK

www.liverpooluniversitypress.co.uk/littman

Managing Editor: Connie Webber

Distributed in North America by
Oxford University Press Inc., 198 Madison Avenue,
New York, NY 10016, USA

First published in Hebrew 1999 as Ḥeirut al haluḥot
First published in English translation 2006
English edition first published in paperback 2008

Catalogue records for this book are available from the
British Library and the Library of Congress

ISBN 978-1-904113-04-1

Publishing co-ordinator: Janet Moth
Original translation: Shalom Carmy
Copy-editing: Connie Webber
Proof-reading: Philippa Claiden
Index: Margot Levy and Connie Webber
Design: Pete Russell, Faringdon, Oxon.
Typeset by Hope Services (Abingdon) Ltd

Printed in Great Britain by
CPI Group (UK) Ltd, Croydon, CR0 4YY

This book is dedicated to the memory of
ARIELLA DIM-GOLDBERG
RIVKA SCHATZ-UFFENHEIMER
SARI FOIERSTEIN
and
ORNA ZOHAR-ROTHBLIT

———

These truly exceptional women, my intellectual and spiritual partners, illuminated and enhanced my teaching and research—indeed, my whole life. Free in spirit, their souls soared to new heights, radiating light all around them. But the bodies to which their souls were shackled failed them, and they died far too young.

.

Preface

THE WORDS 'hasid' and 'hasidism' have become so familiar to people interested in understanding the Jewish world that their meaning is rarely discussed. Little thought is given to understanding exactly what hasidism is, and where and when it has flourished. This book is devoted to explaining the origins of the hasidic movement and its spiritual and social consequences.

What are the distinguishing features of hasidism? What innovations does it embody? How did its founders see it? Why did it arouse opposition? What is the essential nature of hasidic thought? What is its spiritual essence? What does its literature consist of? What typifies its leadership? What is the secret of its persistence through the centuries? How have scholars explained its origins? Is hasidism mysticism, or a response to changing social circumstances? What is its connection to kabbalah? To Shabateanism? To messianism? What is its relationship to the traditional structures of authority in the Jewish world? This book is concerned with all these questions.

Hasidism is best studied through its highly articulated literature, and it is not possible in a single book to discuss the hundreds of volumes that constitute this hasidic library in any depth. For this reason I focus on the fundamental positions and the factors of primary importance—the substantial issues that recur in the literature of the movement, including how hasidim have seen themselves over the centuries, how they have constructed a new spiritual and social ideal, and how that ideal has stood the test of reality. The goal is to present the main characteristics of the hasidic movement and to examine the social implications of its mystical ideas.

I hope that this book will encourage those who wish to gain greater knowledge of the subject to continue their study of the hasidic literature and the various scholarly theories concerning it.

*

The Hebrew word *ḥasid* has three meanings. It can mean a person who, in the name of love of God and imitating his ways, is punctilious in observing religious commandments, in the sense of the verse 'God is righteous in all his ways and *ḥasid* in all his deeds' (Psalm 145: 17). It can also mean one who acts with special kindness (*ḥasid*) towards others. Finally, it can mean one who follows the teaching and leadership of another person, both literally and figuratively.

Let me immediately expand on these definitions. The first meaning corresponds to the English words 'piety' or 'pietism'. It refers to an attachment to God's ways impelled by ascetic rigour and a sense of conscious withdrawal from this world. This spiritual quest for attachment to God and proximity to the higher world implies the rejection of accepted limits and greater freedom in determining the relationship between body and spirit. The second meaning is connected to compassion and charity, to loving kindness that derives from a sense of all-encompassing religiously inspired social responsibility. The third meaning, 'to be a *ḥasid* of ', corresponds to the English terms 'follower' or 'disciple'. In the hasidic movement, all these three meanings converge. In its origin the movement derives from the first meaning, that of mystical pietism and devotion to God. Its growth was connected to the second meaning—responsibility and loving kindness. Its spread was crucially connected to the third meaning—the establishment of hasidic congregations.

The hasidic phenomenon is not easily characterized. It encompasses mystical arousal and spiritual revival; a historical turning-point and a polemical background; an original spiritual world, new conceptual vocabulary, and social phenomena. It implies both continuity with kabbalistic tradition and ideological innovation. It owes its origins to a variety of creative personalities—mystically inspired charismatic leaders and socially innovative and productive religious thinkers who from the eighteenth century on have produced a rich and multi-faceted literature that to this day continues to attract followers to the hasidic way of life. The complexity of their work precludes simple linear description, so in the chapters that follow certain elements may recur as particular details are reconsidered in different contexts.

The main discussion is divided into thirteen chapters, followed by a succinct summary. The book concludes with a glossary of hasidic concepts, a list of the hasidic texts on which the discussion is based, and a comprehensive bibliography of scholarly works on kabbalah and hasidism.

Contents

Publisher's Note on the Translation and Transliteration

THE Hebrew-language version of this book originated as a series of lectures broadcast by Israel's University of the Air (a project of the Israeli army radio station Galei Tsahal in co-operation with the army's Education Division) and published by Israel's Ministry of Defence. The present volume derives from a skilful translation of that text by Shalom Carmy of Yeshiva University, New York, but has been heavily edited and reworked in collaboration with the author to meet the needs of an English-speaking readership less familiar with the basic concepts under discussion.

In reworking the text, every effort has been made to make the mystical language and concepts that are central to hasidic thought as accessible as possible to the non-specialist. The same term may therefore be translated in different ways in different contexts so as to capture the breadth and multivocality of the hasidic vocabulary. A glossary has been provided to act as an aide-memoire.

The system adopted for transliteration of Hebrew reflects the type of book it is, in terms of its content, purpose, and readership. It therefore adopts a broad approach to transcription, rather than the narrower approaches found in the Encyclopaedia Judaica or other systems developed for text-based or linguistic studies. The aim has been to reflect the pronunciation prescribed for modern Hebrew, rather than the spelling or Hebrew word structure, and to do so using conventions that are generally familiar to the English-speaking Jewish reader.

In accordance with this approach, no attempt is made to indicate the distinctions between *alef* and *ayin*, *tet* and *taf*, *kaf* and *kuf*, *sin* and *samekh*, since these are not relevant to pronunciation; likewise, the *dagesh* is not indicated except where it affects pronunciation. Following the principle of using conventions familiar to the majority of readers, however, transcriptions that are so well established as to have virtually entered the English language have been retained in that form where they appear in the English text, even though the strict transcription rules have been applied in transliterating the Hebrew form; thus, for example, where the English has 'Maggid' and 'Rabbi', the corresponding transliterated forms are *magid* and *rabi*. Likewise, the distinction between *ḥet* and *khaf* has been retained, using *ḥ* for the former and *kh* for the latter; the associated forms are generally familiar to readers, even if the distinction is not actually borne out in pronunciation, and for the same reason the final *heh* is indicated too. As in Hebrew, no capital letters are used, except that an initial capital has been retained in transliterating titles of published works (for example, *Shulḥan arukh*).

Since no distinction is made between *alef* and *ayin*, they are indicated by an apostrophe only in intervocalic positions where a failure to do so could lead an English-speaking reader to pronounce the vowel-cluster as a diphthong—as, for example, in *ha'ir*—or otherwise mispronounce the word.

The *sheva na* is indicated by an *e—levush, kelipah*—except, again, when established conventions in Anglicized usage dictate otherwise (e.g. B'nai Brith).

The *yod* is represented by *i* when it occurs as a vowel (*bereshit*), by *y* when it occurs as a consonant (*yesodot*), and by *yi* when it occurs as both (*yisra'el*).

Names have generally been left in their familiar forms, even when this is inconsistent with the overall system.

ONE

The Origins of Hasidism

L ET US BEGIN by considering a remarkable historical phenomenon. Hasidism originated in eastern Europe in the second third of the eighteenth century, crystallized and flourished there from the turn of the eighteenth century to the end of the nineteenth, and continues to flourish to the present day, despite the tremendous challenges associated with the confrontation with modernity in the twentieth century and the murder of a large part of the hasidic world in the Holocaust. There are significant hasidic communities today in Europe, Israel, North America, South America, and Australia. No other movement in modern Jewish history has managed to sustain itself over three centuries in such a variety of historical and linguistic locales and contexts, and in such different social, cultural, and existential circumstances. One is bound to ask why this should be so. But to answer this question one has to start from the beginning.

Hasidism originated in south-east Poland, in districts which the eighteenth century knew as Volhynia and Podolia and which were later incorporated into Galicia, Ukraine, and Poland. It started around the charismatic figure of Israel Ba'al Shem Tov (1698–1760),[1] and within several decades had spread throughout eastern Europe—from White Russia, Poland, and Lithuania to Moravia, Hungary, and Romania; it never had a single geographical centre or exclusive focus of leadership. In the earliest stages, starting around the middle of the eighteenth century, hasidic groups—congregations focusing on a charismatic leader—were established by such followers of Israel Ba'al Shem Tov as Pinhas of Korets, Nahman of Horodenka, Nahman of Kosov, Mikhal of Zloczow, Jacob Joseph of Polonnoye, Menahem of Bar, Dov Baer of Mezhirech, and others, all of whom derived their status from their charismatic

---

[1] Charisma is 'the quality of an individual's personality by virtue of which he is separated from ordinary mortals and is treated as if he were endowed with supernatural, superhuman qualities, or at least with specific extraordinary qualities': see Weber, *Theory of Social and Economic Organization*, 358–9 and *On Charisma*, 12. On Israel Ba'al Shem Tov see Dubnow, 'The Beginnings', and Ch. 5 nn. 1–3 below.

authority and mystical experiences. These small groups were connected to one another by an awareness of shared religious renewal. This fragmented network steadily grew, so that by the end of the eighteenth century we find hasidim in White Russia led by Shneur Zalman of Lyady, hasidim in Poland led by Elimelekh of Lyzhansk and Jacob Isaac of Lublin, and hasidim in Moravia led by Shmuel Shmelke Horowitz of Nikolsburg. The leaders of hasidism in Hungary, Romania, and the Ukraine included Levi Isaac of Berdichev, Barukh of Medzibozh, Hayim Haikl of Amdur, Hayim of Czernowitz, and Nahman of Bratslav. Each of these hasidic centres developed its unique character, helping to make hasidism a broad movement. By the middle of the nineteenth century, following a series of conflicts and disputes, the number of hasidic centres had grown and further new leaders had emerged: Simhah Bunem of Przysucha, Menahem Mendel of Kotsk, Mordecai Joseph Leiner of Izbica, Isaac Meir Alter of Ger, Tsevi Hirsch of Zhidachov, Israel of Ruzhin, Abraham of Sadgora, Isaac Eizik of Komarno, and Tsadok Hakohen of Lublin. This list is not exhaustive.

Such broad diffusion precluded uniformity. The various hasidic communities differed in their way of life, social identity, and spiritual orientation, but they were bound together by a shared consciousness of spiritual renewal, mystical insight, and charismatic leadership. Many hasidic groups interacted with each other, although not a few were engaged in mutual polemic. They also produced an impressively distinctive body of literature.

The search for common denominators unifying the various hasidic groups yields four factors:

1. *A relationship to the Ba'al Shem Tov*. Direct and indirect identification with the spiritual legacy of Israel Ba'al Shem Tov, who is universally regarded as the founder of hasidism, and with his disciples and their disciples as bearers, interpreters, and disseminators of his teaching.

2. *Tsadik and community*. The establishment of a community whose members accept the authority of a charismatic leader or 'tsadik' (literally, a 'righteous person'), whether they are geographically close to him or at some remove (even in another city or country). The tsadik links the terrestrial world of his followers with the supernal worlds, worlds with which he enjoys unmediated contact. The link between the tsadik and his followers is intimate, based on charismatic leadership of the community in a spirit of holiness. All members of the community are equal in their relationship to the tsadik, which fosters a strong sense of brotherhood. This mystical–charismatic model of leadership gave those upon whom it was bestowed unlimited authority, but also unlimited responsibility with regard to their community of followers. This intricate

structure, which represented a new development in the Jewish world, would continue to characterize the hasidic movement (subsequent modifications in the leadership model notwithstanding) and be the key determinant of its religious and social significance.

3. *Being and nothingness.* Hasidism understands the divine reality as the coincidence or unity of opposites. Tangible reality is seen as having meaning only in so far as it derives from a divine source; similarly, the hidden world of the Infinite, the divine Nothingness, can only be perceived in the reality of mundane being. This world-view draws upon a kabbalistic dialectic that connects the manifest and the hidden, understanding 'reality' in a way that goes far beyond its simple meaning.

4. *The hasidic congregation.* The symbolic and concrete realities of the tsadik's leadership and of following the kabbalistic tradition were such as to generate a totally new social structure and a way of life that derived from a mystical conception of man's relationship to God—a relationship based on love to the point of *devekut*, meaning total devotion to God to the extent of renouncing the realities of the material world and transcending one's own self in order to achieve true communion with the divine. This was a spiritual objective, but it affected social realities because the congregation's relationship with God was mediated by the tsadik. Because the tsadik was the sole channel of divine mercy and sustenance for his followers, they felt a sense of fraternity in their dependence upon him; the tsadik, for his part, depended on the recognition and support of his followers. This system of mutual interdependence between the tsadik and his hasidim had far-reaching implications and served to distinguish the hasidic community from the broader Jewish community.

In the chapters that follow I devote attention to each of these aspects and to the connections between them. I shall begin, however, by describing the circumstances in which hasidism was created and assessing the innovations it introduced.

*

The hasidic movement that grew up in eastern Europe—originally in Podolia, Volhynia, and eastern Galicia—is viewed as a turning-point in Jewish social history because it posed a significant challenge to the traditional frameworks and religious outlook of the Jewish world. By the last decades of the eighteenth century, the small circles of hasidim which had developed around the Ba'al Shem Tov in the 1740s and 1750s had become a substantial force; by the early nineteenth century they had become a mass movement. Hasidic social and religious ideals had been embraced by a significant number of the Jews of Ukraine, Galicia, Poland, Russia, Hungary, and Romania, and hasidic writings had become a point of reference for Jewish study by the intellectual elite.

The first historians to seek an explanation for this unprecedented expansion tied the rise of hasidism to economic and social conditions and crises. Simon Dubnow and Ben-Zion Dinur, both eminent historians of Jewish eastern Europe, believed that hasidism had emerged in response to the severe crisis experienced by Polish Jewry in the first half of the eighteenth century; however, they differed in their interpretation both of the crisis and of the nature of the response.

Dubnow saw the background for the rise of hasidism as the social and economic distress of Polish Jews following the Chmielnecki uprisings of Ukrainians against the Poles in 1648–9 and the associated pogroms perpetrated against the Jews. The decline in Polish power following the uprisings led to a decline in the institutions of Jewish self-government that the Poles had supported. Despair among the Jews at these events was compounded in the 1670s by the failure of the Shabatean messianic movement, leading to spiritual decline and to alienation from the traditional values upon which communal relationships depended. The inability of the rabbis to provide proper leadership at a time of such social and political instability led to a general perception among the uneducated masses that religion had failed them. Hasidism, in this view, was a response to a spiritual vacuum; in Dubnow's words, a response to 'the deep needs of the despondent soul', which provided answers in the wake of 'the terrible despair that came after the defeat of the messianic movement'. For Dubnow, the 'great and wondrous success' of hasidism was the way in which it responded to the individual's need for contact with the divine, thanks to the innovations of its founder, Israel Ba'al Shem Tov.[2]

Dinur likewise saw the rise of hasidism in the context of 'two severe crises in Judaism: the failure of the Shabatean movement and the attenuation of Jewish self-government in Poland'.[3] In his view, the increasing domination of communal institutions by despotic figures led to the emergence of an alternative leadership of preachers proclaiming a new social message; in other words, hasidism was a response to social oppression and economic exploitation by a corrupt leadership. But he also recognized a fundamental messianism in the ideology of the hasidic movement, a reaction to the spiritual crisis stemming from the failure of Shabateanism and its promise of imminent redemption. In sum, he

---

[2] Dubnow, *History of Hasidism* (Heb.), 35, 36.
[3] Dinur, 'The Origins of Hasidism', 86.

characterized the basis of hasidic ideology as 'the transfer of rule and decisive influence in the communities to a leadership possessing prophetic authority'.[4]

These explanations, however, do not adequately account for the uniqueness of the hasidic phenomenon. The next generation of scholars—historians such as Jacob Katz, Israel Heilperin, and Yeshayahu Shahar—challenged the theories of Dubnow and Dinur on the grounds that hasidic sources do not in fact testify to an awareness of social tension or to distinctively hasidic initiatives for social reform. Moreover, the economic and social conditions in which hasidism emerged were not essentially different from those experienced by Jews elsewhere, while hasidism constituted an unprecedented development. Likewise, they pointed out that the hypothesis of spiritual crisis cannot account for the spread of hasidism in time and space. If hasidism emerged only in response to localized economic distress and specific social and religious circumstances, why has it continued to exist long after these conditions changed? The survival of hasidism in widely differing historical and social settings, in different places and periods, would seem to require a distinction to be drawn between the causes of its emergence and growth and the factors encouraging its wider dissemination.[5]

In recent years, scholars such as Gershon Hundert and Moshe Rosman have shed new light on the economic and social context in which hasidism emerged. In contrast to the earlier unambiguous depictions of distress, their work has shown that Polish Jewry in the middle of the eighteenth century enjoyed relative prosperity and security. But even if we accept that contemporary economic factors were of relatively little importance in the rise of hasidism, there is little doubt that the earlier social and religious crises had left their mark on Jewish society, and that hasidism may have been a response to this. However, these background crises are not sufficient to explain its distinctive characteristics.[6]

The circumstances in which hasidism emerged—the tragic confrontation with Shabateanism and its after-effects, and the decline of the Jewish

---

[4] Ibid. 159.

[5] For different interpretations of early hasidism see Dubnow, *History of Hasidism* (Heb.), 8–38; Dinur, 'The Origins of Hasidism'; Ettinger, 'The Hasidic Movement'; Katz, *Tradition and Crisis*, 225–44; and Mahler, *Hasidism and the Jewish Enlightenment*. For a critique of the nexus between economic and social distress and the rise of hasidism see Katz, *Tradition and Crisis*; Shahar, *Criticism of Society and Leadership* (Heb.), 62–79; and Etkes, 'Hasidism as a Movement'.

[6] For studies of Polish Jewry that take issue with the accepted portrayal of its difficult economic situation see Hundert, 'Some Basic Characteristics of the Jewish Experience in Poland', and Rosman, *The Founder of Hasidism*, 19–27, and contrast with Brawer, *Galicia and its Jews* (Heb.), 53–104, 141–96. Cf. Weinryb, *The Jews of Poland* and see also Teller, 'Economic Activity of Polish Jewry' (Heb.).

autonomy—are neither a necessary nor a sufficient explanation of its subsequent influence. The breakdown of communal institutions and spiritual and social authority that resulted from the rise of Shabateanism may have led to a decline in moral values which enabled the emergence of new forces, but these processes did not determine the nature of the new phenomenon.[7]

Hasidism originated in a mystical awakening that altered conceptions of the relationship between man and God. It was the product of an eruption of charismatic piety that drew its legitimacy from a consciousness of contact with superior realms.[8] This awakening occurred in the first half of the eighteenth century in ascetic circles of men known as hasidim who followed the practices developed by the kabbalistic disciples of Isaac Luria of sixteenth-century Safed, known by the acronym formed from his Hebrew title, Ha'elohi Rabi Yitshak ('The divine Rabbi Isaac'), as the Ari ('Lion') or even the Ari Hakadosh ('Holy Lion'). Like their predecessors, these groups ascribed great importance to mystical experiences and recognized the authority of visionaries. They came into being as a result of the wide dissemination of kabbalistic literature, with its paradoxical image of the kabbalist as simultaneously the conserver of sanctified tradition and an inspired innovator.[9] This image appears to have attracted would-be kabbalists to withdraw from everyday life in order to reach higher levels of consciousness through mystical practices. Following this ideal led man to 'see himself as if he were not . . . to think that he is not in this world',[10] or, as one unambiguous formulation has it, 'Man must see himself as nothing and forget himself altogether.'[11]

Withdrawal from the world gave the kabbalists the freedom to formulate new conceptions and mystical practices and to redefine the limits of reality. The kabbalistic view distinguished manifest reality from hidden reality, body from soul, exile from redemption. It sharpened the difference between the bounds of reality and the broad horizons of the spirit, eschewed submission to worldly values, and sought the freedom to explore new realms of mystical illumination. Members of these groups sought to formulate *kavanot* (expressions of mystical intent) and *yihudim* (literally 'unifications': meditations

---

[7] For an assessment of different approaches to hasidic historiography as it pertains to the emergence of the movement, see Weiss, 'Some Notes on the Social Background of Early Hasidism'; Rapoport-Albert, 'Hasidism after 1772'.

[8] On the idea of charisma and its meaning for religious leadership, see Weber, *On Charisma*; id., *Theory of Social and Economic Organization*, 64–6, 358–73; id., *The Sociology of Religion*, pp. xxxiii–xxxv, 40–60; Barnes, 'Charisma and Religious Leadership'; Shils, 'Charisma, Order and Status'; id., *The Constitution of Society*, 110–19.

[9] For the kabbalistic background to the rise of hasidism, see Dinur, 'The Origins of Hasidism', Elior, 'Hasidism: Historical Continuity', and Ch. 3 below.

[10] *Tsava'at harivash*, 17.   [11] *Magid devarav leya'akov*, 186.

aimed at restoring the ultimate unity of the divine purpose) which could affect the supernal world mapped out in the kabbalistic vision and restore the mystical order of the universe to its primeval form. Their aim, in accordance with this world-view, was to bring about the redemption of the Shekhinah and its unification with the Kudsha Berikh Hu (the masculine aspect of the deity), and to elevate to their rightful place the *nitsotsot* or 'sparks of holiness' scattered through the universe in consequence of the breaking of divine vessels when God contracted himself (a process known as *tsimtsum*) in order to make space for the world he was creating.[12]

In order to enter the mystical world, the kabbalists aimed to transform the self (*ani*) into the divine Nothingness (*ayin*—in Hebrew these two words are an anagram of the same three letters). They therefore distanced themselves from the wider community and the material world so as to experience divine inspiration more intensely and draw closer to God. Considering themselves 'precious individuals' (*anshei segulah*), they called themselves 'holy societies' (*ḥavurot kedoshot*); others called them 'kabbalists, pietists, ascetics, tsadikim, and hasidim'. They were known for their charismatic piety and a consciousness of close proximity to the divine. This kabbalistically charged atmosphere nurtured inspired figures who were considered to have been granted special spiritual gifts such as the quality of prophecy, or the ability to transcend the boundaries between heaven and earth. Early hasidism thus bore strongly the imprint of the charismatic personality. Its later development and wide acceptance reflect the aptitude of its gifted teachers in bringing the influence of kabbalah and the mystical renaissance to an ever-widening circle of adherents.

The spiritual transformation introduced by hasidism, originally affecting small circles within the Jewish world, gradually effected a social transformation of far-reaching consequences. Social relationships came to be seen in a different way as the new concepts of hasidism took hold. Concepts originally applied to the ecstatic mystical relationship between man and God—'unification' with God, 'devotion' to God, 'love' of God, and the 'annihilation of being' in the presence of God—came to be applied by the group to relations between themselves: there is talk of 'brotherly love', 'selflessness', 'devotion to comrades', 'unification with comrades', and so forth. These same concepts also came to be used to define the relationship of the group to its charismatic leadership, as can be seen in such expressions as 'devotion to the tsadik' and 'unification with the tsadik'. These concepts were developed to express the new social relationships that hasidism engendered, and particularly the new form of relationship with the religious leadership.

[12] On *kavanot* and *yiḥudim* see Jacobs, *Hasidic Prayer*; Werblowsky, *Joseph Karo*, 70–9, 100–1, 162.

Early hasidism was thus characterized by respect both for supernally inspired charisma, recognized both by those endowed with it and those witnessing it, and for the new hasidic teachings that saw the divine presence as suffusing the whole universe, thereby blurring accepted distinctions. Similarly, the capacity for mystical elevation, so as to transcend the boundaries between heaven and earth, divine and human, introduced a new fluidity into the concept of divinity that resulted in a similar breaching of borders of authority in the terrestrial realm and the undermining of traditional social frameworks.

The spiritual renewal produced by the ecstatic arousal and charismatic inspiration of the early hasidim, the product of immediate contact with the divine realm and the kabbalistic tradition, challenged traditional Jewish values. It created a new intellectual world that redefined the relationship between God and man. Through the power of charisma and the authority of mystical tradition, through a set of oral and written religious concepts, the leaders of hasidism produced far-reaching changes in religious outlook and social institutions.[13]

The transition from individual mystical experience to a comprehensive doctrine relevant to ever-broadening social circles occurred, as I have already mentioned, among groups influenced by Isaac Luria and the kabbalists of sixteenth-century Safed and the associated Lurianic 'rules of conduct'. They tried to live in the spirit of the sixteenth-century Safed mystics who taught, following Luria's teachings as recorded by his disciple Rabbi Jacob Tsemah in *Shulḥan arukh shel ha'ari*: 'He who wishes to learn the true wisdom [i.e. kabbalah] must conduct himself in the way of the pious [*derekh ḥasidut*].' The meaning of this phrase, which elicited spontaneous responses throughout the Jewish world, will be discussed in Chapter 3. For the moment, let us note only that hasidism moulded a mystical world outlook that drew upon the kabbalistic tradition, published and unpublished, and upon the mystical life of the elite groups; and that this generated new social and religious frameworks of divine authority, spiritual partnership, and mutual responsibility.

Contrary to the conventional depiction of hasidism, it was not understood by its leaders as a social revolution, despite its eventual far-reaching social consequences. Nor was it at all a populist revolution, despite the prevalent

---

[13] For different views of spiritual renewal and the mystical meaning of hasidism, see Buber, *Befardes haḥasidut* and cf. id., 'My Way to Hasidism'; Scholem, *Major Trends in Jewish Mysticism*, 325–50, and '*Devekut* or Communion with God'; Schatz-Uffenheimer, *Hasidism as Mysticism* and 'Man's Relation to God and World'; *EJ* vii. 1383–1432, s.v. 'hasidism'; Tishby and Dan, 'Hasidism' (Heb.); Tishby, 'The Messianic Idea' (Heb.); and Elior, *The Paradoxical Ascent to God*, and 'The Paradigms of *Yesh* and *Ayin*' in Hasidic Thought'.

image created under the impact of Haskalah critique and Marxist historiography. Hasidism was the creation of mystically oriented individuals deeply conscious of the experience of exile and yearning for redemption. They were also deeply conscious of the ultimate meaningless of subjugation to worldly matters (the realm of 'being') and yearned for the freedom of the higher worlds (the realm of Ein Sof, 'Divine Endlessness', also known as Ayin, 'Nothingness'). The resurgent consciousness of this kabbalistic dialectic led to the emergence of new leaders who embodied its ideals. Seeing themselves as 'sons of the supernal world', as people 'who conduct themselves as if they were not in this world and consider themselves as nothing', they imbued hasidism with an openness to spiritual arousal, charismatic affect, and mystical revelation, and instigated a way of life based on kabbalistic tradition.[14]

The hasidim of the Ba'al Shem Tov differed from similar groups in earlier periods in that their spiritual assumptions were intended for and appealed to a much wider audience. They assumed an all-embracing divine presence that made closeness to God a possibility for all. The notion that 'all is God'—in the words of the prophet Isaiah, that 'the whole earth is filled with His glory', or as the Zohar puts it, 'there is no place devoid of Him'—led them to address all men in all ways, in all places, and at all times. Previous groups who had dedicated themselves to the study of the Zohar and Lurianic kabbalah had focused only on the supernal worlds and distanced themselves from the broader community, seeing these teachings as esoteric and directed solely to the elite. Hasidic teachers, in contrast, reinterpreted and reworked the kabbalistic literature, adding new layers and innovative social and religious interpretations. It was on this basis that they instructed their followers to see themselves as 'belonging to the higher world' and enjoined then 'to pay no attention to the people who dwell in this world, for all this world is like a grain of mustard by contrast with the higher world'.[15]

In so far as God was grasped as omnipresent, kabbalistic hasidism was bound up with an attachment to the supernal worlds and withdrawal from this world, with the estrangement from material values required in order to regard 'being' as 'nothingness'. As this paved the way to the recognition of mystical authority and to disregard for conventional social and religious structures, traditional hierarchies were discarded in favour of a new religious and social order.

The emergence of hasidism was thus a profound religious development within the kabbalistic tradition. With the acceptance of charismatic authority came new leadership structures, a mystical consciousness that regarded the

---

[14] See Maimon, 'On a Secret Society'.   [15] *Tsava'at harivash*, p. 2, §6.

revealed world and the hidden world as interchangeable, and a surge of spiritual inspiration that led to the development of new concepts. To borrow an
old rabbinic play on words, the founders of the hasidic movement moved
from the traditional world which lived in the spirit of the Ten Commandments engraved (*harut*) on the tablets of stone brought down by Moses from
Mount Sinai as the divine word to one in which they spoke out in the name of
the new freedom (*herut*) that they saw as implicit in the divine word. That is
to say, they based the right to innovate and challenge the existing order on
mystical experiences transcending the borders between heaven and earth
(experiences such as 'the ascent of the soul', 'divine inspiration', 'utterance of
the Shekhinah in human speech', or 'revelation through Elijah'), and on conceptions of God, divine worship, the source of religious legitimacy, and social
conduct inspired by kabbalistic tradition. Their claim to leadership derived
from their close and unmediated experience of divine being and their understanding of how this crucially affected human existence.[16]

Hasidism succeeded because it changed from being concerned solely with
the religious renaissance of individuals to being a model of religious and
social organization with mystical foundations. Its leaders saw themselves as
incorporating the two poles of spiritual experience: as endowed with divine
inspiration yet as the personification of self-abnegation, self-sacrifice, and
humility, directly responsible for the well-being of their community while
yearning for seclusion from the community in order to attain communion
with the divine. Thus, as their writings indicate, they saw themselves simultaneously as being 'beyond nature', as 'nothing', as 'tabernacles of the
covenant', or as 'protagonists of freedom', but also as leaders whose souls
were bound up with those of the community they were representing. They
saw themselves as divinely inspired leaders who hear the words of the messiah and transmit his teachings, as redeemers who have experienced revelation and can therefore propose an experience of spiritual partnership and
brotherhood relevant to wider circles of society.[17]

[16] On the relationship between mystical thought and freedom, see Scholem, 'Religious
Authority and Mysticism', and Elior, *Jewish Mysticism*.
[17] See Jacobs (ed.), *Jewish Mystical Testimonies*, 148–55, 196–216, 217–23, 224–44. On the creative inspiration derived from mystical experience and its significant role in hasidic leadership see
Chs. 10 and 11 below.

The Hasidic Library

For in truth the entire Torah is only letters and each and every Jew, according to his standing and value, engenders permutations of the individual letters.

Or hame'ir, 38b

ANY survey of the multifaceted nature of hasidism and its intricate relation to kabbalistic tradition should begin by noting the variety of written sources that the hasidic movement created, a veritable library that reflects both the forceful new ideas that shaped hasidism and the conflicts it engendered. This literature, which started to develop in the last third of the eighteenth century and has been published in an almost continuous stream down to the present, affords a great variety of perspectives on the hasidic world.

From its inception, the hasidic movement gave oral and written expression to a wide range of new ideas. Not everything said was written down, not everything written down was edited, not everything edited was published, and not everything published has reached us; even so, a most impressive library has survived. Written sources cannot of course capture social and historical reality in all its complexity, yet despite their limitations they have been of critical importance in disseminating hasidic ideas and in shaping the perception of hasidism among its followers and among its opponents. In the sense that the literature produced by the hasidic movement shaped its conceptual world, it may be considered a prime factor in defining its spiritual and social identity.

Hasidic literature of the eighteenth and nineteenth centuries written and published in Hebrew can be classified into six distinct genres: *derush* (homilies); *hanhagot* (manuals for a hasidic way of life); polemical literature; letters; hasidic tales; and contemporary hasidic historiography and memoirs. These genres flourished at different times, and differ in their purpose, style, authorship, and readership. Each also illuminates a different aspect of the hasidic reality. In addition to these published Hebrew-language sources, documents in Russian, Polish, and Ruthenian dealing with various aspects of the hasidic world have survived in archives in eastern Europe, but few of these have been published. This chapter will focus principally on the eighteenth- and nineteenth-century Hebrew sources constituting the first five categories, although some mention will also be made of the twentieth-century sources that constitute the sixth category.[1]

HASIDIC *DERUSH*

Hasidic leaders used the traditional Jewish genre of *derush*—homilies, commentaries, and sermons on the weekly Torah reading—as a way of presenting hasidic insights into the nature of reality in a familiar form. Dozens of volumes of hasidic *derush* were written in the eighteenth and early nineteenth centuries, and literally hundreds from the middle of the nineteenth century to the present; together they reflect the different facets of hasidic thinking as it has evolved through its 250-year history.[2]

The Ba'al Shem Tov—like other great religious innovators, from Jeremiah and Jesus down to Jewish mystics of the sixteenth to eighteenth centuries such as Isaac Luria, Shabetai Tsevi, and Jacob Frank—did not write down his own teachings. The first volume of hasidic *derush, Toledot ya'akov yosef*, was published in 1780, almost half a century after the inception of hasidism.[3] Its author was Jacob Joseph of Polonnoye, the major disciple and disseminator of the Ba'al Shem Tov's teachings, who lived in the region known as Podolia. This work, which comprises a commentary on each week's Torah reading, includes many homiletical insights cited in the Ba'al Shem Tov's name. These are based on summaries, made from memory, of his oral discourses over about a quarter of a century; most were delivered on sabbaths and holy days, when writing is forbidden by Jewish law, which obviously did not facilitate clear formulation or reliable transmission. Many hasidic leaders, from the Ba'al Shem Tov and the Maggid of Mezhirech, through Menahem Mendel of Kotsk, Mordecai Joseph Leiner of Izbica, Israel of Ruzhin, and Menahem Mendel Schneerson, the last Rebbe of Lubavitch, likewise delivered their teachings spontaneously in discourses on sabbaths and holy days and did not write them down. The works of hasidic leaders that have

[1] See *EJ* vii. 1413–16 s.v. 'hasidic literature'. On hasidic literature see Dubnow, *History of Hasidism* (Heb.), 375–433, which is still of great value, despite its many deficiencies. See also Tishby and Dan, 'Hasidism' (Heb.), 816–20, and Dan, 'Hasidism' (Heb.), for discussion of the literature. On the types of hasidic literature and scholarly attitudes towards them, see Elior, 'The Minsk Debate' (Heb.), and Gries, *Book, Author and Story in Early Hasidism* (Heb.).

[2] See Dan, Liebes, and Reem (eds.), *Gershom Scholem's Library* (Heb.), i. 513–624; a major part of vol. ii is devoted to hasidic literature: see pp. 697–838.

[3] On *Toledot ya'akov yosef*, see Nigal, *Leader and Congregation* (Heb.), and the introduction to Jacob Joseph of Polonnoye and his works in Nigal's annotated edition of *Tsofenat pa'ane'aḥ*.

survived are thus mostly written from memory by disciples who heard the original oral formulation, often with additional changes introduced by editors and proof-readers.[4]

Hasidic *derush* from the earliest years is known to us mostly from the books that began to appear somewhat later, from the 1780s on. The publication of hasidic literature before this time was constrained by opposition to mystical ideas within the Jewish community as a consequence of the disastrous consequences of the antinomian Shabatean and Frankist movements of the late 1750s,[5] as well as, to some extent, by government censorship.[6] The first hasidic books were thus not published until the 1780s, though they in fact reflect the thinking of earlier periods, dating back to the end of the 1730s. Their subsequent publication was undertaken by Solomon of Lutsk—a disciple of Dov Baer, the Maggid of Mezhirech, himself a disciple of the Ba'al Shem Tov—who set up a printing press in Korets for this purpose.[7]

The second work of hasidic *derush* to be published, *Magid devarav leya'akov*, was by the Maggid of Mezhirech himself. Published about eight years after his death, it was a compilation of his remarks as written down and edited by his disciples in the region known as Volhynia. The comments of Solomon of Lutsk as publisher at the beginning of the book make it clear that it was intended to express the Maggid's interpretation of the Ba'al Shem Tov's teachings. It is known that Levi Isaac of Berdichev played a major role in the writing and editing, but it is difficult to identify precisely all the other disciples involved in the various stages of production.[8]

These two books represent the rise of two distinct schools of hasidic tradition: the Podolia school of Jacob Joseph and his followers in such towns as Khmelnik, Luntzitz, Medzhibozh, Nemirov, Shargorod, and Rashkov; and the Volhynia school led by Dov Baer of Mezhirech and his followers in Berdichev, Korets, Lutsk, Zaslaw, and Zhitomir. Though both schools are based on the ideas of the Ba'al Shem Tov and his circle, the geographical distance between them is reflected in an ideological distance too. Each school originated with direct disciples of the Ba'al Shem Tov who claimed to have preserved oral and written traditions. But whereas Jacob Joseph of Polonnoye

---

[4] See Gries, *Book, Author and Story in Early Hasidism* (Heb.), 17–44.

[5] See Scholem, *Sabbatai Ṣevi*; id., 'Redemption through Sin'; Balaban, *On the History of the Frankist Movement* (Heb.), 125; Heilperin, *Records of the Council of the Four Lands* (Heb.), 410, 205.

[6] See Lieberman, 'On Legends and on Truth with Regard to Hasidic Printing' (Heb.); Shmeruk, *Essays on the History of Yiddish Literature* (Heb.), 176–8, 242.

[7] On Solomon of Lutsk see Gries, *Book, Author, and Story in Early Hasidism* (Heb.), 53–6.

[8] On *Magid devarav leya'akov*, see the introduction to the 1976 critical edition by Rivka Schatz-Uffenheimer.

sought to render his master's words quite literally, Dov Baer of Mezhirech was more expansive in his approach and aimed at a more spirited interpretation of the Ba'al Shem Tov's mystical teachings.

Despite points of contact between the two traditions, it is obvious that from the very start the Ba'al Shem Tov's words were interpreted in different ways. To understand the variety of emphases and concepts that emerged within the hasidic world in the last sixty years of the eighteenth century, one must begin with the differing traditions to be found in the earliest genre of hasidic writing, the *derush* literature.

The major volumes emanating from the circles of Jacob Joseph of Polonnoye, the Maggid, and the Ba'al Shem Tov's own family were published between approximately 1780 and 1820. Among those deserving mention are *Magid devarav leya'akov*, *Or ha'emet*, and *Or torah*, from the Maggid's circle; *Toledot ya'akov yosef*, *Ben porat yosef*, *Tsofenat pa'ane'aḥ*, and *Kutonet pasim* by Jacob Joseph of Polonnoye. Among works by disciples of the Maggid one should list *Peri ha'arets* by Menahem Mendel of Vitebsk; *Tanya: likutei amarim* by Shneur Zalman of Lyady; *Kedushat levi* and *Shemuah tovah* by Levi Isaac of Berdichev; *Or hame'ir* by Ze'ev Wolf of Zhitomir; *No'am elimelekh* by Elimelekh of Lyzhansk; *Yosher divrei emet* by Meshulam Feivush Heller of Zbarazh; *Ḥayim vaḥesed* by Hayim Haikl of Amdur; *Me'or einayim* by Menahem Nahum of Chernobyl; and *Ḥesed le'avraham*, which includes the teachings of Abraham 'the Angel', son of the Maggid of Mezhirech, and of Abraham of Kalisk. Among works by those close to Jacob Joseph are *Teshuot ḥen* by Gedaliah of Luniets and *Divrei moshe* by Moses of Dolina. Works by relatives of the Ba'al Shem Tov include *Likutei moharan* by Nahman of Bratslav, and *Degel maḥaneh efrayim* by Moses Hayim Ephraim of Sudylkow. Most of these works are presented as homilies and comments on the weekly Torah reading.[9]

The very extensive library of hasidic *derush*, only a few volumes of which have been mentioned here, attests to the enormous spiritual and mystical renewal that characterized the hasidic world. This renewal created an unparalleled wealth of innovative concepts. At its heart, however, all the hasidic *derush* literature expresses a palpable awareness of the hidden divine presence that suffuses the manifest world. Time and again it touches on the intimate relationship between the concealed essence and the revealed entity, between God and man, in consequence of the divine reality that animates all dimensions of being; the kabbalists described this reality as manifesting itself in the form of letters, sparks, *sefirot*, or thoughts.

---

[9] For the bibliographical history of these hasidic books, see Dan, Liebes, and Reem (eds.), *Gershom Scholem's Library* (Heb.), i. 513–624.

The various works of hasidic *derush* base themselves directly or indirectly on the Ba'al Shem Tov's teachings and engage in rich dialogue with earlier homiletic literature and works of kabbalistic ethics. Yet although they ostensibly share the same spiritual world and kabbalistic vocabulary, each of these compositions represents an innovative unfolding affected by the author's personal circumstances and existential conditions within the hasidic world of his time.

HANHAGOT

Readers of the first books of hasidic *derush* encountered difficulty with the genre. Because the novel insights of hasidism were often woven into an exegetical tapestry of kabbalistic teachings, ethical literature, and centuries of homiletical tradition, it was impossible to identify them without a thorough knowledge of biblical allusions and interpretative modes and a great deal of patience. Since relatively few readers had these prerequisites, the spread of hasidism in this early period was hampered rather than helped by such hasidic writings as were available.

As awareness of this difficulty grew during the 1790s, hasidic editors and compilers began to review the hundreds of pages that had been published by their predecessors and extract from them the ideas attributed to the Ba'al Shem Tov. These editors, some of whom are known while others remain anonymous, abandoned the traditional exegetical framework of weekly commentaries on the weekly Torah reading, focusing instead on the embellishment of contemplative and ritual practices which had been introduced with a view to expressing in daily conduct the spiritual values inspired by the new mystical awareness. These hasidic practices, known as *hanhagot*, were published in pamphlets and small books: among the best known are *Tsava'at harivash*, *Keter shem tov*, *Likutim yekarim*, and *Hanhagot yesharot*. Though often overlapping in content and form in consequence of their shared sources, they enjoyed wide circulation and went through many editions. Undoubtedly they encouraged the emergence of a separate hasidic identity and the further dissemination of hasidism.[10]

In effect, the *hanhagot* derived from the homiletical *derush* literature, but whereas in the latter the information on the new hasidic practices was scattered through other material, these new publications collated them and gave them a literary form that delivered a specific spiritual message. This clarified the nature of the hasidic innovation: the increased mystical

[10] On the *hanhagot* literature, see Gries, *The Hanhagot Literature* (Heb.).

spirituality associated with the new consciousness of the presence of the divine in all things, and the new way of life thus engendered.

Many of the *hanhagot* are introduced by preliminary phrases such as 'One must consider', 'One must understand', 'One must imagine', 'One must contemplate'—phrases implying a change in consciousness rather than merely a change in behaviour. That is to say, they are presented in a way that is designed to inculcate a reassessment of meaning: a new mode of serving God, a new way of defining man's purpose in this world, and new spiritual horizons. The change related more to the *kavanah* or intent with which the practice was to be performed—the contemplation of its mystical significance—than to its actual performance. This emphasis on intent became the hallmark of the hasidic identity.[11]

POLEMICAL LITERATURE

Whereas the genres already discussed reflect eighteenth-century hasidism as seen from within, the polemical literature presents the views of its opponents, who came to be known as mitnagedim (from the Hebrew term for opposition), in the last third of the eighteenth century and in the first decades of the nineteenth century. (Somewhat paradoxically, the mitnagedic polemical literature began to appear a decade before the first hasidic writings.) Mordecai Wilensky's two-volume *Hasidim and Mitnagedim* collects the major printed and manuscript sources, including *Shever poshe'im*, *Zemir aritsim*, and various writs of anathema and excommunication.[12]

The polemical literature constitutes a prime resource for understanding the development of hasidism because it shows how the rabbinic establishment reacted to the challenge it posed. It comprises a great variety of sources: circulars, critical attacks, satire, insult, and intellectual treatises. It highlights the difference between how hasidism saw itself and how it was perceived by others, and also provides evidence both of the dissemination of hasidic ideas and the burning of hasidic manuscripts and books. Overall, this literature demonstrates the conflict between tradition and change, the tensions it engendered in conventional religious and social structures, and the ways in which they were transformed as a result. The conflict derived from the lingering suspicions of Shabateanism and the undermining of the established

---

[11] See Elior, 'Hasidism: Historical Continuity'.

[12] For mitnagedic polemic, see Wilensky, *Hasidim and Mitnagedim* (Heb.); an English translation of part of this book can be found in Wilensky, 'Hasidic–Mitnaggedic Polemics'; Mondshine, 'The Two Incarcerations of the Old Rebbe' (Heb.), 17–108; see also Nadler, *The Faith of the Mithnagdim*; Etkes, *The Gaon of Vilna* (Heb.).

order by the new charismatic leadership.[13] It was further intensified when hasidic leaders, for kabbalistic reasons, abandoned the Ashkenazi liturgical rite used throughout Europe in favour of the Sephardi rite used by the kabbalists of sixteenth-century Safed and established their own synagogues.[14]

The polemical texts demonstrate the causes of the conflict and enable us to see it from the perspective both of the hasidim and their traditionalist opponents, the mitnagedim. The frequent hyperbole of the polemic necessitates a certain scholarly caution, but its strength and vitality enable us to learn much about the complex intellectual and social issues involved and to feel the intensity of the spiritual life of Jews in eastern Europe.

It is the extreme positions expressed that make the polemical literature especially interesting. We learn of the fears, the sense of insult, the outrage, and the resentment of those defending the old order against hasidism, and of the self-confidence, self-awareness, and self-righteous reaction of those seeking to defend the new ways inspired by mystical traditions. The polemical literature clarifies the topics that so angered the mitnagedim, and shows how the hasidim reacted to the accusations levelled against them. It also shows the similarities between the two camps, stemming, paradoxically, from the very matters about which they disagreed. The disputes will be discussed in more detail in Chapter 7; here I will simply emphasize the significance of the documents for the historical understanding of hasidism.[15]

In addition to the early polemical reactions to hasidism as a distinct social phenomenon in the eighteenth century, the mitnagedim later produced theoretical works that confront hasidism from a more moderate perspective. Hayim of Volozhin's *Nefesh haḥayim* (1824), for example, confirms the hasidic conception of God but rejects the forms of worship introduced by hasidism;[16] Pinhas of Polotsk's *Keter torah* (1788), by contrast, stresses conflict and censure.[17] Alexander Zederbaum's *Keter kehunah* (1867), a historiographical work describing hasidic practices, is an important source of information about the evolution of Polish hasidism; likewise Solomon Maimon's autobiography, published in Berlin in 1793, which provides a retrospective description of the court of the Maggid from the viewpoint of a maskil who had been a hasid in his youth.[18] There are also Russian government documents that preserve

[13] See Elior, 'R. Nathan Adler and the Frankfurt Pietists'.

[14] On the changes in hasidic prayer see Wertheim, *Laws and Customs in Hasidism*, 83–110, and the introduction to Jacobs, *Hasidic Prayer*.

[15] See Wilensky, 'Hasidic–Mitnaggedic Polemics'; Nadler, *The Faith of the Mithnagdim*.

[16] See Lamm, *Torah lishmah*; Etkes, 'The Methods and Achievements of R. Hayim of Volozhin' (Heb.); Ross, 'Rav Hayim of Volozhin' (Heb.).

[17] See Nadler, *The Faith of the Mithnagdim*.   [18] See Maimon, 'On a Secret Society'.

statements made by each side about the other, as well as valuable evidence of how they were viewed by others.[19]

LETTERS

Letters had a significant impact on the spread of hasidism. We can identify three main types:

Letters written by hasidic masters. The most important letter to have survived is the Ba'al Shem Tov's letter to his brother-in-law, Gershon of Kutow, which contains autobiographical testimony about his mystical consciousness. The Ba'al Shem's letter, known both as *Igeret hakodesh* (the Holy Epistle) and *Igeret aliyat haneshamah* (the Epistle of the Ascent of the Soul),[20] never reached his brother-in-law, but it was published in 1781 as an appendix to *Ben porat yosef*. It will be discussed in Chapter 4 in connection with the Ba'al Shem Tov's mystical concept of language. Other letters depict the spiritual world of hasidism, the crucial importance of mysticism in hasidic courts, and the social atmosphere in the 1770s and 1780s. Those of Meshulam Feivush Heller of Zbarazh, published in *Yosher divrei emet*, attest to the great influence of the hasidic manuscripts which had reached him.[21] So too the letter of Zekhariah Mendel of Jaroslaw, sent from the court of Elimelekh of Lyzhansk, which portrays the hasidic lifestyle of the 1770s and 1780s and its mystical atmosphere. These letters provide vivid testimony to the spiritual quality and social reality of hasidism and are an excellent source for understanding the self-image of hasidism at this stage in its development. They also had contemporary importance, in that their powerful language and descriptions often encouraged those who read them to try the hasidic way of life for themselves.

Letters defending the innovations of hasidism. Hasidic leaders often wrote letters in response to criticism from within and from without; they also wrote letters dealing with the concerns of their hasidim, public affairs, and mystical leadership. The letters of Shneur Zalman of Lyady, a particularly prolific writer who dealt with all these issues, are collected in *Igerot ba'al hatanya uvenei doro*. Other letters emanating from his circle are found in *Igerot kodesh*.[22]

---

[19] For Hebrew translations of the Russian documents see Mondshine, 'The Two Incarcerations of the Old Rebbe' (Heb.), 17–108.

[20] An English translation of the letter from the 1781 edition can be found in Jacobs (ed.), *Jewish Mystical Testimonies*, 182–91 (Zekhariah Mendel's letter, mentioned below, is translated ibid. 208–14).   [21] See Krassen, *Uniter of Heaven and Earth*.

[22] See *Igerot kodesh*, ed. Levin; *Igerot kodesh: kuntres miluim*. Further letters written by Shneur Zalman of Lyady are collected in Mondshine, 'The Two Incarcerations of the Old Rebbe' (Heb.), 17–109.

Letters dealing with the problems of hasidic succession shed light on the tensions engendered by charismatic mystical leadership. Important examples of this are the many letters written by Shneur Zalman's disciple, Aaron Halevi, and his son, Dov Baer, disputing their respective claims to inherit his leadership. Likewise, the letters of Nathan Sternharz, disciple of Nahman of Bratslav, to the hasidic master Moses of Sovran, and the exchanges between Shneur Zalman of Lyady, Levi Isaac of Berdichev, and Barukh of Medzibozh reveal something of the rivalry that developed within hasidic circles in the absence of accepted standards of legitimacy and authority. Such letters are evidence of a fascinating chapter in the formation of hasidic dynasties and of the difficulties in bequeathing the mystical legacy. Communal issues also figure in letters from Levi Isaac of Berdichev, Aaron Halevi of Starosielce, Isaac of Humel, Menahem Mendel of Lubavitch (known as the Tsemah Tsedek), and other tsadikim. Such letters are important for conveying the historical testimony of disinterested bystanders as well as of those who contributed to the correspondence; they also give us the personal perspective of the writers within the hasidic circle on those who helped forge the hasidic revolution.[23]

Letters from hasidic émigrés to Israel. During the 1770s several hasidic leaders felt moved to experience for themselves the mystical reality of the land of Israel. Among them were Abraham of Kalisk (whose writings were published in *Ḥesed le'avraham* together with those of Abraham ben Dov Baer of Mezhirech) and Menahem Mendel of Vitebsk (author of *Peri ha'arets*), both leaders of Byelorussian hasidism. They continued to correspond regularly with their colleagues in the hasidic leadership and with their hasidim. Itinerant fundraisers carried letters between the hasidic centres in Europe and the growing hasidic communities of Safed and Tiberias. Many of these letters, dating from the 1770s to the 1820s, have survived. From this literature we can learn about the network of relations between the tsadik and his community, as well as about disputes and tensions among the leaders. But side by side with personal and public polemics, general letters directed to particular hasidic communities, and accounts of fundraising and the distribution of money, there are also private letters, never intended for publication. The areas touched on include the nature of the relationship between the tsadik and his followers, the complex relations among hasidic leaders, the interaction between the hasidic community in Israel and that in Europe, and the varieties of hasidic existence in this period of expansion. We also learn of material and spiritual distress and gain an autobiographical perspective on mystical inspiration and spiritual leadership.[24]

[23] For the text of some of these letters see Jacobs, *Seeker of Unity*.

[24] On the epistolary literature, see *Peri ha'arets*, by Menahem Mendel of Vitebsk; Hillman,

The epistolary literature of the nineteenth and early twentieth centuries is frequently reproduced in memoirs, and contains important autobiographical evidence of the tensions affecting the hasidic world as well as sources of authority and areas of vulnerability. The publications in which the various letters are collected, and the additions and deletions that have sometimes been made in them, reflect the interests and purposes of those who compiled them.

HASIDIC NARRATIVE

In the 1740s and 1750s the Ba'al Shem Tov achieved fame as a storyteller, and the genre of hasidic narrative is thus closely linked with him. Individual stories began to find their way into print around the end of the eighteenth century and in the first decade of the nineteenth century in such publications as *Keter shem tov*, *Kedushat levi*, and *Degel mahaneh efrayim*. The great collections of hasidic stories, however, *Shivhei habesht* ('In Praise of the Ba'al Shem Tov') and the stories of Nahman of Bratslav, were first published in 1814/15.[25]

Two principal types of hasidic story may be distinguished: those told by the tsadik to his hasidim, and those told by the hasidim concerning the tsadik. The former are an attempt by such masters as the Ba'al Shem Tov, Nahman of Bratslav, Simhah Bunem of Przysucha, Menahem Mendel of Kotsk, and Israel of Ruzhin to communicate the new hasidic-kabbalistic world taking shape. They are a profound artistic articulation of their mystical outlook, interweaving the revealed and the concealed and blurring the boundaries between being and nothingness. In these enigmatic stories the tsadikim seek to communicate their ideas relating to the divinity and divine worship. They give metaphorical narrative expression to their frustration with the limits imposed by mundane reality and offer mystical ways of overcoming the constraints of time and space. At times the tsadikim use their stories to express their spiritual concerns. Sometimes they express the difficulties involved in

Letters of the Author of the Tanya (Heb.); Barnai (ed.), *Hasidic Letters* (Heb.); id., 'Historiography of the Hasidic Immigration to Erets Yisrael'; Katz-Steiman, *Early Hasidic Immigration* (Heb.); Wilensky, *Hasidic Settlement in Tiberias* (Heb.); Haran, 'Inner Ideological Conflicts' (Heb.) and 'R. Abraham of Kalisk and R. Shneur Zalman of Lyady' (Heb.); and Karlinsky, *Counterhistory* (Heb.), 180–5, 200 and 'The Beginnings of Orthodox Hasidic Historiography' (Heb.).

[25] See *In Praise of the Ba'al Shem Tov*, ed. Ben Amos and Mintz; Hebrew–German and Yiddish–German editions of *Shivhei habesht* are available in *Die Geschichten vom Ba'al Schem Tov*, ed. Grözinger; *Nahman of Bratslav, The Tales*, ed. Band. On Buber's rendering of R. Nahman's tales see Schleicher, 'A Theology of Redemption' and Urban, 'The Hermeneutics of Renewal'.

leadership. The relationship between the doctrines of the storytellers and their stories and parables is complex. In some cases the story is an indirect reflection of a subject that cannot be dealt with directly, whether for personal or for mystical reasons.[26]

The second kind of story, in which hasidim talk about their tsadik, was popular throughout the nineteenth century. Some take the form of a dialogue, some are more of a collective memory of mystical events or experiences. Often they are hagiographical narratives recounting the eminence of the tsadik and his miraculous deeds in stereotypical fashion. Such narratives are replete with accounts of the tsadik's mystical powers, extraordinary intelligence, penetrating insight, magnificent deeds, social awareness, and compassion for his flock. They attest to the meaning of charismatic events for those who witnessed them or heard about them from others and also serve to disseminate the uniqueness of the tsadik, thereby attracting new followers. These narratives are therefore very much part of the evolution of the concept of the tsadik and its institutionalization; to put it another way, the tsadik flourished along with the hasidic story. The stories offer a vivid encapsulation of what has come to be known as 'tsadikism', and give clear narrative expression to the social dimension of hasidism, that is, the relationship between the tsadik and his followers. The combination of elements these stories offer— conventional hagiography, heroic tales, legends, and miraculous deeds, together with the historical evidence of living memory, immediate impressions, and records of thought and interpretation—played a major role in forming hasidic consciousness and helping that social consciousness take root.[27]

The stories told by hasidim, unlike those transmitted by the masters, are not directly tied to hasidic teachings. Instead they articulate the complex relationships of the hasidic world, and in particular the glorification of the tsadik by his followers and their total dependence upon him. They also highlight the moments of crisis that accompany charismatic leadership and membership of a hasidic community. One must beware of treating these stories as historically reliable, for they often derive from stereotypical hagiographic forms. At the same time, they attest to the images of tsadikim and hasidim in various periods, and sometimes reflect deep poetic truths relating to genuine experiences.

[26] See Devir-Goldberg, *The Tsadik and the Palace of Leviathan* (Heb.); Dan, *The Hasidic Story* (Heb.).

[27] For hasidic tales, see the introduction to Buber, *Tales of the Hasidim*, i. 1–34. For the debate about Buber's approach, see Buber, *The Hidden Light* (Heb.), ch. 1; Scholem, 'Martin Buber's Interpretation of Hasidism'; and Schatz-Uffenheimer, 'Man's Relation to God and World'.

Many of the stories are heavily dependent on earlier works celebrating the lives of mystical leaders and often consist of the reworking of motifs from earlier sources such as *Shivhei ha'ari*, written in praise of Isaac Luria.[28] They therefore have to be studied with care: the combination of reality, fantasy, conventional turns of phrase, and popular narrative forms requires careful, critical, sensitive investigation.[29] Moreover, the compilers of these stories were frequently not disinterested parties, but rather were themselves connected to the hasidic court around which the plot revolves. One such author is Michael Frumkin-Rudkinsohn, author of *Kehal hasidim* and other collections of hasidic tales; accusations against him of forgery and various other criminal acts by Ephraim Dinard and Yosef Kohen Tsedek must throw doubt on the reliability of his work.[30]

Scholars of the genre discuss these matters in detail. Some consider this literature to be the principal source for understanding hasidism, in so far as it transmits its strength and liveliness. But others sharply dispute this position, claiming that the homilies of the earlier period (from around 1780) offer deeper insights, and that one cannot use ideas that figure in the later literature (the first collections of hasidic tales were not published until 1814) as a way of understanding earlier periods. The leading exponent of the first position was Martin Buber; we find his ideas in his *In the Orchard of Hasidism*,[31] in the introduction to his great collection of hasidic tales *The Hidden Light*,[32] in the introductions to the anthologies he compiled in German at the beginning of the twentieth century of the tales of the Ba'al Shem Tov and of Nahman of Bratslav,[33] and in his responses to the criticism of other scholars. Thus *In the Orchard of Hasidism* argues:

That which defines the uniqueness and greatness of hasidism is not doctrine but a way of life that creates a community. Since hasidism is not in fact a teaching but a way of

---

[28] See Dan, 'On the History of the Praise Literature' (Heb.).

[29] On characteristics of the hasidic story, see Dan, *The Hasidic Story* (Heb.); Nigal, *The Hasidic Narrative* (Heb.); cf. *Degel mahaneh efrayim*, 19 ('Vayera'), 55 ('Vayeshev'). On the stories of R. Nahman see Green, *Tormented Master*, appendix on his tales; Piekarz, *Bratslav Hasidism* (Heb.), 83–131; Dan, 'A Bow to Frumkinian Hasidism'; Oron and Heidenberg, *From the Mystical World of R. Nahman of Bratslav* (Heb.); and Schleicher, 'A Theology of Redemption'. On other stories told by tsadikim to their followers see Devir-Goldberg, *The Tsadik and the Palace of Leviathan* (Heb.). Cf. Band, 'The Politics of Scripture'.

[30] Dan, *The Hasidic Story*, 195–212; id., 'A Bow to Frumkinian Hasidism'; Nigal (ed.), *Tales of Holy Men* (Heb.), 87–109.

[31] *Befardes hahasidut* (1945); an English version—not an exact translation—was published in 1948 as *Hasidism*.

[32] *The Hidden Light* (Heb.); English trans. in Buber, *Tales of the Hasidim*, introduction.

[33] On Buber's anthologies see Urban, 'The Hermeneutics of Renewal'.

life, the primary source for knowing it is its legend, and only then comes the theoretical literature. The intellectual literature is the commentary, while the legend, i.e. the life, is the source.[34]

Gershom Scholem took the opposite position: 'The development of hasidic life was affected and moulded profoundly by the ideas found in this theoretical literature, while it certainly was not influenced in the beginning by the legends'.[35] Rivka Schatz-Uffenheimer also participated vigorously in the ensuing debate.[36]

Current research on the tales of the tsadikim tries to bridge the gap between the different points of departure discussed above. Scholars focus on the complex relations between story and doctrine; on stories of tsadikim as a source for early hasidic history; and on identifying elements in the narratives that are not found in the discourses. Tales told by the tsadikim are considered from the vantage point of intellectual history and mystical creativity, while tales told by hasidim about the tsadikim are studied as testimony to the consciousness of the hasidic community. Popular hagiographies and hasidic stories are further considered from the point of view of folk narrative and oral history, revealing dimensions that are concealed by the more intellectual discourse of the homiletic literature.[37]

HASIDIC HISTORIOGRAPHY

In the twentieth century the encounter with the modern world and with academic studies of hasidism has given rise to a new genre of hasidic literature: hasidic historiography. The studies of hasidism produced by such historians as Heinrich Graetz, David Kahana, and Simon Dubnow did not meet with the approval of hasidic leaders, and they felt compelled to produce alternative histories. Like scholarly historians, they embraced the principle of basing themselves on documents and primary sources, but when the conclusions were not to their liking they had to adduce alternative sources, sometimes relying on spurious or invented documentation. The most notorious example is the Harson Geniza, a collection of letters purporting to be from the time of

[34] *Befardes haḥasidut*, 22–4. See further Buber, 'My Way to Hasidism'.

[35] *Explications and Implications* (Heb.), 368.

[36] The relevant articles are all listed in the introduction to Buber, *Tales of the Hasidim*, i. 1–34. For the debate about Buber's approach, see Buber, *Befardes haḥasidut*, ch. 1; Scholem, 'Martin Buber's Interpretation of Hasidism'; and Schatz-Uffenheimer, 'Man's Relation to God and World'.

[37] See Schleicher, 'A Theology of Redemption'; Devir-Goldberg, *The Tsadik and the Palace of Leviathan* (Heb.); Urban, 'The Hermeneutics of Renewal'.

the Ba'al Shem Tov and Shneur Zalman of Lyady that was purportedly 'dis-covered' as a consequence of the plundering of government archives after the October Revolution in Russia. The forgers' objective was to revise the image of the Ba'al Shem Tov and early hasidism as depicted in the scholarship based on *Shivḥei habesht*. The Habad Lubavitch rabbinate of the time con-firmed the authenticity of the forged letters, and Joseph Isaac Schneersohn, the sixth Lubavitcher Rebbe, went on to produce his own version of early hasidic history based on these documents and family traditions. However, his history does not stand up to critical examination; it is but a revision of the past in the service of contemporary needs.[38]

*

To understand the hasidic world one needs to consider all the available liter-ature, not just a single genre. One must also be aware of the multilayered and multivocal character of this literature, as well as its source and context. The same text can be revealing in different ways. Take, for example, the hasidic tales: the enigmatic narratives told by the tsadikim, emerging from the unique truth of the individual soul, differ from the charismatic stories repeated by their hasidim based on subjective impressions and hagiographical stereotypes. Taken together, they shed light on what the tsadikim sought to inculcate as well as on what their followers absorbed, and on the different shades of reli-gious and social outlook that developed as the hasidic circle widened. The homiletic *derush* literature reveals the polyphony of the hasidic spiritual renaissance and its dialectical ties to the kabbalistic tradition. It also exposes the mystical awakening that accompanied the rise of hasidism, and the attempt to provide a systematic conceptual framework for the mystical experience. The polemical literature sheds light on the profound social and religious tensions that hasidism generated and shows how the traditional circles from which it arose fought the threat implicit in charismatic leadership and in deviation from the established order. From the *hanhagot* we learn about the hasidic self-image at a time when the movement was still searching for its spiritual and intellectual identity and when the social consequences of its innovations in these fields had yet to be felt. The letters of hasidic leaders highlight a whole range of problems of a more reflective nature. These include the difficulties of communicating mystical values to the masses; the challenges facing tsadikim from within the hasidic community as well as from

---

[38] For the Harson documents and hasidic historiography, see Hillman, *Letters of the Author of the Tanya* (Heb.), appendix on the Harson Geniza; Raphael, 'The Harson Geniza' (Heb.); Elior, 'The Minsk Debate' (Heb.), 180–3; Rapoport-Albert, 'Hagiography with Footnotes'; and Bartal, 'Shimon the Heretic' (Heb.).

without; the intense spiritual arousal effected by mysticism; the dissemination of kabbalistic traditions; and the blurring of boundaries between the divine and the human. Taken together, the various literary sources reviewed above thus reflect the ideological and social tensions that accompanied the emergence of hasidism in consequence of the clash between the freedom of thought embedded in the new mystical teachings and the authoritarian structure of the traditional Jewish community. Each of these genres—*derush*, *hanhagot*, polemics, letters, and stories, together with the more recent historiographical literature, memoirs, and hagiography—thus contributes something different to our understanding of the hasidic spectrum.[39] Each presents serious methodological problems, however, and must be scrutinized with a critical eye. Problems associated with writing and publishing in the shadow of mitnagedic censure, government censorship, and power struggles within the hasidic world itself have affected both style and content. Delays between writing and publication affect interpretation. Of necessity, there is a gap between historical reality and its literary representation, which may be further exacerbated by the intervention of editors and typesetters in the textual record. For all these reasons, the great library of hasidic sources, reflecting the multiple forms of hasidism that evolved in its long history, must be approached with caution. Due consideration must be given to the identity of the authors and their personal circumstances and objectives, no less than to the dates of writing and publication. The scholar who wishes to explore the nature of hasidism must engage in precise investigation of textual variants in different editions in order to ensure the reliability of transmission.

Information on the hasidic world-view is also to be found in sources not of hasidic provenance. These include archival documents from the eighteenth and nineteenth centuries; records of communal organizations and holy fraternities; contemporary legal decisions as preserved in rabbinic responsa; maskilic critiques;[40] popular sources, such as memoirs, narrative lore, and the journals of travellers and missionaries; and government sources such as census returns, tax records, and other official documents. In drawing on this literature it is important to distinguish between internal and external sources, date of writing and date of publication, original purpose and later utilization. A critical understanding of hasidic history demands familiarity not only with

---

[39] See Zinberg, *A History of Jewish Literature*. Classification and description of hasidic literature according to period and scholarly orientation can be found in the Scholem Collection in the National and University Library Jerusalem; see the catalogue: Dan, Liebes, and Reem (eds.), *Gershom Scholem's Library* (Heb.), i. 513–696, ii. 697–838.

[40] See Feiner, 'The Turning Point' (Heb.); Wodziński, *Haskalah and Hasidism in the Kingdom of Poland*.

the vantage point of its creators but also with their contemporaries, whether supporters or opponents.[41]

The idea that there is no such thing as 'history'—no way of presenting a faithful description of reality and no way of establishing 'what really happened' or the facts 'as they really are', a notion first formulated by Hayden White in 1978[42]—has become increasingly influential in the world of scholarship. A single narrative can never express the totality of spiritual, material, cultural, and social realities at a particular time and place. Every historical account is the result of a selection of details from an enormous totality. No tale is separate from its teller, whether in the past or in the present. History is never divorced from story, and any story is only one voice among others vying to represent reality. As history and the telling of history are indivisible, the demand to recount the past 'as it really happened' is meaningless. Society has come to recognize that the concept of 'history' that speaks in a single hegemonic voice has been replaced by the notion of rival voices recounting the past from a multitude of viewpoints, all of which carry merely relative weight. Only such multivocality can represent the experiences, thoughts, strengths, weaknesses, and substantially different vantage points of leaders and followers, powerful orators and their silent audiences, dissenters and those whom they opposed. This requires the researcher to use the greatest possible range of sources in order to allow the articulation of different voices, and to enable events to be presented from a variety of viewpoints. Our discussion will engage such a variety of perspectives as they emerge from the full range of hasidic literature and other literary sources, and from contemporary documents.

[41] For examples of the use of such materials see Rosman, *The Founder of Hasidism*; Assaf, *The Regal Way*; Mondshine, 'The Two Incarcerations of the Old Rebbe' (Heb.), 17–108.

[42] See White, 'The Question of Narrative in Contemporary Historical Theory' in id., *The Content of the Form*, 26–57.

THREE

Mystical Societies and the Spread of Hasidism
Internalizing and Reviving the Kabbalistic Myth

> Man is a ladder planted on earth whose head reaches heaven and the angels of
> God ascend and descend it.
>
> *Toledot ya'akov yosef*, 50

HASIDISM emerged as a social reality in the second third of the eighteenth-century in Podolia and Volhynia, but the concept of hasidism as a way of life inspired by the yearning to achieve intimacy with God is an ancient idea. There are references from the Hasmonean period (167–32 BCE) to 'the early *hasidim*' who engage in lengthy preparations for prayer.[1] In the twelfth and thirteenth centuries the term appears in the context of the *hasidei ashkenaz*, ascetics who were punctilious in the performance of the divine commandments of the Torah. The title *hasid* was applied to pious figures of the period, such as Judah the Hasid and Samuel the Hasid.[2] However, there is no direct link between ancient and medieval hasidism and the later forms inspired by kabbalah and the teachings of the Ba'al Shem Tov.

Hasidism as a way of life adopted in response to mystical awakening and the conceptual world of the kabbalah belongs to the sixteenth century. In *Shulḥan arukh shel ha'ari*, written in Safed in 1587 by disciples of Isaac Luria, we find a concise formulation of the new mystical way and the way of life it entails: 'Whoever wishes to learn the True Wisdom [*ḥokhmat ha'emet* = kabbalah] must conduct himself piously [literally, 'following the *derekh hasidut*', or hasidic way] and therefore must be careful in his practices, even those that are halakhically permitted.' The two principal concepts under discussion here are *ḥokhmat ha'emet* and *derekh ḥasidut*. The first refers to the

---

[1] Mishnah *Berakhot* 5: 1.

[2] On *hasidei ashkenaz* see Scholem, *Major Trends in Jewish Mysticism*, 80–118; Soloveitchik, 'Religious Law and Change'; Dan, *Jewish Mysticism*, vol. ii: *The Middle Ages*.

theoretical speculative background of mystical teaching, the second to the daily devotional practice derived from the mystical tradition.

Ḥokhmat ha'emet denotes the kabbalistic tradition that began in the late twelfth century with the enigmatic book *Sefer habahir*; the kabbalah of Provence, Catalonia, and Castille; the Zohar; and the mystical writings of Moses Nahmanides (Ramban) and Solomon ben Abraham Adret (Rashba). This kabbalistic tradition continued to develop through the late medieval commentators on the Zohar in the fourteenth and fifteenth centuries, reaching its acme in the sixteenth century among the Spanish exiles and their descendants in Turkey and in Safed.[3] The major figures who generated and disseminated the sixteenth-century kabbalistic world-view were Solomon Molkho, Joseph Karo, Solomon Alkabets, Moses Cordovero, and Isaac Luria, and their disciples Hayim Vital, Joseph Ibn Tabul, Israel Sarug, Elijah de Vidas, Eleazar Azikri, and Isaiah Horowitz ('the Holy Shelah').[4]

Seeking to discover the inner meaning of reality, these kabbalists devoted creative religious energies to deciphering the concealed structure that lies beyond historical realities so as to explain that which otherwise seemed inexplicable, chaotic, arbitrary, or cruel.[5] They wrote many books presenting their mystical conceptions of how the divine world and the human world are interrelated, aiming to demonstrate the link between the manifest, physical world and the hidden realm of the Torah and the divine commandments it embodies. This hidden realm was framed in terms of mythical traditions transformed by mystical insight and given new meaning in terms of the realities of daily life. On this view, acts performed in fulfilment of the divine commandments of the Torah became acts of theurgic significance with crucial impact on the higher worlds.[6]

The sixteenth-century kabbalistic tradition transformed the biblical conception of God into something far more complex. It perceived in divinity a process of reciprocity with the human world, which it interpreted in terms of

---

[3] On the stages of the historical formation of kabbalistic thought, see *EJ* x. 489–653 s.v. 'kabbalah'; Scholem, 'The Historical Development of Kabbalah', in *Kabbalah*, 8–86; Tishby, *Wisdom of the Zohar*; Dan, *The Early Kabbalah*; Liebes, 'How the Zohar Was Written'; and Idel, *Kabbalah*.

[4] On Shlomo Molcho see Aescoly, *Jewish Messianic Movements*, 273–304, 382–436. On Joseph Karo and the Safed kabbalists, see Solomon Schechter, 'Safed in the Sixteenth Century'; Werblowsky, *Joseph Karo*; and Fine, *Safed Spirituality*. On Safed in the 16th century see Werblowsky, *Joseph Karo*; Elior, 'Messianic Expectations'; and Fine, *Safed Spirituality* and *Physician of the Soul*. See also Pechter, 'The Concept of *Devekut*' (Heb.).

[5] See Elior, 'Exile and Redemption', and 'The Doctrine of Transmigration in *Galya Raza*'.

[6] On the nature of kabbalistic thought, see Scholem, *Origins of the Kabbalah* and *On the Kabbalah and its Symbolism*; Liebes, 'The Messiah of the Zohar', 'Zohar and Eros' (Heb.), and '*De Natura Dei*'; Elior, 'Different Faces of Freedom'; Dan, *On Holiness* (Heb.); Idel, *Kabbalah*.

states of exile and redemption, both cosmic and terrestrial. This conception, which derived from an esoteric interpretation of the Torah, visionary insight, and mystical lore, viewed the divinity and the Torah as a multilayered, simultaneous revelation linked to the manifest human world through a dialectical process. The essential unity of the divinity is perceived as having been damaged by a cosmic catastrophe in the heavenly temple that split the ineffable name asunder and caused sparks of the divine to fall and be dispersed through the world or to become inaccessible, a heavenly calamity paralleled by exile on earth. The divinity was split into a masculine element and a feminine element, respectively the Kudsha Berikh Hu and the Shekhinah, but the power of human intent and prayer can restore the primal state of divine wholeness. At the same time, the divine realm is perceived as embodying both the Infinite (Ein Sof), which lies beyond apprehension, and ten *sefirot* ('spheres'), which are perceptible aspects of the divine. Kabbalah further divides the hidden reality into the 'side of holiness' (*sitra dekedusha*) and the 'other side' (*sitra ahara*) of satanic impurity, parallel to the states of redemption and exile in the higher worlds and on earth, and seen as being influenced by human actions and intentions. The processes and interactions binding and separating God and man have their origins in holy texts and sacred rituals based on mystical interpretations of the Torah and its commandments and gave rise to a set of symbols, metaphors, and concepts seen as existing simultaneously in the deity, in the human soul, and in the Scriptures. These texts lie at the heart of kabbalistic study and mystical contemplation.[7]

The conception of the divine realm as dependent on purposeful human action and intention altered man's role in the divine scheme of things from one of passive obedience within the confines of the manifest world to one of active intervention in it through intention, deed, prayer, mystical unification, and attachment to God. In the kabbalistic mythos, humanity is in a reciprocal relationship with the supernal worlds. The kabbalists determined a link between the 613 parts of the human body, the 613 divine commandments of the Torah, and the 613 parts of the divine chariot, such that fulfilling each of the Torah's 613 commandments has a specific corresponding effect in the supernal world. Human consciousness thus becomes an active factor in the divine realm, uniting and separating its different dimensions and participating in the cosmic struggle between the Shekhinah and the *kelipot* (the 'husks' concealing the sparks of holiness), between sanctity and impurity, exile and redemption.[8]

---

[7] For the kabbalistic vocabulary see Scholem, *Major Trends in Jewish Mysticism*, 244–86; Elior, 'Messianic Expectations'; Tishby, *Wisdom of the Zohar*, 229–43.

[8] See Tishby, *The Doctrine of Evil and the Husks* (Heb.); id., *Wisdom of the Zohar*, 371–421, 447–548, 1155–1212.

It was this new status accorded to man in the kabbalistic mythos, whereby human thought and deed were perceived as having real impact on the sefirotic world, that justified the religious stringencies that came to be known as *darkhei ḥasidut*, 'paths of piety'. A life aimed at achieving the reunification of the divine realm through human intent, meditative prayer, and ritual required distance from the material world, freedom from the bounds of conventional language, and a not insignificant degree of imagination, autonomous spirituality, and intellectual liberty. The goal was participation in the redemption of the Shekhinah, and the way to attain this was by *devekut*. This was to be achieved through an ascetic minimalization of bodily demands and by striving to achieve a state of ecstasy that would move the spirits in the higher worlds. This devotion engendered the internalization of an altered consciousness focused on a commitment to restoring the divine unity: to redeeming the sparks of divinity dispersed in the world; bringing together the scattered elements of the divine world; repairing the damage to the heavenly temple; and restoring the divine throne. It was expressed in a new form of religious worship that specifically linked the details of the Torah commandments given to man in the terrestrial domain to the elements of the divine chariot in the heavenly domain.[9]

The kabbalistic literature in which these concepts were developed in the Middle Ages and the early modern period was composed in different places and under diverse historical circumstances. It includes texts dealing with the divine and with man's relation to the divinity, as well as with new ideas about the Torah, the divine commandments, the Hebrew language, and prayer, all of which are directed to bridging the gap between the revealed and the concealed. But the major achievement of kabbalah, with its theosophical, theurgic, ecstatic, ascetic, and mystical elements, was its profound transformation of the concept of the divinity in relation to human acts and thoughts. This led to new interpretations of ideas regarding the splitting off and reunification of the components of the godhead as well as of exile and redemption, equanimity and passionate attachment, in heaven and on earth.

Since the kabbalistic literature was largely written by Jews in exile from the Holy Land, it is not surprising that it is replete with cosmic, mystical, messianic, and historical ideas connected with exile and redemption. The experience of exile and the yearning for redemption were not constant: they waxed and waned with the vicissitudes of the times. The greater the sufferings of exile, the deeper the yearning for redemption; the more life seemed arbitrary, punishing, and senseless, the greater the search for consolation, and the more intense the effort to find a mystical dimension to experience. The effort to

---

[9] See Tishby, *Wisdom of the Zohar*, 673–749.

escape the sense of exile, the confinement in the material world, and the bodily constraints implicit in the domain of 'being' engendered the quest for a higher reality, a longing for redemption, and an ongoing concern with the abode of the spirit, freedom, and the domain of 'nothingness'.[10]

The expulsion of the Jews from Spain and Portugal that began in 1492 imposed great suffering on the exiles and their descendants. This unprecedented catastrophe, taxing body and soul, underscored the sense of exile and engendered alienation from tangible reality; redemption was to be found only in the superior worlds. Exile was seen not as the consequence of political and religious factors but rather of cosmic events and meta-historical processes; this bestowed significance on suffering and offered hope for change.[11] The kabbalists of the sixteenth century gradually reinterpreted the chaos and arbitrary nature of history as a predetermined, perceivable process of cosmic importance: when reformulated as the 'birthpangs of the messiah' (*hevlei mashiah*), Jewish suffering became a stage in the transition from exile to redemption. This interpretation drew on an ancient tradition recorded in *Lamentations Rabbah*, according to which the messiah was born on the day that the Temple was destroyed, thereby linking crisis and birth, destruction and redemption, catastrophe on earth and the intensity of the yearning directed to the divine realm. In the first decades after the expulsion, the exiles impatiently awaited redemption: if the pain of the expulsion was the 'birthpangs of the messiah', then the birth of the messiah, in fulfilment of the hope for imminent redemption, was inevitable.[12]

But the hope for imminent redemption was disappointed. By the opening decades of the sixteenth century it became clear that exile would not be swiftly followed by redemption. In consequence, the trauma of exile and the yearnings for redemption underwent a mystical metamorphosis and were transposed from the earthly plane to the heavenly domain. It was now the Shekhinah that was in exile, and the Jewish longing for redemption became a longing for the redemption of the Shekhinah. The deeper meaning of this inversion becomes clear once one understands that if the exiled one is the Shekhinah, it is God who is in exile; whereas previously God was depicted as the Redeemer, the Jewish people was now the redeemer. Redeeming the exiled Shekhinah, or freeing her from the *kelipot* that conceal her and from the influence of the *sitra ahara* (the heavenly projection of the earthly exile), became the main concern of kabbalistic literature. In the kabbalistic view it is

---

[10] See Scholem, *The Messianic Idea*; Baer, *Exile* (Heb.); Elior, 'Exile and Redemption'.

[11] Regarding the spiritual crisis of the Iberian expulsion, see the introduction to Scholem, *Sabbatai Sevi*; id., *Major Trends in Jewish Mysticism*, 244–51; and Elior, 'Breaking the Boundaries' and 'Exile and Redemption'.   [12] See Scholem, *Sabbatai Sevi*, 1–102.

the deity who is captive, broken, and seeking redemption, while man is the potential redeemer and restorer of worlds. The kabbalists transformed the arena of the contest: although they could not change the desperate situation in which they found themselves in exile, they were able—through prayer, study, and meditation on the unity of the deity—to affect the struggle taking place in the heavenly spheres. They believed that once equanimity had been restored in heaven, the earthly situation would change too and exile would give way to redemption.[13]

All this was revealed to Joseph Karo in a mystical vision by a *magid*, a mentoring angel revealed in his spirit who claimed identity with the Shekhinah as the exiled daughter of Zion (Bat Tsiyon). Karo experienced the *magid* as the vocal embodiment of the Mishnah, which introduced itself by saying, 'I am the Mishnah speaking to you, I am your soul, I am an angel . . .'. We know that Karo experienced this revelation in 1533, on the eve of Shavuot—according to the Zohar, the mystical wedding night of the Shekhinah and the Kudsha Berikh Hu:

He first said: My devoted beloved . . . who have taken it upon yourselves to crown me [le'atereni] on this night, for it is many years that my wreath has fallen and I have no consolation, and I am cast down to the earth embracing the dust. Now you have restored my wreath to its place . . . and the sound of your Torah and the vapour of your mouths ascended before God and penetrated several firmaments . . . I am the Mishnah . . . through you I have been elevated this night . . . Therefore my children, be strong and rejoice in my love, in my teaching, in my reverence, for if you could surmise an infinitesimal measure of the sorrow that is mine you could have no happiness in your hearts . . . Therefore be courageous and of good cheer my sons, my devoted beloved, and do not cease from your study . . . Therefore stand on your feet and raise me up and recite aloud as on Yom Kippur the verse blessed be the name of the glory of His kingdom for ever [Barukh shem kevod malkhuto le'olam va'ed] . . . and ascend to the land of Israel for all times are not the same . . . It is through you that I was elevated this night.[14]

This revelation formed the basis of the kabbalistic vision of reciprocity in the relationship between man and God, and it led to the development of a mystical dimension that added new purpose to the kabbalistic ethos. It evolved around the exile and redemption of the Shekhinah, concepts which

---

[13] On the conceptual reversal of exile and redemption, see Elior, 'R. Joseph Karo and R. Israel Ba'al Shem Tov' (Heb.). On the historical experience of the Jews in exile see Israel, *European Jewry*, ch. 1.

[14] For the words of the Shekhinah (or the *magid*) to Karo, see *Magid meisharim*, 18; *Shenei luḥot haberit*, vol. iii, *Masekhet shevuot*, §5; an English translation can be found in Jacobs (ed.), *Jewish Mystical Testimonies*. See also Werblowsky, *Joseph Karo*; cf. Elior, 'R. Joseph Karo and R. Israel Ba'al Shem Tov' (Heb.).

were linked to the 'breaking of the vessels' (a cosmic process through which the divine world itself is exiled) and the 'restoration' (or 'restitution') of the supernal worlds. These processes were viewed as representing the cosmic battle between the *sitra aḥara*, emblem of evil, impurity, exile, enslavement, chaos, and destruction, and the *sitra dekedusha*, embodiment of the yearning for good, the domain of sanctity, freedom, harmonious order, and a salvation whose true colours have yet to be revealed.

In resolving this dualistic conflict between good and evil, holiness and defilement, between Shekhinah and *kelipah*—ultimately between exile and redemption, life and death, and slavery and freedom—human deeds and intentions were regarded as crucial. The ancient concepts of *kavanah*, *yiḥudim*, *devekut*, and *tikun* were given new meaning in the conceptual world of kabbalah. Redemption, Shekhinah, holiness, and the higher worlds are situated at one pole, corresponding to the imperatives of kabbalistic prayer, continual study, spiritual elevation, contemplation, self-sacrifice, *devekut*, and *yiḥudim*. Exile, *sitra aḥara*, *kelipah*, impurity, and the mundane world occupy the other pole, corresponding to the requirements of withdrawal, equanimity, estrangement, asceticism, and self-abnegation. The redemption of the Shekhinah was tied to study and prayer characterized by *devekut*; to prayer with particular intentions; to the performance of commandments with the intent of elevating the divine sparks; in a word, to religious activity for the sake of restoring the world and redeeming the Shekhinah. The subjugation of the *kelipah* and the *sitra aḥara* would follow from the abandonment of material concerns, the punctilious performance of divine commandments with proper intent, additional stringencies, piety, *hasidut*, asceticism, and equanimity. The groups that elected to live according to the way of *hasidut* occupied themselves with *hokhmat ha'emet* in order to accelerate the end of exile and the coming of redemption by redeeming the Shekhinah from the *kelipot* or husks enfolding, concealing, and entrapping her.

To summarize the argument so far: from the late 1520s on, groups of Spanish exiles and their descendants engaged in the study of kabbalah in order to redeem the Shekhinah, following the path of *hasidut* that meant turning one's back on this world and engaging instead in the realm of holiness, Shekhinah, spiritual life, and redemption. In the circles of Joseph Taitazak and Solomon Molkho in Salonika in the third decade of the sixteenth century, and of Joseph Karo, Solomon Alkabets, and Moses Cordovero, who came to Safed from Turkey a decade later, a dualistic myth of the supernal world developed. This conception is marked by the struggle between defilement and holiness, *kelipah* and Shekhinah, exile and redemption. The idea of the exiled daughter of Zion, Bat Tsiyon—a concept identical with that of the

Shekhinah, sometimes represented as *atarah* ('wreath' or 'crown'), Keneset Yisra'el, the bride, or the captive woman—became a multilayered symbol representing in the heavenly sphere the earthly experience of suffering in exile and hope for redemption. It promised the potential of metamorphosis from bad to good, from separation to unity, from distress to hope, and from exile to redemption. It was in this context of an intense sense of exile and yearning for redemption that the kabbalists evolved the idea of redeeming the female Shekhinah from the power of the *kelipah*—the impure, exile, and separation—and bringing about its unification with its male counterpart Kudsha Berikh Hu so as to restore a state of unity. In the second half of the sixteenth century Lurianic kabbalah added concepts which connected the exile and the 'breaking of vessels' to the redeemed 'restored world' (*olam hatikun*) and the elevation of the divine sparks. This reinforced the concept of dualistic conflict in the higher worlds being reflected in the human world and emphasized the power of human thought and action carried out with the intent of achieving 'restitution', 'mending', and 'restoration' and resolving the mystical conflict of forces on high.[15]

The social expression of this myth was the formation of circles of mystics who devoted themselves to studying kabbalistic texts, praying with the intention of mystical unification, and taking upon themselves all kinds of stringent religious practices. Their purpose was to hasten the redemption of the Shekhinah by withdrawing themselves from this world—the world of *kelipah* and *sitra ahara*, evil and exile—and seeking proximity to the higher realms, the sphere of the *sitra dekedusha*, good and redemption. To this end they introduced new customs in prayer and ritual: meditations of intent (*kavanot*), formulas to help them restore the divine order (*tikunim*) and understand the essential unity of God (*yihudim*), and mental techniques to help them overcome the bounds of corporeality and achieve a closeness with God (*devekut*). The intention of this intellectual activity was to tilt the scales in the struggle between the cosmic powers of good and evil, exile and redemption, subjugation and freedom. The outcome of this struggle, they believed, determined the fate of the Shekhinah and the fate of the heavenly and the earthly Keneset Yisra'el.[16]

These practices derived from the esoteric writings of early kabbalistic masters of the twelfth and thirteenth centuries, from the Zohar, from the extensive kabbalistic literature written between the thirteenth and sixteenth centuries, and from the charismatic behaviour of outstanding spiritual

---

[15] See Scholem, *Major Trends in Jewish Mysticism*, 244–86; id., *On the Kabbalah and its Symbolism*, 118–57.

[16] Schechter, 'Safed in the Sixteenth Century'; Faierstein, *Jewish Mystical Autobiographies*.

personalities. Such were the kabbalists Solomon Molkho, Joseph Karo, Solomon Alkabets, Moses Cordovero, and Isaac Luria, who incorporated the kabbalistic mythos into their way of life. Subsequent generations of disciples, including Eleazar Azikri, Hayim Vital, Abraham Galante, and Israel Sarug, established sacred societies whose members took on stringent and ascetic halakhic practices in order to assist in the battle between *kelipah* and holiness, to restore and mend the worlds, to weaken the power of the *sitra aḥara*, strengthen the power of the sacred, and hasten the redemption of the Shekhinah.[17]

Their peers and disciples quickly adopted the new practices, giving them public currency in much wider circles. These included wearing two pairs of tefilin; using highly sharpened, 'polished' blades for the ritual slaughter of animals; wearing garb consisting of four white garments, to symbolize the reign of the *sefirah* of Hesed; wearing extremely long prayer-shawls; replacing the regular Ashkenazi liturgy with the Sephardi liturgy that had been used by the Holy Ari in Safed; fasting and self-mortification in order to facilitate withdrawal from the world; frequent ritual immersion; and rigorous asceticism, purification, and isolation to attain greater distance from the dominion of the *sitra aḥara* in the material world. All this in addition to the regular study of kabbalah with the purpose of drawing closer to the supernal world through *kavanot* and *yiḥudim*, fervent prayer with appropriate intent, and other customs connected to properly motivated supererogation, replete with symbolic meaning referring to the sefirotic universe, the heavenly temple, and the priestly service, all with the intent of having an effect on the higher worlds.[18]

Further dissemination followed once the ideas of the kabbalists and the practices of the sacred societies and those inspired by them were put into writing. The innovations that reflected the mystical reality of the circles who had revived in their consciousness the spirituality of the Zohar were soon to be found in books being published in every part of the Jewish world, such as *Sefer hamefo'ar* (Salonika, 1529); *Pardes rimonim* (Kraków, 1592); *Reshit ḥokhmah* (Venice, 1579); *Tomer devorah* (Venice, 1589); *Sefer ḥaredim* (Venice, 1601); *Ta'alumot ḥokhmah* (Basle, 1629); *Magid meisharim* (Lublin, 1646); *Emek hamelekh* (Amsterdam, 1648); *Shenei luḥot haberit* (Amsterdam, 1649); *Ḥayat hakaneh* (Amsterdam, 1658); *Shulḥan arukh shel ha'ari* (Safed, 1587);

---

[17] See Fine, 'Pietistic Customs from Safed' and *Safed Spirituality*. On the leaders of the sacred societies and their members see Werblowsky, *Joseph Karo*; Fine, *Physician of the Soul*; Zak, *Moses Cordovero's Gates of Kabbalah* (Heb.).

[18] Cf. *Shivḥei ha'ari*; *Magid meisharim* (1960 edn.), 'Instructions', pp. 21–2, and the pietistic rules of conduct collected in Schechter, 'Safed in the Sixteenth Century'.

Sefer gerushin (Venice, 1602); and *Nagid umetsaveh* (Amsterdam, 1712). Some material survived in manuscript—for example, *Galya raza*, written in 1543–53 by an unknown author; the anonymous sixteenth-century work *Sefer hameshiv*; *Ets hayim*, printed in 1784; the early seventeenth-century *Sefer haheziyonot* ('Diary of Dreams') by Hayim Vital, first published by Aaron Ze'ev Aescoly in Jerusalem in 1954 (a similar work, called *Shivhei rav hayim vital*, was published in Ostraha in 1826); and *Or yakar*, by Moses Cordovero, not printed until the twentieth century—as did various *takanot* (collections of rules) of kabbalistic groups, which spread through the Jewish world in this form in various editions. From the sixteenth century onwards, dissemination of these practices and the mystical ideas underlying them led to a wave of religious renewal in intellectual circles and the formation of further groups devoted to the study of kabbalah, to prayer directed towards the redemption of the Shekhinah, and to a life of piety aimed at eschewing materialism in favour of spirituality. Between the sixteenth and the eighteenth centuries, kabbalistic fraternities spread throughout the Jewish world, from Turkey and Safed to the Balkans, Italy, Podolia, and Galicia. They produced a rich harvest of new liturgical practices, prayers, and religious ceremonies, intensive mystical study, and halakhic innovation.[19] The main effort was directed towards internalizing the new concepts through the study of kabbalah and a life of piety.[20] In order to attain this redemptive consciousness and to articulate its detailed ritual system, the kabbalistic fraternities frequently cut themselves off from the community. Concerned to maintain their esoteric way of life, they rejected traditional sources of authority and established separate frameworks for prayer and study, for ritual slaughter and charity, and for purification and sanctification. Their justification for their exclusive socioreligious practices was that the goal of influencing the superior realms, through the study of kabbalah, prayer with special intent, innovative Zoharic rituals, and a life of piety, demanded consecration and asceticism and the maintenance of much more severe standards than was the practice in the traditional community. The effort needed to exert an impact on the higher worlds required them to distance themselves from the conventional order so as to create a separate sacred space, both symbolic and tangible.[21]

---

[19] Many of the 9,060 Jewish books that were printed in the course of the 18th-century printing revolution were the product of the resurgence of mysticism and its expression in mystical-moral and liturgical literature. See Winograd, *Thesaurus of the Hebrew Book* (Heb.).

[20] See the description of Luzzatto's pietistic circle in Ginzburg (ed.), *R. Moses Hayim Luzzatto* (Heb.); for an English biography of Luzzatto see Ginzburg, *The Life and Work of Moses Hayyim Luzzatto*. Cf. Tishby, *Investigations* (Heb.), iii. 625–994.

[21] See Elior, 'R. Nathan Adler and the Frankfurt Pietists'.

Over the sixteenth, seventeenth, and eighteenth centuries, reactions to the spread of kabbalah and the rise of ascetic mystical groups varied. Some communities tried to restrict the pietistic way of life to the select few, although in general the members of the esoteric groups who dedicated themselves to the study of kabbalah for the sake of the Shekhinah did not seek public influence and did not represent a threat to the communal establishment. This changed, however, with the appearance of the Shabatean movement in the last third of the seventeenth century.[22] The significance of Shabateanism for hasidism will be discussed in Chapter 7; here it is sufficient to note that the nature of the many closed, separatist groups took on new significance with the emergence of this eschatological movement, which undermined the social order by yoking kabbalistic tradition to immediate (not future) messianism.

The hasidism of the Ba'al Shem Tov evolved in the mid-eighteenth century in the world of the kabbalistic circles that were concerned with the 'Torah of truth' and lived according to the 'way of *ḥasidut*'.[23] Its founders, however, did not confine themselves within the bounds of the mystical tradition of the dualistic struggle and the attempt to affect the higher worlds. These mystical innovators set out to contribute something new to the mystical outlook and its implications on earth. The novelty of the Ba'al Shem Tov's approach was that it replaced the dualistic mystical perception of good and evil, exile and redemption, with a new holistic perception based on three essential theological elements: the entirety of the divine presence everywhere; the accessibility of the hidden divine realm to every member of the community; and the essential equality of all modes of divine worship.[24]

The novelty of the hasidism of the Ba'al Shem Tov derives from its fresh interpretation of biblical concepts. Take, for example, the idea of God's glory filling all the earth (Isaiah 6: 3). By taking this verse literally—by maintaining that *all* is divinity and that the tangible physical world is merely an illusion— hasidism linked the divine realm with the terrestrial one. Similarly, a new point of departure in divine worship is reflected in the hasidic concept that '*all* people' can address the immanent, ever-present God, and that this can be achieved through any form of divine worship, taking the verse 'In all your

---

[22] See Heilperin, *Records of the Council of the Four Lands* (Heb.), 205, 418, and Balaban, *On the History of the Frankist Movement* (Heb.), i. 125–6, on various measures that the Jewish communities took against the spread of kabbalistic writings.

[23] On kabbalistic-pietistic associations in the 18th century, see Maimon, *Lebensgeschichte*; Dinur, 'The Origins of Hasidism'; and Elior, 'R. Nathan Adler and the Frankfurt Pietists'. On the pietistic associations that were acting under the auspices of the community see Gelber, 'History of the Jews of Brody' (Heb.); Reiner, 'Wealth, Social Status and Torah Study' (Heb.).

[24] On the novel hasidic conception of God and man, see Elior, *The Paradoxical Ascent to God*, 1–5, 49–97.

ways know Him' (Proverbs 3: 6) to be a reflection of the unlimited power of human thought. Many of the ideas presented by the founders of hasidism in regard to mystical devotion resemble those of the kabbalists of Safed and their successors, but now they were no longer limited to esoteric circles or to a dualistic perception of God. The hasidic innovation was the interrelationship between the new holistic conception of God (his glory fills *all* the earth, divine vitality ebbs and flows at *all* times, and *all* is divine) and a new holistic conception of society—a concern for '*all* men', 'the entire community of Israel', where every person is viewed as a 'child of the superior world', and as partaking of 'comradely love'—which opened the world of kabbalah to ever-widening circles. This openness derived from the idea of an immanent, all-embracing divinity, a view of God as perpetually animating existence and present in all reality, defined as that which can be grasped in thought and language. Exile and redemption were reinterpreted as being and nothingness, that which is revealed and that which is concealed, divine and human thought. The innovation of hasidism was the understanding of the holistic nature of the divine presence and its accessibility to all through the power of the human mind, and the concomitant extension to the ordinary person of spiritual demands previously addressed only to the elite. Whereas the ritual stringency of the esoteric groups of scholarly mystics had made them closed by their very nature, hasidism was open and voluntary: each charismatic leader or tsadik gathered around him an egalitarian community, or *edah*. Practices derived from the new mystical consciousness now served to confront the dual meaning of an existence that united being and nothingness while acknowledging the equal divine reality in every being, irrespective of physical barriers. These conceptual systems were now accessible to anybody. All were invited to approach them in any way possible, in the new awareness that the illusory manifestations of the world concealed a hidden divine essence.

Hasidism is thus the continuation of the chain of Jewish mysticism that extended from the ancient *heikhalot* literature[25] to the late twelfth-century kabbalah of Spain and Provence, the Zohar of thirteenth-century Spain, the mysticism of the exiles from Spain that culminated in sixteenth-century Safed, and finally to the diffusion of kabbalistic ideas in the seventeenth century and their expression in Shabateanism and in the kabbalistic piety of the

---

[25] *Heikhalot* literature is concerned with describing the attributes of the celestial temples in a mystical-poetical way. This literature was composed between the second and fifth centuries CE. The hagiographical tradition on Israel Ba'al Shem Tov notes that he studied this literature as a means of transcending boundaries and engaging with mystical experience in the upper world. See Loewenthal, *Communicating the Infinite*, 7–10.

first half of the eighteenth century. The kabbalistic literature was a treasury of midrashic and mystical traditions perpetuating the legacy of the mishnaic and talmudic periods, and the laboratory for new ways of describing the messianic future in the light of divine–human relationship. From the twelfth century on, this literature laid down a fourfold thesis: beyond the manifest world there exists a concealed world; beyond the manifest meaning of sacred texts there lies a secret meaning; beyond human language there is a hidden, divine language; and beyond the manifest life of man, limited in time and space, there is a hidden life in the higher worlds which are free of such limits. The basis of all things is this hidden, divine reality that, ordinarily, cannot be perceived; however, thought, through its manifestation in language and sacred texts, is a window onto that reality. The divine order of time, stretching from exile to redemption, stands behind the arbitrary time that determines the tangible order of events. The hidden realm in its various manifestations is revealed in the human soul, in thought, in waking and dreaming consciousness, in manifest language and concealed language, and it can be reflected in this world through symbolic and ritual expressions. The growth of hasidism belongs to the continuum of kabbalistic history concerned with exile and redemption. Its background was the cultural constellation inaugurated by the diffusion of Safed mysticism, resulting from its publication during the sixteenth and seventeenth centuries.[26]

But hasidism is not only a continuation of kabbalistic tradition; it is also a revolution in its meaning and application. The kabbalistic tradition had reshaped the concept of God in the image of man and man in the image of God and transformed man into the redeemer and God into the redeemed; the Ba'al Shem Tov combined this with a new spiritual approach which connected human thought, formulated in ordinary language, with the enigmas of divine dialectic, formulated in the letters that incarnate the divine spirit. In doing so it made the mystical perception of kabbalah relevant to every person in every place and every social context.

The hasidic masters did not view kabbalah as the property of the elite or the few. The mystical view of exile and redemption and of the linguistically mediated encounter between the human spirit and the divine spirit, with all its implications for the ritual reality of the sacred tongue, was seen as relevant to everyone, without limitation or precondition. This hasidic innovation establishes a complex interaction between kabbalistic theology, with its dialectic of thought, speech, and action, creation and nothingness, and the religious destiny of each individual. That destiny stems from the revelation of

[26] On the relationship between kabbalah and hasidism, see Elior, 'Hasidism: Historical Continuity', and also Chs. 5–7 of the present volume.

the spiritual element in the world of speech and the world of action in its relation to the divine dialectic.[27]

The cosmic ideas of domains of exile and of redemption mediated by a
world of language and speech were redefined as finite and infinite, being and
nothingness, division and unity, subjugation and freedom. In the hasidic
interpretation, 'exile' meant the manifest world as isolated from its divine origin and treated as a tangible reality in the categories of time and space. This
was a literal way of separating the unity of thought, speech, and action from
its relation to the Infinite. 'Redemption' meant grasping the world from the
divine perspective, unifying thought, speech, and action in their divine
source, seeing through tangible, physical being to the abstract, divine endlessness. It meant bestowing upon man the divine freedom of infinity, regarding
existence as an esoteric reality expressed in a dynamic unity of opposites that
is ever changing in the human spirit.

---

[27] On the dissemination of kabbalah in hasidic teachings see Loewenthal, *Communicating the
Infinite*, 1–28; Elior, *The Paradoxical Ascent to God*, 5–7, 139–42.

The Hasidic Concept
of Language
The Window in the Word

I heard in the name of the Ba'al Shem Tov that making a window in [Noah's] ark [*tevah*] means making a window out of the word [*tevah*] of Torah and prayer, to gaze through it from the beginning of the world to its end.

Or hame'ir, 57

MYSTICAL thought assumes that the higher and lower worlds are interconnected. The higher world is concealed, but is intimated in the lower world that is manifest. The essential unity is to be perceived in the oppositions in the manifest world; the variety within it reflects the concealed world from which it draws life and sustenance. Each world includes the other, and every aspect of each exhibits deep reflections of the other and their infinite interrelationship. The common ground of these mutual relations is language.

According to Jewish mystical doctrine, the source of language is divine. For this reason it is infinite, varied, eternal, and creative. The transition from the concealed to the revealed takes place through language; it is the revelation of God's creative power. We comprehend his infinity through his creation, understood in the Jewish mystical tradition as the infinite flow of letters from the hidden summit of being to the lowest level in this world. Creative power is thus contained in the letters of the sacred divine language, unifying the abstract with the concrete in so far as reality is an elaboration of the expression of divine speech. The letters of the divine speech exist simultaneously in heaven and on earth; they are its energizing vital source and the necessary condition for its existence. The incessant and infinite permutation and combination of the letters in divine speech expresses both the infinite possibilities of divine being and the infinite possibilities of human thought, for the letters are the common denominator of Creator and creation. Each letter is a link between the higher worlds and the lower worlds. Mysticism unifies the earthly and divine meaning of the letters and reveals their hidden significance. In studying holy texts and the prayers derived from them, the mystic is able to go beyond the spatio-temporal bounds of their written form; by focusing his attention on the letters themselves, he is able to look through them to the higher worlds.[1]

For the Jewish mystic Hebrew is the key to deciphering the secrets of Creator and creation and to influencing the higher worlds, because it is the language of both divine creation and human perception: 'These twenty-two letters with which God . . . founded [and created His world]'.[2] In the ancient mystical text *Sefer yetsirah* (Book of Creation), written by an anonymous author in the early centuries of the Common Era, the process of creation is explicitly linked to the letters of the Hebrew language. The transition from abstract, creative divine power to the concrete reality of enduring creation sustained by 'divine breath' is effected through letters and ciphers, the source of both divine creativity and human perception. Jewish mystical tradition therefore has a distinctive attitude to the Hebrew language in all its aspects: its letters singly and in combination, the diacritical vowels and cantillation marks, the shape of the letters and their sounds. The transition from abstract to concrete and vice versa comes about through language; the Hebrew letters are seen as the physical manifestation of divine speech, as the creative force that perpetually engenders and sustains the universe, as a world within time whose validity transcends time.

The creative power of language, which moves all being from chaos to creation, is an axiom of many Jewish mystical doctrines. It derives from the description of Creation in Genesis, with its identification of divine speech with terrestrial existence: 'And God said let there be light—and there was light.' There is a rabbinic tradition that the world was created in ten utterances or speech-acts. A similar mystical tradition holds that it was created by means of thirty-two channels of wondrous wisdom, comprising the twenty-two letters and first ten numbers. This tradition in itself reflects the creative possibilities implicit in language, in that it plays on the connections between words sharing the same three-letter root *s-p-r*: these are *sipur* (narrative), *mispar* (number), *sefer* (book), *sapir* (sapphire, a term that occurs frequently in the mystical *Sefer yetsirah*, referring to the heavenly throne and heavenly tablets that were quarried from sapphire), and *sefirah* (a perceptible aspect of the divine):

---

[1] On the mystical conception of language, see Bialik, 'Language Closing and Disclosing'; Scholem, 'The Meaning of the Torah'; Elior, 'Different Faces of Freedom'; and Dan, *On Holiness* (Heb.), 31–58, 108–30.

[2] *Sefer yetsirah* 5: 4, 1: 1. For a comprehensive study of the book see Liebes, *The Creative Mysteries of the Book of Creation* (Heb.). For an English translation see *The Book of Creation*, ed. Kaplan.

With thirty-two wondrous paths of wisdom Yah, the Lord of Hosts, the God of Israel, the Living God, King of the Universe, Almighty God, merciful and gracious, high and exalted, dwelling in eternity, whose name is Holy, engraves and creates His universe with three *sefarim*: with text [*sefer*] with number [*sefar*], and with narrative [*sipur*]. Ten *sefirot* of infinite nothingness and twenty-two foundation letters . . . Ten *sefirot* of nothingness. Their measure is ten, which has no end: a depth of beginning; a depth of end; a depth of good; a depth of evil . . . a depth of above; a depth of below . . . The singular master, God faithful King, dominates them all from his holy dwelling until eternity of eternities. Ten *sefirot* of infinite nothingness: their appearance is like that of lightning, their limit has no end. His word in them is running and returning, they rush to His words like a whirlwind and prostrate themselves before His throne. . . . Ten *sefirot* of infinite nothingness. One is the breath of the Living God, blessed and praised be the name of the Life of the Worlds. Voice, Breath, and Speech: this is the Holy Spirit [*ruaḥ hakodesh*]. Two: Breath from Breath with it God Almighty engraved and carved the twenty-two foundation letters.[3]

The Hebrew language, the language of the Torah, embodies the word of the Creator and his infinite power through the divine word that perpetually sustains reality. Language consists of letters (*otiyot*), a word whose root, *ata*, means 'to come' (see, for example, Isaiah 21: 12), indicating that the letters come forth incessantly from the infinite divine source, from the depths of the creative consciousness. It is an infinite becoming because the word comes into being in each encounter between the word, or signifier, and the thing it signifies, between the spirit creating the letter and the spirit perceiving it, between the super-temporal idea and its specific manifestation in time and place.

Through language, the eternal, infinite, holy spirit (the Hebrew term is *ruaḥ*, which also means breath, wind, divine spirit, human spirit, living spirit, soul, life, and animation)—is connected to the spirit of man, the spirit of life, spirituality, and creativity. It stretches between the depths and heights of human experience, and to the spirit of the living God that includes all these. Sanctified by its divine source, language thus transcends its syntactical structure and human communicative function; it is the link between heaven and earth that exists beyond space and time as well as within it. It is the bridge between the divine and the human, the infinite and the finite, the abstract and the tangible, the spiritual and the physical; for abstraction and concreteness of thought, speech, and action are attributes of both divine and human language. Letters and numbers are the concrete, finite expression in this world of the creative divine spirit that is abstract and infinite. By virtue of its origins, language allows the human spirit to transcend the bounds of its material existence.

---

[3] *Sefer yetsirah* 1: 1, 6, 9, 11; 2: 1.

Hasidic tradition often cites the Ba'al Shem Tov's words concerning the creative language common to God and man, the divine source of the letters and their eternal vivifying power:

It is from the holy letters that the root and animation of man derive. For whatever is, in reality gets its being and existence only from the letters, out of which heaven and earth and all they contain were created. As is well known, the Ba'al Shem Tov explained the verse 'For ever, O God, Your word stands in heaven' (Ps. 119: 89) to mean that even now the entire life of creation and all existence springs from the holy letters that are God's word standing always in heaven to give them life. For otherwise, all would return to chaos, as it would have no sustenance.[4]

The power to create reality by the flow of letters from the infinite to the finite, from nothingness to being, from the spiritual to the physical, from the inconceivable to that which can be apprehended, is not the exclusive dominion of the deity. God creates the world through the utterance and permutation of letters, by inscribing, carving, and combining them as recorded in *Sefer yetsirah*; but man also combines letters to create words through language, generating in his mind new meanings and permutations that expand the bounds of comprehension and the depths of the spirit. The letters of which language is comprised may be regarded as the coincidence of opposites; spiritual and physical, abstract and concrete, concealed and visible, they are overflowing with meaning and yet essentially limited in their power to express the boundlessness of infinity.

Sefer yetsirah describes the letters as constantly 'flowing' from their infinite divine source, from nothingness: 'It is called nothingness because it is not conceived, neither in terms of its cause, nor in terms of itself. Its cause is the primal cause which is called the primeval cause because it preceded the universe; it is not a physical entity.' The Hebrew word for letter, *ot*, also means a sign or symbol, a marker that signifies an eternal meaning, as when one speaks of 'the sign of the covenant'. A symbol incorporates past, present, and future, the temporal and the eternal. The letters emerging from the hidden infinite into the revealed finitude transform nothingness into being, chaos into creation. They establish covenants, so to speak, between the abstract and the concrete, between the formless and the multidimensionality of existence. The apparently limited sign, a finite creation, gives concrete expression to the dialectical duality of divine expansion and contraction. The finite sign points to what is beyond it and testifies to its infinity; for infinite being to be conceivable and meaningful, it must be externalized and given token form in letter, symbol, or sign.

---

[4] *Ba'al shem tov al hatorah*, i. 16.

The letters perpetually emerging from thought into speech—from the infinite to the finite—simultaneously limit, signify, contract, reveal, conceal, and realize the infinite, constantly flowing divine thought, the 'spirit of the living God' that engenders and animates creation. They give literal, concrete expression to the covenant between heaven and earth, to the idea that the infinite, concealed element, ever vital and effusive, is made apparent only in the limitation provided by a finite signifier.

Let us now restate the basic assumption of mysticism. The concealed and revealed are interrelated—spirit and matter, soul and body, nothingness and being, abstract and concrete. The spiritual aspect, hidden from knowledge, animates the revealed reality, and the physical aspect makes possible the manifestation of the infinite aspect. Throughout reality, therefore, letters simultaneously reflect the revealed and the concealed, the concrete and the abstract, the spiritual and the physical, what is contracted and what expands:

Just as there are twenty-two letters composing Torah and prayer, so in all material and physical affairs in the world there are twenty-two letters, through which the world and all that is in it is created . . . But with the letters clothed in the matter of the world, the divine spirit abides under several coverings and garbs and shells.[5]

Divine speech has four distinctive characteristics:

1. It has infinite creative power (according to rabbinic tradition, the world *was created* through divine speech; according to mystical tradition it is *being created* continually through the everlasting divine speech, presented as a stream of letters flowing from above).

2. It is constantly in flux; the flow from the infinite to the finite animates terrestrial existence as the soul animates the body, sustaining its physiological reality and preventing it from reverting to chaos.

3. It exists simultaneously in heaven and on earth, thereby expressing a cosmic linguistic reality: 'For ever, O God, your word stands in heaven' (Psalm 119: 89).

4. It is a dialectical expression of nothingness and being. The letters represent simultaneously the finite, concrete signifier and the abstract, infinite signified, that is to say, both being and nothingness:

'For ever, O God, your word stands in heaven' (Psalm 119: 89): The Ba'al Shem Tov explained that 'your word', when you said 'Let there be a firmament within the water', refers to these words and letters. They stand for ever within the firmament of heaven,

---

[5] *Toledot ya'akov yosef*, 'Bereshit', 8.

wrapped within all the firmaments to vivify them . . . For if the letters withdrew for a moment, God forbid, and returned to their source, then all the heavens would be literally null and void, as if they were not . . . So too for all the creatures in all the worlds . . . Even this physical earth that is literally inanimate, if the letters of the ten utterances through which the earth was created during the first six days withdrew for a moment, they would literally be null and void.[6]

The Torah, understood as God's word, is a key element here. Jewish mystical tradition is founded on the conviction that the divine infinite, which both transcends time and space and permeates time and space (as well as thought, speech, and action) is imparted in the Torah and elaborated through language. Blurring the lines between infinite being and its finite manifestations, between abstract essence and its concrete expression, the sacred language transforms the apparently finite text into a coded form of the infinite divine spirit. The relation between divine being and holy text is not constrained by the laws of nature, human limitations, or rational thought. It is rather like the relationship between God and the world, between the concealed and the revealed, the spiritual and the physical, the esoteric and the exoteric. One might compare it to the relation between time and the clock, between music and its notation, between thought and speech. The perception that the Torah is composed of letters and words which are comprehended in human language and can be deciphered by human beings despite their divine source turned the sacred text into the meeting-place of the infinite and the finite. In the phrase of the kabbalists, it is 'a ladder planted on earth whose top reaches unto heaven', a place where being and nothingness coincide, where human understanding coalesces with its divine source.

Kabbalistic tradition attributed the Torah to a divine source or voice. It ascribed infinite meaning to the finite text and regarded each word and its component letters as an open unit, meaning that it has no determinate content that would dictate a single truth. Jewish mysticism is characterized by this recognition: the overt sense of the written text of the Torah is normative in the world of action, while in the realm of thought it is open to innumerable interpretations. Freedom of interpretation, freedom to explore the myriad possible meanings implicit in the divine word, is a key element in the mystical approach: as a hasidic dictum puts it, the Ten Commandments that God gave Moses on Mount Sinai were to be regarded not as 'engraved on stone tablets' (*harut al haluhot*) but as the freedom (*herut*) to devise inspired interpretations of the infinite sacred text.[7] Finite man seeks the infinite foundation, the spirit of the living God, in the infinity of language and the infinity of the spirit shared by

---

[6] *Tanya*, 'Sha'ar hayihud veha'emunah', 2.   [7] Mishnah *Avot* 6: 2.

God and man: 'Ten *sefirot belimah*' ('infinite abstract spheres', *belimah* meaning literally 'without substance', but also with connotations of constraining, so it is simultaneously flowing/expanding and constraining/holding): 'one is the spirit [or 'breath'] of the living God, blessed be He and the name of the eternal, the voice and spirit and speech and that is the Holy Spirit'.[8]

The mystical tradition maintains a threefold relationship to infinity and the freedom it embodies. First, the infinity of divine being transcends the limits of time, space, and language, but is intimated in the sacred tongue of Scripture. This is expressed in terms such as Ein Sof, *ayin*, the source of all being, and 'the spirit of the living God', sustaining all manifest dimensions. Second, by virtue of its infinite divine source (termed the 'holy spirit'), the Torah embodies an infinity of meaning, represented as having 'seventy facets'. Third, the infinity of human thought and its creative potential is reflected in the infinity of language, the letters, reading, writing; as described in *Sefer yetsirah*, 'voice and spirit and speech, and this is the holy spirit'.

The dialectical relationship between the infinity of meaning stored in the text and the finite disclosure at the overt level parallels the relation between God and the world, between the freedom of thought and the limits of speech and action. The principle of divine infinity (the signified) is expressed as effusion, abundance, expansiveness, and concealment; this is referred to as essence, idea, light, sparks, abundance, spirit, or nothingness. The principle of physical finitude (the signifier) relates to the element of limitation, contraction, and disclosure, referred to by the kabbalists as *levush* (literally 'garb', meaning 'external appearance' or 'concrete form'), vessel, boundary, letters, judgement, and contraction of the bodily or of being. Divine infinity can be perceived only when contracted into a vessel—that is, given form through its garb, or expressed in essentially limited form by letter, cipher, sign, or corporeality. The *levush* or concrete form is defined in terms of the level of reality in which it exists or to which it is passing. Divine infinity, embodying thought expanding without bounds and perpetually creative effusion, is clothed in a world that 'hides' it in order to reveal it discriminately. The kabbalists derive the etymology of *olam* (world) from *he'elem* or *ne'elam*, that which is hidden; they explain the process of creation by saying that 'the hidden is the cause of revelation and revelation is by dint of the hidden'. The infinite expansiveness of the divine spirit contracts, withdraws, and conceals itself in the world, just as the infinity of human thought is garbed in language with its finite signs. Divinity is comprehended as a process in which the infinite, limitless, divine essence constantly moves from nothingness to being: from abundant effusion to limit and judgement, from chaos to creation, from hidden revelation to

[8] *Sefer yetsirah* 1: 9.

revealed concealment, from boundless expansion to contracted existence, from idea to speech, and from abstract spirit to physical matter. For the sake of revelation it contracts itself in the cycles of nature, in letters, symbols, and signifiers, in material representations that can be grasped through the limits of understanding and the confines of language. This is a two-way process, for in kabbalistic thought each element seeks to return to its source, and each individual entity to its root: the spirit confined in its embodied form seeks to expand again and revert to its original state. Among the terms employed for this return from the concrete to the abstract are *bitul hayesh* (annihilation or transcendence of being), *hafshatat hagashmiyut* (stripping away of corporeality or divestment of materialism), *histalekut* (withdrawal), *hafshatat hamahshavah* (stripping away of thought), and *devekut* (attachment to or communion with the divine). Terms for the transformation in the other direction, from the abstract to the concrete, include *hamshakhah* (drawing down) and *shefiah* (effusion).[9]

In hasidic writings, the two-way nature of this process is often represented by the phrase 'And the holy creatures [*hayot*] ran back and forth', from Ezekiel's vision of the divine chariot (Ezekiel 1: 15). In the hasidic interpretation, *hayot* was read as *hiyut* ('animation'), an allusion to the divine animation, expanding and withdrawing, creating and annihilating, forming the universe and stripping away corporeality. This perpetual, dialectical process is a movement from the infinite to the finite and back, from nothingness to being and from being to nothingness. Each constricted element seeks to return to its expansive, abstract source, and each abstract element seeks to take on physical garb and be revealed in limited manifestation. Thus in the mystical tradition of *Sefer yetsirah* we find a dialectical relationship between hidden infinity and revealing finitude, or between the concealed essence that emanates and expands incessantly and the revealed garb which delimits it. The infinite is ever the hidden source of life for the manifest and the condition of the finite, while the finite is the condition of the disclosure and the partial conception of the hidden and the expression of the infinite. Nothingness is the condition of being, and being is the condition for the disclosure and conception of nothingness. Hidden thought is the condition of speech, and speech (oral or written) is the condition of the disclosure of thought.

The word *ruah*, as a designation for divine being, means spirit and inspiration, creating spirit and sustaining spirit, divine breath or life force, as well as

---

[9] On the hasidic mystical vocabulary see Elior, *The Paradoxical Ascent to God*, 143–66; Loewenthal, *Communicating the Infinite*, 100–38; Schatz-Uffenheimer, *Hasidism as Mysticism*; Green, *Tormented Master*, 285–336; Piekarz, *Between Ideology and Reality* (Heb.) and *Ideological Trends in Hasidism* (Heb.).

the spirit of unbounded freedom, omnipotent, infinite, and eternal, the spirit of wisdom and insight and holiness. In the divine being there is an identity of thought, speech, action, freedom and creativity, spirit and life, ideas that constitute separate categories of human existence. It is the purpose of mystical thought, however, to unify and to attain contemplative attachment to the divine coincidence of opposites—that is, to uncover this creative identity in human consciousness and to pursue the divine perspective. This divine perspective consists in the unity of thought, speech, and action in their relation to freedom and creativity, spirit and life, wisdom and creation, and in the dynamic relations of revelation and concealment, expansion and withdrawal, emanation and contraction, ebb and flow. The quest to contemplate the hidden divine element that perpetually animates the manifest universe is identical with the quest for the abstract infinite divine element embodied in the concrete, finite letter in speech, voice, and writing, as described in *Sefer yetsirah* and in the creation and freedom of the human spirit.

An interesting testimony to the mystical conception of language is found in the Ba'al Shem Tov's letter to his brother-in-law, the kabbalist Gershon of Kutow, who was living in the land of Israel. This letter, which describes in the first person an experience of mystical ascent, was inspired by visionary mystical literature. Written in the early 1750s, it did not reach the addressee, but was published in 1781 by Jacob Joseph of Polonnoye as an appendix to his *Ben porat yosef*, under the title *Igeret aliyat haneshamah*. Additional manuscript copies that surfaced subsequently were published in the twentieth century.[10] Following the description of his ascent in a dream to the heavenly 'world of souls' the Ba'al Shem Tov illuminates the relationship of mystical language to the higher worlds as explained to him in his vision:

Let me inform you of this, and may God be your help . . . particularly in the holy land: when you pray or study, in all that emerges from your mouth, you shall have the appropriate intentions, for each and every letter contains worlds and souls and divinity, and they ascend and are bound together and become unified [with the divinity]. Then the letters become unified [and form a word] and become truly unified in the divinity, and you thus include your soul with them in every aspect of the above, and all the worlds become unified so that there is then a great joy and immeasurable delight. As you would understand the joy of groom and bride at a minor level [*bekatnut*] so much more at this

---

[10] The two most important variants can be found in *Rabbi Israel Ba'al Shem Tov* (Heb.), ed. Kahana, 99, published in 1901 and based on a manuscript found in the library of Isaiah of Donovich, a disciple of the Maggid of Mezhirech, and Mondshine, 'An Early Version of the Besht's Epistle on his Heavenly Ascent' (Heb.), 233–6, published in 1982 and based on MS 8°5979 in the National Library in Jerusalem. An annotated English translation is published in Jacobs (ed.), *Jewish Mystical Testimonies*, 182–91, taken from *Ben porat yosef* (Korets, 1781), 100*a*–*b*.

supreme level . . . This vision was while awake, not in a dream, in full sight and not in riddles.[11]

The mystical significance of this perception of language and its heavenly origin becomes clearer within the context of the letter and a similar text in *Tsava'at harivash*, which will be discussed below, after presenting the epistle:

You will no doubt marvel and rejoice, as I too marvelled, about the vision that God showed me, the wonderful matters that are known to you respecting the ascent of the soul. I saw wondrous things the like of which I had not seen from the day I attained maturity. What I saw and learned when I ascended there it is impossible to tell or to say even face to face. But when I returned to the lower Garden of Eden I saw many souls of the living and the dead, known and unknown to me, without number, 'back and forth', to rise from world to world, as is known to the initiated, with great joy that the mouth cannot recount and the corporeal ear is too heavy to hear . . . The delight was great, literally like the giving of the Torah, which is impossible to conceive physically. I was confounded and shaken by this vision, for I thought perhaps this is for me and the time has come, heaven forbid, to leave the world, and that is why this was appropriate. So I sorrowed over myself and over my friends who were destined to die outside the land of Israel. But then I entered the palace of the King Messiah and I saw face to face what I had not seen from the day I became mature. They revealed to me that it was not for me, and they revealed to me wonderful and awesome profundities of Torah that I had not seen or heard, nor had any ear heard for many years. It occurred to me to ask whether the joy and jubilation was because of the imminence of His good advent and when He would come. To which His lofty response was that it could not be revealed. But [He said], know that when your teaching becomes famous in the world and what I taught you and you attained and they too can have unifying intentions [*yiḥudim*] and ascents like you, then all the shells will be consumed and it will be a time of propitiation and salvation. I wondered and sorrowed about the length of time and when this could possibly happen. But I heard three nostrums and three holy names that are easy to learn and explain and this appeased me. I thought that in this way other men of quality could reach my level. That is, they would be able to elevate their souls to heaven and learn and attain what I had. But I was not permitted to reveal this during my life. I asked on your behalf to instruct you and they did not permit [this] at all, so that I am sworn from there about this matter. And this I inform you and may God be your help . . . particularly in the holy land: when you pray or study, with every utterance and all that emerges from your mouth, you shall understand [intend] and unify, for each and every letter contains worlds and souls and divinity, and they ascend and are bound together and become unified with divinity. Then the letters become unified and form a word and become truly unified in the divinity, and you thus include your soul with them in every aspect of the above, and all the worlds become unified so that there is then a great joy and immeasurable delight . . . This vision was while awake, not in a dream, in full sight and not in riddles.[12]

[11] *Igeret aliyat haneshamah*, based on *Rabbi Israel Ba'al Shem Tov* (Heb.), ed. Kahana; bracketed material is from Mondshine, 'An Early Version' (Heb.). Cf. the version in *Ben porat yosef*.

[12] *Igeret aliyat haneshamah*, based on Mondshine, 'An Early Version'.

The Ba'al Shem Tov's multifaceted discussion clearly documents the spiritual transformation experienced when passing from one reality to another, whether when awake or while dreaming, in an 'ascent of the soul'. It indicates an intense inner experience of a higher reality in which limits are overcome. It reveals something about the vision of a new world that evolves as a consequence of the heavenly experience, a vision which annuls distinctions between past, present, and future, between sign and signified, between the written text and its internalization. It testifies to the blurring of the differences between the higher and lower worlds that accompanies the mystical elevation and expands the limits of the human spirit. The Ba'al Shem Tov's words, studded with substantial allusions to earlier mystical texts that come to life in his mystical consciousness, express his yearning to be liberated from the limits of his physical being and finitude. However, he is not only speaking of himself. He also aims to unify the human soul with the divine reality by disclosing the eternal, unbounded nature of language: each letter contains infinite spiritual manifestations: 'worlds and souls and divinity'.

The Ba'al Shem Tov's conception of language is rooted in the relationship between the infinity of the divine spirit and the infinity of the human spirit; it views language as linking the divine and the human. This conception is anchored in a view of the letters as a system of divine forces containing the infinite light and as the concrete manifestation of the abstract, divine nature. The spirit captured by the vessels of the sacred tongue is then liberated through the unification of the divine spirit and the human spirit. The version recorded in *Tsava'at harivash* displays another dimension: the unification and conjugation (*zivug*) with the world of speech, with the divine spirit speaking in man, is interpreted as unification (*yihud*) with the Shekhinah:

The Ba'al Shem Tov said about the verse 'And you will make a window [*tsohar*] to the ark [*tevah*]' [Gen. 6: 16] that every word [*tevah*] should shine [*matshir*]. For in each letter there are worlds and souls and divinity that ascend and are bound together and unified with each other and with divinity. Then the letters become unified and form a word and become truly unified in the divinity, and a man should include his soul in each aspect, and then all the worlds become unified so that there is then a great joy and immeasurable delight. That is the meaning of 'lower, second and third levels shall you make it'—worlds and souls and divinity contain three worlds. One must hearken to each word spoken by the Shekhinah, and in a similar manner to every word spoken in the world of speech, whenever one is speaking. That is the meaning of making a *tsohar*, that it should emerge brightly and please his creator. This requires great faith [*emunah*] as the Shekhinah is called the faithfulness of the nursemaid [*emunat omen*].[13]

---

[13] *Tsava'at harivash vehanhagot yesharot*, found among the papers of Isaiah, Rabbi of Janov, who witnessed and listened to the Ba'al Shem Tov and Dov Baer the Maggid of Mezhirech (Zolkiew, 1793).

The Ba'al Shem Tov's understanding as revealed to him in the mystical ascent reported in his letter forges a link between human language and the divine essence, and delves into the meaning of the sacred tongue and the power of the immediate experience of the ascent. Not only are all created beings animated and sustained by letters, but 'in each letter there are worlds and souls and divinity'. This concept is almost certainly tied to *Sefer yetsirah*, which proposes 'world, year, soul' as categories referring to place, time, and human life respectively, in their specific concreteness and infinite abstraction. Another kabbalistic source restates the *Sefer yetsirah* motif: 'All worlds, all years, all souls are full of letters . . . The whole world is full of holy letters.'[14] This phrasing may have influenced the Ba'al Shem Tov when he speaks of *letters* (finite, but conceived by man through the infinity of Hebrew, the sacred language), *worlds* (both the infinite superior and eternal world and the earthly world), and *souls* (both the infinite, transcendent, and the souls of finite human beings), *divinity* (infinite, creative, and changing), and proposes the unity of concrete and abstract in the letters of language. God discloses his infinite essence through the letters that are, so to speak, receptacles for the divine light, containing simultaneously the concealed higher worlds and the manifest world. The purpose of the spiritual quest is to contemplate the divine essence hidden in the letters as expressed through their physical manifestation in the spoken and the written word and consolidated through them: 'a man should include his soul in each aspect, and then all the worlds become unified and ascend so that there is then a great joy and immeasurable delight. That is the meaning of "lower, second and third levels shall you make it"—meaning worlds and souls and divinity.'[15]

The biblical mention of a window in Noah's ark (*tevah*) was understood by the Ba'al Shem Tov to imply that the word (also *tevah*) must also be illuminated and made to shine, for each letter contains worlds and souls that ascend and are bound together and unified with each other and with divinity, and then the letters become unified and form a word and achieve true unity with the divine. For example, acronyms formed from the initial letters of several words (*rashei tevot*) may be reinterpreted or expanded in a different way so as to throw new light on their meaning, or whole words may be interpreted as if they were acronyms. In the hasidic tradition, 'Making a window for the ark' means 'giving brightness to the words of Torah and prayer from the world of thought'.[16] Since words have been severed from the totality of their spiritual and cosmic contexts, from their relationship to the source of their life and their creative power, they must be opened up so that they can be penetrated

---

[14] *Otsar gan eden haganuz*, cited in Scholem, *The Kabbalah of Sefer hatemunah*, 193–5.
[15] *Tsava'at harivash*, p. 23, §75.   [16] 'Orah lahayim', 18*a*.

by the all-encompassing light. The concrete, physical, earthly, and finite must be illuminated through the abstract, spiritual, divine, and infinite that is concealed within it. To put it another way, the finite sign, word, and utterance must be illuminated in order to make visible the infinite signified, the glow of divine light that vitalizes its inner being.

A word (*tevah*) is open to multiple levels of interpretation, just as the biblical *tevah* (as Noah's ark is called in Hebrew) had multiple levels, following the divine injunction to construct it 'with lower, second, and third stories'.[17] The mystical tradition mandates enlightenment—the decoding of the seemingly physical meaning of the words to uncover their genuine divine essence—to open a glowing window into their esoteric being, to illuminate what is behind them. The sacred text reflects the duality of concealment and revelation, with each letter containing the whole in miniature, indicating its processes and contradictions, descending from the divine source to the earthly manifestation and then ascending again: 'Each and every letter contains worlds and souls and divinity, and they ascend and are bound together and become unified with divinity. Then the letters become unified and form a word.'

Divine infinity is embodied in words; the multilayered holy text is understood to be a concrete covering for the abstract, divine essence. The letters are the physical manifestation of the inconceivable Supreme Being, specific vessels containing the infinite divine light. Letters further imply narrative (*sipur*), and the root *s-p-r* is connected to unity, inclusion, and attachment (*devekut*). ('A woman *conversing* [*mesaperet*] with her husband' is a rabbinic euphemism for sexual intimacy, itself perceived as a theurgic force for attaining divine unity.) *Tevah* has many meanings in Hebrew, and the Ba'al Shem Tov seems to make use of them all. This word refers to letters and words, to Noah's ark, or to a floating ark concealing in itself the divine spark, passing vertically and horizontally beyond the limits of time and space. He speaks of the *tevah* as a container or treasure chest that preserves hidden or unknown strata of language, as a resonating chamber for language's manifold meanings and connections. He likewise evokes the image of letters hovering in the air when he depicts the words of prayer wafting up from earth to heaven. The relationship between the word-receptacle and the glowing window is also compared to the relation between womb and seed, that is to say, between the covert condition of life and the overt condition of life, between matter and spirit, body and soul. The letters, in the sense of spoken words, are regarded as receptacles or vessels containing worlds, souls, and divinity. In human

---

[17] Gen. 6: 16.

thought and speech these pass from concrete to abstract and vice versa. Fervent prayer or recounting a story in sanctity, with the intention of becoming one with God through concentrating on the hidden meaning, allows the opening of the containers of language; they open a window into the word, engender unity, *devekut*, and conjugation with the Shekhinah, which is known in kabbalistic tradition as 'the world of speech' or 'hidden speech'. They allow the movement from being to nothingness and entry into the supreme palaces. For the Ba'al Shem Tov, the Shekhinah, 'the world of speech',[18] speaks within the human individual. In other words, the multivalent metaphors of sexuality, speech, narration, unification, and attachment bring the divine and the human together.

In the Ba'al Shem Tov's teaching, the words spoken in the holy tongue of prayer and Torah intersect with the divine plane of the world of speech (*olam hadibur*) connected to the Shekhinah; when man's voice is charged with the holy tongue, the Shekhinah speaks within him. Divine speech and human speech are interwoven, for the 'world of speech' is a kind of resonating box through which that world communicates from within. In other words, the manifest human speech reciting holy scriptures or sacred texts is the concrete disclosure of the hidden divine voice; the inwardness of the infinite light within the letters is revealed in human speech.

The *olam hadibur* resonates in man when he opens the window onto the letters of language, laying bare its divine essence. From another perspective: when man annuls his independent conception and turns his self (*ani*) to nothing (*ayin*), then his consciousness is filled by the spirit of God speaking in man: '"It is not in heaven" (Deut. 30: 12): This is his mighty Shekhinah that the Holy One imparted his Shekhinah among us, in the mouths of his people the house of Israel as the holy Zohar states that the Shekhinah dwells in the mouth of man.'[19] In the Ba'al Shem Tov's words, the window in Noah's ark becomes a source of light illuminating the verbal 'ark', uncovering the infinite significance of 'worlds and souls and divinity' behind the finite representation of the sign. Some kabbalists regard each letter as a gateway to the higher worlds; for some, every word symbolizes and points to the world of the *sefirot*; some go further in their freedom to read the hidden meaning of the text and find the divine letters in all manifestations of reality. Some emphasize the joy that arises from interaction with the cosmic depths of the letters, and the ecstatic element in the language of prayer through which man passes from the finite to the infinite. Some visualize cosmic forms to the letters; others ascribe

---

[18] On the 'world of speech', see Schatz-Uffenheimer, *Hasidism as Mysticism*, and Elior, 'R. Joseph Karo and R. Israel Ba'al Shem Tov' (Heb.). Cf. *Degel mahaneh efrayim*, 243–4 ('Ekev').

[19] *Hesed le'avraham*, 'Likutim', 52*b*.

to them musical forms; some associate different colours with the different *sefirot* and holy names; others emphasize the interrelationship between divine speech and human speech, between the infinite element that is identical with infinite thought and the concrete element that is identical with the letters. The relationship to the straightforward meaning of the text is that of a creative metamorphosis that seeks to replace the univocal literal meaning with a new interpretation that discloses its multiplicity of meaning.

The letters of language, speech, and prayer become the window through which the infinite world is perceived. Letters and words are associated systematically with the individual *sefirot* that are interpreted as the foundations of being. Note that the word *sefirot* is etymologically connected not only to the words for numbers, books, and narrative but also to the word for *sapirim* (sapphires), hinting at a mirror-like illumination reflecting the divine spirit in terrestrial letters, opening a shining window on to language. Thus the Ba'al Shem Tov connects the ten *sefirot* of *Sefer yetsirah* 1: 1 with the twenty-two letters about which *Sefer yetsirah* 2: 1 says that 'He engraved them, weighed them, permutated them, and formed the soul of every creature that would ever exist.' By combining the individual letters or digits into language—in the form of book (*sefer*), story (*sipur*), divine sphere (*sefirah*), and number (*mispar*)—he created a window onto the infinite, through which the divine is also manifested in human reality. The *sefirot* are connected to the sapphire pavement of Exodus 24: 10 and the sapphire foundations of Isaiah 54: 11 and Ezekiel 1: 26.[20] These represent the exalted infinity of divine abstraction inconceivable by man. They correspond to the spirit, soul, and divinity that cannot be grasped by man without a mediating, physical form to conceal their infinity. The letters and numbers that unite the concrete with the abstract are the form of divine revelation that can be grasped in the human world. As a physical being, man has no perception of or contact with the 'sapphire pavement', the divine world of *sefirot* and the ancient source of the holy written language. The ten *sefirot* are beyond conception, abstract and infinite without definable essence, and therefore have no clear-cut interface with the human world other than that provided by the letters and numbers which, infinite themselves, manifest the infinite spirit. Man is called upon to recognize the dual nature of the letters and numbers as symbol and essence, as sound and sense, as signifier and signified, to recognize the infinite meanings of language in its various transformations as it unifies being and nothingness and mediates between the divine and human spirits.

---

[20] The sapphire is the 'divine material' on which the divine letters of the ten commandments were engraved, and its source is the divine throne of sapphire from which the tablets were hewn. *Sifrei* Bamidbar, end of 'Beha'alotekha'; *Pirkei derabi eli'ezer*, ch. 46.

The dialectical conception upon which the hasidic view of language is based sees language as the concrete, contracted manifestation of the abstract, infinite, divine being that requires concealment for the sake of revelation. According to this depiction of God as contracted, as it were, in the letters of the Torah, the hidden divine reality animates language and endows it with eternal, multi-layered existence and infinite significance. Language, whose origin is divine and whose units are names, letters, hints, meanings, and secrets connected with the nature of the universe, is perceived as an essential representation of the mutual relationship between the divine and the human, a specific dialectical relationship according to which the hidden nothing is the condition of the manifest being, and concrete being is the condition for the manifestation of abstract nothingness. In other words, the tangible entities of language—words, letters, signs, vocalization—serve as vehicle and garb for the hidden divine essence, the 'spirit of God', while the divine essence of language—which is designated as light, glow, 'window', or infinite nothingness—is dependent on its articulation in words and letters.

Jewish mysticism regards the deity as a dynamic, dialectical process linking the abstract and the palpable, nothingness and being, creation and chaos. This process is conceived as ebb and flow, or as expansion and withdrawal, and the eternal reciprocity of becoming and annihilation as enacted in human thought and language. The letters and their permutations are perceived as a two-way movement. The letters are a physical manifestation of the solitary thought of the infinite, which acquires a distinctive character and establishes created being as it moves from the abstract to the concrete; in the same way, the letters and their permutations provide a means of influencing the higher worlds through a process of dismantling continuous speech units, renouncing determinate meaning, obscuring distinct characteristics, and transcending consciousness of created reality.

Letters simultaneously disclose the creative divine substance and conceal it; they are the building-blocks of the universe. Language is a condition of existence and a condition of movement from world to world. It is language that separates chaos from creation, for chaos is nameless, lawless, and limitless, without measure, number, or calculation. Creation is a network of being suffused by the divine speech that unifies matter and form and which must be omnipresent in order that the world may continue to exist; a kind of oath that commits the components of the universe to persistence, or a covenant of word and number that guarantees the continuity of the world. The operative processes are *tseruf* and *peruk*, construction and deconstruction: *tseruf* is the transformative movement from the abstract to the concrete; *peruk* is the return from the concrete to the abstract. As words are factored into their constituent letters, the letters return to their divine source; creation returns to nothingness. Differentiation becomes meaningless as it dissolves into the unitary origin; the articulation of human speech is understood as but echoes of the divine voice. In kabbalistic terminology, the movement back towards the source that makes the concrete abstract is called *yiḥud*; it is a process in which language is returned from a state of differentiated construction to one of undifferentiated deconstruction. For the divine voice to pass from the infinite to the finite it must be formed into letters, which coalesce into words and separate into the components of reality. In the movement from the finite to the infinite, by contrast, there is a transition in the opposite direction. *Yiḥudim* are permutations of letters, without meaning in themselves, designated *shemot* or *azkarot*—names or mnemonics, devoid of semantic value, functioning in performative ritual language or in amulets and nostrums. The recitation of these words transcends the need for meaning and dissolves language and consciousness; it returns the distinct elemental parts to their unified source and transforms being into nothingness. The mystical tradition conceives of language as sacred tongue because it unifies the hidden divine and the concrete and palpable and the movements from nothingness to being and from being to nothingness: 'The letters of the Torah hint at spirituality and the highest *sefirot*. Each letter has a spiritual form and all the names and words have a higher source from a supreme holy place.'[21]

The Ba'al Shem Tov, who was, by his own definition, 'a man who lived beyond nature', and saw 'letters, souls, worlds, and divinity' throughout the universe, was a kabbalist attached to the 'luminous infinite inwardness within the letters'. He was a mystic who used the letters to achieve mystical ascent and experienced higher reality through letters transparently showing him their divine infinite being. As a *ba'al shem* (master of the divine name), he employed the letters for magical purposes, as a means to bring heavenly powers down to earth. He functioned within the realm of the occult, whose essence is the activation by human beings of forces regarded as supernatural, through names and letters. He turned language into an arena of religious activity, for the transition from the hidden to the revealed and vice versa takes place through the continuous formation and dissolution of letter permutations.

Kabbalistic tradition teaches that God had contracted himself into the letters of the Torah, the Torah being the very substance through which he created the world. The thesis of contraction (*tsimtsum*) of the divine light into letters which then persisted as a written sacred Torah and as an oral sacred tongue engenders a mode of study and thought known as *devekut ba'otiyot*, 'attachment to the letters': 'He should study in the morning with *devekut* and

---

[21] *Shenei luḥot haberit*, i. 10.

desire, to cleave unto the inner infinite light within the letters . . . And then a man should know this great principle, that there is no partition separating him from his God during Torah study and prayer.'[22] 'Just as there are twenty-two letters of speech [meaning, the letters that combine to form the spoken word] in Torah, and prayer, so in all material and physical affairs in the world there are twenty-two letters through which the world and all that is in it was created: as it has been said, "Bezalel knew how to combine the letters by which heaven and earth were created . . . For the letters expanded from above below, and that is how He made all creatures with the twenty-two letters".'[23]

The letters are not only the vehicles of divine creation but also essential components of creation in its totality. Hence connecting to the divine light in the Hebrew letters is the way to withdraw from materiality, to ascend to higher worlds and to become attached to the deity. *Devekut ba'otiyot*, or identification with their content in the course of concentrated contemplation, allows the transformative divine power and the transformative human power to amalgamate and lets the ebb and flow of divine animation coalesce with human thought.

The Ba'al Shem Tov's concern with 'the luminous infinite inwardness within the letters', and their infinite creative power, is what led him to emphasize the importance of uncovering the divine element that animates all layers of reality through the infinity of human thought: 'I heard from my teacher that the primary occupation of Torah and prayer is that one should attach himself to the inner infinite spiritual light within the letters of the Torah and the prayer, and this is what is called study for its own sake.'[24] 'Wherever one sees or hears even a personal conversation about material affairs he may take for himself from there some intimation of wisdom, and he can divest [himself of] the corporeal form and perform holy permutations to attach his soul to the sublimity of his divinity, may He be blessed.'[25] The unifying bond between God, man, and the world is wrapped up in the letters of 'God, Torah, and Israel are one', for the letters of the Torah that express the infinite divine speech within the parameters of the finite text are the letters of divine speech that create the world, and they are the letters that serve as man's tools of understanding and creativity, remembering and forgetting, imagination and freedom.

[22] *Toledot ya'akov yosef*, 'Bereshit', 22.   [23] Ibid.

[24] Ibid., 'Vayetse', 89.   [25] *Or hame'ir*, 'Vayishlaḥ', 25.

Israel Ba'al Shem Tov's Uniqueness Myth, Bibliography, Facts, and Image

> The God-fearing, wholesome man . . . remembers at every moment before
> Whom he stands and divests himself of corporeality as if he is above this world
> and beyond the order of time.
>
> *Or hame'ir, 39b*

I N the minds of his hasidic followers in the eighteenth and nineteenth centuries, the reputation of Israel Ba'al Shem Tov soared beyond the bounds of historical reality and acquired mythological status unconstrained by time, place, the written record, or biographical evidence. Within a short time of his death, the known historical facts of his life[1]—based in part on direct testimonies and in part on written sources—found their way into oral traditions that circulated in the 1760s and 1770s and merged with hasidic mystical traditions in the homiletical literature that began to appear from 1780 on. They continued to be written down in the decades that followed, and were published in the hagiographical literature in praise of the Ba'al Shem Tov that began to appear after 1814.[2]

As hasidism spread, so the mythical dimensions of the Ba'al Shem Tov expanded as traditions recorded by the early generations of his disciples relating to his teachings and outlook, his charismatic personality, his mystical practices, his ability to illuminate the hidden world, and his prowess as a 'master of the Name' with the power to heal by virtue of his contact with the sacred

---

[1] The facts known about the Ba'al Shem Tov's life were first discussed at length in the writings on hasidism of Simon Dubnow, Ben-Zion Dinur, Martin Buber, and Gershom Scholem, and to some degree in the earlier books by Heinrich Graetz and Abraham Kahana. Moshe Rosman's recent comprehensive biography surveys the history of research in this field, adding previously unknown facts from Polish sources and developing the field in new directions. In recent years Moshe Idel, Immanuel Etkes, and I have written about the sources of the Ba'al Shem Tov's ideas and their religious and social context; see the bibliographical references in these sources.

[2] See *In Praise of the Baal Shem Tov*, ed. Ben Amos and Mintz; Dresner, *The Circle of the Ba'al Shem Tov*; Rosman, 'In Praise of the Ba'al Shem Tov'.

found their way into oral narratives.[3] Written sources attested to 'the new way in which he initiated in the worship of God', his direct and indirect legacy as a religious innovator, and his skill in using parables to communicate religious messages. The various traditions concerning him rapidly fed into one another in an ever-growing torrent that obscured the line between fantasy and reality.

The traditions concerning the Ba'al Shem Tov were disseminated in the first instance through the books of his disciples Dov Baer (the Maggid of Mezhirech) and Jacob Joseph of Polonnoye, which were published in the 1780s, and subsequently through books based on these and additional sources that were published in the 1790s. From then until the 1820s, an expansive literature was published that served to establish the nature of hasidism. *Shivḥei habesht*, the first hagiographical treasury of Ba'al Shem Tov legends, was published in 1814; new editions appeared many times in the years that followed. It includes depictions of the Ba'al Shem Tov as a wonder-worker, traditions about the origins of hasidism, and fascinating historical material on the first half of the eighteenth century. Another book published in this period, *Degel maḥaneh efrayim*, by the Ba'al Shem Tov's grandson Moses Hayim Ephraim of Sudylkow, contains first-hand accounts of aspects of the Ba'al Shem Tov's life, and transmits anecdotes and family traditions in his name.[4]

Shortly after the homiletic works of the Maggid and Jacob Joseph were published, editors known and unknown began to disseminate abridgements and anthologies. The editors combined the two traditions indiscriminately and added material of their own choosing. The bibliographical record shows clearly that in the written sources the different traditions of the disciples overlapped. The dates or places of publication do not necessarily establish the chronology of sources, and comparison of the various anthologies shows the extent to which the traditions merged. The titles the editors chose for these collections and anthologies added further confusion. For example, readers

---

[3] For literary reflections of the Besht's mythic figure see the following hasidic works: *Magid devarav leya'akov*, by Dov Baer of Mezhirech, and the introduction by Solomon of Lutsk (pp. 1–7); *Me'irat einayim*, by Nathan Neta Hakohen of Kalbiel and Shimon Menahem Mendel Wodnik of Govartchov, i. 11–32; *Toledot ya'akov yosef*, by Jacob Joseph of Polonnoye; *Tsava'at harivash*; *Keter shem tov* (sayings of the Besht); *Degel maḥaneh efrayim*, by Moses Hayim Ephraim of Sudylkow (Jerusalem, 1994 edn.); *Shivḥei habesht*, in the editions by Jaffe (1814) and by Mondshine (1982); and *Shenei hame'orot*, by Samuel of Kaminka. See also Dan, 'On the History of the Praise Literature' (Heb.); and Reiner, '*Shivḥei habesht*: Transmission, Editing, Printing'.

[4] Moses Hayim Ephraim was the son of Odel or Edel, the daughter of the Besht (her unusual name, was interpreted as an acronym of a strange verse *esh dat lamo* (Deut. 33: 2) '[at his right] a host of his own'). Moses Hayim Ephraim was born in 1748 and lived in his grandfather's house until the latter's death in 1760. Moses himself died in 1800; his recollections of his childhood offer a picture of mid-18th-century life.

would have assumed that books with titles such as *Hanhagot yesharot* ('Righteous Practices') or *Likutim yekarim* ('Precious Collections') had been handed down by the founding fathers of hasidism, not compiled by editors, and likewise that *Tsava'at harivash* was indeed the Ba'al Shem Tov's testament, whereas in reality it was, at best, inspired by his teachings. However, as a digest of the teachings ascribed to the Ba'al Shem Tov by various sources it was certainly important and influential.[5]

In fact, the primary charismatic and hagiographical material about the Ba'al Shem Tov is to be found in the traditions conveyed in the books of Jacob Joseph of Polonnoye. It was he who was largely responsible for the autobiographical mystical document known as *Igeret hakodesh*, which appeared in his *Ben porat yosef* (1781), as well as for a significant portion of the hagiographical anecdotes that were later published in *Shivhei habesht* (1814). His *Toledot ya'akov yosef* (1780), *Tsofenat pa'ane'ah* (1782), and *Kutonet pasim* (1866) also disseminated the Ba'al Shem Tov's theoretical teachings and articulated the mystical conceptions introduced in his circle during the second third of the eighteenth century.[6]

Other important transmissions of the Ba'al Shem Tov's doctrine come from the circle of Dov Baer, the Maggid of Mezhirech. Between the death of the Ba'al Shem Tov in 1760 and his own death twelve years later, Dov Baer significantly expanded the theoretical concepts of hasidism and deepened the perception of its social significance. The disciples he gathered around him— among them Levi Isaac of Berdichev, Shneur Zalman of Lyady, Shmuel Shmelke Horowitz of Nikolsburg, Elimelekh of Lyzhansk, Hayim of Amdur, Menahem Mendel of Vitebsk, Ze'ev Wolf of Zhitomir and his son Abraham 'the Angel', Abraham of Kalisk, and Solomon of Lutsk—intensified the spread of hasidim. The Maggid's teachings began to be published, on the initiative of his students, in 1781, in books such as *Magid devarav leya'akov*, *Or torah*, and *Or ha'emet*, and in anthologies such as *Tsava'at harivash* and *Likutim yekarim*; they also appeared in the writings of Ze'ev Wolf of Zhitomir (*Or hame'ir*, 1790), Levi Isaac of Berdichev (*Kedushat levi*, 1798, and *Shemuah tovah*, 1888). Shneur Zalman of Lyady's *Tanya: likutei amarim*, published in 1797, was regarded by its author as a systematic formulation of his teacher's

---

[5] On hasidic bibliography see Friedberg, *The History of Hebrew Print in Poland* (Heb.); Schatz-Uffenheimer's introduction to her edition of *Magid devarav leya'akov*, 9–23; and Gries, *The Hanhagot Literature* (Heb.) and *Book, Author and Story in Early Hasidism* (Heb.). See also the references in Ch. 2 above, and Dan, Liebes, and Reem (eds.), *Gershom Scholem's Library* (Heb.), i. 513–696, ii. 697–838.

[6] See Nigal, *Leader and Congregation* (Heb.) and id., *Teachings of R. Jacob Joseph of Polonnoye* (Heb.).

ideas, which were in turn an elaboration of those of the Ba'al Shem Tov. Students close to hasidic circles in the last third of the eighteenth century undoubtedly had access to various versions of the Ba'al Shem Tov's ideas in manuscript form. Most were published between 1780 and 1814; some appeared later, in the nineteenth century. However, given the alterations that may have been introduced by copyists and editors, the relationship between the printed form and the original doctrines is often unclear.

It is probably both pointless and impossible now to unpick the rich tapestry woven at that time in an effort to establish the Ba'al Shem Tov's reputation for spirituality and to disseminate his teachings. In the minds of subsequent generations of hasidim, all the doctrines transmitted in his name became as one; the different approaches originally articulated by the circle of the Maggid in Volhynia and the circle of Jacob Joseph of Polonnoye in Podolia became inextricably intertwined. *Keter shem tov* is an anthology of the Ba'al Shem Tov's sayings culled from Jacob Joseph's *Ben porat yosef* and *Tsofenat pa'ane'aḥ* by his disciple Aaron ben Tsevi Hirsch Kohen of Opatow. *Magid devarav leya'akov* overlaps with *Likutim yekarim*. There is similar overlap between *Tsava'at harivash* and *Hanhagot yesharot*, and between *Tsava'at harivash* and *Shemuah tovah*. The mixture of traditions handed down in these and other works, some published and some available only in manuscript, shaped the image of the hasidic teaching associated with the Ba'al Shem Tov as disseminated by the first two generations of his disciples.

Hence one may regard the hasidic literature published between 1780 and 1814, with its many different genres and approaches, as representing the complexity of the movement in its formative years. The different approaches that developed during the forty-five-year period (1735–80) in which the Ba'al Shem Tov, the Maggid, and Jacob Joseph led, taught, and wrote but did not publish, and the varied traditions emanating from the works published in the following thirty-five years (1780–1814), are less important than their common denominator: a sense of mystical inspiration and spiritual awakening inspired by the Ba'al Shem Tov and his disciples but anchored in kabbalistic traditions concerning the unity of opposites in language. The Ba'al Shem Tov's distinctive mystical identity, manifested in a radically unconventional way of looking at the world and in the blurring of accepted distinctions, led to the transformation of the vocabulary of divine worship, a novel approach to the relationship between God and man, and a conception of charismatic leadership and communal fraternity that challenged existing structures of authority and was to revolutionize traditional Jewish society.

This corpus of hasidic works that came into being around the beginning of the nineteenth century encompassed, as we have seen, a variety of sources and genres: homiletical literature, hagiographical literature, codes of conduct, biographical and autobiographical material, stories, and letters. Together, they established a multidimensional portrait of the Ba'al Shem Tov as spiritual leader that reached mythological proportions. Some aspects of this mythical image were inspired by depictions of the personality of the Ari in the seventeenth-century hagiography *Shivḥei ha'ari*, in Hayim Vital's manuscript of *Sefer haḥeziyonot*, and in the introduction to his *Ets ḥayim*, which was composed in the sixteenth century and published in the eighteenth century after circulating widely in manuscript form. Aspects relating to his mystical testimony concerning revelations from higher worlds were influenced by *Sefer haḥeziyonot*, by Joseph Karo's journal *Magid meisharim*, by Eliezer Azikri's *Sefer ḥaredim*, and by other autobiographical works by Safed kabbalists.

From the various hasidic traditions it is clear that the Ba'al Shem Tov's circle was in awe of him and considered him to have mystical powers, consistent with his view of himself as 'living beyond nature' and being conversant with the higher worlds. He was regarded as a 'master of the Name', treating ailments of body and soul by spiritual means; as a mystic who inspired a spiritual renaissance through his own mystical elevation; and as a charismatic who could influence the revealed realities of this world through his immediate contact with the hidden reality of the divine realms. He was a consummate storyteller, able to convey obscure messages through apparently simple parables, and to fascinate his audience through the drama of his mystical experiences. Unquestionably, the novel ideas he engendered inspired a rich literature that resonated throughout the hasidic world. He was a religious innovator who left a unique mark on his environment.

Although the bulk of the biographical, mystical, and social traditions that characterized the development of the hasidic world in its early stages have been available in print for over two hundred years, only a small portion of them have received scholarly attention. The Ba'al Shem Tov's teachings have engendered surprisingly little discussion, and there has been little study of their relationship to other aspects of his personality. It seems to me that this is primarily because the mystical character of hasidism was incompatible with the rational intellectual concerns of the mitnagedic and maskilic movements and of traditional academic scholarship. The mitnagedim did not study hasidism because they aimed to preserve the ways of the traditional Jewish world; they opposed hasidism for undermining its foundations in the name of charisma.[7] The maskilim did not study hasidism because they sought to advance enlightenment; they viewed the hasidim as benighted irrationalists

---

[7] See Ch. 1 n. 1 and Ch. 7.

and as obstacles to their own critique of the traditional.[8] Academic scholars did not study hasidism because they were daunted by the bibliographical thicket surveyed above, as well as by the host of philological and methodological problems associated with the confusion of sources and traditions and the variety of genres.[9]

In recent years the academic discourse has changed, and there is now more openness to multiple perspectives. There is greater understanding of the inseparability of rational and meta-rational elements, fact and fantasy, the legendary and the spiritual truths of consciousness; the role of dreams and visions in generating changes in spiritual life and religious innovations; idiosyncratic points of view are tolerated alongside the general consensus. There is a new awareness of the relationship between facts, vantage point, and impressions; of the complex interactions between fantasy, narrative, and history; and of how a historian's interests affect both the choice of data and their interpretation. Hence the time is possibly ripe to analyse the totality of hasidic teachings as perceived by those who absorbed them and were responsible for disseminating them in all their richness in the course of the eighteenth century—the scribes, copyists, editors, and printers—rather than merely focusing on the original intent of the founders (now in any case shrouded in the mists of historical remoteness), or on the findings of early scholarship that was motivated by the negative attitudes of historians committed to partisan ideologies.[10]

An important work compiled in the 1920s by Menahem Mendel Wodnik of Govartchov, *Ba'al shem tov al hatorah*, gathers together all the hasidic traditions available at the time, including citations of the Ba'al Shem Tov in the works of Jacob Joseph and the Maggid and their disciples. Teachings explicitly attributed to the Ba'al Shem Tov by those who knew him are brought together with commentaries on the Torah culled from the nineteenth-century hasidic author Isaac Eizik of Komarno, author of *Otsar hahayim, Heikhal haberakhah, Zohar hai, Notser hesed*, and *Netiv mitsvoteikha*, who recreated the Ba'al Shem Tov in his imagination, claimed him as his direct teacher, and rewrote his doctrine clearly, perspicuously, and systematically. *Ba'al shem tov al hatorah* is arranged as a commentary on the Torah and compares the insights of 210 hasidic commentators (all listed in the back of the book) on individual scriptural verses. This systematic arrangement facilitates examina-

---

[8] See Feiner and Sorkin (eds.), *New Perspectives on the Haskalah*; Wodziński, *Haskalah and Hasidism in the Kingdom of Poland*; Feiner, *Haskalah and History*, 91–115.

[9] For a list of academic contributions on hasidism see Dan, Liebes, and Reem (eds.), *Gershom Scholem's Library* (Heb.), i. 515–44.

[10] For scholarship on hasidism see Ch. 13 below; see also Feiner, *Haskalah and History*; Bartal, 'The Imprint of Haskalah Literature'; and Wodziński, *Haskalah and Hasidism*.

tion of the differing traditions. Each comment is printed separately, and clearly attributed; moreover, the insights deriving from the first three generations of hasidic scholarship—the Ba'al Shem, his disciples, and his disciples' disciples—are printed in a different typeface to those of subsequent generations of scholars (post-1814) whose insights derive from mystical identification and interpretative licence rather than a direct historical connection with the founders of the movement. Some material (for example, that on prayer) is arranged topically rather than following the order of the biblical text, facilitating direct access to major subjects in hasidic thought. The editor also offers valuable insights into the relationship between the sources.

Wodnik's editing is a tour de force of bibliographical thoroughness. His accumulation of all the relevant sources is exhaustive, and his sensitivity to subtle distinctions enables him to deftly assess the relative weight of the different traditions and establish chronological order with accuracy. He comments in closing—after having cited literally hundreds of quotations—'Many statements like this, quoted in the name of the Maggid, were really made by the Ba'al Shem Tov.'[11] In support of this assertion he cites the almost intractable confusion between the authentic ideas of the Ba'al Shem Tov as presented in the various editions of his disciples and those imposed by subsequent editors and others involved in disseminating the tradition.

None of the many studies of the Ba'al Shem Tov has answered the key question: what caused him to become the founder of hasidism?[12] The corpus of historical, bibliographical, intellectual, and social research as listed in the bibliography to the present volume is considerable, but little attention has been paid to the discrepancy between our knowledge of his later years and the virtual absence of knowledge about his earlier years. Other than the fact of his birth in 1698, little is known about the first thirty-five years of his life. We know only that his parents were elderly and that he was orphaned young. Neither the Ba'al Shem Tov nor his disciples mention his childhood, youth, education, or family. In particular, there is no reference to a social environment that might have influenced him or to the places where he studied, and no mention of flesh-and-blood teachers. There is therefore reason to surmise that he gained his education in unconventional ways; indeed, his idiosyncratic freedom

---

[11] *Ba'al shem tov al hatorah*, ii. 277.

[12] Regarding scholarly perspectives on the Besht, see Dubnow, 'The Beginnings'; Scholem, 'The Historical Image of R. Israel Ba'al Shem Tov' (Heb.); Elior, 'R. Joseph Karo and R. Israel Ba'al Shem Tov' (Heb.); Idel, *Hasidism*; Rosman, *The Founder of Hasidism*; Elior, 'The Paradigms of *Yesh* and *Ayin* in Hasidic Thought' and 'Der Baal Schem Tov, zwischen Mägie und Mystik'; and Etkes, *The Besht*. See also the references in Ch. 6 below.

of vision may be attributed to the absence of contact with a traditional authoritative structure. This may have fostered his sensitivity to the connection between the manifest and the hidden, his penetrating affinity for the realms of the imagination, and his characteristic disregard for conventional intellectual limits and traditional social demarcations.

From the mid-1730s on, the situation changed abruptly. Suddenly the Ba'al Shem Tov appears to be at the centre of a group of men who see him as a source of inspiration and authority. These men, referred to in *Shivḥei habesht* as *anshei segulato* ('his treasured people') all outranked him in family background, social status, and education. For example, Jacob Joseph was a rabbi in Sharogrod and Polonnoye; Dov Baer of Mezhirech was a *magid* (popular preacher and storyteller) in Rovno in Volhynia; Mikhal of Zloczow was a *magid* in Brody in Galicia, and his son-in-law Moses Shoham was rabbi of Dolina; Gershon of Kutow, brother-in-law of the Ba'al Shem Tov, was a kabbalist in the Brody *kloyz*; and Aryeh Leib was a preacher in Polonnoye. Pinhas Shapira, who was a preacher in Korets, Nahman of Kosov, also a preacher, and Meir Margaliyot, the rabbi of the Ostraha district, were also closely associated with the Ba'al Shem Tov. Notwithstanding this, all of them recognized his primacy and regarded him as the undisputed leader of the mystical group that served as the foundation of the movement.[13] They saw him as having extraordinary mystical and spiritual qualities, as being endowed with inspiration and the gift of prophecy. The teachings he inspired changed their lives because they affected their spiritual and social perspective and commitments; but they adopted his ideas, disseminated his teachings, and built the hasidic movement under his inspiration. Inspired by his vision, they turned their energies to increasing his following. Each made his contribution to the development of the hasidic movement, yet the Ba'al Shem Tov alone was regarded as its founder.

The ideas attributed to the Ba'al Shem Tov in the books of Jacob Joseph, Dov Baer, and their disciples establish unequivocally his originality and exegetical imagination, his ability to find new significance in sacred texts and reveal their mystical dimension. Above all, one gets a sense of the Ba'al Shem Tov's ability to blur the borders between the divine and the human, between the fantastic and the real. He was capable of transcending the limits of time and place, unifying the abstract and the concrete, rendering indistinct the distance between the text written long ago and the voice speaking in the present, overcoming the gap between the symbol and what it symbolizes, and overturning conventional social hierarchies. He was a man whose soul

[13] On the circle of the Ba'al Shem Tov, see Heschel, 'R. Pinhas of Korets and the Magid of Mezhirech'; Rapoport-Albert, 'Hasidism after 1772'.

ascended to heaven, conversed with the inhabitants of the higher worlds, and learned their wisdom; he strolled in the Garden of Eden, but inspired his followers on earth with a profound sense of freedom, imagination, and creativity powered by the infinite resources of language as the link between man and God. He saw himself as part of the mystical chain of people who cross the line between earth and heaven—prophets and kabbalists, thinkers and visionaries, redeemers and messianic figures—and return inspired with novel ideas that reconfigure the relations between the heavenly and the earthly, new knowledge of God, and original insights that transform the world. The basis of his innovative authority was the intensity with which his consciousness breached the bounds of imagination and reality, sanity and madness, self and other, human and divine. The revolution that the Ba'al Shem Tov engendered is anchored in the blurring of distinctions: between the 'infinite light in the letters' and human language; between the heavenly abundance and the terrestrial delimitation; between the endowing divine and the receiving human; between sacred and profane; between the higher world and this world; between the heavenly 'world of speech' and the human being in whom that world speaks; between the individual human being's soul and that of his neighbour; between life and death. In other words, the innovation was in transcending the discriminations that mark physical reality, obscuring the distinctions upon which tradition is based, and blurring the difference between divine thought and human thought, between the spiritual space of the individual and of the totality.

The Ba'al Shem Tov maintained that his doctrine was inspired by heavenly teachers such as the messiah and the prophet Ahijah the Shilonite, whom he encountered during his ascents to the higher worlds and his sojourn in the Garden of Eden.[14] In *Shivḥei habesht* he is depicted as involved in the study of the mystical chariot tradition and the Holy Names, exemplifying his freedom in transcending conventional limits. In the conceptual world of the Ba'al Shem Tov, the differences between imagination and reality, between signifier and signified, are erased. Different realities are brought together under a single rubric. There is no distinction between past, present, and future, between being and nothingness, between mortals and immortals. His disciple Jacob Joseph of Polonnoye, who describes the Ba'al Shem Tov's ascent, often quotes his statements on this theme:

I heard from my master the Ba'al Shem Tov that, when they brought him beneath the Tree of Knowledge of Good and Evil, there were many Jewish persons with him. Later,

---

[14] See *Avot derabi natan*, 39, on Ahijah who was Elishah. On Ahijah as the heavenly teacher of the Ba'al Shem Tov, see the various hasidic traditions in *Ba'al shem tov al hatorah*, i. 19, 79, 124; *Keter shem tov* (Brooklyn, 1981 edn.), 35, 40, 47, 163.

when they passed him beneath the Tree of Life there were fewer. Finally, when they introduced him to the inner Garden of Eden, there was hardly anyone with him.[15]

Everything we know about the Ba'al Shem Tov is testimony to his blurring of the boundaries of identity between self and other, the hidden and the revealed, the earthly and the heavenly. He clearly perceived the dual face of reality, informed by earlier writings in the mystical tradition, notably the Zohar (Book of Splendour), Karo's journal *Magid meisharim*, and Vital's description of his teacher 'the Holy Ari' in the rich hagiographical literature that had been published from the end of the sixteenth century onwards. While being very much of this world, he also saw himself as a visitor to the Garden of Eden and a denizen of higher worlds, conversant with those dwelling therein and disseminating their Torah: as he himself wrote, in the work that has come to be known as *Igeret aliyat haneshamah*: 'I ascended, level after level, until I entered the messiah's palace.' He saw himself as the 'agent of the community' (*shaliah tsibur*), who goes up to heaven on Rosh Hashanah on a shamanist mission to defend Israel and to combat Samael, the evil one.[16] He reported contact with Jesus and with Shabetai Tsevi, viewing the latter, according to *Shivhei habesht*, as a 'spark' of the messiah (see Chapter 12 below). He gave new meaning to prophetic and mystical texts, defining the religious quest in terms of Ezekiel's chariot vision, and telling his community that 'every man should see himself as belonging to the superior world'.[17] He is cited as saying: 'When one is worshipping in the aspect of greatness [*begadlut*] one should feel possessed of great potential, ascending in one's thought and breaking through all the firmaments at once, rising above the [various classes of] angels. That is perfect worship'.[18] So, too, he brought the worshipper closer to the Shekhinah when he said: 'One should think that the whole earth is filled with the Creator's glory and His Shekhinah is always [with the human being] . . . And one should consider that he may gaze upon the Shekhinah just as he gazes upon physical things.'[19] One of his constant refrains was that a person is where his thoughts range, and he thought that attachment to the Shekhinah, the 'world of speech', was attainable by every person: 'It is a high attainment when one always thinks that one is with the Creator, may He be blessed, and encompasses Him on all sides . . . and one should be so attached . . . that one gazes upon the Creator with the eye of his intellect'; 'it is a high level for a person to see the Creator constantly with the eye of the intellect as one gazes upon another person, and he should consider

[15] *Ben porat yosef*, 17b.

[16] On shamans who intervene on behalf of their community in the heavenly realm or in the world of the dead see Eliade, *Shamanism*, 181–214.

[17] *Tsava'at harivash*, 23.   [18] Ibid. 50, §137.   [19] Ibid.

that the Creator too looks back in the same way . . . This should be always in one's thoughts.'[20]

When the Ba'al Shem Tov writes, in *Igeret aliyat haneshamah*, that 'every letter contains worlds and souls and divinity', he turns the routine letters of speech into divine experiences accessible to human consciousness, and transforms language into the interface between the divine and the human. His representation of reality is based on the divine coincidence of opposites: the duality of being, the relativity of being and nothingness, the overcoming of divisions between people, the conception of language as the bridge between God and man, the correspondence between the 'divine spirit' and the human spirit, the identity between divine creative thought—revealed in the Torah and in creation—and human creative thought, revealed in language and its derivatives in the world of thought and the world of action. The details of these ideas will be discussed in Chapter 6; here it should merely be noted that all his teachings demonstrate a desire to bring the divine and the human closer to each other and to undermine hierarchical distinctions. He seeks to make the divine coincidence of opposites accessible to all, and argues against conventional conceptions based on sensory experience. The overall intensity of mystical experience aiming to unify the earthly and the heavenly and to transcend the limits of sensual apprehension is captured in such phrases as 'man is planted on earth and his head reaches heaven, and the angels of God ascend and descend on him' and 'the behaviour of the spiritual man is above nature', and in concepts such as 'annihilation of being', 'withdrawal from corporeality', 'turning self to nothing' (*ani* to *ayin*), 'cleaving unto and inclusion in God', 'unification of superior levels with inferior ones', 'elevation of worlds', 'drawing the divine down to the physical', and 'turning nothingness into being'. The Ba'al Shem Tov regarded the notion of reality—defined in terms of time and space, bound by the limits of sensory experience, but detached from its divine source—as an illusion, as no more than a 'mustard seed' in relation to the superior world or the dialectical unity of opposites that expresses the divine perspective. The profound sense of freedom as well as the quest to overcome limits and categories can be discerned in his attitude towards 'authoritative truth' and to the standard discriminations that underlie the traditional world-view. In the consciousness of one who lives in the presence of the divine, all manifestations of reality are merely relative, dialectical, paradoxical, and mutable.

Solomon of Lutsk, publisher of *Magid devarav leya'akov* and a disciple of the Maggid, describes in his introduction how the unifying outlook of the Ba'al Shem Tov ties together the higher and lower levels of reality in human

---

[20] *Keter shem tov*, vol. i, 42 and 58.

consciousness: 'For he uncovered the precious glory of this wisdom [kab-balah], on every detail he displayed abundant knowledge concerning the eternal ways of the superior world and its unification with the inferior world in each motion and manner and utterance and act.'[21] Various articulations of the Ba'al Shem Tov's doctrines illuminate the relationship between revealed and concealed, the quest for a paradoxical and dialectical vision of reality, a preference for the subjective world over the concrete world; moreover, there is a distinct tendency to reject the conventional. He tends to unify opposites and abandon accepted frameworks and prevalent values; the aspiration to spiritual freedom and the preference for charismatic, visionary authority are conspicuous. The tendency to expand man's spiritual and existential horizons emerges from the blurring of boundaries between heavenly and earthly ('the eternal ways of the superior world and its unification with the inferior world'; 'that every person should see oneself as belonging to the superior world'). It emerges from the acosmic perspective that negates the world's autonomous status ('all is divine'; 'being is a total falsehood'), and from the dialectical perspective grounded in the duality of existence (the power of the agent over the act; nothingness and being). Manifest reality is interpreted as having a hidden essence. Man is conceived as belonging to the superior world; man's existential experience is interpreted in connection with a God-suffused reality; man's thought is identified with God's thought, and 'man is where his thoughts are'. Human speech is tied to the divine 'world of speech'; the language in which 'each letter contains worlds and souls and divinity' is viewed as the holy tongue shared by God and man ('the Shekhinah, the world of speech, speaks through man'; 'Torah, God, and Israel are one'). This recognition of the divine nature of human language implies that the simple meaning of Scripture, composed of the letters of divine speech, embodies hidden meaning, just as the manifest physical world is interpreted as covering and concealing the divine entity it embodies.

Unquestionably, the Ba'al Shem Tov saw himself and was seen by others as one who had crossed the divide between the terrestrial and the celestial and had attained unmediated contact with those dwelling in the higher worlds. We know this from his words, as quoted by his grandson: 'I swear to you here that there is a man in this world who hears words of Torah from the Holy One Blessed Be He and His Shekhinah'.[22] A letter written by Menahem Mendel of Vitebsk in 1786 similarly testifies to the unique impression made by the Ba'al Shem Tov on his contemporaries: 'The word of God came in the hand of the Ba'al Shem, and he decreed and it was established [cf. Job 22: 28]. There was only one like him, among the ancients there was none like

---

[21] *Magid devarav leya'akov*, 2.   [22] *Degel maḥaneh efrayim*, 282.

him, and after him none like him.'[23] The Ba'al Shem Tov's distinctiveness, as one who lives in two worlds, emerges likewise from the various traditions about his 'ascent of the soul' to hear the messiah's Torah and stroll in the Garden of Eden, about 'man who lives above nature', about 'withdrawal from corporeality', about man 'who is nothing', and who 'attaches himself to inner spiritual infinite light within the letters of the Torah'.[24] Ultimately the Ba'al Shem's new approach, which his disciples made accessible to all, transcended his individual mystical experience and went beyond the world of the elite: hasidism became the possession of the Jewish masses.

[23] *Peri ha'arets*, 60.   [24] See *Degel maḥaneh efrayim*, 282–5.

The Hasidic Revolution

And greater than the seen is the unseen, more wonderful than what is, is the
mystery of nothing on high. Visit me O my God and let me see what hides
behind the border of the eye.

Merahok, 146

THE innovations of hasidism were connected to the personality of the Ba'al
Shem Tov, the teachings ascribed to him, and the spiritual and social
transformation that gradually took place in their wake. Specific aspects will be
elaborated in later chapters; this chapter offers a brief outline of his personality and teaching as portrayed by his contemporaries and in various literary and
historical sources.

We can list five characteristics that set the Ba'al Shem Tov apart from his
peers. First, he was an inspiring leader. The respect accorded him by his
peers is evident in the works of Jacob Joseph of Polonnoye and Dov Baer of
Mezherich. Further evidence is provided by Polish sources: records from the
town of Medzibozh show that the Jewish community there chose to grant
him residence rights, exemption from local taxes, and financial support in
recognition of his status as a spiritual figure, healer, and mystic.[1]

Second, he was an ecstatic mystic, visionary, and charismatic, attentive to
the inner experiences of his soul. He felt a sense of immediate contact with
the divine that he was able to communicate to those around him. This
emerges powerfully from autobiographical remarks in *Igeret hakodesh* and
from comments made by such figures as his grandson, Moses Hayim
Ephraim of Sudylkow, Meir Margaliyot of Ostraha (who knew him when he
first emerged as a leader), Solomon of Lutsk (who published many of the
major works of his disciples), and his disciples.[2]

---

[1] Rosman, *The Founder of Hasidism*, 159–70. For Polish documents about the Besht, see id.,
'Medzibhoz and R. Israel Ba'al Shem Tov' (Heb.), and *Founder of Hasidism*, ch. 4 (pp. 63–82).

[2] Meir Margaliyot (or Margulies) was the rabbi of Ostrog (Ostraha) from 1777 to 1790. As a
young man he met the Besht and considered himself to be one of his followers: in his book *Sod
yakhin uvoaz* (Ostrog, 1794), he describes him in a tone of admiration and reverence. He
continued to support hasidic issues and hasidic teachers all his life. See Scholem, 'The Historical

Third, he was a 'master of the Name', able to cure physical and psychological complaints by using names of God and by combining Hebrew letters—the letters of the divine language—to activate supernatural powers. The magical use of language linked healer and patient in cosmic harmony; transcending the individual, it endowed suffering with meaning and nurtured hope of change by dint of a cyclical determinism. Evidence of the Ba'al Shem Tov's skills in this field is found in hasidic literature on the general subject of 'masters of the Name', in *Shivḥei habesht*, and in Polish documents that describe him as a 'doctor of kabbalah', or as a healer using names and nostrums.[3]

Fourth, he was a powerful communicator, skilled in using stories and parables to demonstrate the relationship between the revealed and the concealed. The Ba'al Shem Tov's ability to communicate new ideas powerfully and with precision is attested by his grandson and by members of his circle and disciples, and by the many teachings, sayings, and parables quoted in his name.[4]

Finally, he was a spiritual innovator who introduced ideas that were to transform the Jewish world. The Ba'al Shem Tov's ideas on mysticism, ecstatic prayer, and language not only inspired religious revival among his contemporaries but have also withstood the test of time. His teachings survived him and have continued to attract devotees in large numbers ever since.[5]

The first four characteristics listed above all relate to the use of language: mystical language, magical language, the language of imagination, and the language of narrative. His skills in this area were no doubt very significant in inspiring followers. His words appear to have created a sense of spiritual renascence that imbued the individual with a feeling of having had contact with the divine. While this was clearly a major factor in the spread of hasidism

Image of R. Israel Ba'al Shem Tov' (Heb.); Green, *Tormented Master*, 53 n. On aspects of the Besht's personality, see Scholem, 'The Historical Image'; Elior, 'R. Joseph Karo and R. Israel Ba'al Shem Tov' (Heb.); and Etkes, 'The Besht as Mystic' (Heb.).

[3] Scholem, 'The Historical Image of R. Israel Ba'al Shem Tov' (Heb.); Elior, 'Der Baal Schem Tov, zwischen Mägie und Mystik'; Idel, *Hasidism*, 75–81; Etkes, *The Besht*, 15–53; Rosman, *The Founder of Hasidism*, 16, 118, 120–6, 134–5, 148–54.

[4] See Buber, *Tales of the Hasidim*; stories of the Ba'al Shem are collected in *Keter shem tov* and *Degel maḥaneh efrayim*, and can be found throughout the works of Jacob Joseph of Polonnoye.

[5] The spiritual innovations of the Ba'al Shem Tov are collected in *Ba'al shem tov al hatorah*, ed. Wodnik, a two-volume work containing all teachings cited in the name of the Besht in hasidic literature. For analysis of the fundamental concepts in hasidic thought that were generated by Israel Ba'al Shem and his disciples see Schatz-Uffenheimer, *Hasidism as Mysticism*; Scholem, '*Devekut* or Communion with God' and *Major Trends in Jewish Mysticism*, 325–50; and the following entries in *EJ* vii, s.v. 'hasidism': 'history' (pp. 1390–1403), 'basic ideas' (pp. 1403–7), and 'teachings' (pp. 1407–13). See also, by Elior, 'The Paradigms of *Yesh* and *Ayin* in Hasidic Thought', '"The World Is Filled with his Glory"' (Heb.), 'Der Baal Schem Tov, zwischen Mägie und Mystik', and the index to *The Paradoxical Ascent to God*.

during the Ba'al Shem Tov's lifetime, it was the fifth dimension—his spiritual innovations and teachings, transmitted as the legacy of a quasi-mythical figure—that exercised crucial influence after his death.

THE BA'AL SHEM TOV'S TEACHINGS

Too little attention has been given to the distinctiveness of the Ba'al Shem Tov's teachings and their tremendous impact on the development of hasidism in its various forms in subsequent generations. Flowing in part from kabbalistic tradition and in part from his extraordinary mystical consciousness, they can be summarized as a series of interrelated concepts.

Divine vitality is present in every being and is the basis of its existence

The assumption of the omnipresence of God—a thesis that scholars call 'divine immanence'—stresses the constancy of the divine vitality concealed in all dimensions of manifest being. 'The whole earth is full of his glory and there is no place void of him . . . divinity is in every place.'[6] In abandoning the distinction between superior and inferior levels of reality, the assumption of divine omnipresence closes the gap between God and man. The idea that all physical existence requires the divine presence—that God is the essence that animates physical form—demands recognition of the infinite abundance of divine vitality flowing through all dimensions of the physical world. God is present in every thing, in every act, in every utterance or thought. Taken to the extreme, this makes the concept of 'manifest reality' as separate from God devoid of meaning: all is divinity. 'Thus the worlds do not maintain in God any substance at all from the aspect of his truth, in so far as there is nothing besides him.'[7]

Reality may be perceived from a human perspective or a divine perspective

From the human perspective, looking at the world with 'eyes of flesh', one generally sees only manifest reality; or to put it another way, physicality is a screen that conceals the omnipresent divine vitality. Looked at from the divine perspective, however, with 'eyes of the intellect', all is divinity; the physical world is revealed as without substance. What the human eye sees is illusion—barriers to understanding created by the imagination. If reality comprises both revealed and concealed dimensions, human knowledge and divine knowledge are in reality indivisible. The objective must be to see with 'eyes of intellect' rather than with 'eyes of flesh' in order to grasp the true essence of reality from a divine perspective.

---

[6] *Magid devarav leya'akov*, 240.   [7] *Sha'arei ha'avodah*, vol. ii, gate 3, ch. 22, p. 42b.

The Ba'al Shem Tov formulates this approach in his 'parable of the barriers', which describes the relations between God and man in terms of a king and his son. The son is made to recognize that appearances are meaningless, and that it is the divine infinite, hidden from the eye, which constitutes true being. He reaches a state in which he realizes that the barrier he perceives between himself and his father is an illusion:

I heard [it] from my teacher, of blessed memory, speaking before the blowing of the shofar. 'There was a wise and great king who did everything through illusion, walls and towers and gates. And he commanded that people come to him through the gates and towers, and that royal treasures be scattered at each gate . . . His loving son made a great effort to reach his father the king, and then he saw that there was no barrier dividing him from his father, *for it was all illusion.* And the application of the parable is obvious . . . For when one knows that God's glory fills all the earth, and that every motion and thought is from Him, then with this knowledge all evil agencies collapse, since there is no barrier or curtain separating man from Him, may He be blessed . . . *For all concealment is but an illusion. In truth everything is of His substance.'* (emphasis added)[8]

The individual must strive to understand that the physicality that seems to separate him from God is irrelevant. God is the essence of being, the sole autonomous existence. 'When a person knows this great principle, that there is no separation between him and his God, during Torah study and prayer even when strange thoughts enter one's mind, these are garments and coverings within which God hides, in any case; in so far as he knows that God is hiding there, it is not hiding.'[9]

'Being' implies the simultaneous existence of the physical and the spiritual in dialectical relationship

The existence of any entity implies the existence of its opposite. Revelation implies the existence of concealment, physicality implies the existence of the spiritual. Being implies animating infinite nothingness, contraction implies expansion, garb implies essence, matter implies form. The manifest physical element is illusory; only the hidden divine element is genuine. Physical existence is but a cover for the infinite light, a receptacle containing the divine presence. The word *olam* (world) is derived homiletically from *he'elem* (concealment); on this view, the world is but a concealment of the divine light that makes possible its manifestation. It is the concealed divine element that animates the revealed reality; the physical element is merely a material manifestation that allows the hidden divine reality to be perceived. All existence is

---

[8] *Ben porat yosef*, 70c; cf. 111a. Interesting variations of the parable are recorded in *Degel maḥaneh efrayim, haftarat* 'Ki tavo' (pp. 257–8) and *parashat* 'Vayelekh' (pp. 264–5).

[9] *Toledot ya'akov yosef*, 'Bereshit', 22b.

thereby understood as the coincidence of opposites that are at the same time mutually interdependent: divine substance and physical manifestation, spiritual content and material form, divine unity and concrete plurality, infinity and finitude, nothingness and being. Divine perfection lies in the infinite unification of opposites through simultaneous composition and decomposition at physical, metaphysical, and epistemological levels. Human perfection lies in the recognition of this unity of opposites and the internalization of this recognition in the service of God.[10]

Every physical phenomenon has at its root a divine entity, a hidden truth that lies beyond the manifest reality

This idea lies at the heart of hasidism: no aspect of reality can be taken at face value, for every manifestation of reality conceals its divine essence. To put it another way, that which is manifest is actually a manifestation of the hidden divine essence. Ze'ev Wolf of Zhitomir formulates this well, admonishing man 'not to see anything in the world as it appears, but raise your eyes to the heights, meaning the aspect of your contemplation and study, to see only the divinity clothed in all things of the world. For there is nothing besides Him, and there must be hidden holy sparks at all levels of being, granting them vitality.'[11] Man must aim to see himself and the world not as concrete manifestation but as abstract essence, to transcend the physical in all its variety and perceive the spiritual in its unity. He must use 'the eye of the intellect' rather than 'the eye of flesh' to redirect his focus from being to nothingness, from external garb to inner essence, from matter to spirit, from the 'word' to the 'window', from colloquial speech to the word of God it embodies.

Accomplishing this transition means going beyond the illusory limits of physical consciousness and becoming aware of the divine presence animating the universe. From a divine perspective, this is the only reality. Many different terms are used in hasidic writing to refer to this effort to reveal the spiritual basis of physical reality—a revelation predicated on abandoning ordinary sensory experience and focusing instead on the divine presence. It is known variously as *bitul hayesh* ('nullification of being'), *hafshatat hagashmiyut* ('divestment of corporeality'), *hitbonenut* ('contemplation'), *avodah begashmiyut* ('worshipping [God] through the physical'), *mesirut nefesh* ('self-surrender'), *ha'ala'at nitsotsot* ('elevation of sparks'), and *devekut* ('becoming one with God').[12]

---

[10] Elior, *The Paradoxical Ascent to God*, 25–37, 73–97.   [11] *Or hame'ir*, 'Pekudei', 85.
[12] See Schatz-Uffenheimer, *Hasidism as Mysticism*, index, for these concepts and also the indexes in Elior, *The Paradoxical Ascent to God*, and Loewenthal, *Communicating the Infinite*.

The transition from the mundane to the divine is achieved through the power of human thought

By virtue of its divine source, human thought is able to overcome the limits of physical perception and recognize the essential nothingness in being: 'By thought man can attain great limitless conceptions, for thought too is infinite.'[13] In Hebrew, thought is termed *ayin*, 'nothingness', a word closely related to Ein Sof, the Infinite, a way of defining God as the absence of finitude. Thought is itself infinite, abundant, and unlimited. Being of divine origin it strives by nature to return to its divine source, thus affording man the possibility of overcoming the barriers that seemingly place the divine presence beyond human apprehension. The power of thought allows man to become one with God and permits perception beyond the limits of the senses. The Ba'al Shem Tov maintains that 'when a man thinks about the higher worlds, then he is in the higher worlds, for where a man's thoughts range, there he is'.[14]

On this view, the ability to attain the divine perspective on the universe depends solely on the human mind and the ability to attain states of altered consciousness. As a divine power, thought is able to penetrate to the truth beneath appearances: 'Man must believe that God's glory fills the earth and all human thoughts contain his being and each thought presents a divine entity.'[15] This approach also reflects the blurring of boundaries between the divine spirit and the human spirit: creative human thought, expressed linguistically, is infinite, and by virtue of its infinity is identical with the infinite creativity of the divine.

The vitality of creation derives from its origins in divine effluence in the form of divine speech, the letters of the word of God that constantly animate the universe

The Ba'al Shem Tov perceived 'worlds and souls and divinity' in every letter.[16] The infinite light of the divine vitality in the universe, its sparks embodied in the letters of the holy tongue, is apprehended by man through language. Language is the unification of the abstract and the concrete: 'We hold this principle: that there is no place void of Him and His glory fills the whole earth, and all utterances that are spoken or actions done by necessity contain the letters of the Torah and holy sparks that animate them.'[17]

Language is the bridge that connects the divine and the human. Through the letters whose source is divine—through which God created the world and brought it forth from nothingness, from unity to multiplicity, from the

---

[13] *No'am elimelekh*, 25a.   [14] *Tsava'at harivash*, 11 (= p. 21, §69).

[15] *Ben porat yosef*, 50a.   [16] *Igeret hakodesh*; *Ben porat yosef*, 128a.

[17] *Or hame'ir*, 126b; *Shir hashirim*.

hidden to the revealed, from higher to lower, from abstract to concrete—man ascends from being to nothingness, from corporeality to spirituality, from physical multiplicity to spiritual oneness:

In prayer one must invest one's power in the utterances and move in this way from letter to letter until one becomes oblivious to corporeality and thinks of the letters combining and permutating with each other, and this is a great delight . . . Afterwards one arrives at the dimension [*midah*] of nothingness, meaning that all his physical powers are annulled and that is the world of Emanation.[18]

The process of movement from nothingness to being that constitutes 'creation', designated *tseruf ha'otiyot* (the 'joining of letters') or *hitlabeshut* ('enrobing', or taking on physical form), can be contrasted with what happens in prayer. Here concentration on the letters enables consciousness to traverse the opposite path, passing from being to nothingness in a process called *peruk ha'otiyot* ('separating the letters') or *hitpashetut* ('abstraction'). Physical reality is disrobed, so to speak, and ascends through the levels of apprehension from being to nothingness. The letters are the roots of existence; they are the imprints of the divine speech accessible to man. Divinity, as embodied as the 'world of speech' in the *sefirah* of Malkhut (i.e. the Shekhinah), resonates in man and allows him to overcome the limits of his physical existence through the acts of thinking and speaking that constitute prayer. Hasidic commentators understand 'the king fettered by the tresses' in the Song of Songs (7: 6) as the divine king imprisoned in the thoughts of man such that only contemplative thought and speech-acts resulting from great concentration on their divine purpose can liberate him from his captivity—an interpretation that is typically hasidic in its abandonment of conventional distinctions between the divine and the human.

Every person, at all times and in all places, can contemplate the hidden divine root of manifest physical being and come closer to the divine essence

Just as God is present at all times and in all places—as is implicit in the Psalmist's phrase 'the whole earth is full of His glory and there is no place void of Him'—so man can always draw closer to him. Man has an absolute obligation to devote himself to recognizing that the idea of the world as an autonomous entity is an illusion; the sole reality is the divine presence. The Ba'al Shem Tov taught that man must strive to do this in every thought and action, as implied in the verse 'In all your ways know him.'[19] The expansion of religious worship to all areas of human life—known as *avodah begashmiyut* (literally, 'worship through corporeality', but perhaps better translated as 'the

---

[18] *Keter shem tov*, ii. 17*b*.   [19] Prov. 3: 6.

task of seeking God in the material world')—accorded religious significance even to profane activities, by virtue of the thought that illuminates them and the intention that accompanies them:

In truth, where one's thought ranges, that is where one is. In truth, his glory fills *all* the earth and there is no place vacant of him. In all places that a man is, that is where he will find attachment [*devekut*] to the Creator in the place where he is, for there is no place void of him . . . In *all* places is divinity.[20]

This crucial expansion of the concept of religious worship derives from the thesis of divine presence in every place, every utterance, and every thought, as this omnipresence brings with it the obligation of attachment to God at all times and in all ways. Furthermore, man is connected to the divine reality— variously conceived as sparks, letters, Shekhinah, the 'divine stature' (*shiur komah*), *sefirot*, lights, and ideas—in a number of ways, thereby obscuring the distinction between the human and the divine:

Man is one of the limbs of the Shekhinah so that the totality of world completes the *shiur komah* . . . For everything in man and all his events are within Shekhinah. He should know to unify this dimension and to combine it with the superior dimension above it. This is about man in principle . . . that the perfect man can unite the Holy One Blessed Be He and His Shekhinah at every step and in every act that he performs even in the physical realm, in his eating and occupations and business dealings, all for the sake of His unification, and to know the dimension of the Shekhinah. About this Scripture says, 'Know the God of your father.'[21]

It is the power of speech that links man and the Shekhinah, the divine presence known also as 'the world of speech'.[22] There is a mutual relationship of revelation and concealment, speech and thought, the human voice and the spirit of God. The divine power to create and the human power to abstract are linked through the letters of language that unite the hidden with the revealed and the divine with the human:

For just as there are twenty-two letters of speech and Torah and prayer, so in all material and physical affairs in the world there are twenty-two letters through which the world and all that is in it was created. Within these letters dwells the divine spirit, for His glory fills all the earth and all that it contains, and there is no place void of Him, only there is concealment. When those who know are aware of this concealment it is not concealment any more.[23]

---

[20] *Magid devarav leya'akov*, 240; emphasis added.

[21] *Degel mahaneh efrayim*, 'Va'ethanan', p. 232.

[22] On the Shekhinah as the 'world of speech' see *Degel mahaneh efrayim*, 'Ekev', 243–4; *Magid devarav leya'akov*, 44, 52, 55, 71, 183; Schatz-Uffenheimer, *Hasidism as Mysticism*, 204–14.

[23] *Toledot ya'akov yosef*, 'Bereshit', 22*b*.

Hasidic literature uses a variety of terms to signify the unification with the divine element that animates physical reality, which can be achieved through concentration on the letters of divine being: 'nullification of being', 'attachment', 'contemplation', 'stripping away of the material', and 'worship through the material'. It is this attempt to achieve spiritual unification with the divine through thought, meditation, and the letters of speech and language that constitutes the essence of hasidic worship.

The hasidic conception of the essential unity of the divine and the human developed from kabbalistic theology. Kabbalism envisaged the presence of God in the world in the form of divine sparks that were scattered through the universe during a process termed the 'breaking of the vessels'—a crisis within the godhead that disturbed the divine harmony of the cosmic order and precipitated existential exile. The divine sparks thus scattered through the universe can be redeemed from their exile and restored to their divine source by the power of human thought and intent. Hasidism augmented this kabbalistic vision by emphasizing the ubiquity of the divine sparks and the necessity of serving God by working to seek their elevation at all times, in every way, through every thought and deed. For the hasidic masters, there was no object, place, or time incapable of serving as part of the religious duty imposed upon man to reveal the divine root of all existence. Everything, from the simplest physical actions to the loftiest religious deeds, offers man the opportunity to redeem the sparks and to mend the world, to engage in *yiḥudim* (literally 'unifications', meaning acts designed to achieve such reunification) and to know God. Contemplative awareness can discover the divine spark in all areas of life and turn each realm into a pathway leading to *devekut*: 'There is no thing great or small that is separate from Him, for He is present throughout reality. Therefore the perfect person can achieve supreme *yiḥudim* (unifications) even in his physical actions, such as eating and drinking and business intercourse.'[24]

Laying bare the metaphysical foundations of being by 'elevating the sparks' or 'finding God in the material world' involves uncovering the divine roots of reality in sacred language. This requires recognition of the relativity of sensory perspectives; of the dual nature of language in consequence of its letters being the embodiment of the divine speech that animates being; of the duality inherent in reality because of the simultaneity of 'being' and 'nothingness'; and of the need to transcend the physical world in order to achieve attachment to the divine. The ideas of *bitul hayesh* ('negating being') and *hafshatat hagashmiyut* ('abstracting [the essence of] physicality') imply the transcendence of physical reality in order to uncover the divine element that

---

[24] *Toledot ya'akov yosef*, 'Naso', 474.

animates it. In other words, revealing the divine substance in being requires recognition of its essential nothingness.

This mystical doctrine aimed at seeking out the concealed life-source and recognizing the insignificance of that which is manifest is expounded in detail in the works of Jacob Joseph of Polonnoye and the Maggid of Mezhirech and their disciples, and in the two volumes of *Ba'al shem tov al hatorah*. Its goal is to reveal the divine essence that underlies and animates the physical world, thereby eliminating the distinction between the revealed and the concealed and between man and God. In the hasidic world-view, consciousness itself oscillates between perceiving physicality and perceiving its divine essence; the recognition of 'being' and 'nothingness' are thus determinations of the observing intellect rather than products of sensory experience.

This doctrine was almost certainly influenced by the Ba'al Shem Tov's own mystical experiences. By all accounts, he claimed to have had direct contact with the higher worlds and immediate experience of the divine presence. In his view, 'each letter contains worlds and souls and divinity'; every word, every physical phenomenon, can be a 'window' allowing the light of the life-giving divine infinity to shine through and reveal that things perceived by the senses as discrete are in reality part of the divine totality. Physical 'reality' is in fact transparent; God is always present but not normally perceived. God dwells in human thought and the divine 'world of speech' speaks in man. 'Man is one of the limbs of the Shekhinah', and it is possible to go beyond the limits of 'reality', which are but illusions imposed by the senses, so as to see its true divine essence.

The Ba'al Shem Tov was certainly influenced by kabbalism in developing his mystical orientation and articulating his experiences. But whereas the kabbalistic tradition elevated the mystical elements to the distant domains of the higher worlds and saw divine revelation as remote from the human world, the mystical vision of the Ba'al Shem Tov focused on what man and God have in common: ideas, speech, and letters—the creative power vested in language common to God and man. Kabbalism focused on esoteric concepts: *atsilut* ('emanation'), *sefirot* ('divine spheres'), *tsahstahot* ('shinings'), *heikhalot* ('shrines'), *shemitot* ('cosmic septennials'), *adam kadmon* ('primeval man'), *partsufim* ('countenances'), and *butsina dekardinuta* ('illumination emerging from darkness'). The Ba'al Shem Tov stressed instead the divine aspects of man ('for man is a limb of the Shekhinah') and the human aspects of God. For the Ba'al Shem Tov, God is perceived as 'dwelling in the letters' and is portrayed as the 'world of speech' resonating within man.

Whereas kabbalism relegated mystical practices to an elite who separated themselves from the community and followed a pious way of life in order to devote themselves to sacred matters, the Ba'al Shem Tov saw every Jew as having the mystical potential to recognize the animating divine essence that suffuses everything. Whereas Lurianic kabbalah applied the term *olam* ('world') to the divine, the Ba'al Shem Tov used it to describe the Jewish collective, based on the mystical categories of *Sefer yetsirah*: 'The world is complete divine stature and a single divine countenance in the mystery of world, year, soul.'[25]

The Ba'al Shem Tov took this position because the experience of a permeating divine presence and an awareness of the divine reality concealed behind every manifest being were fundamental to his outlook. The duality of revelation and concealment is also apparent in the fact that the divine language of Creation shares the same letters as the language of human thought and speech. To emphasize the concept of a divine reality present everywhere and accessible to all, the Ba'al Shem Tov quoted the Zoharic saying, 'No place is devoid of Him.' The idea that there is no place devoid of the divine presence nor any circumstances in which it is not present means that God is ever present in human thought; the implications of this are huge, since that which springs from a divine source is itself divine. No thought or utterance, no act or being, is outside the province of divine presence; hence no person is unable to take part in the spiritual dialogue between the revealed and concealed. This is stated very clearly in *Magid devarav leya'akov*:

Everything is the expansion [*hitpashetut*] of the Creator whose glory fills every part of the universe. One should elevate the inwardness in that thing, every person according to his capacity . . . In every gesture the Creator resides, for it is impossible to make any motion or utterance without the power of the Creator, may He be blessed. This is the meaning of the verse: 'The whole earth is full of His glory.'[26]

Similar ideas are expressed in *Tsava'at harivash*. From this concept of the all-inclusiveness of the divine presence, the hasidic masters inferred the totality of human access to God. Just as God is everywhere, so all may approach God through their thoughts and achieve unity with him: 'Every Jew, contemplating . . . how God literally fills the higher and lower [levels] and heaven and earth literally, the whole universe is literally full of His glory'.[27] That is to say, everyone, in every way, in any place and time, is allowed to approach the sacred so long as one meditates on the 'power of the agent over the object', recognizing the relationship of being to nothingness, and directing one's thoughts to living in the presence of God, who is both revealed and concealed: 'Everyone must worship God in all His aspects, for everything is for the sake of the Highest,

---

[25] *Toledot ya'akov yosef*, 'Kedoshim', 337.   [26] *Magid devarav leya'akov*, 44.
[27] *Tanya*, 120.

because God wants to be served in all modes . . . God can be served in every thing.'[28] This conception, which saw in each person 'a divine portion from above',[29] which asserted that 'everyone was created on earth below to do great and wondrous things . . . to hint at the higher world',[30] and which did not hesitate to say that 'everyone can reach the level of our teacher Moses of blessed memory',[31] reflected a new perception of man as part of an outlook that overturned conventional hierarchies which discriminate among different people and modes of worship.

The idea that every individual is a sanctuary for the divine essence that fills the universe with its glory accords equal value to all members of the community and all modes of worship by virtue of the radical claim that 'God wants to be served in all modes . . . God can be served in every thing.' As early as 1906 Martin Buber noted that 'hasidism is kabbalah that has become ethos', meaning a written mystical heritage that has turned into a source of inspiration, a way of life, and a comprehensive transformation of consciousness for many. Buber's discussion in *In the Orchard of Hasidism* and the concluding chapter of Scholem's *Major Trends* are based on this insight. However, further enquiry into the nature of the relationship between hasidism and kabbalah demonstrates that, despite the fact that they share a common conceptual basis, there are significant differences in applications and implications.

Certainly, hasidic thought is moored in the kabbalistic tradition: kabbalah perceived the deity as a dynamic, multi-dimensional being; as a dialectical coincidence of opposites; as a continuous, infinite process unifying the dichotomy between becoming and nullification, revelation and concealment. In kabbalistic literature this is expressed by such terms as 'ebb and flow', 'expansion and withdrawal', 'nothingness and being', 'emanation and contraction', 'creation and annihilation', 'concretization and abstraction', terminology that expresses the dynamic nature of divine being in its various processes and the dialectic of opposites in its alterations. Kabbalistic thought ascribed great significance to the paradoxical dynamic posed by the coincidence of opposites, but confined it to the transcendent world, concealed beyond human apprehension. The innovation of hasidism was to apply this celestial set of concepts to the human world, a world of thought and consciousness and religious worship. The Ba'al Shem Tov saw the hidden divine immanence as the sole essential reality and regarded physical existence as illusory. In other words, he translated the kabbalistic dialectic into one of human enlightenment: the concepts of emanation, greatness, essentialization, and attachment pertain to a

---

[28] *Tsava'at harivash*, 1a (= p. 1, §3).   [29] *Magid devarav leya'akov*, p. 62, §41.
[30] *Me'irat einayim*, p. 24, §§57, 59. *Ba'al shem tov al hatorah*, i. 57 (p. 25, §59).
[31] *Likutei yekarim*, 1c.

state in which human consciousness experiences the divine essence that unifies opposites, while contraction, smallness, withdrawal, and separation pertain to a state in which it perceives only the physical manifestations in their isolation.

The founders of hasidism based themselves on the kabbalistic tradition but revolutionized its limits. Mystical experience and the new way in which they interpreted reality as the perception of superior worlds, seeing beyond the concrete ('the whole earth full of His glory'), were blended with an appeal to 'all persons' ('the whole world is a complete stature and a single countenance'). The implication of the divine presence being everywhere and accessible to all people was a blurring of distinctions between Jews: all were to be regarded as limbs of the Shekhinah, capable of revealing God in every thought and action ('in all your ways know Him'). Hence the hasidic call to 'distance [oneself] from physicality and imagine that one is only divine animation . . . and perceive the superior source of all things'.[32]

All this constitutes a fundamental transformation in the perception of the relationship between man and God. Whereas the kabbalistic tradition saw access to the divine as restricted to a knowledgeable elite, hasidism saw it as open to all. Indeed, in the hasidic view, the distinction between man and God is itself illusory: 'humanity is a limb of the Shekhinah' and 'the whole world is a complete stature and one face'. Hasidic teaching overturns the customary theological distinctions between God and humanity ('My thoughts are not your thoughts', Isaiah 55: 8), between heaven and earth ('The heavens are God's', Psalm 115: 16), between Creator and creature, between people and their neighbours. On the contrary, human thought is seen as divine. Man is linked to God because language and consciousness, spirit and creativity, are all founded on the letters of divine speech; creativity becomes the portion of all. Hasidism made mysticism a universal legacy when it proclaimed: 'One should always be attached to God with a wondrous *devekut* . . . And one should know that his worship and attachment to the Creator blessed be His name can elevate all the worlds.'[33] In bringing about this spiritual revolution it also caused profound changes in social reality.

---

[32] *Magid devarav leya'akov*, preface, 6.   [33] Ibid. 6.

SEVEN

Hasidism in the Context of its Time

Paradox is a characteristic of truth. What common opinion has of truth is sure-
ly no more than an elementary deposit of generalizing partial understanding,
related to truth even as sulphurous fumes are to lightning.

Count Paul Yorck von Wartenburg[1]

T HE mystical outlook and religious devotion engendered by the study of
    the 'true wisdom' of kabbalah led the Ba'al Shem Tov and his circle
increasingly to *darkhei ḥasidut* ('pious ways'—a devout and ascetic way of life
in keeping with kabbalistic principles), and to the establishment of their own
social frameworks compatible with their esoteric spirituality and practices.
However, they were not unique in this. The spirit of the time was such that
other groups were also deeply interested in kabbalistic literature, and equally
committed to pietistic practices. The following formulation from *Nagid umetsaveh* is typical of statements found in seventeenth- and eighteenth-century
works such as *Shulḥan arukh ha'ari* and *Sha'ar hakavanot* and in kabbalistic
prayer-books:

You will find in this book all the esoteric commandments and customs and pious per-
formances and acts of *tikun* [i.e. acts aimed at restoring the world to its proper order] in
the books of our master R. Isaac Ashkenazi Luria of blessed memory, the inner meaning
of each commandment and its *tikun* . . . We found in his book several matters about
which he taught that they are permitted according to the law . . . but they are practices
of piety [*darkhei ḥasidut*] and necessary for those occupied with the True Wisdom [kab-
balah].[2]

Committed as they were to *darkhei ḥasidut*, all these groups considered
themselves *ḥasidim*; at the time, the term was certainly not limited to followers of the Ba'al Shem Tov. In fact it had been used since the sixteenth century
to designate members of a pious elite committed to devout religious observance, people punctilious in the performance of divine commandments and
devoted to long hours of meditative prayer in accordance with kabbalistic

---

[1] From the correspondence of Count Paul Yorck von Wartenburg and Wilhelm Dilthey, as
quoted in Scholem, *Sabbatai Ṣevi*, 1.   [2] *Nagid umetsaveh*, preface.

rites. By the eighteenth century, though, it had actually come to have some-what negative connotations because the various groups of *ḥasidim* that had emerged in response to the messianic ferment of the times were seen as a de-stabilizing influence within Jewish society. The growing belief that introducing mystically inspired prayers and rituals to replace the common custom would hasten the redemption of the Shekhinah and the dawn of the messianic age inevitably brought its proponents into conflict with the traditionalrabbinic authorities, and it was for this reason that they were considered a threat.

The link between kabbalah and messianism is complicated. Briefly stated, the suffering of exile engendered a yearning for messianic redemption and nourished spirituality, which led in turn to the adoption of a kabbalistically inspired, mystical world-view. This new-found spirituality expressed itself in a multitude of ways in the Middle Ages and the early modern period, with significant social consequences. The very 'revelation' of the Zohar in the thirteenth century contributed to this, in so far as studying the kabbalistic mysticism of the Zohar was considered to bring redemption closer and hasten the coming of the messiah.[3] In the sixteenth and seventeenth centuries, the link between kabbalah and messianism was further reinforced by the wide dissemination of works of Lurianic kabbalah written in Safed; kabbalah became the very substance of the messianic age. As the daily concerns of the practical reality of exile (the main focus of halakhah) gave way to an eschat-ology oriented towards a celestial reality beyond the limits of time and space, so the study of the norms and practices of halakhah was gradually replaced in certain mystical circles with the study of kabbalah. As long as these new mystical concerns were limited to small groups of kabbalists they had no broad social repercussions, but when they began to lead to changes in accepted customs—to segregation from the community in the name of greater sanctity, and to the rise of charismatic and mystical modes of leadership—the social consequences were significant.[4]

The idea of charismatic leadership with mystical authority and a messianic orientation proved enormously popular in the seventeenth-century Jewish world. The key factor here was the messianic expectation aroused by plague, wars, and the pogroms associated with the Chmielnecki rebellion of 1648–9;

---

[3] The quotation marks around 'revelation' relate to the fact that the Zohar was written in Spain in the 13th century but purported to be an ancient text, written by the 2nd-century sage Rabbi Simon bar Yohai under mystical inspiration and deliberately hidden for a thousand years; its future revelation was presented in the book itself as a sign of the beginning of the messianic era. See Scholem, *Major Trends in Jewish Mysticism*, chs. 5 and 6, and Tishby, *The Wisdom of the Zohar*, vol. i, introduction.

[4] On the nature of kabbalistic hasidism, see Dinur, 'The Origins of Hasidism'; Elior, 'R. Nathan Adler and the Frankfurt Pietists'; Rosman, *The Founder of Hasidism*, 27–41.

the misery that followed the assassination at that time of many thousands of Jews in the Ukraine was interpreted as part of the tribulations of a pre-messianic era. When Shabetai Tsevi, deeply affected by the news of the massacre, declared himself 'king messiah' in 1666 after reading the tragic record preserved by Nathan Neta Hanover in his *Yeven metsulah* which was published in Venice in 1653, he aroused widespread public hope of redemption from the sufferings of exile. When the news of his messianic aspirations reached the Ottoman authorities, however, they ordered him to retract all such claims, to demonstrate his retraction by converting to Islam, and to leave the Ottoman lands: they were not disposed to welcome an additional monarch to the realm, even if the competitor was merely the mystical-messianic king of the Jews.[5]

The obvious absurdity of an apostate messiah caused great despair among Shabetai Tsevi's many followers. Their reactions were varied. Some explained his apostasy as an act of obedience to a divine revelation, and therefore chose to convert to Islam as well; such was the apostasy of the three hundred families of the Donmeh, the Shabatean faithful in Salonika, in 1683.[6] Others reacted by dedicating their time to the study of the Zohar and its interpretation in Shabatean kabbalah, in an attempt to explain the discrepancy between external reality and the hidden messianic reality ultimately to be disclosed. Shabatean kabbalah offered new ideas concerning divine redemption and the war against the *kelipah*; its proponents saw exile and redemption as a dualistic cosmic struggle between the forces of good and the forces of evil, and developed original theories about the relationship between God and man in the revealed and concealed reality. Chief among them was the concept of 'sacred deceit' (*mirmah dekedushah*), which justified sin as a way of deceiving the powers of evil. In this view, apostasy was not a cardinal sin but rather a subterfuge undertaken for the sake of the holy mission of redeeming the soul of the messiah in order to confuse the forces of evil concealing this spark of divinity in the husks of the *kelipah*. Both consequences of this approach—apostasy and immersion in kabbalah—drew the ire of the established community. The Va'ad Arba Ha'aratsot (the Council of the Four Lands), the central leadership of east European Jewry at that time, issued bans of excommunication against the Shabateans throughout the seventeenth and

---

[5] On Shabetai Tsevi see *EJ* xiv. 1219–54. On Shabateanism, see the following by Scholem: *Sabbatai Ṣevi*, *Studies and Sources on the History of Shabateanism* (Heb.), and *Studies on Shabateanism* (Heb.); see also Liebes, *The Secret of Shabatean Faith* (Heb.); Elior (ed.), *The Dream and its Interpretation* (Heb.); and Goldish, *The Sabbatean Prophets*.

[6] See *EJ* vi. 142–58 s.v. 'Doenmeh'; cf. *Shirot vetishbaḥot*; Balaban, *On the History of the Frankist Movement* (Heb.), i. 44–53.

eighteenth centuries. In 1714, in response to the growing numbers of mystics, pious Shabateans, and others who called themselves *hasidim* or *ma'aminim* ('believers') and were engaged in studying mystical texts, it published prohibitions against studying kabbalah in any form before the age of 40.[7]

Despite the paradox inherent in the apostasy of the messiah, and to a large extent precisely because of it, Shabatean groups continued to flourish in Salonika, one of the great Jewish communities of that time. Eventually a new messianic movement was to emerge from these residual groups under the leadership of Jacob Frank, a Jew from Podolia who entered the circle of the Donmeh in Salonika between 1753 and 1755 and absorbed their teachings. In 1755 Frank returned to Podolia in order to disseminate Shabatean ideas there and in Galicia.[8] As an expression of their rejection of exile and endorsement of the messianic era, Jacob Frank and his followers openly questioned the legitimacy of traditional Judaism and its authorities, and preached heresy, anarchy, and antinomianism. They called themselves *ma'aminim* ('people of faith'), 'Zoharites' ('believers in the Zohar'), and 'anti-talmudists'. The spirit of the times was such that they attracted many supporters. In Galicia and Podolia, in Poland, Bohemia, Romania, and Germany, thousands of Jews joined the Frankist movement, and hundreds converted to Christianity in the belief that this would hasten the dawn of the messianic age while also enabling them to live freely as believers in the new messianic world inspired by Shabetai Tsevi, untrammelled by opposition from the rabbinic establishment. It is known that 530 families converted in a public ceremony in Lvov in 1759, and others did so later in Warsaw. Frankist sources claim thousands of converts, but no exact figures are known.[9]

The apostasy of Shabetai Tsevi thus generated tendencies to separatism as people sought mystical solutions to the suffering of exile. They were variously labelled *hasidim*, *ba'alei sod ha'emunah* ('masters of the secret faith'), Shabateans, Frankists, Zoharites, anti-talmudists, ascetic pietists (*perushim*), or simply 'believers'. The rapid proliferation of such groups in various places aroused a great sense of tension, menace, and dread within established Jewish communities. In the ensuing panic, many people who were merely seeking

---

[7] See Heilperin, *Records of the Council of the Four Lands*, 418, 205; Balaban, *On the History of the Frankist Movement* (Heb.), i. 125–6.

[8] Podolia came under Ottoman rule between 1672 and 1699, and in consequence the Jews of Podolia developed close ties with Salonika in Greece, the largest Jewish community of the time, which was likewise under Ottoman rule. These close ties—commercial, legal, cultural, and spiritual—continued even after Podolia was taken over by Russia in 1772.

[9] See Balaban, *On the History of the Frankist Movement* (Heb.), i. 95–151; *Hakhronikah*, ed. Levine, p. 56, sects. 47–8; Elior, '*Sefer divrei ha'adon*' (Heb.).

spiritual enrichment through mystical contemplation and cultivating messianic hopes without rejecting the traditional order were accused of being covert Shabateans and therefore dangerous subversives.

This had significant consequences for the new religious movement that was developing in the mid-eighteenth century around the Ba'al Shem Tov in Podolia and Galicia. Because at that time these areas were also the focus of Frankist Shabatean activity, the new hasidic groups also aroused anxiety and fear. They were suspected of being yet another manifestation of Shabateanism, even though there was (and still is) no evidence that their leaders had any direct ties to Shabateanism or to its paradoxical mystical beliefs.[10]

The apostasy of the Shabateans in Ottoman Salonika, the Donmeh, had made a deep impression on the established community all over the Jewish world. The Va'ad Arba Ha'aratsot, the central institution of Ashkenazi Jewry until its dissolution in 1764, devoted many sessions to the conflict with Shabateanism. The first bans of excommunication were issued in the 1720s; by the 1730s, accusations of Shabateanism were being made throughout the Jewish world. Thus, the Italian kabbalist Moses Hayim Luzzatto (1707–47), also known by the Hebrew acronym Ramhal, a prolific poet and playwright and author of grammatical studies and mystical writings including the famed *Mesilat yesharim*, was dogged by such accusations in every city he went to; all over Europe his books were banned and buried.[11] In the 1750s a controversy involving Jonathan Eybeschuetz (1690–1764), the rabbi of Prague suspected of Shabateanism and of ties to a circle of Jewish Christians, rocked the Jewish world; the apostasy of his son Wolf did nothing to calm the storm. Virulent anti-Shabatean campaigns were conducted by Jacob Emden (1697–1776),[12] son of Tsevi Ashkenazi (known as the Hakham Tsevi) who was himself ardently anti-Shabatean,[13] and Moses Hagiz;[14] these are documented in their works. They attacked Nehemiah Hayon, Judah Leib Prossnitz, and Jonathan Eybeschuetz as Shabateans, and publicly condemned the Amsterdam rabbinate for supporting these and other rabbis suspected of practising Shabateanism or writing controversial works of a Shabatean orientation. The polemical literature on both sides left its imprint on the hasidic world. From the Shabatean side this literature includes compositions such as *Va'avo hayom el ha'ayin* (1724) and *Raza demehemnuta*, of unknown authorship; works by known Shabateans such as Samuel Primo, Abraham Michael Cardozo,

[10] See Elior, 'Hasidism: Historical Continuity'.
[11] See Ginzburg (ed.), *R. Moses Hayim Luzzatto* (Heb.); *EJ* xi. 599–604.
[12] See Schacter, 'Rabbi Jacob Emden'.
[13] On Jacob Emden's father Hakham Tsevi, see *Megilat sefer*.
[14] See Carlebach, *The Pursuit of Heresy*; Schacter, 'Rabbi Jacob Emden'.

Nehemiah Hayon, and Hayim Malakh; and works written by authors suspected of Shabateanism, such as Jacob Koppel of Mezhirech and Joshua Heshel Tsoref, author of *Sefer hatsoref*, which circulated in manuscript form.[15] The anti-Shabatean tracts included *Shever poshe'im* (1714), *Leḥishat saraf* (1726), *Shevirat luḥot aven* (1756), *Sefer shimush* (1758), *Sefer hitabekut* (1762), *Minḥat kenaot*, *Gaḥalei esh*, and many more. There were also refutations of the accusations, such as *Luḥot ha'edut* (1755) and others. Rabbinical courts, from Brody to Satanow and from Amsterdam to Frankfurt, occupied themselves with considering testimonies concerned with the influence of Shabatean writing and practices; the stormy process of issuing bans and of accusation and refutation through letters and books became routine.[16]

It is not easy to characterize Shabateanism, or even to identify it: theory and practice were frequently neither consistent nor in harmony. It seems, however, that support for Shabateanism was rooted in the conviction that Shabetai Tsevi's messianic activity (and subsequently that of his successor Barukhyah Russo (d. 1720) in Salonika, and later of Jacob Frank) had overturned the traditional order. Believers in Shabetai Tsevi and in the 'God of Shabetai Tsevi' maintained that the era of exile had ended and the messianic age had started—notwithstanding the fact that there was no apparent indication of redemption. The faithful were to be liberated from the chains of external reality, and Judaism was to be redeemed from the era of exile and enter the epoch of redemption. Accordingly, the time had come to replace the 'old' Torah—the Torah of exile, of the Tree of Knowledge and of halakhah—with a new Torah, the Torah of the Tree of Life and kabbalah, which was regarded as a redeeming doctrine and as an expression of the new world of freedom. One of the fundamental manifestations of this idea, which was based on Isaiah's eschatological prophecy 'for a new teaching will come forth from Me',[17] was to abandon the conventional distinction between what is forbidden and what is permitted, on the grounds that it was merely a consequence of the chasm between the external reality of exile and the inner reality of redemption. However, not all who defined themselves as Shabateans, or who were suspected of being so by others, really lived according to these principles. Most did not subscribe to the extremist ideas of a new Torah, of 'holy sin' (*mitsvah haba'ah ba'aveirah*).[18] They did not really believe that 'the

---

[15] See Scholem, 'Redemption through Sin'; id., 'The Shabatean Movement in Poland' (Heb.).

[16] See Heilperin, *Records of the Council of the Four Lands*, 332–432; Carlebach, *The Pursuit of Heresy*; Schacter, 'Rabbi Jacob Emden'. On excommunication in the 18th century, see Ferziger, *Exclusion and Hierarchy*.

[17] Isa. 51: 4 (*Vayikra rabah* 13: 3).   [18] See Scholem, 'Redemption through Sin'.

time has come to violate the Torah for the sake of God',[19] or accept the concept of a new deity in the form of a divine messiah, and these ideas made little difference to their lives. There were exceptions: the Donmeh, who converted to Islam in order to pursue their life as free messianic Jews, and the Frankists, who converted to Christianity from similar motives.[20] But there were many others who lived outwardly in accordance with the forms of the traditional world while expressing, directly or indirectly, in their inner life and religious rituals, the sense that, by dint of their faith in the inception of a redeemed age and the messianic status of Shabetai Tsevi, the bounds of that old world had disintegrated.

Shabatean views were to be found among mystics and ascetic pietists, but also at the heart of the rabbinic establishment: Solomon Ayllon of Amsterdam (1660–1728), Jonathan Eybeschuetz of Prague, Moses Hayim Luzzatto of Padua, and Nathan Adler of Frankfurt were all accused of being Shabateans, as were many other authorities. However, because of the persecution of Shabateans following the conversion of Shabetai Tsevi and groups of his followers to Islam, adherence to Shabatean theology and practices associated with the beginning of the messianic age was often clandestine. In any event, the reality of defining mystical and pietistic practices as Shabatean was complicated; the key problem was the lack of an obvious criterion that distinguished Shabatean pietists and mystics from others. All studied kabbalah and lived in accordance with esoteric ritual practices and 'paths of piety' that led to exceptional sanctity. All chose to form separate congregations for prayer. All adopted Zoharic practices that could elevate the 'divine sparks' so as to hasten the redemption of the Shekhinah and generate the final revelation of the messianic era. The Shabateans did so in the belief that the messiah had already come, and that the more sins they committed (as a way of disguising their true intent), the faster the messiah would be revealed again and bring about the ultimate messianic redemption. Others did so in the hope of a redemption that was yet to come and respected the traditional boundaries in their practices. However, this did not translate itself into an obvious criterion for differentiating between them in practice.

As the Shabatean movement continued to grow, it posed an increasing threat to the traditional community. In 1756/7, the rabbis of Podolia and Galicia excommunicated the Shabatean followers of Jacob Frank. The

---

[19] Ps. 119: 126, as interpreted homiletically in Mishnah *Berakhot* 9: 5. See Scholem, 'Redemption through Sin'.

[20] See Scholem, 'Jacob Frank' (*EJ* vii. 55–71); Brawer, *Galicia and its Jews* (Heb.), 195–275, and also Isaac ben Zvi's introduction to *Shirot vetishbahot shel hashabetayim* and Elior, '*Sefer divrei ha'adon*' (Heb.).

Frankists responded by challenging leading rabbis in public disputations conducted under the supervision of the Church. In 1759 hundreds of them publicly followed Jacob Frank's example and converted to Christianity in the cathedral of Lvov; many more followed them in a public conversion in Warsaw. The Church authorities suspected the sincerity of Frank's conversion, however, and in 1760 he was tried and sentenced to imprisonment in the fortress of Czestochowa; in 1772 the Russians conquered Czestochowa and set him free. From the time that Frank was released from prison in 1772 until his death at the end of the century, many apostates flocked to join him.[21] The traditional Jewish leadership, unable to distinguish between the different separatist movements and anxious to protect the community from the kabbalistic and messianic trends that were leading in some instances to apostasy and anarchy, reacted strongly. They imposed a total ban on changes in ritual practice, and anyone who tried to set up separate groups for prayer and for the study of the kabbalah was excommunicated.[22]

Hostility towards manifestations of kabbalistic piety is rife in the contemporary literature. Such attacks are directed against ascetics, Shabatean pietists, Shabatean Frankists, and the hasidim of the Ba'al Shem Tov. General attacks on unnamed pietistic kabbalists appear, for example, in *Mishmeret hakodesh* by Moses of Satanow (1746), in the preface to Solomon of Chelm's *Merkevet hamishneh* (1751), in Jacob Emden's *Mitpahat sefarim* (1768), in Joseph Steinhardt of Fuerth's *Zikhron yosef* (1773), and in Ezekiel Landau's *Noda biyehudah* (1776). Such texts are discussed at length by Simon Dubnow in his *History of Hasidism* and by Mordecai Wilensky in *Hasidim and Mitnagedim*. A particularly interesting example, discussed by Dubnow, is to be found in a preface written by Solomon Isaac Heilperin (b. 1727), rabbi of Zwaniec in Podolia around 1770, to the collected responsa of his father Jacob Heilperin, published as *Beit ya'akov*. While he was aware of the differences between Shabateans, Frankists, and hasidim, his depiction reflects the assessment of the kabbalistic-hasidic phenomenon by its eighteenth-century opponents. Heilperin, who attended the 1756 public disputes with the Frankists and observed in person the events that agitated the Jewish world of his time, begins by quoting his father (who had died in 1738) on the early part of the eighteenth century:

My late father's response [concerning the recitation of prayer according to the Sephardi pronunciation of Hebrew, adopted in kabbalistic circles which followed the Lurianic

[21] See *Hakhronikah*, ed. Levine; Balaban, *On the History of the Frankist Movement* (Heb.); Brawer, *Galicia and its Jews* (Heb.); Elior, '*Sefer divrei ha'adon*'.

[22] See Elior, 'R. Nathan Adler and the Frankfurt Pietists'; Wilensky, 'Hasidic–Mitnaggedic Polemics'.

custom of praying according to Sephardi liturgy] fulfilled the rabbinic dictum that 'the sage is superior to the prophet'. For he anticipated the sect of believers in Shabetai Tsevi, may the name of the wicked rot, the messiah of defilement [*mashiah lefi tumah*, a play on *mashiah lefi tumo*, meaning one who testifies without an ulterior motive]. In the generation of my father this sect was like the wild boar, with cloven hoofs stretched forward as proof of their purity,[23] they fasted and mortified themselves mightily, showing themselves as pious and ascetic . . . Verily their prayers swelled to heaven, only they began to change our text of prayer . . . Then they broke down the fence and ate on the four fast days [commemorating the destruction of Jerusalem and the Temple], arguing that these had now become days of festivity [see Zech. 8: 18 ff.]. When my father and teacher heard of this, he prophesied that ultimately they would throw off the yoke of the commandments in their entirety. Some years later, after his demise, I myself saw that as he predicted, so it was, as all know about the apostasy in Lvov [of the Frankists in 1759] at the gathering of all the rabbis of the Lvov district to debate at the church with that wicked sect. I too was compelled to participate when I was head of the rabbinical court of Bratushany . . . How many troubles confronted us when the members of the sect stood against us, brazenly, in their hundreds, to destroy us with false libels and empty slander . . . They conducted themselves lawlessly: some embraced Islam and some Christianity. They left the community [of Israel] with their wives and sons and daughters, children and adults, compelling little schoolchildren to convert against their will, who wept among their families [see Num. 11: 5], as I saw with my own eyes when I was in Lvov at that time. They called themselves *mitnagedim* [opponents] meaning that they opposed the Talmud, in order to flatter the Christians, who also do not suffer the Talmud for well-known reasons . . . Now, in our generation, for our many sins, the leprosy spreads, to cast away the Oral Law, the Talmud, and talmudic authorities and seize instead the kabbalah books, calling themselves *hasidim*, and pray according to the Sephardi liturgy. Some of them wrap themselves in white linen and pace backwards on a ladder that reaches to the heavens . . . They are idle and dissipate their days in the smoke of the pipe, and have appointed ritual slaughterers to slaughter with extra-sharp knives.[24]

Note the confusion and historical irony here: although the Shabateans of the early and mid-eighteenth century were called hasidim and *perushim* (ascetics), the Frankist Shabateans called themselves mitnagedim, and this at the very same time as Shabatean connections were imputed to the hasidim of the Ba'al Shem Tov by their persecutors, who were also known as mitnagedim. No doubt this lack of terminological clarity has contributed to the confusion in

---

[23] A kosher animal has cloven hoofs and chews the cud (Lev. 11: 7). The pig, or boar, has the first trait but not the second. The rabbis took the recumbent pig, which displays its 'kosher' feet while hiding his mouth, as an emblem of hypocrisy (*Bereshit rabah*, 45).

[24] Dubnow, *History of Hasidism* (Heb.), 484–5; Scholem, *Explications and Implications* (Heb.), 294; Hundert, *Jews in Poland–Lithuania in the Eighteenth Century*, 203–4; Rosman, *The Founder of Hasidism*, 133–4.

identifying the various kabbalistic and pietistic groups that flourished in the eighteenth century.[25]

During the Ba'al Shem Tov's lifetime, his followers were never banned as a distinct group, although they did arouse hostility and criticism. The text cited above, for example, implicitly and explicitly links the hasidim of the Ba'al Shem Tov with kabbalistic practices and Shabateanism. As the movement grew and consolidated after the Ba'al Shem Tov's death in 1760, under the leadership of Dov Baer, the Maggid of Mezhirech, so did the opposition. By 1772, writs of excommunication began to emanate from Vilna in Lithuania and from Brody in Galicia that clearly linked hasidism with Shabateanism. The hasidim were dubbed 'the chronic leprosy' and 'suspects' (hashudim, a pun on hasidim deriving from the fact that, in Lithuanian Yiddish, 'sh' and 's' are interchangeable). The attacks were motivated primarily by the suspicion that the hasidim were Shabateans; in other words, they were considered a new manifestation of the phenomenon against which community authorities had struggled incessantly throughout the eighteenth century. The community scribe who copied the 1772 ban of excommunication in Brody wrote: 'When this letter reached us, we were frightened of what we saw and heard, that the fire roaring among us for some years is still dancing among us in the form of wicked groups.'[26]

Analysis of the writings of the hasidic masters and their disciples indicates that the accusation of Shabateanism was baseless. Hasidism did not link itself to Shabetai Tsevi in any way and did not follow Shabatean writings or doctrines. It did not exchange the present for the future, or the Tree of Knowledge (signifying law-abiding obedience to the traditional halakhah) for the Tree of Life (signifying the subversive interpretation of the mystical kabbalah). It did not assign a central role to an actualized messiah, or to an immediate, reality-altering redemption that would justify 'violating the Torah for the sake of God'. It adhered to the regimen of the divine commandments and did not adopt the idea of the 'holiness of sin'. On the contrary, it tended to a kabbalistically inspired rigour in matters of ritual. There is no evidence, direct or indirect, of significant contact between hasidim and Shabateans, although of course the founders of hasidism lived in a world on which

---

[25] On the geographical, historical, and cultural proximity between hasidism and Shabateanism and its significance, see Heilperin, *Records of the Council of the Four Lands* (Heb.); Balaban, *On the History of the Frankist Movement* (Heb.); Scholem, 'The Shabatean Movement in Poland' (Heb.); Brawer, *Galicia and its Jews* (Heb.); Gelber, 'History of the Jews of Brody' (Heb.); and Elior, 'Hasidism: Historical Continuity'.

[26] Wilensky, *Hasidim and Mitnagedim* (Heb.), i. 44; on the ban of Brody in 1772, see Hundert (ed.), *Essential Papers*, 47, 66, 365; Elior, 'R. Nathan Adler and the Frankfurt Pietists', 168.

Shabateanism, with its desire to transcend the limits of the traditional world, its yearning for charismatic leadership, and its belief in actualized messianism, had left its mark. Shabateanism had also shown the way to an anarchistic, antinomian, paradoxical, dialectical world-view that conceptualized a new relationship between the revealed and the concealed and understood exile and redemption in innovative ways.

The Shabatean system of concepts proved very influential. Among its innovations were such enduring ideas as 'descent for the sake of ascent', 'the holiness of sin', 'the time has come to violate the Torah for the sake of God', 'light is only revealed from within the darkness', 'the staff transformed into the serpent', and 'the serpent-messiah' (because the two Hebrew words have the same numerical value, the followers of Shabateanism considered them semantically equivalent too); another innovation was the doctrine of the Tree of Life, free from concepts of prohibition and sin. Through charismatic leadership—visionary, prophetic leaders hearkening to the new divine voices of the messianic age and therefore not subservient to normative authority—these Shabatean innovations continued to reverberate. As I have already said, although there were no demonstrable ties between the Shabatean hasidim and the hasidim of the Ba'al Shem Tov, it is not unreasonable to assume that at a time when the traditional world was being shaken to its foundations because of the messianic revolution inspired by kabbalistic tradition and charismatic arousal, groups in such close geographical, chronological, and intellectual proximity would have influenced each other in matters both social and spiritual.

The first ban against the hasidim of the Ba'al Shem Tov was issued in 1772—the year in which the apostate messiah Jacob Frank renewed his activities in Podolia and Galicia after his release from prison—and more were to come over the next two decades. The bans of excommunication issued against the hasidim are instructive regarding the differences between the hasidim and their opponents. The major claims made against them in the various bans and polemical pamphlets may be summarized under six headings:[27]

- *Rejection of prevailing Ashkenazi traditions in prayer.* The main problems were the use of the Lurianic prayer-book, which incorporates elements of

[27] On anti-hasidic compositions, see *Zemir aritsim*; see also the two volumes of Wilensky, *Hasidim and Mitnagedim* (Heb.), in their entirety, for *shever poshe'im*, writs of excommunication and polemics. For hasidic reactions to attacks by their opponents, see Hillman, *Letters of the Author of the Tanya* (Heb.), and *Igerot kodesh* ('holy epistles'), by the Habad rabbi Dov Baer (the 'Mitteler Rav'), by the third rabbi, popularly known as the author of *Tsemaḥ tsedek*, and by Shneur Zalman of Lyady.

Sephardi ritual practice such as daily bestowal of the priestly blessing; recitation of the *Sim shalom* formula in the last benediction of the Amidah in all daily prayers, not only in the morning Amidah; and recitation of the Kaddish and *Barekhu* at the conclusion of the evening Amidah. In order to implement these innovations and to pray loudly and ecstatically, the hasidim established separate *minyanim*, outside the traditional community framework.[28]

• *Rejection of prevailing Ashkenazi traditions in ritual.* The innovations here included donning two pairs of tefilin; donning tefilin at the afternoon prayer; knotting the tefilin worn on the arm in an unusual way; and wearing white clothing as everyday dress.[29]

• *Rejection of prevailing Ashkenazi traditions in religious norms.* Excessive fasting, self-mortification, and asceticism were a further force towards separatism, as was the introduction of more rigorous practice in other areas. In particular, new rigour in the laws of ritual slaughter, requiring the use of specially honed knives, meant that hasidim would not eat meat prepared by other Jews. This effectively further segregated them from the community.[30]

• *Rejection of prevailing Ashkenazi spiritual priorities.* Hasidim studied kabbalah and mystical moral literature in preference to the traditional texts, and abandoned the various restrictions and prerequisites that normally limited these pursuits to the elite.[31]

• *Contempt for the Torah and its scholars.* Hasidim did not accept rabbinic authority, and actively encouraged young men from traditional yeshivas to join hasidic groups.[32]

• *Subversive activity.* Shabateanism, heresy, and undermining the order by which communities had lived from time immemorial.

The first four accusations were not unjustified: these were unquestionably hasidic practices. They derived their legitimacy from two principal sources.

---

[28] On different hasidic customs and their kabbalistic sources, see Wertheim, *Laws and Customs in Hasidism*, and Elior, 'R. Nathan Adler and the Frankfurt Pietists'.

[29] On kabbalistic innovation, see Scholem, 'Tradition and New Creation'. For the source of these changes, see Isaac Luria's 'Manner of Life', in *Sefer toledot ha'ari*, ed. Benayahu, 315–39.

[30] See Shmeruk, 'The Social Significance of Hasidic Ritual Slaughter' (Heb.); on ritual slaughter see Wilensky, 'Hasidic–Mitnaggedic Polemics', 253–7; Elior, 'R. Nathan Adler and the Frankfurt Pietists', 163–7.

[31] See Weiss, *Studies in East European Jewish Mysticism*, esp. the chapter 'A Circle of Pneumatics in Pre-Hasidism'; Schatz-Uffenheimer, *Hasidism as Mysticism*.

[32] See Wilensky, 'Hasidic–Mitnaggedic Polemics'.

The first was the kabbalistic tradition, and in particular the practices of the Lurianic kabbalists of Safed; the second was the personal charisma of the movement's leaders, who allowed themselves to innovate by authority of their mystical inspiration—through visions and dreams, or through 'ascent of the soul'—and religious fervour. If the new spirituality that arose within them led them to formulate new ritual responses, they saw no need to seek approval from the traditional leadership. Following patterns established by their kabbalistic predecessors, they simply regarded the traditional hierarchy as irrelevant to their conception of the nature of religious obligation and spiritual creativity inspired by the mystical tradition. Although their opponents regarded these changes as an attempt to overthrow the existing order, for the hasidim they were first and foremost an expression of personal spirituality and a quest for spiritual freedom. Aspiring to have contact with the divine in their everyday life, they introduced new practices in the conviction that this would help them achieve their aims. The problem was that the changes introduced by the hasidim led to their segregating themselves from the community, which undermined the traditional leadership structure. As such, they disturbed the community's sense of solidarity and aroused sentiments of menace and anarchy. What the hasidim saw as increased rigour in halakhic standards designed to hasten the messianic era was perceived by their opponents as covert Shabateanism designed to shake the Jewish world to its foundations.

The fifth criticism—contempt for the Torah and its scholars—was not strictly justified. The hasidim certainly recognized the value of Torah study, and in no way did they see themselves as denigrating the Torah or those who devoted their lives to studying it. Many of the hasidic masters in fact belonged to the scholarly circles of the traditional world, but the rabbinical establishment, distressed at the rejection of its leadership, chose to interpret it as lack of respect for the Torah. It could not accept that the mystical ideas that stemmed from the kabbalistic tradition blurred the boundaries between the human spirit and the divine and led to a reliance on alternative sources of authority. It was not the interest in mysticism per se that posed the problem; as one of today's foremost authorities on hasidism, Mendel Piekarz, points out, the Torah scholars of the time opposed hasidism not because of its spiritual approach (some of them were themselves interested in kabbalistic writings and mystical inspiration) but because they saw it as a movement that was resolved 'not to be satisfied with preaching and protests alone, but to change the situation fundamentally, by organizing new social and religious units around a leading personality whose authority differed from that of the rabbis . . . and derived from his personal qualities and the holy spirit bestowed upon him'.[33] The traditional rabbinical leadership refused to recognize the legitimacy of these changes in sources of authority in consequence of the emphasis placed on kabbalah. Viewing this development as one of contempt for the Torah and its scholars, they fought it with all their might. Changes in liturgical practice, deviation from congregational custom, and the unprecedented diffusion of kabbalah were met with suspicions of Shabateanism and anarchy. Mindful of the recent threat, leaders of the established community closed ranks to persecute and excommunicate in order, as they saw it, to safeguard the Jewish future.

The hasidim, by contrast, saw themselves, not as undisciplined innovators but as perfectly faithful Jews. Their higher level of observance, which followed accepted Lurianic practice, was motivated by a devotion to the higher worlds and anchored in written kabbalistic norms that had an established sanctity. The words of Shmuel Shmelke Horowitz, rabbi of Nikolsburg, an important hasidic leader and disciple of the Maggid of Mezhirech, are quoted by Wilensky as representative of this perspective: the hasidim were 'Godfearing and perfect in following the customs of the Ari . . . who stand at the heights of the universe and receive the tradition of Elijah . . . Can one say of them that theirs are new customs unimagined by our forefathers?' Along with his rejection of the accusations of innovation, Shmuel Shmelke also condemned the restrictions imposed by the Brody ban to the effect that only 'well-known' individuals whose qualities were attested by 'the congregation' were permitted to adopt the Lurianic liturgy in their prayer. Thus, he continued, 'One who fears God, even though he is not well known, should be allowed to serve God in prayer with all his strength and to be rigorous in any way possible, be it in his clothing or his offering at the house of the Lord. He can do much or little, so long as he directs his heart to heaven.'[34]

Accusations of Shabateanism and of contempt for the Torah were likewise dismissed vigorously by Shneur Zalman of Lyady, a disciple of the Maggid who was a rabbi in White Russia, a celebrated halakhic scholar, and the author of a contemporary version of the *Shulḥan arukh*, as well as being a hasidic leader immersed in kabbalah: 'Whoever hears this cannot help laughing.'[35] He also protested sharply at the criticism of Lurianic practices and the mystical exultation and enthusiasm associated with hasidic prayer; in his responsa and in letters to his hasidim and disputants, as collected in *Igerot ba'al hatanya uvenei doro* and *Igerot kodesh*, we find testimony to both the magnitude of the spiritual revolution brought about by hasidism and the

[33] Piekarz, *The Rise of Hasidism* (Heb.), 383. See Ch. 10 below for examples of Piekarz's contention.

[34] Wilensky, *Hasidim and Mitnagedim* (Heb.), i. 84–8.   [35] Cf. Gen. 21: 6.

intensity of criticism it aroused. These writings also highlight the conflict concerning the status of kabbalah as the source of public religious renewal. Levi Isaac of Berdichev, rabbi of Pinsk and Zelechow and one of the Maggid's leading disciples, engaged in written disputation with Rabbi Judah Katzenellenbogen of Brisk, forcefully protesting at the unjustified imputations of the mitnagedim. He insisted that the innovations of which the hasidim were accused all derived from well-established practices ascribed to great kabbalists and authors of kabbalistic treatises. The goals of these practices were to strengthen Torah values and the love and fear of God, certainly not to detract from them.

A study of the detailed arguments levelled at the hasidim shows clearly that all the 'innovations' for which they were attacked are indeed to be found in kabbalistic literature from the sixteenth century on, and that they derived from such famous religious authorities as Joseph Karo, Solomon Alkabets, Isaac Luria, Elijah de Vidas, and Isaiah Leib Horowitz, the Holy Shelah. That is to say, the hasidim did not in fact initiate new practices, but merely adopted those developed by Isaac Luria and the kabbalistic circles of Safed that preceded him. Such practices had in any case long been accepted in elite circles of Ashkenazi Jewry—pious ascetics such as the members of the *kloyz* of Brody or the Vilna Gaon, who subscribed to the very same practices with the concurrence of their communities. This did not prevent them participating in bans against the hasidim of the Ba'al Shem Tov and forbidding others the kabbalistic practices that they themselves followed. The problem, it would seem, was the background of Shabatean turmoil; the rabbis were concerned that access to the kabbalistic tradition should remain the exclusive right of the elite possessing the approbation of the community. It was this that motivated the attacks on innovation.[36]

Those who counted themselves among the hasidim of the Ba'al Shem Tov did not see themselves as rebels, deviants, or transgressors; they considered themselves bearers of a sanctified kabbalistic tradition, and as such beyond the control of the community. In their view, the changes they were making in halakhah and custom, such as the replacement of the common Ashkenazi custom with the *darkhei ḥasidut* and the Sephardi liturgy found in kabbalistic prayer-books, were intended to foster holiness, to inspire fear of God, and to inculcate stringent observance of the divine commandments—all this in an attempt to expand the domain of holiness in order to redeem the Shekhinah.[37] Since these changes were based on mystical inspiration bestowed upon the

[36] See Elior, 'R. Nathan Adler and the Frankfurt Pietists'.

[37] For an example of such self-perception in the writings of Meshulam Feivush Heller of Zbaraz see Krassen, *Uniter of Heaven and Earth*; Jacobs, *Seeker of Unity*.

select few and were adopted only by members of their esoteric circle, the hasidic innovators did not believe that they needed the consent of the community or its leadership. They therefore ignored the bans issued by the communal rabbis, or protested against them and continued on their path; they considered themselves free to pursue their mystical interests while being completely devoted to the halakhic tradition, subject only to the authority of the spirit in matters relating to kabbalah.

From the standpoint of the community leadership things looked very different. The changes in laws and customs on the basis of kabbalistic tradition, the exaggerated scrupulousness regarding ritual slaughter and purity, and the excessive piety and asceticism were viewed as an intolerable deviation from the bounds of traditional custom. Similarly, the establishment of separate congregations was seen as a challenge to the integrity of the prevailing order and as an assault on the unity and authority of the community and its time-honoured traditions. The celebrated eighteenth-century halakhist Ezekiel Landau of Prague, known as the Noda Biyehudah, who fought the hasidim because he suspected them of affinities with Shabateanism and because he opposed the establishment of new liturgical formulas, referred to them as innovators 'lately arrived [Deut. 32: 17] to alter in our countries the customs of our holy forefathers'. The leaders of the communities determined to stamp out sectarianism and the changes in custom that accompanied it. Suspecting the motives of the innovators, they began to avail themselves of bans of excommunication to strengthen their hand.[38]

Tensions were intensified by the lack of terminological clarity I have already mentioned surrounding the term *ḥasid*. It was originally used by established scholars who had the backing of the community and passed their days in *kloyzen* that were under the supervision of the community. However, it was also appropriated by those who formed separate *minyanim* outside the community's domain: by covert and overt Shabateans, but also by the followers of the Ba'al Shem Tov, who likewise detached themselves from the traditional community and formed new congregations.

The decision to persecute the hasidim was a response to the twin insult of the changing of customs accepted for generations and the formation of separate congregations, which was seen as a critique of communal policy and an attack on its legitimacy; moreover, both were seen as masking a new outbreak of Shabateanism. These suspicions were intensified by the fact that the locales in which the hasidic congregations were growing were the same as those in which circles of Shabatean and Frankist mystics and pietists were

[38] See Wilensky, 'Hasidic–Mitnaggedic Polemics'; Nadler, *The Faith of the Mithnagdim*; Ferziger, *Exclusion and Hierarchy*.

still active in breaking down the bounds of tradition in the name of Shabatean faith and the messianic era.

As we have seen, tension had surrounded the Shabatean circles from the early eighteenth century on. It was later fuelled by the apostasy of the Donmeh and the anarchic heretical activity of Barukhyah Russo, Shabetai Tsevi's successor in Salonika, who sent emissaries to spread Shabateanism in Podolia and Galicia.[39] The sense of conflict was also connected with the public hounding of Moses Hayim Luzzatto, who was suspected of Shabateanism by Moses Hagiz and other rabbis throughout Europe, with the support of Eliezer Rokah, the rabbi of Brody.[40] It was further tied to the activity of Hayim Malakh and his colleague Jacob Vilna, who had studied in Salonika with Russo and went on to spread Shabateanism in Podolia and Galicia, and also to the publication in 1731 of the popular work *Ḥemdat yamim*, which was allegedly Shabatean.[41] The tensions were heightened by the sharp debates between Jonathan Eybeschuetz and Jacob Emden in the 1750s[42] and the polemics against Nehemiah Hayon and Leib Prossnitz, Eybeschuetz's teacher.[43] The conflict intensified with the publication of Shabatean works emanating from Eybeschuetz's circle, most notably the controversial *Va'avo hayom el ha'ayin*, which aroused the attention of rabbinical courts and was subsequently banned.[44] Then came the Brody anti-Frankist anathema of 1756, with its accusations of licentious behaviour and rejection of the divine commandments, and the great Frankist apostasy of 1759.[45] Other manifestations became more acute in the late 1760s and early 1770s, when the Shabatean leader Jacob Frank was intensely engaged in disseminating his anarchic, nihilistic doctrine in Podolia and Galicia through emissaries, letters, and books.[46] It is probably no coincidence that the first bans against hasidism were issued in a period of increased Frankist activity in Poland and Galicia, Moravia, and Germany; the Frankists' 'red epistles' encouraging the public to join the apostate groups created a climate of anarchy and an antinomian undermining of tradition that was deeply troubling to the establishment.[47] All these events took place, as we have seen, in the very same period and regions

[39] See Scholem, 'The Shabatean Movement in Poland' (Heb.).

[40] See Carlebach, *The Pursuit of Heresy*; Gelber, 'History of the Jews of Brody'.

[41] See Fogel, 'The Shabatean Character of *Ḥemdat yamim*' (Heb.).

[42] See Schacter, 'Rabbi Jacob Emden'; Liebes, *The Secret of Shabatean Faith* (Heb.), 326–9.

[43] See Liebes, *The Secret of Shabatean Faith* (Heb.), 70–6.

[44] See Perlmutter, *Jonathan Eybeschuetz* (Heb.); Liebes, *The Secret of Shabatean Faith* (Heb.), index, s.v. 'Va'avo hayom el ha'ayin' (p. 460).

[45] See Balaban, *On the History of the Frankist Movement* (Heb.), i. 118–27; Brawer, *Galicia and its Jews* (Heb.), 216.

[46] See Brawer, *Galicia and its Jews* (Heb.), 210–75.   [47] See ibid. 269–75.

in which hasidism was consolidating; it is small wonder that the leaders of the traditional community became suspicious of any kind of innovation.

Support for the various Shabatean circles, both overt and covert, was sufficiently strong to cause concern about all types of kabbalistic piety with separationist tendencies. In the early 1770s, any move to change accepted practice increased the suspicion that the traditional world was under siege, and the establishment started to attack all manifestations of deviation. Unable to distinguish among the various groups committed to kabbalistic pietism, they decided that any group sponsoring separate prayer and practices was suspect unless it functioned with communal approbation. Excommunication was the primary weapon in determining the boundaries of common identity for the congregation and opposing spiritual divisiveness of any kind.

Elijah ben Solomon, the Gaon of Vilna, excommunicated the hasidim in 1772 on the grounds that 'the sect of hasidim is replete with the heresy emanating from the sect of Shabetai Tsevi'. This claim, cited in his name in the anti-hasidic treatise *Shever poshe'im*, was to be repeated many times in the polemical literature. In the following year, Joseph Steinhardt (1720–76) rabbi of Fuerth, published a condemnation of 'the congregation of hasidim and *perushim* who diverge in their deeds and practices from the holy congregation'.[48] He participated actively in the persecution of Shabateans, and later in the proceedings that led the Frankfurt community to excommunicate the pious kabbalist and halakhic authority Rabbi Nathan Adler for deviating from the established Ashkenazi custom, praying according to the kabbalistic liturgy, and adopting stringent practices, thereby arousing suspicion of Shabatean leanings. (It is noteworthy that Adler's disciple, the great Rabbi Moses Sofer of Pressburg, known as the Hatam Sofer, regarded him as the greatest spiritual figure in his generation.[49]) Rabbi Shneur Zalman of Lyady was imprisoned in Russia as a result of mitnagedic slander. Rabbi Levi Isaac of Berdichev was deposed from his rabbinical positions in Pinsk and Zhelekhov and was hounded by mitnagedim led by Avigdor ben Hayim, rabbi of Pinsk. Rabbi Jacob Joseph of Polonnoye, a leading disciple of the Ba'al Shem Tov, was deposed from his rabbinical office in Shargorod in Podolia. Other hasidic kabbalists, in various communities throughout the Ashkenazi world, were excommunicated in a similar manner during this period.

One must not forget that the issue at stake was not only a question of religious principle; since the hasidic innovations impinged on matters of communal authority, they had significant social and economic implications too. When hasidim insisted on their own ritual slaughter, the community was

[48] *Zikhron yosef*, introduction; see Elior, 'R. Nathan Adler and the Frankfurt Pietists', 152–3.

[49] Katz, *Halakhah and Kabbalah* (Heb.), 353–86.

deprived of the income from the associated communal taxes. When they prayed separately, they did not pay the communal candle tax or synagogue tax. When they supported their own tsadik, they stopped supporting the local rabbi. These and other similar social and economic elements caused deep communal resentment.[50] Even if the original reason for segregation was inspired by spiritual motives and mystical aspirations, the rejection of traditional authority had very real social and economic consequences. Inevitably, the establishment of a new order implied criticism of the existing order and its values. That was sufficient to provoke the opposition of those from whom the new group was separating: with the challenge to their practices and the desertion of their synagogues—not to mention the economic consequences— they felt themselves very much the offended parties.

The hasidism of the Ba'al Shem Tov, open to 'all men', teaching that 'every man should serve God in all His ways', and holding that 'every Jew, whoever he may be should contemplate that God literally fills the higher and lower worlds, and heaven and earth literally, so that His glory fills the universe literally',[51] did not explicitly subscribe to a sectarian polemical position and did not exclude any portion of the community. Separation from the community for prayer was not an act of social criticism, but rather the outcome of a mystical world-view seeking to achieve a change in religious consciousness, to reach higher levels of sanctity, and to live the kabbalistic ethos in its hasidic interpretation. Nevertheless, from the 1770s on, the hasidim were perceived as rebels who threatened to undermine the unity of the community and its value system.

The hasidic circles that flourished in eastern and central Europe in the last third of the eighteenth century were not persecuted and excommunicated solely for what they were—'those who seek the nearness of God', in the words of that most penetrating mitnaged, Rabbi Hayim of Volozhin[52]—but rather because their opponents and persecutors thought they were lawless Shabateans, undisciplined revellers, and social dissidents. Changes initiated out of mystical passion and the spiritual impulse of uniting with higher worlds were interpreted as rebellion against the congregation and as a rejection of the foundations of the traditional world, primarily because of the dread of the Shabatean groups that were still active at that time and in that place.[53]

*

---

[50] Wilensky, *Hasidim and Mitnagedim* (Heb.); Bartal, 'Maskilic Criticism' (Heb.).

[51] *Tanya*, 120.

[52] See Etkes, 'The Methods and Achievements of R. Hayim of Volozhin' (Heb.).

[53] For new documents and new evaluations of mitnagedim and hasidim, see Mondshine, 'The Two Incarcerations of the Old Rebbe' (Heb.), 17–108; Etkes, *The Gaon of Vilna* (Heb.), 84–160; and Nadler, *The Faith of the Mithnagdim*.

It is commonly suggested that the conflict between hasidim and mitnagedim was a class struggle between the scholars and the ignorant or between an intellectual elite and populist circles. This allegation, rooted in the historiography of maskilim who were closely affiliated with mitnagedic circles, is in my view entirely baseless. Hasidism originated in a mystical world-view, and the rationalist maskilic ideology quite simply denied its legitimacy. In reality, hasidim and mitnagedim shared the same social background and often belonged to the same families.[54] Some examples will suffice. The hasidic writer Meshulam Feivush Heller of Zbarazh, author of *Yosher divrei emet*, was the brother of Abraham Heller, author of *Zerizuta de'avraham* and a member of the Brody *kloyz*. Shmuel Shmelke Horowitz, rabbi of Nikolsburg and disseminator of hasidism in Moravia, was the brother of Pinhas Horowitz, rabbi of Frankfurt and author of *Sefer hafla'ah*; both were students of the Maggid of Mezhirech, and also kin of Abraham Katzenellenbogen, the mitnagedic rabbi of Brisk. Jacob Joseph of Polonnoye and Hayim Zunzer, a leader of the Brody *kloyz*, were related by marriage. Gershon of Kutow, brother-in-law of the Ba'al Shem Tov, was a member of the Brody *kloyz*. The hasidic leader Judah Leib Eger, author of *Torat emet*, was the grandson of the eminent halakhic authority Akiva Eger of Posen.[55]

Both camps boasted prominent scholars of eminent family stock, men of great spirituality, thinkers, authors, and rabbis. The differences between them were not related to intellectual stature, social status, scholarship, or ancestry. They derived from principled positions regarding the boundaries of the human spirit, mystical revival, and the place of kabbalistic tradition. These principles led in turn to different opinions regarding the limits of the authority of the traditional world, the powers of the congregation and its leadership, and the degree of spiritual freedom that ought to be granted to members of the community. The hasidic position, as shaped by the mystical approach of its masters, aspired to a dynamic religious experience in a God-suffused universe; kabbalah and the mystical way of life was to be accessible to all. This view emphasized the freedom of the spirit to open new horizons and brought to the fore a mystical, charismatic leadership drawing upon novel sources of legitimacy.[56] The traditional leadership, by contrast, was seen as imposing bounds

---

[54] On the social closeness of hasidim and mitnagedim, see Scholem, 'Two Testimonies' (Heb.); Hisdai, 'The Beginnings of Hasidim and Mitnagedim' (Heb.).

[55] On the connection with the kabbalists of the Brody *kloyz*, see Scholem, 'Two Testimonies' (Heb.); Gelber, 'History of the Jews of Brody' (Heb.); Reiner, 'Wealth, Social Status, and Torah Study' (Heb.).

[56] For differences between charismatic leadership and rational leadership, see Weber, *On Charisma*; Shils, 'Charisma, Order and Status'.

to limit that freedom by its determination to preserve the traditional order and its unwillingness to countenance change in matters of practice or interpretative freedom. It insisted on limiting public interest to this-worldly reality; the realm of divine infinity was to be accessible only to an elite (*yeḥidei segulah*) under the aegis of the community and with its permission. It recognized only the rational legitimacy of the official communal leadership, acting in accordance with the traditional hierarchical order to which spiritual and social egalitarianism was alien.[57]

The difference between hasidim and mitnagedim concerned the limits of spiritual liberty, mystical accessibility, the purpose of spiritual life, and the right to decide the boundaries of spiritual and social stratification—who is entitled to determine which members of the community can study kabbalah and live according to pietistic custom or play a role in a movement of spiritual renaissance. The mitnagedim maintained that the traditional community had decisive authority to adjudicate these questions. In their view it was the established order, represented by rabbinic authority, that bore the responsibility for preserving the tradition and passing it on in determinate, well-attested forms connected to conventional social norms and ancient custom. The hasidim, by contrast, believed that each individual could participate in deciding the bounds of his spiritual concern and his relationship to a world whose only concrete reality is its divine essence and whose external manifestations are mere illusions and shallow conventions of relative significance. When Shneur Zalman of Lyady wrote in his homiletic work *Torah or* that 'although the worlds seem to us as being, in truth they are absolute falsehood',[58] because in fact 'all is divine', he was perhaps not merely expressing a radical mystical outlook but also casting doubt on the traditional order and its hierarchical structures. By its very nature, the standpoint of mystical totality—which recognizes only the truth of the divine reality and strives for a renewed encounter with the divine word beyond the bounds of tradition—perceives the established social order as mere illusion: 'What we see of the being of the world is only an illusion'.[59] Even if this mystical outlook was not expressed with a view to effecting change in the social order, the focus on supernal worlds and higher realities entailed consequences for the mutual relations between God and man and a critique of the normative order founded on a sanctified tradition.

---

[57] For a literary depiction of the struggle between the mitnagedim and the hasidim, see S. Y. Agnon's story 'The Banished One' (*Hanidaḥ*); for a good English synopsis of the story see Band, *Nostalgia and Nightmare*, 96–9. Cf. Zweifel, *Peace on Israel* (Heb.), i. 58–60, 72–96.

[58] *Torah or*, 'Ki tisa', 172.   [59] *Boneh yerushalayim*, 54.

EIGHT

The Unity of Opposites
Being and Nothingness

> That externality gives way to the essence, that is the foundation of the entire
> Torah: that being is reduced to nothingness.
>
> *Torah or*, 'Megilat ester'

IN the last decades of the eighteenth century and first decades of the nineteenth, hasidic mysticism reconceptualized the relationship between God,
man, and divine worship around the dialectical opposition of being (*yesh*) and
nothingness (*ayin*). Reality as a whole—indeed, the totality of human experience—came to be understood as reflecting a divine unity of opposites: finite
revelation and infinite essence; manifestation and concealment; the revealed
and the concealed. It is this unity of opposites that constitutes the divine
mystery—the tension and flow between the manifest, tangible reality known
as 'being', and the infinite, vitalizing divine presence known as 'nothingness'
that animates the dynamic duality of existence. As Levi Isaac of Berdichev
put it: 'For nothingness conducts itself in all ways as above nature, and being
conducts itself according to nature, for what is concealed hints at nothingness
and what is revealed hints at being.'[1] No entity is as it seems to be; everything
has a hidden essence, and reality is but a point of departure for process and
metamorphosis.

The relationship between finite and infinite, between being and nothingness, was a prime concern for many hasidic thinkers. The circle of the
Maggid of Mezhirech and his disciples, for example, emphasized the mystical
and dialectical meaning of 'two opposites in one subject'. In their attempt to
understand finite being as infinite nothingness, they perceived the world as
nihility: the only 'being' is God, the source of existence. Bratslav hasidism, by
contrast, emphasized the paradoxical coexistence of being and nothingness—
emanation (*atsilut*) and concentration (*tsimtsum*)—in God and in reality.
Other hasidic circles focused more on understanding the links between
heaven and earth, God and man. Thus, Habad regarded the dual nature of

---

[1] *Kedushat levi*, 1a.

the divine as the key to understanding divine and human reality; the concept of dialectical opposition underlies a world-view in which the tsadik transforms himself into nothingness and nothingness into being, thus embodying in his own existence the coincidence of opposites of being and nothingness. Such is the conception found in the doctrine of the tsadik formulated by Abraham the Angel, the son of Dov Baer of Mezhirech, and Jacob Isaac, the Seer of Lublin.

In kabbalistic thought, 'nothingness' and 'being' represent the two poles of a divine process based on the dynamic unity of opposites: revelation and concealment, presence and withdrawal, emanation and contraction, ebb and flow, direct light (*or yashar*) and reflected light (*or ḥozer*). Emanation, effusion, direct light, and abstraction are concepts that represent the transition from nothingness to being—the transformation of the concealed into the revealed, the infinite into the finite. The concepts of contraction, withdrawal, and reflected light represent the transition from being to nothingness, from finite to infinite, from the limited to the unbounded, from plurality to unity. These oppositions appear to be a static contradiction in the spirit of the verse 'God made this contrasting to that',[2] but in fact they represent a dynamic unity of opposites that manifests itself in dialectical movement from abstract to concrete and from concrete to abstract. There is constant tension between the impulse to manifest the divine will in absolute being (i.e. divine immanence in the world) and the impulse for being to give way to the concealed nothingness (i.e. divine transcendence). It manifests itself within the godhead, which itself embodies a dialectical process of nothingness and being, and also in human thought, seeking as it does to connect the tangible and the abstract, the revealed and the concealed, the divine presence and divine absence, and vice versa. This is articulated in the idea of God as a coincidence of opposites: 'Before Him, may He be blessed, who is omnipotent, being and nothingness are equal.'[3] Man's task is to respond to both expressions of the divine will, and to perceive nothingness as being and being as nothingness.[4]

*

[2] Eccles. 7: 14. [3] *Avodat halevi*, 1a.

[4] On mystical concepts in hasidism, see Buber, 'The Beginnings of Hasidism', and 'My Way to Hasidism'. Compare James, *Varieties of Religious Experience*; Weiss, *Studies in Bratslav Hasidism* (Heb.) and *Studies in East European Jewish Mysticism*; Zeitlin, *In the Orchard of Hasidism and Kabbalah* (Heb.); Scholem, '*Devekut* or Communion with God'; Elior, 'The Paradigms of *Yesh* and *Ayin* in Hasidic Thought'; Dan, *The Teachings of Hasidism*; Tishby and Dan, 'Hasidism' (Heb.); and Schatz-Uffenheimer, *Hasidism as Mysticism*, and 'Man's Relation to God and World'.

These questions are widely discussed in hasidic literature, but most particularly by the disciples of the Maggid of Mezhirech. Within that circle, one of the most systematic and comprehensive developments of hasidic teaching in this area is that of the Habad school, which was led by Shneur Zalman of Lyady (1745–1812). It emerged in the 1780s, at a time when hasidism was rapidly disseminating its teachings, both orally and in writing, and developing a broad social base even while retaining its force as a movement of religious revival and renewal. The very name Habad has mystical connotations, in that it derives from Hokhmah, Binah, and Da'at—Wisdom, Knowledge, and Understanding—which, according to one enumeration, are the three highest *sefirot*, or qualities, of the divine, and allude to Exodus 31: 3, where divine spirit is mentioned, along with wisdom, knowledge, and understanding.[5]

The bedrock of Habad thought is the dialectical nature of being. This implies that every entity embodies simultaneously a set of oppositions: the infinite essence is concealed beyond the realm of appearances of finite reality. This duality, which characterizes all dimensions of reality and human experience, is an expression of the dual nature of the divine being. The divine is depicted as a dialectical process, including within it oppositions—ebb and flow, expansion and limitation, hidden vitality and external garb (*hitlabeshut*) or form, negation and concretion, concealment and revelation, unity and multiplicity, being and nothingness. Kabbalistic vocabulary has many terms for this bidirectional duality in its attempt to represent the mystical reality of the divine being who unites the dimension of creation with that of chaos, being and nothingness, matter and spirit, revealed and concealed.

On this view, divinity comprises two conflicting yet interdependent aspects. One aspect is embodied in the infinite, expanding boundlessly, that is beyond apprehension; a power that is creative and life-giving in a manner that transcends all delimitation, confinement, or form. This aspect is called *hitpashetut*—a term that conveys ideas of expansion, infinity, nothingness, and abstraction. The second aspect is embodied in contracted being, manifested in its limitation and confined within its form. This distinct, bound reality is referred to as *tsimtsum*, literally, 'contraction' of the divine essence and its manifestation as finite being.

These two aspects delimit each other in so far as the mundane, visible phenomena are dependent at root on the divine infinity, referred to as 'nothingness', from which they draw their vitality, their essence, and their reality. By contrast, the divine infinity requires the limitation engendered by physical being in order to be manifest. In other words, 'being' is the tangible expres-

<hr />

[5] See Elior, *The Paradoxical Ascent to God*, 1–48; Loewenthal, *Communicating the Infinite*, 29–63.

sion of the divine nothingness, while 'infinite nothingness' is the vital force energizing or animating every finite physical being.[6]

The conceptual world of Habad hasidism is based on the kabbalistic notions of 'lights' and 'vessels', 'direct light' and 'reflected light'. However, whereas in kabbalistic thought these ideas pertain to the celestial realm—the world of the *sefirot* and the stages of creation and emanation—in Habad thought they refer to the mundane, human realms as well. As such they are applied to every aspect of religious creativity, be it the apprehension of God and his worship, or the Torah and its divine commandments, and they are the perspective from which all reality is interpreted.

The processes of concretization and annihilation expressed in 'being' and 'nothingness' are continuous. Emanation, overflowing, and creation reflect the transformation of nothingness into being, the passage from the infinite to the finite, from unity to multiplicity and complexity. Contraction, withdrawal, and annihilation are connected to the transformation of being into nothingness—restoring the finite to the infinite, returning the limited to its abstract source—and entail the transition from multiplicity to unity. Shneur Zalman of Lyady offered a concise definition of this process: 'For this is the purpose of the creation of worlds from nothingness to being, in order to transform the aspect of being into the aspect of nothingness.'[7]

In effect, Habad turned the kabbalistic concepts of creation and annihilation into a model that could encapsulate the human–divine nexus of thought and comprehension. Hasidic masters maintained that all things embody simultaneously a coincidence of opposites. Every thought, every action, every reality or image embodies its opposite because beyond every being there is nothingness, and beyond the manifest appearance of finite reality there is its infinite essence. Nothing is monolithic: no entity is solely physical and no entity is simply divine. Every entity embodies both the divine element that is its life-force and the physical element that conceals it through its very manifestation. Every entity combines the expansive, divine element, the light and revelation, and also the physical, restricted element—the vessel and the concealment. Reality was perceived not as something stable and finite, but rather as an expression of the expansive divine essence restricted in its physical form.

The mutual relationship between the infinite divine being that is the vitality of the universe and the physical world that is its finite form is best

---

[6] On the mystical teachings of Habad hasidism, see Schatz-Uffenheimer, 'Anti-Spiritualism in Hasidism' (Heb.); Elior, 'Habad', and *The Paradoxical Ascent to God*; Loewenthal, *Communicating the Infinite*; Jacobs, *Seeker of Unity*; and Teitelbaum, *The Rabbi of Lyady and the Habad Sect* (Heb.).   [7] *Torah or*, 'Vayetse', 44.

formulated by the Maggid of Mezhirech's disciple Menahem Mendel of Vitebsk, author of *Peri ha'arets*:

Nothing persists unless God, may He be blessed, vivifies it. In every thing there is the expansiveness of the Creator, and that is the meaning of His contracting His Shekhinah—that He dwells in the lower worlds . . . The [concrete] physical aspect of every thing is only the vessel and the boundary that limits the vision and taste and odour. And this spirituality is the vitality of the Creator that is drawn to and confined by the corporeal.[8]

If being and nothingness are interdependent and inseparable, then being, which is tangible, depends on its source in the divine nothingness from which it draws its vitality, the very possibility of its existence; divine nothingness cannot be revealed without the limitation of being in physical reality. The hasidic masters concluded from this that man must see his life as an encounter with the divine unity of opposites. One must therefore confront reality with a contemplative and interpretative attitude, recognizing that the apparent limits of being are just that: apparent, and limited. Rather, one must constantly seek out the divine vitality, the infinite energy of the 'nothingness' that energizes all being. One must transcend one's consciousness so as to appreciate the concealed divine reality behind manifest physical existence. Everything physical must be understood in terms of its spiritual source. The apparently physical entity, seemingly self-sustaining, must be deconstructed in order to reveal its divine source. This way of looking at the world, in total contradiction to sensory experience, is variously known as *hafshatat hagashmiyut* ('divestment of the corporeal'), *hitbonenut* ('contemplation'), *bitul hayesh* ('annihilation of being'), *avodah begashmiyut* ('worship through the corporeal'), and *devekut* ('devotion').

The divine soul, also known as the 'contemplative consciousness' or the 'eye of the mind'—synonyms for the apprehension of truth from the divine standpoint—became the subject of a religious quest for the nothingness concealed within being. The human soul, like the divinity, is conceived as combining these two contradictory aspects: the 'divine soul' (*nefesh elohit*) and the 'bestial soul' (*nefesh behemit*). The divine soul strives to elevate everything to the spiritual level, to strip away materiality so as to reveal the divine element underlying the concrete manifestation. The bestial soul (also known as the 'eye of the flesh'), by contrast, seeks descent into the material world, to convert the spiritual into the physical. Whereas the divine soul seeks to return to its divine source and to revert from being to nothingness, the bestial soul seeks physicality in an attempt to distance itself from its source.

---

[8] *Peri ha'arets*, 44 (*Peri ha'arets* includes the teachings of Menahem Mendel of Vitebsk and letters written by Abraham of Kalisk.)

The dynamic process linking these two opposing movements, described in the language of Ezekiel, chapter 1, in the phrase 'the *ḥayot* ran back and forth' (reading the word *ḥayot*, 'creatures', as *ḥiyut*, 'vitality'), can, in the hasidic view, be operationalized through divine worship, which itself comprises two contradictory processes. Through the process of *hafshatah*—abstraction, or the superior *yiḥud* (unification)—one expresses the desire of the divine soul to transform being into nothingness by means of contemplation, *devekut* (devotion), *hitpa'alut* (ecstasy), and the transcendence of corporeality through prayer. Through the process of *hamshakhah*—influx, or the lower *yiḥud*—one expresses the desire of the bestial soul to transform nothingness into being by drawing down the abstract into the concrete by performing the divine commandments of the Torah.

The transcendence of corporeality requires the suppression of individuality through true humility, for ascent on the ladder of spiritual comprehension depends on the diminution of the self: 'During worship one must understand that there is nothing besides God and that man, in himself, has no substance at all . . . and he must always remember . . . that the worlds and his body and his soul have no substance at all.'[9] The purpose of abstraction is to internalize the recognition that all is divine: that physical beings have no independent existence, and that the culmination of the drawing down of divine vitality into the material world is in fact to reveal that divinity and restore it to its source. The Maggid of Mezhirech explains this concept as follows: 'For in every being it is the divinity that animates it . . . If a man wishes to prepare himself for the divine effusion then it is most important that he understand and thoroughly consider that there is nothing in him besides the divinity that animates him, and that without this he is as naught, and then he is prepared for divine inspiration.'[10] His disciple Menahem Mendel of Vitebsk expresses it concisely: 'one should not pay attention to the corporeality of things but to their interior spiritual nature'.[11]

The spiritual elevation associated with abstraction requires the transcendence of selfhood. The goal of hasidic worship is thus to deny the existence of being separate from divinity and to turn being into nothingness that is engulfed by the infinite. As Shneur Zalman of Lyady put it: 'The principal matter is to reach the level of nothingness that is included in the Infinite, may He be blessed, and to annul one's reality.'[12] Another disciple of the Maggid of Mezhirech, Abraham of Kalisk, similarly advocates transcending the self in order to become closer to the divine nothingness:

---

[9] *Sha'arei ha'avodah*, pt. 4, ch. 39.   [10] *Magid devarav leya'akov*, 197.
[11] *Peri ha'arets*, 6 (letters).   [12] *Ma'amrei admor hazaken haketsarim*, 61.

For the purpose of Torah and wisdom in thought, speech and action is to attain the level of nullity, and he should make himself as nothing. Wisdom is found in nothing [*ayin*; a standard play on Job 28: 12: 'From where [*ayin*] is wisdom found?'], and nothingness is its root, and from this principle are derived humility and low spiritedness . . . for nothingness serves as unification [*yihud*] of a thing and its opposite.[13]

The way to comprehending nothingness and the unification of a thing and its opposite is 'contemplative worship', also called 'unifying of the divinity' (*yihud ha'elohut*). Habad hasidism regarded this contemplative worship, or the intellectual investigation of the nature of being and nothingness, as a universal obligation. The Hebrew term for contemplation, *hitbonenut*, is derived from the same root as the word for insight, *tevunah*. Its purpose is to endow man with an intellectual vision capable of going beyond the bounds of his ordinary consciousness and his physical existence, a vision that will enable him to transcend the limits of being so as to recognize the unity concealed beyond the manifest multiplicity. Rational contemplation of what is, by nature, suprarational is achieved through the study of kabbalistic theosophy in its Habad interpretation: 'Through contemplation of the being's emergence from nothingness, one understands the opposite: how being is nothingness and insignificant.'[14] The purpose of contemplation is comprehension of the paradoxical acosmic truth: that all being is divine, and that the entire universe is thus the manifestation of the divine reality, appearances to the contrary not withstanding. In the Habad perspective, revealing the divine unity of all reality in accordance with kabbalistic exegesis is no less important than obeying the divine commandments, and is imposed on all as an absolute duty. Only when the divine essence of reality is understood can human beings truly aspire to transcend the limitations of being and achieve communion with the divine. In the words of Shneur Zalman of Lyady:

Through contemplation of the greatness of the Infinite, blessed be He, before whom everything is as if it were nothing, the soul is inflamed to the precious majesty of His greatness . . . like sparks of fire, a bold flame ascending on high, separating from the wick and the wood to which it lays hold . . . And then the soul arrives at its literal consumption.[15]

In the act of contemplating God, the individual is distinct from the object of contemplation. In the act of consuming passion and devotion to God, man and the object of his yearning are united. The difference lies in the transition from adopting the divine perspective on reality—before God, everything is as if it were nothing—to mystical inclusion in the divinity, a unification and

---

[13] Abraham of Kalisk, in a letter printed in *Peri ha'arets*, 16.

[14] *Ma'amrei admor hazaken haketsarim*, 15.   [15] *Tanya*, 140.

ecstatic elevation in which man coalesces with God. 'That is the true *devekut*, to become one substance with divinity, to be swallowed up within Him, that it be considered impossible to be a separate entity on his own at all. That is truly the injunction of cleaving unto God.'[16]

For Habad hasidism, the desired ecstatic result of contemplative worship and the acquisition of knowledge illuminated by truth is the mystical act of *devekut*—the union and inclusion that comes with the passionate, all-consuming love of God. Habad literature powerfully evokes the experience of going beyond the bounds of conscious reality towards a limitless divine reality in which all distinctions are void:

To cleave unto Him, may He be blessed, is to be included in the aspect of His essence and substance . . . to be drawn into the body of the King . . . This love is called 'with all your might' [Deut. 6: 5] which is without a limit . . . until he attains the aspect of love with all one's might, meaning to be included and attached to His essence and substance literally . . . that there shall be total unification with His essence and substance.[17]

Habad hasidism thus presented a paradoxical point of departure. It sought to persuade man that sensory experience is illusory and that truth is to be found in the abstract intellectual experience, founded upon love and faith, contemplation and comprehension. To resolve the apparent contradiction between the apparent reality of tangible being and the affirmation that the divine, identified with nothingness, is present in every entity requires oscillation between being and nothingness. Human sensory experience is of no consequence, and this world is of no consequence because it does not exist in and of itself; it is the concealed, infinite divine essence, designated nothingness, that is the true being, and it is this nothingness that man encounters in transforming being into nothingness:

The principle is that one should be as if he were not. His body and soul must be totally vacant, to be effaced from this world and from the world to come, in every way and in every place, for the sanctification of His name, may He be blessed. He has no other desire and does not turn in any direction but towards Him . . . For what has he for himself . . . as he has annihilated himself totally as a result of his contemplation of the Creator's greatness.[18]

These last quotations from hasidic writing exemplify the mystical point of view that informed hasidism: the overwhelming awareness of the presence of the living God and the immediate access to the omnipresence of the divine— 'the universe is filled with His glory'—that the mystical world-view cultivated. Mysticism has recently been defined by one of the leading scholars of

---

[16] *Seder hatefilot*, i. 26a.   [17] *Torah or*, 'No'aḥ', 17–18.
[18] *Peri ha'arets*, 76 ('Kedoshim').

the discipline, Bernard McGinn, as 'the ongoing search for a heightened consciousness, or awareness, of the presence of the living God—the God who
makes a difference not only in what believers think, but also in how they
struggle to live.'[19] This mode of thought overcomes the distinction between
the tangible and the abstract through the awareness that divinity is at the core
of all things, although it appears to be absent. When man transcends his
physical existence and goes beyond what he sees with his own eyes, the eyes
of the flesh, in order to experience the world through his abstract intellectual
eyes, he thereby transforms being into nothingness and nothingness into
being. Or one might say that through the power of the divine soul he renders
physical being null and void, and envisages the divine infinite as the only true
being. The disciples of the Maggid in general, and the masters of Habad
hasidism in particular, were known to articulate this acosmic negation of the
separate existence of palpable reality:

Before the universe was created He and His name alone existed, and after He created
everything nevertheless, according to the truth of contemplation there is nothing in the
world other than Him. All is within Him and He is within everything, He forms it and
sustains it, so that it is as if there were only Him and His name.[20]

The blurring of the boundaries between the human and the divine, between
being and nothingness, is intensified through the contemplative path that
leads to the transcendence of being, and through the ecstatic love that leads to
unification (*yihud*), to *devekut*, and to inclusion in the divine (*hitkalelut*). It
reaches its climax in the paradoxical thought that overturns conventional conceptions and expresses the mystical yearning for the unification of the divine
and the human.

---

[19] McGinn, 'Selective Affinities'. For more on the notion of mysticism employed here, see id.,
The Foundations of Mysticism, pp. xiii–xx.   [20] *Peri ha'arets*, 118; cf. *Torah or*, 'Ki tisa', 172.

NINE

'For indeed all is null and void'
Transcending Being

This is the path that a man ought to choose for himself: in any place where he
looks or listens, let him see and hear nothing but divinity clothed there.

Or hame'ir, 7b

I N the last third of the eighteenth century, the followers of the Ba'al Shem
Tov began to disseminate the idea that access to the divine was not
restricted to an elite: anyone prepared to follow the hasidic path could help
elevate the divine sparks and redeem the Shekhinah. Following the hasidic
path entailed an awareness of the divine presence throughout the universe,
and the concomitant recognition that every action and thought can reveal and
elevate the Shekhinah. Divinity is ever present, waiting to be revealed
through purposeful intent; all that is required is the necessary transformation
of consciousness through the meditative strategies of *kavanah* and *yiḥud*. The
basic concept here derives from the kabbalistic tradition of cosmic conflict:
ideas of struggling with the *kelipot*, the material husks that conceal the divine
core, so as to elevate the divine sparks and redeem the Shekhinah from exile;
but hasidism recast this tradition in terms that emphasize the presence of the
divine in every place and time. In so doing it strove to expand the circle of
participants contributing to the redemption of the Shekhinah through mystical intent and contemplative awareness. Mystical experience or spiritual
status were not prerequisites of the new hasidic way of life. It was open, at
least in its original formulation, to everyone.

Ultimately, the implication of the mystical teachings of the Ba'al Shem
Tov and his circle was social change. The idea of an omnipresent divinity,
suffusing all individuals equally and open to the creative spiritual response of
every individual, would inevitably lead to the breakdown of social barriers.
Hasidism originated as an egalitarian movement, oblivious to social status
derived from lineage and intellectual standing. Even with the subsequent
emergence of the tsadik, this egalitarianism was maintained in the relationship between the individual hasidim and the tsadik, the living focus of their
congregation. It stood in stark contradiction to the traditional social and

religious order, with its authoritative and coercive leadership structure and an established hierarchy, which recognized different rights and duties on the basis of differences in status.[1]

The openness and accessibility of hasidism at the social level was a reflection of the concepts of 'all the universe' being filled with God's glory, 'all' being God, and 'every path' giving access to him. In contrast to this accessibility, those who chose the hasidic path faced rigorous demands in the religious sphere because the basic point of departure stood in contradiction to conventional human experience. Man relates to the tangible world through his senses, but hasidism maintains, by contrast, that the physical reality perceived by the senses is merely an illusion; in reality, 'all is divinity'. The hasidic injunction to recognize the emptiness within all tangible plenitude (*bitul hayesh*, rejecting that which is material) and the fullness of the void ('all is divinity') is thus fraught with difficulties.

To resolve the tension between the awareness of 'the universe filled with His glory' and the yearning for the divine infinite presence known dialectically as 'nothingness', on the one hand, and the enormous weight of physical existence known as 'being', the hasidic masters formulated a series of concepts that challenge the stability of the prevalent perception of reality by rejecting the distinctions upon which it rests. They offered guidance in this mystical dialectic through sermons, discourses, aids to contemplation, letters, books, and stories and parables open to interpretation in a variety of ways. Their goal was to help their followers achieve the transformation of consciousness that makes it possible to transcend being—to make the transition from the human perspective, which recognizes only the physical, to the divine perspective, for which all is divine. The spiritual objective is total immersion in a reality suffused by God, and total equanimity towards physical reality. As the Ba'al Shem Tov enjoined his followers, in order to achieve this spiritual transformation one must withdraw from the world: 'one must see oneself as a son of the higher world', for this world is 'no more than a mustard seed'.[2]

The discussion on how to achieve this state of consciousness focused on two extreme mystical attitudes: the ascetic and the ecstatic. Concern with the ascetic focused on the need to withdraw from the world and realize its insignificance (thereby seeing 'being' as 'nothingness'). The 'reality' of this world is illusory; one should therefore ignore the world of the senses and turn one's back on physical existence. But following an ascetic way of life must go hand in hand with a concern for the ecstatic: one must increase one's aware-

---

[1] On the structure of traditional Jewish society in Europe see Katz, *Tradition and Crisis*.

[2] *Tsava'at harivash*, p. 2, §6.

ness of the concealed world as a God-suffused reality, and let this influence one's consciousness, feeling, thought, and imagination (thereby seeing 'nothingness' as 'being'). One must see the realm of nothingness as the world of the divine and genuine plenitude and approach it with love, self-sacrifice, and fervour. In other words, the objective of hasidic devotion is an ecstatic-erotic orientation transcending boundaries and seeking unification with the deity.[3]

Seeing the domain of physical and social being as bereft of spiritual horizons, the hasidic masters expressed their attitude to tangible reality in terms that expressed their alienation from it. They regarded it with ascetic equanimity (*hishtavut*) and advocated a policy of withdrawal (*histalekut*) from worldly concerns and the rejection of material concerns (*bitul hayesh*). They tried to transcend it by stripping away the material husks so as to reveal the divine core, a concept expressed variously as *hitpashetut hagashmiyut* and *hafshatat hagashmiyut*. By contrast, their yearning to expand the spiritual horizon of human experience and become one with the divine world was expressed in ecstatic-erotic terms, an objective variously expressed as communion (*devekut*), unification (*yiḥud*), contemplation (*hitbonenut*), enthusiasm (*hitpa'alut*), inclusion (*hitkalelut*), and abandonment of the soul (*mesirut nefesh*). Reference is also made to 'smallness' and 'greatness' of spirit (*katnut* and *gadlut*) in the context of distancing oneself from the world and coming closer to God. All these terms are connected to deliberate alterations of consciousness—intellectual attempts to transcend one's sensory experience of the physical world and become one with the concealed divine being through contemplative thought, ascetic disposition, and mystical love.[4]

The goal of this spiritual activity was to transcend individual experience, with its petty physical constraints, and to recognize that behind apparent multiplicity lies essential unity—the divine vitality concealed within the revealed reality. One must understand that the apparent independence of being is illusory and adopt an attitude of indifference to the external expression of various concrete properties. In other words, the goal of religious life became the awareness of the nearness of God and his all-embracing presence in all manifestations of being.

The hasidic masters formulated the effort to remove the barriers to this awareness in terms of three successive levels. The lowest level was to with-

[3] On nothingness and being, asceticism and ecstasy, see Elior, 'Between *Yesh* and *Ayin*'; Idel, *Hasidism*, 107–27.

[4] On annihilation of being, equanimity, cleaving to God, contemplation, and abstraction from corporeality, see Buber, *Befardes haḥasidut*, and 'The Beginnings of Hasidism'; Scholem, '*Devekut* or Communion with God'; Schatz-Uffenheimer, 'Man's Relation to God and World'; Dan, 'Hasidism' (Heb.); Tishby and Dan, 'Hasidism' (Heb.); and Elior, 'R. Joseph Karo and R. Israel Ba'al Shem Tov' (Heb.), and 'The Paradigms of *Yesh* and *Ayin* in Hasidic Thought'.

draw from this world and develop an attitude of rejection and indifference to its material benefits. The second level was to recognize the dialectical nature of being, and to go beyond the manifest reality to reveal its divine core. The highest level was to devote oneself entirely to the divine world, to transcend the physical constraints of individual being and recognize one's ultimate unity with God in *unio mystica*. One who attains the highest level regards reality from a divine perspective and is able to engender far-reaching transformations by virtue of his spiritual enlightenment.

To achieve the first level, one must free oneself from the chains of reality and human sensory experience. This is embodied in the concept of *hishtavut* (equanimity), which means that all common distinctions pertaining to human existence are to be regarded with equal indifference, in accordance with a position ascribed to the Ba'al Shem Tov in *Tsava'at harivash*. All values and concepts relating to concrete existence are to be regarded as meaningless. The consequence is profound: liberation from the routine limits of the concrete world and freedom from prevalent social expectations.

It says, 'I have set [*shiviti*] God before me always' [Ps. 26: 8]. *Shiviti* implies equanimity [*hishtave'ut*]. Whatever occurs should be equal to him, whether people praise him or despise him, and so too with all other matters . . . let his thought cling to the higher [world] . . . and let him not consider at all the affairs of this world, and let him not think about them at all, in order to separate himself from corporeality . . . Let him think that he is a son of the superior world, and let not all those human beings who dwell in this world have importance in his eyes, for all this world is no more than a mustard seed compared to the higher world. Thus it should be equal in his eyes if he is loved or hated, for their love and hatred is nothing.[5]

This equanimity regarding the realm of being and the world of the senses—the indifference to mundane considerations, social affairs, and the requirements of the body—facilitates spiritual freedom and consequently the transcendence of the bounds of concrete experience so that the soul can ascend to the realm of nothingness and to celestial dimensions. This spiritual transformation sustains its own dialectic: the losing of one's sense of selfhood through the utter devotion of *devekut*—immersion in the higher worlds and transcending the limits of corporeality in the domain of nothingness, and realization of the freedom to ascend to higher levels of spiritual apprehension—leads in turn to alienation from the values of the mundane world and to the equanimity that brings indifference to the domain of being.

Equanimity is a great principle. Meaning, that it should be the same to him if he is regarded as ignorant or as versed in the entire Torah. What causes this is regular

---

[5] *Tsava'at harivash*, §§5–6.

devekut in the Creator, may His name be blessed, so that because of his preoccupation with *devekut* he has no time to think about these matters, in so far as he is always preoccupied with attaching himself on high, to Him.[6]

Similar frequent exhortations in *Tsava'at harivash* to consider oneself 'as not being in this world' or as 'a son of the higher world' are a clear indication that hasidism in its early stages had a decidedly mystical outlook.[7] Its eyes were firmly fixed on the higher worlds; social reform was simply not on the agenda. On the contrary, 'this world' was regarded as emptiness devoid of substance, a mere husk with no significance of its own. Its inhabitants were likewise insignificant. Human consciousness, associated with the soul and therefore essentially estranged from human existence, strives to reject the limits of physical being in order to reunite with the higher world and the divine being. A mystical approach that regards the higher world as genuine 'being' and rejects this world as devoid of significance is not a conventional point of origin for a social movement. However, the alienation from this world that hasidism proposed was not only a mystical orientation towards other worlds; it also contained an anarchic tendency that challenged the foundations of the traditional world.

Hitbonenut (contemplation) is another major concept relating to transcendence of the physical that is often discussed in hasidic texts. It implies focusing on the spiritual vitality that underlies physical manifestations so as to see in every thing 'its supreme root and source'. The Hebrew word *hitbonenut* derives from *tevunah*, intelligence or insight. It denotes rational kabbalistic investigation of the existence of being and nothingness: confrontation with the chasm separating what is visible to the 'eyes of the flesh' from what is visible to the 'eyes of the intellect', between 'being' as perceived by the senses and interpreted from a human perspective and 'non-being' or 'nothingness' as comprehended by the contemplative consciousness and interpreted from the divine perspective. The transformation in religious thinking is reflected in the emphasis on the contemplative, the yearning to perceive the divine essence beyond physical manifestations and to redefine the essence of spirituality that is revealed through the concreteness that veils it:

The principle is that of the wise man whose eyes are in his head [Eccles. 2: 14], who strengthens the eye of his intellect to divest himself of corporeality . . . until he acquires

---

[6] Ibid. p 3, §10.

[7] On mysticism as an attempt to express direct consciousness of the presence of God see McGinn, *The Foundations of Mysticism*, pp. xiii–xx. On the common characteristics of the mystical state of mind see Stace, *Mysticism and Philosophy*, 79. All the seven characteristics that Stace lists are amply represented in hasidic literature.

within himself a clarity and purity of vision, so that wherever he looks and listens he sees only the spirituality garbed in corporeality.[8]

In order to be liberated from subjugation to the constraints of physical existence and to become a free soul sustained in the expanses of nothing-ness—in order to pass from seeing with the 'eyes of the flesh' to seeing with the 'eyes of the intellect'—one must distance oneself from this world, alienate oneself from social concerns, withdraw from corporeality, and shut one's con-sciousness to external stimuli and routine modes of thought. After reaching this level one is able to divest oneself of one's physical 'garb', to attain true spirituality and concentrate on the divine essence concealed within revealed concreteness:

The principal element of worship is to be uprooted from one's place, one's human sen-suous apprehension, solely in order to grasp the truth ungarbed . . . that is, to become accustomed to contemplate the vivifying spirituality . . . The main apprehension . . . that all reality and its apprehension are nothingness, and that is the origin of all worship.[9]

The purpose of contemplative worship is thus to recognize and acknow-ledge the concealed divine unity of physical reality, to free the spirit from physical subjugation, to decipher the greatness of God 'that fills all worlds and surrounds all worlds', and to comprehend that its apparent distance from man is only illusory. Through contemplation, man strives to comprehend the divine unity of opposites: that the 'real' world one perceives is illusory, and the only reality is the divinity.

The following definition of divine worship by the Maggid of Mezhirech succeeds in conveying the desired reorientation in the realm of religious con-sciousness: 'A man must withdraw from all corporeality so much that he ascends through all the worlds and achieves unity with the Holy One Blessed Be He, until his being is transcended and then he is called a man [adam].'[10] For the sake of this transformation man must turn his back on the physical world and investigate the higher world by occupying himself with kabbalistic study of the hidden dimensions of reality, comprising theosophical treatises on the nature of the deity and the celestial perspective on existence and its divine processes.[11]

[8] Or hame'ir, 'Pekudei', 84a.

[9] Shneur Zalman of Lyady in Igerot kodesh, appended section, p. 10.

[10] Magid devarav leya'akov, 38.

[11] Shneur Zalman's Tanya: likutei amarim (Tanya: Gate of Unity), and Kuntres hahitpa'alut (Tract on Ecstasy) by his son Dov Ber of Lubavitch, are fine examples of kabbalistic studies of the hidden divine dimension of existence. Both are available in English: see Likutei amarim—Tanya, ed. and trans. Mindel et al., and Tract on Ecstasy, trans. Jacobs.

As already noted, the study of kabbalah is a prerequisite for understanding the divine perspective on existence that unifies being and nothingness, discovering the infinite in the finite, and transcending the limitations of human cognition that divide them. Kabbalah opens up the expanses of spiritual freedom and transcends the constraints of the physical. To attain this level, however, one must also follow the path of piety, *darkhei ḥasidut*, which entails withdrawal from this world, solitude, asceticism, a dedication to holiness, and an equanimity achieved by ignoring the world of the senses.

Hasidic literature is replete with behavioral guides that require the individual to reject the material world and engage in contemplation. These are not ends in themselves but means to attain a new level of perception: a mystical awareness responsive to the divine presence rather than to mundane reality, an awareness that will lead to recognition of the hidden divine essence of manifest reality and unification with the divine:

Hold on to this rule. Do not dismiss it from your mind even for a moment. There is no thing in the world in which there is no enrobing of the Shekhinah . . . which dwells in it to give it life . . . Let one not pay attention to the corporeal nature of things but rather to the divinity that is enrobed and concealed there.[12]

In order to concentrate the contemplative consciousness on the divine truth of reality and to understand the nothingness of physical being, one is required to withdraw from the flow of quotidian life and to distinguish the dual significance of reality and its changing essence. In other words, one must see the material as merely the garb of the spiritual, and then strip away the material garb and see the spiritual as the force animating the material:

Because God desires the worship of Israel He first created being out of nothingness; what had previously been infinite became being and was contracted in order that Israel do the reverse, making being into nothingness. That means that [the people of] Israel are to remove the garb step after step until they arrive at the Infinite.[13]

In hasidic thought, the objective content of reality and its manifest essence as interpreted within the set limits of tradition do not determine its significance; rather, it is the spiritual meaning and its divine interpretation, as revealed to human consciousness and constantly changing, that determine the significance of reality. Several things are necessary in order to achieve this change of perspective. One must strive to transcend the sense of reality limited by parameters of time and space ('the entire world is like a mustard seed in the face of the higher world'). One must reject sensory perceptions as creating an illusion of the particular ('remove the garb'), emphasizing difference

---

[12] *Or hame'ir*, 'Rut', 182a.   [13] *Ḥesed le'avraham*, 14b.

instead of the divine unity ('all should be equal in one's eyes'). One must distance oneself from mundane social concerns ('view oneself as belonging to the superior world'). In sum, one must see that understanding the true nature of the world requires indifference to the distinguishing and accidental features of human experience in order to uncover the divine nothingness that is synonymous with expansiveness, boundlessness, and freedom of the spirit.

The hasidic leaders who sought the limitless, the infinite, and the 'world of freedom' within nothingness aspired to transcend the constraints of being. Their position was acosmic: they rejected the cosmos and treated the world as illusory because they sought to regard reality as consisting of two dimensions—essence and appearance, nothingness and being, spirit and matter—while denying its separate existence, its determinate concreteness, and its palpable lack of ambiguity.[14] Devoid of the connection with its life-giving source, the world of matter was rejected as meaningless:

For all the worlds are totally null compared to Him . . . Even though the worlds appear to us as being, this is total falsehood.[15]

When we see the world as being, that is mere imagination.[16]

For there is no reality other than His, may He be blessed . . . The spiritual and material garbs have no reality at all . . . Although there appear to be other things it is all His reality and powers.[17]

For all the worlds occupy no place, to constitute beings and separate things in themselves. They are all, compared to Him, literally nothing, as there is nothing beside Him.[18]

In the acosmic approach advocated by the Ba'al Shem Tov and his followers, the only true being is the divine nothingness. They created an intellectual system and way of life in which the world is regarded as devoid of significance, a 'barrier' produced by mystical illusion. The purpose of hasidic worship is to internalize this attitude through mystical contemplation and reveal the truth. This is illustrated in the Ba'al Shem Tov's 'parable of the barriers':

It is like a king who, through the art of illusion, erected several barriers before his palace to prevent entry, and he made walls and fire and moats, all by means of illusion in the presence of his children. Now his chosen son was wise and took notice of it, realizing that . . . in truth there is no concealment at all, so that the moment one took the risk of walking through the moat the illusion was dispelled and he passed through, and likewise with the other barriers until he entered the king's inner sanctum.[19]

[14] On the acosmic outlook, see Elior, *Theosophy in the Second Generation of Habad Hasidism* (Heb.), index, s.v. 'acosmism', and ead., *The Paradoxical Ascent to God*, 49–58.

[15] *Torah or*, 'Ki tisa', p. 172 (= 86*b*).   [16] *Boneh yerushalayim*, 54.

[17] *Yosher divrei emet*, 14.   [18] *Torah or*, 'Mikets', 64.

[19] *Ba'al shem tov al hatorah*, ii. 253–4.

Undoing the illusory concealment that separates the apparently distinct realms of the revealed and the hidden, of being and nothingness, of matter and spirit, is at the core of the hasidic enterprise. Its objective is to seek out the divine infinity concealed in corporeality and finitude and to fulfil the soul's yearning for freedom from subjugation to matter.

Practical realization of this acosmic, mystical doctrine was not easy.[20] Hasidic literature preserves testimony to this. For example, when hasidim complained of the difficulties of divine worship, of attaining the spiritual freedom needed to transcend being, the master repeated his definition of the desideratum and the nature of the difficulty in its attainment:

In truth all is null and void, and the goal of perception is to annihilate in the heart and mind, for annihilation [*bitul*] is the [correct] perception. However, because in this world people are accustomed to consider only the dense matter [i.e. corporeality] they only look at the material nature of things, which negate and conceal the truth, in so far as it is because of the divine concealment that being appears to us. The principal worship is to uproot from its place and from human sensory perception and to apprehend the true object that is not enrobed . . . In other words, one must become accustomed to contemplate the spiritual life-giving purpose . . . For the main point of contemplation is to approach communion with the life-giving God, and how can one approach nearer when all one's perceptions are literally the opposite inasmuch as they are all limited . . . The primary perception is that all reality and perception of it is nothingness; that is the aim of all worship. But what shall I do for you when you persist in asking that I show you how to perceive nothingness? . . . Truly you [should] believe me that the beginning of worship uproots one from his place, but what can I do when you are not accustomed to look heavenward but only to what is on the earth below? However, the main thing is contemplation, and the more you persist in it the more knowledge and perception are engendered.[21]

Such penetrating remarks testify to the disparity between the normative formulation of the hasidic outlook and its realization, and the great difficulties of an approach that required each individual to overcome the barriers of illusion to encounter God. The sentence cited above—'But what shall I do for you when you persist in asking that I show you how to perceive nothingness?'— indicates that when the demands of withdrawal from mundane reality, transcending being, and achieving spiritual freedom through perceiving the plenitude of nothingness became incumbent upon the community as a whole they presented great problems.

[20] On the confrontation between spiritual standards and the inability of the community to meet them, see Elior, 'Between Divestment and Love of Corporeality' (Heb.). Cf. Loewenthal, *Communicating the Infinite*, 1–28.

[21] *Avodat halevi*, 'Likutim', 98*a*; cf. the version ascribed to Shneur Zalman of Lyady, *Igerot kodesh: kuntres miluim*, 10–12.

The non-specific demand to perceive nothingness beyond being includes an innovative spiritual element that transcends the traditional imperative of the divine commandments. It requires sedulous listening to the hidden word of God, which is interpreted anew in the human spirit. This call is framed in many different ways: as a call to redeem the divine sparks; in the image of the desolate Shekhinah seeking to rise from captivity; as a continuous divine revelation; and as the image of divine thought seeking release from its imprisonment in the human mind. Always there is a demand to breach the apparently finite by dint of the true infinite: to redeem the spiritual from the chains of the material, to respond to the call of the non-specific divine element that transcends the limits of conventional perception, to listen to the divine voice that echoes beyond the limits of the written text and the constraints of accepted tradition. This can be achieved through *avodah begashmiyut*, 'worship through corporeality', meaning the quest for the divine essence in the multifaceted nature of material reality.

It is likely that the absolute mystical and spiritual demand focusing on nothingness, infinity, the unlimited, and that which transcends experience and knowledge, on the 'world of freedom' and the 'world of divine speech speaking through the human', received no more than a partial response. It is obvious that the religious and social totality put forward in the early days of hasidism underwent qualification as the movement developed, for hasidism could not transcend social barriers as it had transcended those between divine reality and corporeal reality. It had to recognize that, even if divinity is omnipresent, not every human being is capable of revealing the divinity within the corporeal; nor are all human beings willing to turn their backs on the comforts of conventional existence in order to try. Yet even if hasidism did not succeed in either transcending the barriers to perception or breaking down social barriers, it can be said to have spanned them with new bridges and carved out new gateways, giving all human beings new ways in which to access divinity. The mystical, dialectical, and acosmic concepts of hasidism focused the attention of individuals and of communities on spiritual values. Whether these were only abstract concepts or values that governed their lives in practice, they undoubtedly affected the boundaries of consciousness and religious discourse in the hasidic world.

As the movement spread, its leaders became aware that the mystical requirements that had originated in elite circles were too challenging for ordinary people. In consequence they came to function more as a guiding spiritual ideal than as a doctrine to be realized in a specific social milieu. Because of the inability of the average hasid to attain such rigorous spirituality, a new division of spiritual and social functions gradually developed.

Henceforth the challenge of breaching the limits of perception, transcending the limits of being, and attaining the spiritual freedom to strive towards nothingness was focused on the figure of the tsadik.[22]

The tsadik encapsulates the duality of reality in terms of nothingness and being. He articulates in his being the unity of opposites and the simultaneity of hidden reality and revealed reality. He embodies mystical values, ranging from equanimity, asceticism, and solitude, which liberate him from the bounds of corporeal reality and subservience to the conventional, to contemplation, divestment of corporeality, transcendence, attachment to God, freedom, and infinity. However, whereas the mystical tradition that preceded hasidism was satisfied with individual, subjective mystical experience, based its requirement of divestment of corporeality on withdrawal from the world, and made communion with God conditional on separation from mundane reality, hasidic thought demanded quite a different stance. Hasidism required the internalization of the divine dialectic of concealment and revelation, expansion and withdrawal, nothingness and being, ebb and flow, freedom and responsibility.

Accordingly, the tsadik does not fulfil his task merely by distancing himself from the corporeal, liberating himself from the bounds of being, and achieving devotion to God through *devekut*. On the contrary: armed with the power of *devekut*, he is obliged to occupy himself with the terrestrial in its social and material manifestations. Paradoxically, the personal realization of mystical objectives is significant only in its social context. Hasidism makes a dual demand of the tsadik, emphasizing the mutuality of the relationship between God and the community. The tsadik is an emissary from the terrestrial world to the higher world, from being to nothingness, for in his separation from the world—in his divestment of corporeality, in his liberation from the bounds of being and the elevation of his soul to the higher worlds—he represents his hasidic followers (often referred to in Hebrew as *olam*, 'the world') or community (referred to as 'friends who hear my voice', '*devekut* of friends', and other similar terms). On the other hand, he is also the link between the higher world and the terrestrial domain. He is the channel through which divine providence flows to his hasidim (the 'world', his 'people', his 'beloved', 'the branches from the root of his soul'). When he brings the divine *ḥesed* (kindness, divine grace, celestial abundance) down to his followers in the material world, he embodies for them the divine presence. In his very being he represents the complexity of reality and the breadth of its horizons, the freedom that enables the individual to rise above the limitations of reality and appreciate the infinity that confers the divine perspective upon the restricted material world. We shall learn more of this in the next chapter.

---

[22] For the doctrine of the tsadik see Chs. 10 and 11 below.

TEN

The Doctrine of the Tsadik

The tsadik should draw God into this world, in order that He will dwell among us and will sustain us, and then he should raise up the Shekhinah.

No'am elimelekh, 8

It is known that God emanated worlds and created being out of nothingness, primarily in order that the tsadik should transform being into nothingness and elevate the qualities of the corporeal to their source.

Ḥesed le'avraham, 9

SINCE the late eighteenth century, the most distinctive and probably most famous feature of hasidic communities has been the leadership of a tsadik. Tsadikim such as Elimelekh of Lyzhansk (1717–86), Jacob Isaac Horowitz the Seer of Lublin (1745–1815), and Nahman of Bratslav (1772–1811) established their courts at that time in Galicia and Poland, as the Habad dynasty did in Russia. In the nineteenth century the practice spread to other areas in which hasidism had taken root: Karlin-Stolin, Chernobyl, Ruzhin-Sadgora, Kotsk, Izbica, Zhidachov and Komarno, Belz, Munkacs, Satmar, and Ger. In their heyday these hasidic courts demonstrated the spiritual inspiration and social potential of the tsadik-led community; in their decay they demonstrated its pitfalls. But the leadership of the tsadik—sometimes known as 'tsadikism'—has continued to be a key feature of hasidism into the twenty-first century, despite the decimating effect of the Holocaust on hasidic communities.

The mystical concepts underlying the tsadik's leadership and its spiritual and social significance are less well known, however. The doctrine was first articulated in the circle of the Maggid of Mezhirech in the 1760s and early 1770s. In the 1780s and 1790s it was developed by his disciples in writing and in practice, and further articulated in the works published by Jacob Joseph of Polonnoye from 1780 on. The spiritual and social implications of these teachings were to have a profound effect in the various hasidic circles.[1]

---

[1] On the doctrine of the tsadik in Jacob Joseph of Polonnoye, see Nigal, *Leader and Congregation* (Heb.), 58–81, and Dresner, *The Zaddik*. For that of the Maggid of Mezhirech, see

Leadership by a tsadik is perhaps the main religious innovation of hasidism. As a revolutionary rethinking of the relationship between God and man, it engendered a totally new view of the world. It required the individual to recognize reality as lying beyond sensory perception, and to decipher and perceive the divine infinite, the no-thingness, which is implicit in being. It rested on principles that blurred the boundaries between hidden and revealed: the physical world is infused with sparks of divinity such that the divine presence is none the less present, even though concealed beyond the limits of human perception. These ideas, which express the innovation of hasidism and its intention to free human beings from the chains of the material world, are embodied and demonstrated in the person of the tsadik and his role in the life of the hasidic community.

Many hasidic thinkers have concerned themselves with these concepts and with the related idea that drawing close to God so as to bring divine abundance into the human realm means transcending the limits of human perception. Different approaches developed as to how this was to be achieved. The Maggid of Mezhirech and his disciples, for example, demanded that all must recognize that the internal must take precedence over the external, 'and this is the basis of the whole Torah, that being be obliterated through nothingness'.[2] In this view, all must grapple equally with the dialectic of nothingness and being; all must try to achieve true selflessness, ignoring the demands of corporeality so as to devote themselves to the contemplation and love of God. Jacob Joseph of Polonnoye, by contrast, speaks of 'material people' (*anshei homer*) and 'spiritual people' (*anshei ru'aḥ*), the former chiefly concerned with material matters and the latter closer to the spiritual dimensions of reality. However, he recognizes their dialectical unity: responsibility for the fate of 'material people', i.e. the community at large, lies with the 'spiritual people', i.e. the figure of the tsadik; in turn, the 'material people' are required to take responsibility for the material welfare of the 'spiritual people'. It is likely that this view gained ascendancy in consequence of the realization that the mystical perspective of the Maggid was simply not attainable by all.

With the emergence of the tsadik, the focus of the system became a single charismatic individual as the embodiment of the ideal. The tsadik represented attainment of a spiritual level that would enable perception of a different reality: the understanding of being as nothingness, and of nothingness as being. It is not clear whether this development occurred solely because the massive expansion of hasidism in the last decades of the eighteenth century

Magid devarav leya'akov, ed. Schatz-Uffenheimer, index, s.v. 'tsadik'. Cf. Lamm, *The Religious Thought of Hasidism.*

[2] *Torah or*, 'No'aḥ', 11*a* (= p. 21).

required changes in its forms, or whether it was a primary element in the hasidism of the Ba'al Shem Tov and his circle which then took a different form as hasidism evolved. Either way, there is no doubt that the emergence of the tsadik—a figure characterized as *medugal beherut*, 'outstanding in [his] freedom'[3]—was a defining characteristic of hasidic mysticism. The tsadik attracted followers by his charisma, building up a community open to the idea of blurring the distinctions between God and man and willing to establish new social structures in harmony with the implications of this view.[4]

The tsadik experiences closeness to God, absorbing and reflecting the divine elements of infinity, knowledge, inspiration, freedom, and benevolence. He represents the paradox of being and nothingness: he recognizes the infinite divinity embodied in being, and the need to go beyond the materiality of being in order to achieve the no-thingness of infinite divinity. He acts by virtue of the mystical inspiration and spiritual freedom associated with an abundance of *hesed* (divine grace), enabling him to breach the boundaries of perception and attain knowledge of God. As an instrument of the divine speech ever renewed through his being, the tsadik represents a vertical blurring of the boundary between this world and the higher worlds. As a human mouth articulating a holy voice within a community of which he is part, he represents a horizontal blurring of boundaries. In his very being he epitomizes the hasidic point of departure and its mystical dialectic: every entity in the material world reflects the divine presence, but when denuded of its divine horizon it is revealed as empty and illusory.

The divine presence is represented in hasidic writing by such terms as fullness, infinity, grace, abundance, unity, nothingness, expansion, magnanimity, infinite letters, the world of speech, Shekhinah, light, sparks, arousal from above, and the constant movement of divine vitality ebbing and flowing. The absence of divinity is represented by such terms as mere being, garment, husk, barriers, separation, smallness, breaking, withdrawal, privation, matter, vessel, darkness, corporeality, and contraction. All these terms are attempts to convey the different aspects of the dialectic underlying the hasidic worldview.

The tsadik embodies the unity of these opposites; he is the tangible expression of the divine duality, of the ebb and flow, of emanation and withdrawal,

---

[3] *Beit ya'akov*, 'Shemot', 14*a*.

[4] On the tsadik's mode of leadership, see Katz, *Tradition and Crisis*, chs. 20, 21, and 22; Ettinger, 'The Hasidic Movement: Reality and Ideals'; Scholem, 'The Tsaddik'; Wilensky, *Hasidim and Mitnagedim* (Heb.), index, s.v. 'tsadik', and id., 'Hasidic–Mitnaggedic Polemics'; Rapoport-Albert, 'God and the Zaddik'; Elior, 'Between *Yesh* and *Ayin*' and 'Between Divestment and Love of Corporeality' (Heb.); and Green, 'Typologies of Leadership and the Hasidic Zaddiq' and 'The Zaddik as Axis Mundi'.

expansion and contraction, nothingness and being, lights and vessels, creation and annihilation. He links the higher world to the earthly world by assuming comprehensive responsibility for the material and spiritual needs of his followers, expressed in terms such as love, abundance, grace, and sustenance. In representing the hasidic community to God, he links the earthly world to the higher world. Achieving this unity of opposites places conflicting demands on the tsadik: to allow being to be understood as nothingness, he must adopt an ascetic approach of indifference to his personal needs and withdraw from the world; to allow nothingness to be understood as being, as expressed in the emanation of the divine abundance in material form, he must adopt an ecstatic approach and immerse himself in the world. An example of the spiritual transformation represented by the tsadik is to be found in R. Nahman's saying about the ecstatic mode: 'The world [i.e. the hasidic community] has not yet tasted me at all; for if they were to hear but one *torah* that I say, with its [proper] melody and dance, they would all attain complete self-annihilation'.[5]

The tsadik's every word and action is construed as creating new links between the divine realm, called 'the superior world', and the human realm of his hasidic following, often referred to in hasidic writing as 'the world'. The tsadik raises this world to the level of the superior worlds by freeing himself from the constraints of reality. He brings the divine world into everyday life by acting as the channel through which the divine nothingness is transformed into material being—the good fortune, abundant sustenance, and lovingkindness bestowed upon the community. Both these tasks are the responsibility of the tsadik as the link between his hasidim and the higher worlds. (The word *mazal*, 'good fortune', is related to *nazal*, meaning 'the trickling down from above'.)

The task of elevating mundane reality to a higher level expresses the mystical tradition of *devekut*; following the ways of kabbalah, it focuses on the inner experience. This is known in hasidic language as *bitul hayesh* and *mesirut nefesh*—terms that express ideas such as transcendence or annihilation of being, divestment of corporeality, and abandonment of one's soul to God. The task of drawing down divine grace and spiritual and physical abundance from the higher worlds to the world below—the tsadik's followers—focuses on the community and personal relationships. It is the realization of these kabbalistic concepts in a social framework that constitutes the innovation of hasidism.

The tsadik is himself a symbol of the divine dialectic. He combines the spiritual involvement of mystical exaltation and encountering the divine vitality

---

[5] *Ḥayei moharan*, no. 340.

with the social involvement necessary to channel the divine vitality to material reality. Seeking attachment to the divine element that transcends time and space, he himself strives to go beyond the bounds of sensory realities. Seeking to channel the divine spirit into the world, he strives to involve himself in routine human activity and social sensibility. In the language of mysticism, the dialectic is sometimes termed (following Ezekiel 1: 14) ebbing and flowing, or running back and forth: the tsadik's distancing himself from the world and from the bounds of reality is the 'running forth'; his intense commitment to the world as a channel for conveying divine grace to his followers is the 'running back'. Hasidism thus established an important new model of leadership involving social responsibility and commitment, combining an all-encompassing attachment to God with an all-encompassing love of Israel, the community of brotherhood in whose name the tsadik acts.

The major characteristics of the tsadik's leadership, in its ideal forms and as actually implemented, are discussed in more detail below, but at this point may be briefly summarized as follows:

* *Charisma.* The tsadik derives his authority from the charisma of divine election, a sense of divinely inspired mission and a consciousness of revelation through immediate contact with higher worlds.

* *Mutual devotion and responsibility.* The relationship between the tsadik and his hasidim is based on an all-embracing nexus of spiritual brotherhood and social responsibility.

* *Embodiment of the divine dialectic.* The tsadik embodies the dialectical tension between transcendence and sublimation, the process of emanation from nothingness so as to bring abundance into the world. He moves between different states of consciousness so as to confront both divine nothingness and physical being.

* *Linking the divine and the material.* The tsadik devotes himself simultaneously to God and to the world. In an attempt to reunite the divine element in the material world with its source in the heavenly world, he strives to elevate the mundane; at the same time he attempts to draw down the divine abundance from on high for the benefit of the world.

CHARISMA

The distinctiveness of hasidic leadership derives from its basis in charismatic authority.[6] The view that the tsadik's authority is based on divine inspiration,

---

[6] The word 'charisma' appears for the first time in the second letter of Paul to the Corinthians

an adhesion to the higher worlds, and divine election derives from Numbers 27: 16: 'Let the Lord, God of spirit to all flesh, appoint a man over the congregation, who will go out before them and come before them, and take them out and bring them in.'[7] Charisma implies endowment with divine grace, the power to make divine attributes manifest in human existence. The charismatic leader enjoys unmediated contact with the divine realm and therefore radiates to his environment a sense of unusual spiritual authority, freedom, awareness, and knowledge.[8] The charismatic quality of the tsadik, as grasped by him and by others, derives from his close relationship to the divine being and his consequent ability to exert a crucial influence on central areas of human existence.

Charisma characterizes every aspect of the leadership of a tsadik. His thought, speech, and action are guided by divine inspiration. He radiates the divine presence in the world. This is apparent in the loving kindness and empathy he shows to all, in his assumption of social responsibility, and in his ability to expound the Torah in a way that opens up new horizons. His charisma may also be reflected in an apparent ability to transcend the limits of time and space and perform miracles, in his internalization of mystical concepts, and in powers of divine revelation manifested within the community. These attributes—spiritual grandeur, creativity, insight, charity, freedom, and love of humanity—attract many hasidim, followers drawn into the circle of all-encompassing divine love and linked to the tsadik and to each other through bonds of mutual devotion and social responsibility. As Elimelekh of Lyzhansk wrote: 'When the tsadik performs wonders, then the holy spirit and holiness rest upon him and all can understand that it is from God.'[9]

Through his charisma, the tsadik manifests the presence of the divine in being and demonstrates the ability to transcend material concerns and draw closer to God:

As to the status of the tsadik, foundation of the world, who is called peace [*shalom*] because he causes the combination of opposites . . . This is impossible save through a tsadik who draws the spiritual abundance of the *sefirot*, with the Infinite light within it,

(1 Cor. 1: 11, 12). On the development of the concept see Shils, *The Constitution of Society*, 112. On charisma as a quality of the tsadik see Ch. 1 n. 1 above.

[7] *Zot zikaron*, 28.

[8] On charisma and religious leadership see Shils, 'Charisma, Order and Status'; Weber, *The Sociology of Religion*, pp. xxxiii–xxxv, 46–60; Barnes, 'Charisma and Religious Leadership'; Weber, *Theory of Social and Economic Organization*, 64–6, 328, 358–73; Shils, *The Constitution of Society*, 110–19; Tucker, 'The Theory of Charismatic Leadership'.

[9] *No'am elimelekh*, 'Bo', 36. See Schatz-Uffenheimer, 'On the Nature of the Tsadik in Hasidism' (Heb.); Willner, *The Spellbinders*; Tucker, 'The Theory of Charismatic Leadership'.

into the vessel called Being [*yesh*]. And it is necessary to draw into it the spiritual light that animates it, which is called Nothingness [*ayin*], for that is the soul that is drawn from the Infinite which is the life of life.[10]

When [the *sefirah* of] Malkhut is revealed in this way, divine revelation comes to the world, and all through the tsadik, who does this because the tsadik has the status of Ayin.[11]

For the tsadik through his faith gives life: meaning that as the tsadik has faith that no place is void of God, he thus brings the grasping of divinity into the world, and this is the meaning of 'the righteous shall live [*yihyeh*] by his faith', as if to say that he will give life [*yehayeh*], as he gives life to the sparks and has faith in God.[12]

Hasidic leadership, and the charismatic authority on which it is founded, are described in hasidic writing as combining a supernal transcending of boundaries with a mundane transcending of boundaries. Prophetic innovation inspired by an intense involvement with higher worlds in a way that transcends time and space is matched by social innovation inspired by an intense involvement with a community in a way that involves *bitul hayesh* and transcends selfhood. In other words, by bringing down divine abundance and performing miracles on behalf of the community by dint of divine inspiration, the charismatic authority achieves the union of two opposites: the being that through true selflessness attains divine nothingness, and the divine nothingness that incorporates and sustains being. In this way the tsadik demonstrates the mystical dialectic: the stripping away of corporeality in order to attain the divine infinite and the drawing down of the divine infinite into corporeality, continuously repeated.

The importance of charismatic authority in the hasidic way of life is discernible in the tsadik's consciousness of himself as an instrument of the divine spirit, sometimes likened to a violin or a trumpet. It is apparent in his assumption of responsibility for the community by virtue of the divine abundance that flows through him, and can be transformed into miracles or into material affluence. It is reflected in the profound certainty of the tsadik's followers that his every action is divinely inspired, that his very being is permanent evidence of divine revelation. For Jacob Isaac Horowitz, the Seer of Lublin, writing at the end of the eighteenth century, the charisma of the tsadik made him the 'sanctuary of testimony': 'His abode should be with us in a manner that will effect miracles and wonders for the benefit of Israel. That is a testimony that the Shekhinah dwells among us, namely that He [God] responds when we call out.'[13] His disciple Tsevi Hirsch Eichenstein of

---

[10] *Toledot ya'akov yosef*, 'Shelaḥ lekha', 136*b*.   [11] *Ḥesed le'avraham*, 12*b*.

[12] Ibid. 11*b*.   [13] *Zikhron zot*, 'Pekudei', 73.

Zhidachov, writing in the nineteenth century, wrote in a similar vein of the charisma of the tsadik: 'We find that with saints who serve God genuinely . . . when the counsel of God appears upon them and a spirit is poured out from above and makes steadfast their righteous right hand and guides their way.'[14] In the twentieth century Habad hasidism has provided strong testimony to the idea that the charismatic authority of a tsadik derives from an unmediated relationship between the divine and the human: the tsadik is an 'infinite substance garbed in flesh and blood; the Rebbe being an infinite substance clothed in the Rebbe's body'.[15] This unmediated relationship with the divine gives the tsadik divine properties that are otherwise lacking in human reality—properties such as pity, loving kindness, mercy, concern, patience, peace, dignity, freedom, a concern for equality and justice, broadmindedness, depth and breadth of thought, and hope.

Hasidic writing is full of references to the charisma of the tsadik. He is 'prepared for the infusion of His holiness upon him and within him'.[16] He 'personifies *devekut* to God so that his soul cleaves to the Eternal Life'.[17] However, the gift of charisma—the heavenly illumination with which the tsadik is privileged, the power to channel the divine nothingness into terrestrial being and corporeal abundance—was considered to be subject to two inner conditions: humility and 'divestment of corporeality' in relation to the transcendent glory of divine being; and a consciousness of mission in relation to his followers in the name of the Jewish people. (Hasidic literature terms this a concern for 'the world' or for the 'welfare of Israel', or 'love within the material world'.) The tsadik had to be a humble man, free from any material concerns of his own, yet willing to be closely involved, spiritually and materially, with his individual hasidim, with the community, and with public affairs.

The early hasidic thinkers formulated the ideal of the tsadik as a divinely inspired leader who assumes total responsibility for the community and maintains a close, continuous relationship of care so as to relieve it of the vagaries of a purely material existence.[18] The paradigm was Moses, who was attached to God and led the children of Israel as a devoted shepherd, huddling them beneath his arms. Elimelekh of Lyzhansk summarized the relationship between the tsadik's devotion to God and his obligation to the community—defined as an emanation of the heavenly upon the earth—in the following manner: 'Through the total *devekut* that the tsadik has he brings

---

[14] *Beit yisra'el*, 40b.

[15] *Kol mevaser*, 32, 48–9.

[16] *Zikhron zot*, 'Pekudei', 73.

[17] *No'am elimelekh*, 'Va'ethanan', 90.

[18] The sense of being 'called to a mission', or the consciousness of accepting a spiritual obligation on behalf of the community, is amply attested in hasidic literature: see Weber, *Theory of Social and Economic Organization*, 362.

down to the community of Israel all that is good, and thus he assembles the assemblies of Jacob who huddle beneath his wings that he may bring the influence to them'; 'the perfect tsadik who always walks with the divine unity brings down the abundance of good and blessing to all Israel . . . for the tsadik must convey the abundance, expand it, and spread it over all Israel'.[19]

The idea of a tsadik possessing unqualified power in the community in consequence of the divine source of his authority was a tremendous innovation. The concept had many positive implications, but also showed itself to be problematic—especially when the system of leadership took a new direction, as it did in subsequent generations, and changed from being based on the charisma of a single individual tsadik to being dynastic. The meaning of this shift is that, while in the first and second generations of tsadikim it was only an individual's exceptional inspiration and commitment that made him a leader, in subsequent generations, from the 1810s on, some men inherited the leadership of hasidic communities solely on account of the greatness of their fathers. Naturally the dynastic heritage could not always perpetuate the exceptional vision of the founders; quite often, brilliant students or other relatives would claim spiritual authority and would compete for the leadership of the hasidic community, contributing to conflicts and tension around the succession of charismatic leadership. Opponents of hasidism were quick to point out the lesser quality of successor generations but overlooked the ideals that nourished the concept and their significant application in various hasidic courts.

MUTUAL DEVOTION AND RESPONSIBILITY

A key feature of hasidic leadership is the intimate relationship of mutual devotion and responsibility between the tsadik and his hasidim. This intimate relationship, termed *hitkasherut vehitkalelut* ('affiliation and absorption'), implies ties of affection, fraternity, and mutual responsibility, and derives from the tsadik's status as the metaphysical link between the celestial and the terrestrial.

The dissemination of hasidism was closely linked to the consolidation of communities in which the tsadik and his hasidim were linked by strong bonds of mutual devotion. The spiritual renaissance engendered by hasidism was linked in no small measure to the emphasis on the tsadik's ability to satisfy the needs of his community, while the tsadik in turn enjoyed the devotion and material support of his hasidim. Tsadikism offered a frame of reference in

---

[19] *No'am elimelekh*, 'Bereshit', 1, 58c.

which material and spiritual sustenance were linked. The tsadik is the focus of faith and of community. He is patron and father figure, a loyal and generous brother, a sustaining mother and nursemaid, a liberator and redeemer. The hasid is the dependent believer, sustained, influenced, protected, liberated, and redeemed by virtue of his membership of a fraternity established on the basis of faith in the tsadik.

The close and caring relationship between tsadik and community is expressed in hasidic writing in many ways, all of which serve to emphasize the benevolence and responsibility of one side and the dependence and frailty of the other. It is likened to the relationship between Moses, the 'man of God', and the congregation of Israel, between nursemaid and infant, between parent and child, between faithful shepherd and dependent flock, between the Creator and his creations—all extremely close ties. The Seer of Lublin summarized the relationship as follows: 'And so all the heads of the generation must investigate the needs of their generation . . . Kings, that is to say rabbis, must be your nursemaids [cf. Isa. 49: 23], that is to say that they must look into your welfare and health like a nursemaid.'[20] Elsewhere in the hasidic literature such phrases as 'unification and inclusion' and 'corporeal saintliness' are used to refer to the all-embracing nexus of spiritual brotherhood and social responsibility. The relationship between the tsadik and his followers is not symmetrical; but it is mutual, continual, and comprehensive. In its ideal form it encompasses respect, love, and attentiveness, an unqualified readiness to respond to human spiritual and material needs: the tsadik accepts social and religious responsibility for an entire community.

The hasidic tsadik, unlike his kabbalistic predecessor, is concerned with far more than the kabbalistic goal of fulfilling a personal mystical ideal. Rather, he tries to combine a life of sanctity with a mission of leadership stemming from a consciousness of social responsibility. By virtue of his immediate contact with divine reality the tsadik is regarded as being 'higher than the masses', but he constantly has to engage with the material world in the concrete social context of his community. He must provide it with leadership, bestow upon it the abundance conferred upon him, and be responsible for its spiritual and material needs. By virtue of his simultaneous contact with the higher worlds and the lower worlds he becomes a mediator between heaven and earth, personifying the divine abundance in physical reality: 'For the tsadik is superior to the masses, and through his source the spiritual abundance passes, so that the light of His sanctity comes to the tsadik.'[21]

The sense of responsibility and close emotional ties—terms such as devotion, care, grace, love, fraternity, and inclusion are used in hasidic writing—

[20] *Zot zikaron*, 74.   [21] *Zikhron zot*, 'Bereshit', 2.

that characterize the relationship between the tsadik and his followers are more usually associated with the intimacy of family relations. In hasidism this relationship acquired two distinct features. The first derived from the idea of the metaphysical unity, albeit asymmetrical, between the tsadik and his followers: 'The tsadik of the generation is our soul, who includes many Jews . . . therefore the tsadikim love [the children of] Israel exceedingly, and give their lives for them, in so far as they love them like themselves, for they include Israel, and they are their lot.'[22] The second feature derived from the idea of metaphysical unity between the tsadik and divinity. By definition, a tsadik, both in his own consciousness and in the minds of his followers, is in direct communication with the divine. The divine abundance that the tsadik enjoys, in his elevation as emissary of the congregation, descends again, through him, for his community.

The tsadik acts in relation to his community of hasidim, all of whom are equally part of it and thus of equal status. The hasidic community, which exists on the basis of the equality entailed by unity and inclusion, is sustained through its relation to the tsadik. This relationship is expressed in hasidic writing by such terms as affinity (*hitkasherut*), devotion, love, and the emanation of abundance. It is a consequence of the tsadik's relationship to the higher worlds, a relationship articulated in terms of his love of and devotion to God and the abundance passing through him to the community. The individual's dependence on the tsadik and on being part of the congregation has crucial significance: 'For the tsadikim who cleave unto God draw down the abundance of holiness and awe [of God] to those who are unified with them.'[23] Likewise the dependence of the tsadik on the hasidim, who are referred to as 'branches of the source of his soul', is the basis of the hasidic leadership structure.

The voluntary binding relationship between hasid and tsadik stems from the intimacy of the tsadik's care for and patronage of his hasidim but has to be constantly cultivated. It is not merely individual: it is part of a totality bound by an egalitarian sense of fraternity, variously termed 'comradely love' or 'attachment'. These concepts, deriving from the mystical fervour of the love of God, became the basis of a social contract from the time that unification with the higher worlds became togetherness in this world. The terms applied to the tsadik's obligation and commitment to the community's material and spiritual concerns, reflecting God's promise to his creatures in the lower worlds, are 'abundance', 'progeny, life, and sustenance', and 'blessing and drawing down'. The hasid's relation to the tsadik and the mutual relations

---

[22] *Zot zikaron*, 11–12.   [23] Ibid. 36.

among members of the congregation are described in terms such as affinity, attachment, adhesion, and inclusion. The same terms also refer to the tsadik's obligation towards the higher worlds. The two are enmeshed at the metaphysical level: 'For the tsadik represents the entire generation, like Moses who included the six hundred thousand [who left Egypt; Exod. 12: 37] and he attains the level of nothingness, so that the knowledge of God reaches the world and all the sparks in the mundane are elevated . . . at the lower levels.'[24]

The bonds of devotion between tsadik and hasidim also have tangible ritual expression. For the hasidim this means making pilgrimages to the tsadik's court, offering redemptive donations, associating themselves with him in prayer, confessing before him, and considering themselves first and foremost as members of his community.[25] 'For this purpose one must offer and bind all prayers to the tsadik of the generation.'[26] For the tsadik this means channelling the divine abundance of the supernal world into this world by bestowing blessings on his followers to ease the yoke of corporeality, and elevating this world to the supernal world by means of prayer and devotion to God.

The ideal of tsadikism engendered a sense of partnership and mutual responsibility among its adherents. The tsadik's concern for the physical and spiritual needs of all his followers offered them a true sense of liberty, equality, and fraternity. The role of the tsadik in channelling the heavenly blessings of progeny, life, and sustenance to his followers thus led to the emergence of a social reality very different from the traditional Jewish leadership structure. Even if there was some disparity between the written formulation of the doctrine of tsadikism and its practical realization, it unquestionably exercised great influence in moulding hasidic consciousness and the system of expectations that nurtured it.

The novel relationships that hasidism engendered—the mutual devotion between the tsadik and his followers, and the strong fraternity that developed between the followers themselves in consequence of the equality in their relationship with the tsadik—was a challenge to the hierarchical social order of the traditional world. The devotion to a tsadik who is himself devoted to God and imbued with divine energy generates spiritual energies among his followers that create a sense of mutual responsibility, equality, and fraternity. This

---

[24] Ibid. 27a.

[25] For the evaluation of hasidic leadership and associated practices, such as monetary 'redemption' (*pidyon*), confession, and connectedness, see the mitnagedic documents in Wilensky, *Hasidim and Mitnagedim* (Heb.), index s.v. 'pidyon', and cf. Assaf, *The Regal Way*, index s.v. 'pidyon'; Pedayah, 'On the Evolution of the Social, Religious, Economic Model in Hasidism' (Heb.).

[26] *Likutei moharan*, I, 'Torah', 2: 6.

reality, illuminated by the sanctity of divine presence and encompassing human brotherhood, is well described in a letter written by Abraham of Kalisk, a student of Dov Baer the Maggid of Mezhirech, who went to the land of Israel with a group of hasidim in 1777. The letter, which was addressed to his comrades back in Russia, was published in *Peri ha'arets* (1814):

> One should train oneself to the quality of the higher Wisdom for the benefit of one's comrades . . . For the principle of comradely love is greater than any virtue . . . That is the meaning of Israel being responsible for one another [see *Shevuot*, 39a], so that each is included in his comrade and each can elevate the other by being bound to his out-standing virtue . . . In this unity each soul cleaves unto its fellow, comrades listening to the divine voice . . . All those who, in performing *mitsvot*, cleave unto the perfect human being draw together all those who cleave unto the perfect human being. It is indeed not equally attained, in any event, however all those who are attached to him are more connected to holiness for that reason . . . Thus in the cleaving of comrades hear-kening to the divine voice, surely the mitzvah and the Torah are drawn along with them because of their attachment to people who are attached to God . . . From this one can infer how far the connection and love reach, as if one is bound to the point where one's fellow is bound. It is a special boon that one receives divine providence by virtue of those who cleave unto God, and one is thus prepared for all the benefits and successes in elevating body and soul . . . One should always train oneself to take comradely love into the heart until one's soul is consumed by it, and to prolong the feeling to the point of cleaving unto one another. When they are as one person then the One [God] dwells among them; they will be affected by Him with a multitude of salvations and comforts, and they will be elevated in body and soul.[27]

Hasidism thus proposed a novel ecstatic and social dimension. In addition to the traditional duty incumbent on every Jew to love God with all one's heart and soul,[28] it required devotion to the tsadik and to one's fellow hasidim. This established a new communal ethos in complete contrast to accepted social hierarchy, making all 'as one person' equally devoted to the tsadik and equally included in the community.[29] The tsadik, 'who is called deity [*elohim*] on the model of Moses the man of God [see Deut. 33: 1]',[30] personifies expansiveness, greatness, freedom, care, loving kindness, peace, and truth. He embodies the totality of values for which people yearn: 'Through the tsadik it is revealed to all eyes that there is a God who judges

---

[27] *Peri ha'arets*, Letters, 10–11, 18–19.   [28] Deut. 6: 5.

[29] For descriptions of social reality informed by these ideas see *Keter kehunah* and cf. Assaf, *The Regal Way*; Assaf (ed.), *What I Have Seen: The Memories of Yechezkel Kotik* (Heb.). For crit-icism of the new social patterns, see Wilensky, *Hasidim and Mitnagedim* (Heb.); Hundert, *Jews in Poland–Lithuania in the Eighteenth Century*, 195–210.

[30] *Beit yisra'el*, 13d.

who is superior over all gods.'[31] The emotion of belonging to the hasidic community sparked a deep sense of comradeship, a closeness nurtured by a shared devotion to God that rapidly led followers of a tsadik to prefer the inclusiveness and mystical social solidarity of the hasidic community to the rigid hierarchy of the traditional community. Hasidic tradition contains many testimonies to manifestations of such mystical social solidarity through song and dance; the traditionalists (who came to be known as *mitnagedim*, 'opponents', because of their opposition to hasidism) saw the same manifestations somewhat differently, depicting hasidim 'whose days are all holidays' in a hostile light. The enthusiastic solidarity of a community united through the fellowship of the tsadik—a charismatic leader, accessible to all, who was 'making a new heaven and a new earth',[32] breaking free of the limits of existing order and the shackles of being and personifying the infinite horizon of divine grace—engendered a powerful new social order.

The ecstatic egalitarianism revolving around a mystical focus and associated with the mutual responsibility inherent in tsadikism had broader implications too. Transferred into the social arena, it may well have influenced the founders and pioneers of Zionism to strive in their way to alter the lives of the Jewish people. Many of the early Zionists came from hasidic environments, and there are clear indications of a connection between the revolution of hasidism and that of pioneering settlement in Palestine. Memoirs and autobiographical testimonies of such figures as Aaron David Gordon, Meir Ya'ari, David Hurwitz, and Shlomo Tsemach, as well as other historical and biographical documents associated with the early waves of immigration into Palestine at the beginning of the twentieth century and with Hashomer Hatsa'ir and the kibbutz movement, demonstrate how the religious and social fervour of hasidism could be transformed into fervour for Zionism. The term 'kibbutz' was itself taken from the vocabulary of Nahman of Bratslav (1772–1810), and other terms common in the Zionist vocabulary to express ideas dependent on human initiative—such as *aliyah* ('immigration to the Land of Israel'), *ge'ulat adamah* and *ge'ulat ha'arets* ('redeeming the soil', 'appropriating the land')—were inspired by the mystical concepts used by tsadikim, such as *aliyat nitsotsot* ('elevation of divine sparks'), and *ge'ulat hashekhinah* ('redemption of the Shekhinah'). The influence of tsadikism and the spiritual and social renewal it generated was thus to extend far beyond the hasidic world.[33]

[31] Ibid. 17*b*.

[32] Ibid. 26*d*. See Shmeruk, 'Hasidism, the *Arendars*, and Farm Tenancy' (Heb.) and 'Hasidism and the Kehilla'.

[33] On the historical and social manifestations of hasidic leadership, see Dubnow, *History of*

EMBODIMENT OF THE DIVINE DIALECTIC

In the paradigmatic conception of tsadikism, the tsadik's personality, way of life, teaching, and behaviour exemplify the fundamental duality of hasidism. He can articulate the divine outlook on the essential nothingness of reality by revealing its divine essence. He can also articulate the divine plenitude through the corporeal (progeny, life, and sustenance), and through the presence of divine grace in physical reality. In other words, the tsadik embodies the divine coincidence of opposites—the constant movement back and forth between transcendence and immanence, abundance and contraction, expansion and withdrawal, the individual being of selfhood and the selflessness of going beyond one's self. Because these different qualities all meet in the tsadik, Elimelekh of Lyzhansk refers to him as 'the tabernacle of meeting': 'The tsadik, in his source, clings to the exalted state of solitude and meditation, binding his soul to the higher worlds, and drawing down the abundance. This is the idea of the tabernacle of meeting [*ohel mo'ed*].'[34]

The tsadik must personify the transcendent movement from being to nothingness through selfless devotion to God, and must arouse the flow of nothingness to being that is required in order to draw down the material abundance and spiritual welfare associated with God's loving kindness. For the tsadik to actualize this duality he must himself attain divine nothingness. That is to say, in order to become a channel for the infinite divine abundance known as nothingness, flowing from infinity into the finitude of being, he must transcend the limits of selfhood and attain selflessness: 'it is necessary that the tsadik below . . . refrain from ascribing any standing to himself; he is merely receiving and bestowing on the people who attach themselves to him'.[35]

It is a distinctive feature of hasidism that the two aspects of the divine coincidence of opposites that are embodied in the tsadik have a pronounced social dimension. In the ascent from being to nothingness known as *bitul hayesh*, the tsadik elevates not only himself but the souls of his followers: 'As the tsadik overcomes, raising himself to holiness, he elevates the entire world [his congregation] with him.'[36] When he performs the descent from nothing-

Hasidism (Heb.), 182–211; Aescoly, *Hasidism in Poland* (Heb.); Pedayah, 'On the Evolution of the Social, Religious, Economic Model in Hasidism' (Heb.); Bartal, 'Maskilic Criticism of Economic Aspects of Hasidism' (Heb.); Assaf, *The Regal Way*; Mahler, *Hasidism and the Jewish Enlightenment*; Hundert, *Jews in Poland–Lithuania in the Eighteenth Century*, 160–210; and Rabinowitz, *Lithuanian Hasidism*.

[34] *No'am elimelekh*, 'Vayetse', 15.   [35] *Maor vashemesh*, 'Vayeshev', 39a.
[36] *No'am elimelekh*, 'Vayeḥi', 27.

ness to being known as *hamshakhat hashefa*, he draws down abundance into the material world not for himself but for his community: 'The desire of the tsadik is always that all Israel be full and satisfied with all that is good.'[37] The tsadik's ascent is connected with the elevation of his hasidim, the elimination of their corporeality, and restoration of each soul to its source:

The primary activity of the tsadikim of the generations . . . was to restore the souls of Jews to their source, to remove the screens that separate and the physical lusts, in order to restore the souls to their source . . . The nature of the connection of the souls [of the tsadikim] is by their divestment of corporeality and totally leaving their materiality, in order to bind their souls to the light of the Infinite, may He be blessed. Thus they draw along the souls of Israel to restore them to their source.[38]

The climax of the transition from being to nothingness is embodied in the ecstatic moment of human *devekut* with the divine. The climax of the transition from nothingness to being is embodied in the social ecstasy of inclusion, devotion, and unification of the tsadik and his hasidim.[39] The range of values that the mystical tradition ascribes to the passage from being to nothingness and the consequent elevation in the human–divine relationship—cleaving, inclusion, unification, affinity (*yihud*), and *bitul hayesh*—is transformed into a vocabulary describing the passage from nothingness to being and the abundance, affinity, and drawing down in the network of relations between the tsadik and his hasidim.

LINKING THE DIVINE AND THE MATERIAL

The tsadik is seen as a manifestation of the *sefirah* Yesod, 'the foundation of the world', associated in kabbalistic lore with eternal life, procreation, and virility, and with the divine abundance in the world of spheres.[40] The word has deep resonances from the biblical phrase *tsadik yesod olam*,[41] meaning 'the tsadik is the foundation of the world'. In hasidic writings the tsadik is a

---

[37] Ibid. 28. [38] *Maor vashemesh*, 'Pineḥas', 182*b*.

[39] Jiri Langer described his experience as a young man at the Belz synagogue in Galicia: 'It is as though an electric spark has suddenly entered those present. The crowd, which till now has been completely quiet, almost cowed, suddenly bursts forth in a wild shout. None stays in his place. The tall black figures run hither and thither round the synagogue, flashing past the lights of the sabbath candles. Gesticulating wildly, and throwing their whole body about, they shout out the words of the psalm. They knock into each other unconcernedly, for all their cares have been cast aside; everything has ceased to exist for them. They are seized by an indescribable ecstasy.' Langer, *Nine Gates*, 7. Life as a young man in the hasidic world is described by Jiri Langer in the introduction ('A Youth from Prague among the Chassidim', pp. 3–29), and by his brother Frantisek in the foreword (pp. vii–xxxi).

[40] *Sha'arei orah*, 34. [41] Prov. 10: 25.

channel through which the divine abundance flows to the world. He is the mystical bridge between the spirituality that lies beyond corporeality and the material needs of his community anchored in physical reality. He is 'Israel's source of the triad progeny, life, and sustenance'.[42] He occupies this position because he embodies the divine coincidence of opposites, and it is this that allows him to be the channel linking the divine world and the material world.

This view of the tsadik's role goes back to the Ba'al Shem Tov, who interpreted the rabbinic statement 'the whole world is nourished on account of [bi-shevil] my son Hanina'[43] as meaning 'Hanina my son made a path [shevil] to channel the abundance into the world',[44] thereby denominating the tsadik as the channel through which the hidden abundance of abstract divine ḥesed can flow and be transformed into perceptible ḥesed commensurate to the needs of flesh and blood. His role as intermediary between the worlds is clearly defined:

For the tsadik must connect and unify the higher worlds with the lower.[45]

for the tsadik must always serve God and bind corporeality and spirituality, that is, that in everything he does . . . his intention must be above, for the higher worlds with the intention of the higher unifications.[46]

his entire self, his aim and desire, is only to elevate to the sacred . . . meaning that the tsadik sees that the holiness is down on the earth . . . the tsadik must always be in a state of 'back and forth' like the holy ḥayot [living beings, creatures: see Ezek. 1: 14; the word ḥayot is recast in hasidic writings as ḥiyut, 'vitality'. Thus the tsadik is transforming the divine vitality back and forth].[47]

In linking the divine and the material, the tsadik channels his energies simultaneously in two directions: his influence is felt in heaven as well as on earth. His connection to the celestial plane by dint of the power of his devotion and asceticism enables him to be both the channel through which divine abundance flows to his community ('through his source the spiritual abundance passes') and the emissary representing the community, able to 'receive particular divine assistance for the sake of the world'. This duality—the ability to elevate the mundane while also drawing down divine properties from above—was described by Abraham the Angel, son of the Maggid of Mezhirech, in the following words: 'The purpose is that the tsadik should make being into nothingness and raise the physical dimensions to their source . . . Then all becomes exalted, and thus the vitality of all the worlds comes about through him, from nothingness to being.'[48]

---

[42] No'am elimelekh, 'Vayera', 9.   [43] BT, Ta'anit 24b.

[44] Ba'al shem tov al hatorah, 'Toledot', i. 249–50. [45] No'am elimelekh, 'Terumah', 48.

[46] Ibid., 'Mikets', 23.   [47] Ibid., 'No'aḥ', 4.   [48] Ḥesed le'avraham, 9a.

The idea of the tsadik as the channel through which divine vitality is bestowed on material reality represents a transmutation of the kabbalistic idea of the tsadik as an ascetic recluse. The hasidic idea of a tsadik is a concept replete with religious and social meaning, and its fulfilment requires realization in the leadership of a community. A key feature of hasidism is thus the reconceptualization of the tsadik: whereas the kabbalistic tsadik was an individual who attains communion with God through ascetic withdrawal, the hasidic tsadik is a figure of authority who synthesizes mystical and social dimensions and has both religious and communal commitments.

The Seer of Lublin describes the tension between these two aspects of the tsadik's existence—his yearning to transcend being and become one with God versus the need to concern himself with the material needs of human beings—as follows:

'Go forth from your land' [Gen. 12: 1]: This means that you are to go forth in your thoughts from your corporeality. This means that your desire and will should be not to conduct yourself corporeally . . . 'To the land that I will show you' means that, although your desire is to go forth and refrain from corporeal occupation, you must understand that it is His will that you should be occupied with corporeality as well as the verse says 'Hold on to this but do not abstain from that' [see Eccles. 7: 18]. That is the sense of 'To the land that I will show you'.[49]

The tsadik who rises to higher worlds receives divine assistance for the sake of the world or the community around him in whose name he acts. This enables him to bring down from the higher worlds both earthly and spiritual benefits for his followers in this world: 'One should connect oneself to the tsadikim in each generation, for they are not concerned with their own interests and God is with them. So too they have investigated their humility and have superior assistance particularly for the needs of the world.'[50]

The powers of mystical elevation and the charismatic qualities that the tsadik has—the power to extend the limits of consciousness, the spiritual freedom, the influence over the higher worlds—are not given to him in his own right but only in the context of God's relationship to the Jewish people. 'He [the tsadik] should know that when God responds to him on anything, even with miracles and wonders, it is all God's grace for the benefit of Israel.'[51] Tsadikism made concrete the insight that a genuinely religious life cannot be independent of interpersonal relationships: the connection with the vital centre must be paralleled by a connection with living beings. To put it another way, the love directed towards God must also be directed towards human beings: the tsadik must demonstrate not only his love of God but also

---

[49] *Zot zikaron*, 126.   [50] *Zikhron zot*, 'Mikets', 34.   [51] *Zot zikaron*, 5.

his love of Israel, his willingness for self-sacrifice on behalf of Israel, his sense of identity with his followers.

When charismatic leadership is legitimized by the tsadik's consciousness of his social mission and commitment to the general welfare, the focus of the mystical arena shifts from the higher worlds to the earth. The link between tsadik and congregation is based on the assumption that since ordinary individuals, limited by the bounds of corporeality, cannot meet their spiritual obligations and material needs, they need an intermediary able both to draw down the divine abundance and to represent them before heaven. The tsadik's role as an intermediary between God and congregation, divine and human, spiritual and physical, is mentioned frequently in hasidic writing in the context of channelling the divine abundance. The kabbalistic term for this is 'arousal from above'. The tsadik's role as an intermediary between the congregation and God is referred to in such terms as elevation of sparks, elevation of souls, and elevation of prayers; in kabbalistic terminology this is 'arousal from below'.

For it is known that it is impossible for revelation to come to the world of action [*olam ha'asiyah*, the lowest of the four kabbalistic worlds] unless it first comes to the tsadik . . . as the verse states [referring to Moses], 'I stand today between God and you [see Deut. 5: 5] . . . for it is through him that revelation comes to Israel, for the tsadik is on the level of nothingness.'[52]

The tsadik's mediating function, poised between the higher and the lower worlds, stimulating the 'arousal from above' or the divine flow,[53] is associated with the drawing down of abundance from the spiritual to the physical:

The tsadik must . . . draw down the abundance into the world . . . In this context the tsadikim are called angels, meaning messengers, for they are God's emissaries to benefit His creatures.[54]

Because God's effect is exceedingly great and it is impossible to receive His influence except through an intermediary, that is the tsadik who receives the abundance from on high and he transmits it to all . . . Thus the abundance through the tsadik is a reciprocal loving kindness with the whole world, as he receives the abundance from above and distributes it to all, and it emanates from God.[55]

The effect of the tsadik's mediation between lower and higher realms— termed 'arousal from below' and equivalent to the backward flow envisaged by the kabbalistic concept of *ratso vashov*, 'flowing backwards and forwards'[56]—is to elevate the physical to the spiritual:

[52] *Ḥesed le'avraham*, 28a.   [53] Ezek. 1: 14.
[54] *Zikhron zot*, 'Yeshayahu', 139.   [55] *No'am elimelekh*, 'Bo', 31.   [56] Ezek. 1: 14.

The tsadik is called 'master of return', *ba'al teshuvah* [ordinarily meaning a penitent, one who returns to the right way, but here interpreted as one who returns to the source], because he returns the sparks [to their source]. He is also designated by the [Hebrew letter] vav [literally meaning a hook] because he hooks down the abundance from on high.[57]

The associative world in which the idea of the tsadik was consolidated as pertaining to heavenly spheres has its origins in kabbalistic literature. The kabbalah of the late medieval period saw heaven and earth as linked through a system of divine *sefirot* that affect the earthly realm. On this basis, kabbalah also revealed new mystical meanings for biblical verses. In hasidic writings informed by kabbalistic terminology, the tsadik emerges as a multilayered symbol with cosmic, mystical, and mythological frames of reference drawn from the sacred texts and applied anew within the social reality of hasidism.

As we have seen, the word 'tsadik' resonates from the biblical phrase *tsadik yesod olam*, 'the righteous [*tsadik*] [is the] foundation [*yesod*] of the world'.[58] In kabbalistic terms, the *sefirah* of Yesod is the foundation of both the earth and the celestial worlds, and thus also the connection between them. As the seventh of the *sefirot* (in some enumerations), Yesod is connected to the sabbath and also to oaths: the Hebrew term for oath, *shevuah*, shares the root of *sheva*, the number seven. It is therefore also linked to the oath or covenant between God and man, with which fruitfulness, plenitude, seed, soul, and satisfaction (*sova*, also connected linguistically with *sheva*) are all associated. Yesod is the spine of the kabbalistic system, the core through which everything flows. It is the channel through which being and nothingness flow back and forth, the connection between upper and lower realms.

In kabbalistic literature these attributes are regarded as the province of the divine. In hasidism, 'tsadik' is not only the name of the divine manifestation relating to the seventh *sefirah* signifying divine abundance; all the divine attributes referring to the seventh *sefirah* are applied to the earthly tsadik as well. Kabbalism sees Yesod as the channel for divine abundance, life, and eternity, whereas hasidism attributes this role to the tsadik; the tsadik is described in Psalms as 'flowering like the palm tree',[59] itself a vertical link between heaven and earth. Like Yesod, which kabbalism connects to the biblical Joseph, who provided the hungry with grain, the tsadik channels material benefits to his hasidim. And just as Yesod is the channel through which the divine abundance moves 'back and forth' between higher and lower realms, linking the higher and lower *sefirot* and transforming nothingness into being and being into nothingness, so the tsadik unifies heaven and earth. He is the vehicle for the divine coincidence of opposites: 'It is all by means of the tsadik . . . For there is one

---

[57] *Ḥesed le'avraham*, 23.   [58] Prov. 10: 25.   [59] Ps. 92: 13.

pillar extending from earth to the firmament which lifts up the earthly to heaven . . . Great are the deeds of tsadikim, who make being into nothingness.'[60] Yesod, referred to as 'sabbath', with its connotations of 'oath' and 'sanctuary', symbolizes the promise of fecundity, seed, abundance and unification, growth and flowering, fruitfulness, and longevity; the tsadik is likewise described as the source of abundance, the cause of growth and flowering, engaged in unification with the Shekhinah (the tenth *sefirah*) and unifying being and nothingness. Every verse or image that refers to the *sefirah* of Yesod and its unificatory, creative, fecund powers is likely to be applied in hasidic literature to the tsadik. Any symbolic exegesis in kabbalah that refers to Yesod becomes an allusion to the tsadik.

For it is known that the principle of emanation of the worlds is for the tsadik, as the sages taught: 'The world was only created to be commanded by this person.' For the tsadik is the foundation of the world; through him comes all the good and perfection to the lower worlds, because it is impossible for any revelation to come to the world unless it first comes to the tsadik who has the status of nothingness . . . Through him comes revelation to the world of action [*olam ha'asiyah*] the material world [*olam hageshem*].[61]

The tsadikim of the generation are called foundation of the world for they have the standing of *yesod*, in so far as their good deeds bring all benefits to the world. They are the channel and the pathway by means of which every abundance descends and is divided and every benefit to Keneset Israel.[62]

Hasidism thus projects kabbalistic symbolism on to terrestrial existence and makes the tsadik into the embodiment of divine manifestation. This doctrine was first formulated in the 1770s by Abraham the Angel (1741–76), son of Dov Baer the Maggid of Mezhirech, a hasidic thinker who (perhaps surprisingly) was not himself a tsadik. He was perhaps projecting retrospectively the extraordinary traits and properties of his great father, who formulated the ideas of hasidism under the direct influence of the Ba'al Shem Tov and is considered the perfect embodiment of the dialectical figure of the tsadik. It was soon taken up by disciples of the Maggid who were leading large hasidic congregations—active tsadikim such as Elimelekh of Lyzhansk and Jacob Isaac the Seer of Lublin. It was further transmitted by their disciples Kalonymus Epstein (author of *Maor vashemesh*) and Meir of Stobnitsa (author of *Or lashamayim*), both of whom attributed to the tsadik the characteristics of the divine *sefirah* of Yesod and the power to influence the higher and lower worlds in a supernatural way. This teaching is concisely stated in *Maor vashemesh*: 'The main thing is to bind oneself to a tsadik who can elevate and repair the souls of Israel; this is the tsadik who conforms to the

---

[60] *Ḥesed le'avraham*, 25.   [61] Ibid. 17*a*.   [62] *Maor vashemesh*, 'Vayishlaḥ', 35*a*.

paradigm of the supernal tsadik who connects all things.'[63] The tsadik was seen as having the power to liberate his followers from the shackles of the physical world through his ability to mediate between the heavenly and earthly realities and draw the divine abundance down to this world. Elimelekh of Lyzhansk's *No'am elimelekh* articulates the tsadik's obligation to direct his worship, through his mystical attainment and relationship to the higher worlds, in such a way as to gratify the physical needs of his hasidim. The Seer of Lublin developed this doctrine in new directions, relating the divine dialectic of expansion and withdrawal to the dual nature of the tsadik's existence.

Hasidism was the first religious movement to establish a connection between the mystical relationship to the higher worlds and the ensuing social reality. Before hasidism, the condition for ecstatic ascent was asceticism; the kabbalistic tradition saw withdrawal from society and the rejection of materialism as the necessary condition for mystical elevation to higher worlds. It was moreover a one-directional activity, taking place solely in the private realm. Hasidism added a dialectical opposition to this condition: withdrawal from the community for the sake of contact with the divine can only be justified in terms of the benefits that will flow to the community in consequence.[64]

The hasidic master who 'connects all things' unites in his own being the contradictory values requisite to this achievement. His very existence represents a coincidence of opposites. On the one hand, the tsadik internalizes the ascetic attitude of withdrawal from the world demanded by the hasidic ethos: he is committed to equanimity, solitude, withdrawal, and humility, and to denying himself certain areas of human existence and physical reality in order to pass from being to nothingness and to attain communion with and inclusion in the divine. Yet affinity, inclusion, and unification with higher worlds are not ends in themselves: the goal is rather the return from nothingness to being, to reunite with the community in order to ensure the flow of divine abundance.

With the development of the doctrine of the tsadik, the individual hasid is no longer required to devote himself to God but instead to attach himself to the tsadik, relying on the latter's communion with God. For the doctrine of the tsadik implies the transformation of the direct relation between the hasid and God that characterized early hasidism into an oblique, mediated relationship in which the tsadik is the link between this world and the higher worlds. Hasidim, as individuals and as a community, are not directly connected to

---

[63] Ibid., 'Vayeshev', 39*a*.

[64] See Ettinger, 'The Hasidic Movement: Reality and Ideals'; Rapoport-Albert, 'God and the Zaddik'.

God; in devoting themselves to the tsadik they are included together with him, like Moses, who included the six hundred thousand souls of Israel, and became exalted for them and in their name. When the tsadik returns from nothingness to being, he draws down the divine abundance from the 'supernal blessing' for the benefit of his followers.

Beginning in the 1760s and 1770s, these concepts were elaborated systematically in Mezhirech in the works of Abraham the Angel, Elimelekh of Lyzhansk, and Jacob Isaac the Seer of Lublin, and, by the 1780s and 1790s, in other hasidic courts as well. Both the early hasidic masters and their successors regarded themselves as divinely appointed messengers and as emissaries of the congregation by virtue of being blessed with divine grace. They conceived of themselves as being in the image of Moses 'the man of God' attached to the higher worlds from which he brought spiritual and material abundance, the redeemer who led his people from slavery to freedom and took upon himself responsibility for their welfare. In their interpretation, the humility associated with the biblical Moses[65] became the rejection of selfhood and self-interest. Their concept of leadership was to mediate between the divine and their followers, transforming being into nothingness in interceding for the needs of the community, and transforming nothingness into being in acting on behalf of the community to attract the divine abundance. Elimelekh of Lyzhansk's *No'am elimelekh*, the Seer of Lublin's *Zikhron zot* and *Zot zikaron*, and Abraham the Angel's *Ḥesed le'avraham* repeat the principle formulated by the Maggid of Mezhirech: only the person who can turn the self (*ani*) into nothing (*ayin*) can aspire to attain divine nothingness and convey its abundance for the material welfare of his followers. In other words, the dialectical process presented in hasidic literature connects the transformation of self into nothingness to the transformation of nothingness into being. The former, achieved through the tsadik's divine worship, is the condition for the latter.

When the tsadik who draws abundance wishes to receive the abundance from above he must make himself small through great humility. Then, when his abundance affects the world, he expands and broadens himself to affect the entire world . . . The tsadik must make himself small and submissive when he receives, as it says: 'Wisdom comes from nothingness' [see Job 28: 20]. This means, in one who regards himself as nothing, in such a tsadik is wisdom found, to receive the plenitude from there [from nothingness].[66]

These mystical proclivities had an enormous impact on the teachings that circulated concerning the tsadik, in the form of hasidic tales and elsewhere.

---

[65] Num. 12: 3, 'Now the man Moses was very humble, more so than anyone else on the face of the earth.'   [66] *No'am elimelekh*, 'Bo', 35.

The tales that were disseminated in hasidic circles shed much light on how hasidim perceived the charismatic authority of tsadikim, documenting their attitudes towards the hasidic leadership and the social importance of these attitudes in reality. The homiletic literature written by hasidic leaders demonstrates the mystical concepts that inspired them and the social and religious transformation that took place in their consciousness. Mitnagedic literature shows the strength of the opposition to hasidic leadership and its mystically inspired social innovations. It was not unnatural that hasidic leadership would arouse controversy. Resting as it did on charismatic authority and prophetic inspiration and on a kabbalistic system that had become a social ethos, it deviated radically from traditional rational leadership models. The consequent historical developments had broad repercussions.

*

Gradually, the system of leadership based on the personal charisma of a single individual tsadik took on a new direction and became dynastic. Family status replaced mystical inspiration and immediate contact with higher worlds in the relations between tsadik and community. This naturally had implications for the historical expression of tsadikism. Accounts of hasidic courts and practices dating from the eighteenth, nineteenth, and twentieth centuries are instructive about the changes that occurred in the hasidic way of life. Some autobiographical accounts of hasidic reality show fascinating departures from hasidic theory; others convey the liveliness and intensity of charismatic leadership, while still others demonstrate the dangers of spiritual and social frameworks preserving charismatic leadership models even when unable to provide them with content. The literature of the Haskalah movement mounted an extreme critique of hasidic leadership, to which it ascribed manipulative and populist tendencies.

Certainly, the realization of the mystical ideology of the tsadik provided no shortage of opportunities for criticism. Yet the widespread popularity of the hasidic leadership, imbued with spiritual revival and new patterns of social responsibility, indicates that many people found hasidism a meaningful way of life. Membership of the community was after all voluntary, and charismatic leadership founded on spiritual vocation and social mission was always preconditioned by voluntary acceptance by the community. The religious awakening associated with hasidism—the mystical inspiration stemming from the kabbalistic tradition, the spiritual freedom, the novel outlook on the world, creative enthusiasm, partnership, equality, the alternative social structure that the hasidic community represented, and the comprehensive social responsibility it offered—were a significant lodestone for a large audience. Whereas everyday life entailed a substantial measure of submissiveness and helplessness—what hasidism called *katnut* (pettiness or small-mindedness) in the face of *gashmiyut* (materialism)—hasidism offered the expansive vistas of *gadlut* (greatness) and a spiritual release from the bounds of reality, an aspiration of the finite towards the infinite. The suffering of the material world was replaced by an optimism derived from the recognition that there is more to existence than meets the eye, and that shared social and spiritual responsibility can ease the confrontation with reality.

Scholars of hasidism have written about various aspects of hasidic leadership: its intellectual foundations, its charismatic sources and emotional appeal, its major social and religious frameworks, its prolific literature, vigorous polemics, succession conflicts, and the various disputes among the fragmented dynasties. These new divisions and subdivisions reflected power struggles and competition for honour, status, and authority, as well as elements of decadence and corruption.[67] Scholars influenced by the viewpoint of the Haskalah have emphasized the negative effects of hasidic leadership as a divisive element that split traditional Jewish society, and they have maintained that charismatic leadership undermined the foundations of traditional rational leadership. Others have seen hasidic leadership as an expression of social opposition, while yet others saw it as a stabilizing factor.[68]

The extent of historical variation and the multiple faces of hasidic leadership militate against clear-cut judgements and sweeping generalizations. There is a need for research that recognizes the complexity and changing historical character of the phenomenon. The tsadik was unquestionably the focus and the living pulse of hasidic existence, embodying its sense of freedom and innovation, drawing on contact with the divine and redirecting it to the social arena. But beyond any doubt these elements of hasidic leadership were varied, and some of them were controversial.

While all tsadikim led communities of their own, not all regarded them as necessarily in conflict with the mainstream community or as a substitute for it. Levi Isaac of Berdichev, Isaac Meir Alter of Ger, and Pinhas Horowitz of Frankfurt and his brother Shmuel Shmelke of Nikolsburg all contributed to the strengthening of communal institutions and attempted to unify Jewish society in the face of internal and external change. Hasidic thought and the doctrine of the tsadik as presented by Shneur Zalman of Lyady, Tsadok

[67] See Elior, 'The Dispute over the Habad Legacy' (Heb.)

[68] See n. 32 above, and also Mahler, *Hasidism and the Jewish Enlightenment*; Ettinger, 'The Hasidic Movement: Reality and Ideals'; Hundert, *Jews in Poland–Lithuania in the Eighteenth Century*, 160–210.

Hakohen of Lublin, and Isaac Meir Alter of Ger incorporate an awareness of the needs of the community and the Jewish people and the need for conservatism in public policy. Other tsadikim, such as Jacob Isaac the Seer of Lublin and Mordecai Joseph Leiner of Izbica, place greater emphasis on articulating personal freedom, autonomy, and the rejection of authority and advocate positions liable to weaken, directly or indirectly, the authority of communal leadership.

Hasidic leadership in the twentieth century and beyond has demonstrated that the possibilities of charismatic leadership are by no means exhausted. There is evidence that a tsadik can be a catalyst for expanding his followers' horizons, drawing on a divine vision that pushes back the limits of the human world and sequestered Orthodox positions. A tsadik can be the focus for messianic identification, new intellectual and political activity, and interaction with the modern world, or for the insulation of the hasidic community from change and alienation.[69] The tsadik defines the nature of the hasidic community, for it is through his reliance on the mystical tradition and his evolving relationship to the higher worlds that he influences the attitude of his congregation to this world.[70] Historical and literary evidence, both supportive and hostile, shows the centrality of the doctrine of the tsadik in all areas of hasidic existence. From the eighteenth to the twenty-first centuries, it has embodied the distinctiveness of mystical-charismatic leadership, its potential for spiritual and social creativity, and the alterations of the bounds of earthly experience entailed by its mystical positions.

---

[69] On messianic leadership in 20th-century Habad hasidism, see Elior, 'The Lubavitch Messianic Resurgence'; Berger, *The Rebbe, the Messiah, and the Scandal of Orthodox Indifference*; and Greenberg, 'Redemption after the Holocaust'. For several tragic manifestations of hasidic leadership in the 20th century, see Piekarz, *Ideological Trends* (Heb.); Schweid, *Between Destruction and Salvation* (Heb.).

[70] Testimony to the complexity of the tsadik experience can be found in Elior, 'Changes in the Religious Thought of Polish Hasidism' (Heb.), and Assaf, 'My Small and Ugly World' (Heb.).

ELEVEN

Mystical Spirituality and Autonomous Leadership

God said to him: 'Leave the world of awe, you need not be so punctilious. Better occupy yourself with *devekut* and doing My will. Let awe be secondary for you, for I will be with you . . .'. Awe was no longer the boundary and precaution, but rather love was primary.

Zikhron zot, 'Shemot', 43

H ASIDIC leadership took different forms in the different hasidic centres: there were no fixed paradigms for leadership, no procedures for appointment or succession, no formal obligations or duties, and no supervision or sanctions on behalf of the community. Each tsadik had his own approach to the responsibilities of charismatic authority, to the study of kabbalah, and to the mystical interpretation of the world; each had his own approach to the needs of the individual, the community, and the wider world. Some tsadikim were satisfied with a small circle of followers; others headed hasidic courts that attracted thousands of pilgrims. Some stressed mysticism and the dissemination of hasidic interpretations of kabbalistic ideas; others stressed more philosophical works, such as Maimonides' *Guide of the Perplexed*. Some concentrated on studying halakhah; others focused their energies on alleviating material and spiritual distress and assuming responsibility for their followers' material welfare. Some imposed order and a strong organizational structure on their followers; others were more anarchistic in their approach. Some wrote philosophical works and formulated mystical doctrines; others put their creative energies into stories and fables. Some spoke to the masses; others secluded themselves from their followers. The different approaches derived from alternative conceptions of spiritual commitment and social responsibility, differing intellectual orientations, and differences of personality, ability, and spirit, and they led to tensions and rivalries between the different hasidic courts.

From the last two decades of the eighteenth century on, as the teachings of the founders of hasidism began to be published and disseminated, the next generation of hasidic masters continued the tradition of challenging existing ideas. As each developed his own approach, hasidic congregations split again and again. Thus tsadikim were challenged not only by mitnagedim and maskilim but also from within the hasidic world itself. There were vigorous disputes between Barukh of Medzibozh and Shneur Zalman of Lyady, between the latter and Abraham of Kalisk, between Lublin hasidism and Przysucha hasidism, between the hasidim of Kotsk and those of Izbica, between those of Sanz and those of Sadgura, between Bratslav and Shpole, Gur and Alexander, Belz and Munkacs, and, in our own day, between Habad and Satmar, and between Bratslav and all other hasidic groups.

From the later eighteenth century through the nineteenth century, during the period when hasidism was most identified with the leadership of the tsadik, internal and external opposition was rife. The internal polemic focused on modes of leadership, spheres of responsibility, the tsadik's obligations, and the dissemination of the hasidic perspective among the wider public, as well as on approaches to divine worship inspired by the role of kabbalah in hasidic life. From the outside, hasidim faced opposition from the traditional religious community, now dubbed 'mitnagedim', or dissenters—for tampering with the traditional liturgy and introducing the mystical formulations of Isaac Luria; for abandoning traditional leadership models; and for the social manifestations of hasidism that challenged the conventions of traditional Jewish society. They later also faced opposition from those who aligned themselves with the Enlightenment movement, known as maskilim, on the grounds that tsadikism was a conservative, benighted force preventing progress and enlightenment. Note the irony here: the mitnagedim opposed hasidism on the grounds that it threatened the traditional appointed leadership and undermined the unified basis of the Jewish community (a criticism underscored by the fact that young men of learning were leaving the yeshivas for the courts of the tsadikim); the maskilim opposed hasidism on the grounds that it preserved the old order, which needed to be overturned. Even if the mitnagedim were guilty of exaggeration, there is no doubt that hasidism, offering its followers spiritual renascence within a comprehensive social framework, posed a radical challenge to a traditional leadership that saw these spheres as entirely separate. The viciously explicit polemic that runs through the literature of the period testifies to the dissatisfaction, tensions, and anxieties; conflict was inevitable.

Those who accepted the hasidic way did so in response to its focus on the tsadik, but for a variety of reasons. Some were attracted to the tsadik's commitment to undertake responsibility for 'progeny, life, and sustenance', i.e. to the promise of spiritual and material welfare in return for devotion to the tsadik. Some were drawn to the closeness of the hasidic congregation, while others were affected by the spiritual excitement and mystical intensity that

the tsadik generated. Some were attracted by the tsadik's charismatic personality: depth, erudition, inspiration, and wisdom combined with an approach-
able manner, the willingness and ability to help his followers, the power to
work wonders, and the ability to transmit deeply religious messages through
simple stories. Some turned to tsadikim because they had difficulty coping on
their own with the pressures of life. Some were attracted by the tsadik's daring to challenge religious convention, the boundless freedom that inspired
him, and the revolutionary thought implicit in hasidic doctrine; they saw
hasidic innovations as the expression of a new epoch. Some saw themselves as
enrolling in a movement that combined religious renaissance and social revolution and offered a sense of mutual devotion and comradely love. Some
were impressed by the transformations that tsadikim effected in the world
against a mystical and messianic backdrop. Part of the enchantment of the
tsadik for his followers was that he did as he saw fit; he acted without con-
straint in all that affected the hasidic congregation, its spiritual boundaries, its
practical manifestations, and the new social commitments it entailed. It is
true to say that, from the very inception of hasidism, the spiritual horizons
and autonomous decisions of a tsadik on any matter—spiritual, material,
social, religious, mystical, or messianic—became, for his hasidim, an absolute,
incontrovertible standard.

   This chapter considers how the system of leadership by the tsadik developed in the late eighteenth century in the context of Polish hasidism. It
examines the problems that exercised the hasidic leadership of the time—in
particular, the limits on the authority of leadership based on mystical inspiration, and the problem of continuity of leadership in a period that had not yet
engendered dynastic frameworks—and the nature of the relationship between
tsadik and hasidim in the main hasidic courts. More broadly, I shall examine
the significance of the autonomy introduced by mystical inspiration and an
ecstatic approach, and how this extended the limits of the traditional world.
The prime focus will be on the concepts introduced by the Seer of Lublin,
Jacob Isaac Horowitz (1745–1815) and later continued by Mordecai Joseph
Leiner (1800–54), author of *Mei hashilo'ah*, who formed his congregation in
Izbica, a town in Congress Poland approximately 30 miles south-east of
Lublin.[1]

   The concepts developed by these two hasidic leaders crystallized around
the quest to go beyond the limits of reality as revealed within the traditional

---

[1] On the hasidism of Lublin see *Divrei emet*, *Zikhron zot*, and *Zot zikaron*, by Jacob Isaac
Horowitz; on that of Izbica, see *Beit ya'akov*, by Jacob Leiner; *Dor yesharim*, by Hayim Simhah
Leiner; *Mei hashilo'ah*, by Mordecai Joseph Leiner; and *Ne'ot deshe*, by Samuel Dov Asher Leiner
of Boskowitz.

world on the basis of the values and concepts of the hidden world. The ability to do so came from an ecstatic attachment to God that allowed the tsadik to bridge the boundary between heaven and earth and to be attuned to the divine voice in its infinite renewal. The tsadik had access to a hidden reality beyond the revealed reality, a hidden divine will beyond the manifest will. This involved rapt attention to the divine voice in the present—as revealed in the human soul and in the privacy of the esoteric—rather than mere recall of the voice revealed in the past and henceforth institutionalized in the public domain. This personal revelation made the tsadik a source of authority able to establish new limits; on this view, autonomous deliberation and freedom of thought became social and religious desiderata.

*

The Seer of Lublin established his charismatic hasidic leadership on the basis of an ecstatic relationship with God that he conceptualized as 'the fire of love'. 'Nothing is as intense as hasidism at its inception, the fire of His love burns strongly within a person . . . fire blazing in one's heart, the fire of love for God.'[2] In his view, the fire of this love extends to those who follow the tsadik in his devotion: 'And there is a glow around it, for him and for those who gather around him.'[3] The burning enthusiasm of the tsadik's divine love—seen as associated with the burning bush revealed to Moses in the desert, the fire at Sinai, the glow of the holy living creatures in Ezekiel 1, and the sparks emanating from the living divine element—radiates its glow to those who attach themselves to him. It is transmitted through divinely inspired insights into the Torah delivered to his followers with burning enthusiasm, through the ability to work wonders on the basis of an ecstatic relationship with the divine, and through the ability to mould a socio-religious community on the basis of charismatic inspiration.[4]

The Seer of Lublin's approach to leadership manifested quite self-consciously the charismatic authority with which he was endowed. He developed a comprehensive theory connecting his powers of mystical exaltation to social responsibility and public commitment 'personally and for those surrounding', linking the religious duty of the tsadik with respect to the 'fire of divine love' to his duty to his hasidim with respect to the 'love of Israel'. In other words, by virtue of his devotion to God and the charismatic inspiration

---

[2] *Zikhron zot*, 'Mikets', 33–4. [3] Ibid.
[4] On the spiritual innovation of Polish hasidism, see Elior, 'Changes in the Religious Thought of Polish Hasidism' (Heb.) and 'Between *Yesh* and *Ayin*'.

that enabled him to have links with the higher worlds, he was also charged with the responsibility of conveying God's bounty to the masses: 'That which is paramount concerning the tsadik is his devotion to God, but he must also be concerned with the needs of the community.'[5] However, there is a tension between the Seer's view of himself as a mystic (as expressed in his commentary on Psalm 124: 7: 'Our soul escaped like a bird—this means divestment from corporeality, as a bird flutters in the air, unconcerned with this world'[6]), and the responsibility he felt towards his followers, expressed in such phrases as 'to bring down effluence to the world', 'to plead mercy for Israel', and 'to draw down benefits for Israel',[7] or 'for it is the personal duty incumbent upon the tsadikim of the generation constantly to draw down good affects and great acts of loving kindness for the welfare of Israel'.[8] In his consciousness, the tsadik lives in two worlds: the higher world to which he aspires, and the physical world to which he is sent.[9]

The Seer's approach did not go unchallenged. Most famously, his disciple Jacob Isaac of Przysucha, known as the Holy Jew, distanced himself from his teacher on account of his reservations regarding the latter's charismatic leadership. His own approach to leadership minimized the mystical element and the performance of miracles intended to demonstrate the intervention of divine providence in mundane matters such as responsibility for 'progeny, life, and sustenance'. Seeking instead a deeper asceticism, he advocated solitude and intense study so that each person could focus on the unique demands made of him with respect to knowledge of God and the attainment of wisdom. This approach was most famously continued by his disciple Menahem Mendel of Kotsk, known as the Kotsker Rebbe, whose emphasis on the uniqueness of each human being and insistence on absolute dedication to the search for truth led him to advocate elitist intellectual positions and have little regard for responsibility for the wider community.[10]

The Kotsker Rebbe's approach likewise did not go unchallenged. His disciple Mordecai Leiner advocated an approach closer to that of the Seer of Lublin, trying to overcome the limits of reality while accepting social responsibility in an approach that combines love of God and love of mankind. Like the Seer, he maintained the validity of multiple contradictory perspectives, thereby denying the possibility of unitary truth. With the questioning of

---

[5] *Zikhron zot*, 'Vayetse', 19.   [6] *Zot zikaron*, 11.

[7] *Divrei emet*, p. 123 (first and second quotations), and p. 91 (third quotation).

[8] *Zot zikaron*, 204.

[9] On Lublin hasidism, see Rabinowitz, *Between Przysucha and Lublin* (Heb.).

[10] On the teachings of Menahem Mendel of Kotsk see Heschel, *A Passion for Truth*; on the controversies between the 'Seer' and the 'Jew' see Martin Buber's novel *Gog umagog*.

prevailing norms as primary religious values, all religious duty was called into question.[11]

The tensions between the different hasidic leaders and the attendant disputes, divisions, persecutions, and excommunications thus stemmed both from personal circumstances and from conflicting spiritual and social positions related to the mode of a tsadik's leadership and his mystical authority. The Seer of Lublin, and Mordecai Leiner of Izbica after him, found mystical inspiration in the fact of ever-renewed divine speech, its constant newness in itself challenging the traditional limits of truth. They saw the immediate connection to the higher worlds that characterizes charismatic leadership as constituting freedom from mundane perceptions of reality and likewise from accepted frameworks of authority. In their view, the charismatic leader must interpret the nature of divine will for his own time and place. The traditionally sanctified forms were no longer sufficient because they reflected the divine will as revealed in the past; it was necessary to continue the interpretation of the divine will as it is continuously revealed in the present, beyond the overt sense of the Bible and of halakhah.[12]

The Seer of Lublin expressed this duality—the manifest divine will as opposed to the hidden divine will, and the traditional orientation to past revelation as opposed to the iconoclastic openness to ongoing revelation—in terms of the traditional concepts of *yirah* (awe) and *ahavah* (love). Leiner coined new terminology, using *omek* (depth) and *gavan* (hue, or superficial coloration) to characterize the tension between the ongoing spiritual quest and prevailing convention. Both men were trying to contrast a world-view grounded on written texts and their traditional interpretation with an innovative approach based on interpretation of the divine will in the present, and the freedom to interpret its meaning for the future. The first approach recognizes only the established truth—the sanctified text, the authority of the past, the unambiguous halakhic imperative—which must be regarded with awe. The

[11] On Izbica hasidism, see Weiss, 'A Late Jewish Utopia of Religious Freedom' (on the doctrine of religious determinism of Joseph Mordecai Leiner of Izbica); Schatz-Uffenheimer, 'Spiritual Autonomy and the Torah of Moses' (Heb.); and Faierstein, *All Is in the Hands of Heaven*. See also Gellman, *The Fear, the Trembling, and the Fire*. For the continuation of Izbica hasidism in the teachings of R. Zadok of Lublin, see Brill, *Thinking God*; Magid, *Hasidism on the Margin*.

[12] For a 19th-century non-hasidic perspective on Polish hasidism, see *Keter kehunah*, by Alexander Zederbaum, and compare Trunk, *Poland: Memories and Pictures*, 56–66. Also on Polish hasidism, see Aescoly, *Hasidism in Poland* (Heb.), and Mahler, *Hasidism and the Jewish Enlightenment*. For a summary of the state of research on Polish hasidism, see Assaf, 'Polish Hasidism in the Nineteenth Century' (Heb.). Cf. Hundert, *Jews in Poland–Lithuania in the Eighteenth Century*, 241–67.

second approach recognizes the innovative element of the human spirit in interpreting authority renewed in the present: a new revelation, a new exegesis, the product of continuing *ḥesed* and love capable of overcoming all restrictions; a revelation beyond nature and linked to the higher worlds. The contrast is succinctly captured in alternative vocalizations of the Hebrew word used in connection with the revelation of God's eternal word, *ḥ-r-t*: as we have already seen, vocalized as *ḥarut* it implies that it was 'engraved', and therefore of fixed interpretation; vocalized as *ḥerut* it implies 'freedom'. The former reflects the traditional halakhic approach that pertains to the divine will as revealed or 'inscribed', in the conventional sense of Scripture, in the past; the latter reflects the freedom to see the divine will as ever newly revealed in the present. Devotion to God based on *yirah* is grounded in the normative framework of past revelation and its written formulation; devotion based on *ahavah* is grounded in ongoing revelation and the basic freedom to interpret it continually anew.

The normative framework derives from the manifest divine will as revealed in the overt sense of the text and made accessible through an interpretative authority that supplies laws, rules, and limits. In this framework, religious practice is delimited by authorized halakhic tradition. This limits the scope for autonomous decisions and sets out principles that define human obligations as derived from divine command, itself regarded as 'inscribed on the tablets' and represented by the Ten Commandments. The mystical symbols of the normative traditional perception known as *yirah* or *gavan* are described in the Lurianic vocabulary as 'withdrawal', 'vessels', 'judgement', and 'being', all expressions of limitation. According to this perception, human action is limited by the authoritative halakhic tradition: based on limits and obligations derived from eternal divine command and authoritative human legislation, there is no room for autonomous decisions. The alternative ecstatic mystical framework, known as *ahavah* or *omek*, by contrast, offers endless scope to individuals endowed with spiritual inspiration to decipher the hidden divine will in its boundless meanings. The kabbalistic vocabulary for all this is very broad: the terms used include freedom of infinite expansion, breaching of boundaries, mixing of divine and human realms, inspiration of the Shekhinah, love, unification, divestment of corporeality, eruption of enthusiasm, and religious renewal. Whatever the terms used, they are all rooted in the esoteric tradition that the ever-renewed hidden divine will is accessible to those extraordinary and profound individuals who let their spirit pursue it.

The major contribution of the Seer of Lublin to hasidic thought lay in his novel interpretation of the dialectical relationship between the normative system and the ecstatic system that is fundamental to the kabbalistic concept of God. In his view, the normative framework—the Torah and commandments and traditional standards—binds the community as a whole; the tsadikim, as extraordinary individuals granted the power to go beyond the normal limits of perception and devoted to the love of God and of Israel, are committed to an ecstatic framework based on mystical thinking. They must seek out the hidden will of God as continually revealed through human consciousness and establish new standards and new ways for that love to be manifest.

These two frameworks, pertaining to a manifest divine will and a hidden divine will, are in conflict because they reflect a tension between freedom and subservience, between conformity to limits and continuity and the readiness to relinquish convention and encourage renewal. From another perspective they reflect the tension between autonomous deliberation on the mystical meaning of worship as a way of probing the hidden divine will, and acceptance of the normative framework corresponding to the manifest divine will. To put it another way, they define the observance of divine precepts according to different standards. *Awe* respects limits imposed by authority figures in response to the manifest divine will. It recognizes only the heteronomous imperative embodied in the apparent meaning of the written text and adopts a conservative stance respecting the halakhic norm and assent to accepted tradition, grounded in the sanctity of the past. *Love* breaches boundaries and seeks to determine autonomously the essence of the hidden divine will. This attitude generates an individualistic approach to halakhah, calling for a re-evaluation of how a community should best serve God in accordance with the divine will as revealed in the present. On this view, the true spiritual leader—termed by the Seer of Lublin 'the perfect human being'—is the kabbalistic tsadik who determines the divine desideratum for his own era (as opposed to the divine will in the past), and does so from a position of love rather than of awe. He accomplishes this through powers of autonomous interpretation and moral rectitude that enable him to identify spiritual and moral shortcomings, and through his selflessness and devotion in serving the welfare of the community:

God said to him: 'Leave the world of awe, you need not be so punctilious. Better occupy yourself with *devekut* and doing My will. Let awe be secondary for you, for I will be with you . . .'. Awe was no longer the boundary and precaution, but rather love was primary. For it is from love that enthusiasm comes and love always begets more love, and his wish is always to add delight for God may He be blessed . . . Through love he also loves the lovers of God, namely Israel, and desires that He should enhance their welfare perpetually.[13]

[13] *Zikhron zot*, 'Shemot', 43.

The Seer did not seek to impose this position on his followers at large and did not demand that they follow his path. Rather, he sought to act as an individual, representing the community before God and acting as God's emissary to them. The congregation was required to follow the path of awe and to devote itself to the tsadik; the tsadik was required to purify himself through humility and submissiveness and to follow the path of love that overcomes all limits, attaching himself to the higher worlds in order to channel the divine effluence to the lower worlds. For the Seer, the Psalmist's phrase 'our soul escaped like a bird'[14] expresses the soul's yearning to distance itself from the world and become like 'a castle in the air'; but he recognized that the responsibility of drawing down the divine effluence to his followers obliges the tsadik to adopt a this-worldly perspective and to act within the constraints of time and place. The tsadik's spiritual freedom achieves the mystical exaltation associated with overcoming the limits of being and achieving attachment to the divine; however, attachment to the divine implies spiritual and physical responsibility for the members of the community who devote themselves to the tsadik. It requires him to overcome the disparity between himself and his followers and root himself in the real world.

The Seer's esoteric commentaries *Divrei emet*, *Zot zikaron*, and *Zikhron zot* were written as personal notes. They were not intended for publication and were published only many years after his death. *Divrei emet* was published in Zolkiew in 1830 by his grandson, with an interesting introduction relating to the circumstances of the mystical writing of the book. *Zot zikaron* was published in Lemberg in 1851 from an unedited manuscript. *Zikhron zot* was published in Warsaw in 1869 with divisions according to the weekly Torah readings by his great-grandson but without other editorial intervention. In these works, the Seer discusses the areas in which innovative thinking and deviation from the norm are appropriate for those who have ascended to the higher worlds. He frequently quotes the antinomian verse, 'It is time to act for God, they have transgressed Your Torah',[15] which he explains (adapting Mishnah *Berakhot* 9: 5) to mean that the tsadik determines when it is appropriate to 'act for God' by violating the Torah—in other words, when is it permissible to deviate from the existing normative framework of serving God through awe and develop new modes of serving him based on the intimacy of love. Blurring the boundaries between human and divine suggests new meanings for normative texts and for relationships between human beings.

---

[14] Ps. 124: 7.

[15] Ps. 119: 126. This verse was used by the Shabateans to introduce theological innovations; see Scholem, 'Redemption through Sin'.

The Seer contends that the tsadik can decide when 'a precept fulfilled through sin' is the proper way to serve God. It is he who decides when the physical and spiritual responsibility he has for the congregation by virtue of his closeness to God must outweigh the traditional communal structure of rabbis and lay leaders. In other words, the divine inspiration with which the tsadik is endowed entitles him to determine both the hidden divine will as applicable to this time and place and the consequent religious and social implications:

For there is a tsadik who serves God at the level of awe, and there is a tsadik who ascends from this level to the love of God. Respecting love it says [Deut. 6: 6]: 'And you shall love the Lord your God with all your heart' . . . This is the meaning of 'all your actions should be for the sake of Heaven' [Mishnah *Avot* 2] and this is the meaning of the verse 'in all your ways know Him', even in transgressing [Prov. 3: 6, as interpreted in BT *Berakhot* 63*a*]. The meaning of this is that some people, because of their perpetual awe of sin, have no love, for such a person is always worried and filled with awe lest he be sinning in some matter. This is sometimes necessary. But when it is possible to serve through love that is much better, for that is His primary will . . . So, indeed, a transgression for the sake [of Heaven] is a great thing.[16]

The free thinking implicit in a mystical approach allows autonomous determination of spiritual values, including the rejection of the normative framework of awe (meaning fear of sin), in favour of the spiritual-ecstatic framework of love for God:

All your actions should be for the sake of Heaven . . . hence it is obvious that a transgression for the sake Heaven is a great thing. For the sake of His love, that one understands how through this one may sanctify His name, one does not care if there appears to be a possibility of sin. This is what it means to be a man of God.[17]

Now a person who does not want to learn how to move away from awe of sin cannot achieve love . . . For in love one is not concerned; what matters is only the Creator may He be blessed.[18]

The tsadik's capacity for autonomous judgement in consequence of his intimate relationship with God allows him to determine the relative weight of traditional normative elements and novel spiritual elements and to dare to deviate from accepted practices regarding divine precepts as traditionally interpreted:

For out of the love of God, that which appeared to be so sometimes is altered and that is what is called a temporary suspension of the law [*hora'at sha'ah*] which the tsadik considers to be for the honour of Heaven, then it is permissible to transgress certain commandments and that is a sin for the sake of Heaven.[19]

---

[16] *Zikhron zot*, 'Bo', 47.   [17] Ibid., 'Shemot', 44.   [18] Ibid., 'Pineḥas', 124.
[19] *Divrei emet*, 'Ekev', 133.

The feeling of immediate contact with higher worlds permits the tsadik to breach the boundaries of convention and take responsibility for reassessing divine precepts: in the name of divine love and aware of his community's needs, he redefines that which is sin and that which is divinely ordained. This freedom to redefine and reinterpret God's will attracted those who sensed the potential in this new world opening up before them; but among those who feared that this freedom would undermine the foundations of the traditional world it aroused concern. The writings of the hasidic leaders Elimelekh of Lyzhansk, Jacob Isaac Horowitz of Lublin, Abraham the Angel, Meir of Stobnitsa, and Mordecai Joseph Leiner of Izbica all testify to the increasing importance of subjective consciousness in determining how best to serve God. The new exegetical discussions reflected in the writings of the tsadikim redefined the meaning of awe and love, fulfilment of commandment and sin, certainty and doubt, submission and freedom, equanimity and daring, tradition and change. In short, they produced a new conceptual world.

The Seer's teachings did not win universal approval even among his own hasidim. His disciple Jacob Isaac the Holy Jew of Przysucha opposed the Seer's emphasis on mystical inspiration, on serving God through 'love', and on responsibility for the community. He emphasized instead the intellectual tradition, serving God through 'awe', and the responsibility of the individual. His reservations regarding the manifestation of mystical leadership in wonders and miracles were such as to make him leave his master's court. He tried instead to mould a hasidism characterized by individualistic attitudes, rigorous asceticism, and seclusion from the world. Przysucha hasidism was thus characterized by 'awe' rather than by 'love': mystical meditation in preparation for worship, humility, and Torah study following traditional interpretations.

The Holy Jew and his disciples rejected forms of leadership based on the tsadik's concern for the public good and adopted instead a separatist intellectual position in which the status of the tsadik was defined by his mastery of the Torah as the embodiment of truth. The ideal of leadership based on the performance of miracles as concrete public expression of the tsadik's link to higher worlds therefore gave way to an emphasis on the personal path that each individual must create for himself: intensive learning in the quest for absolute truth, and a sequestered and ascetic way of life. The chief exponent of this view was Menahem Mendel of Kotsk, the Holy Jew's disciple known as the Kotsker Rebbe.

However, the Kotsker Rebbe's approach was in turn rejected by his own disciple, Mordecai Joseph Leiner of Izbica. In Leiner's key work *Mei hashilo'aḥ* (the first part of which was not published until 1860, by his grandson, and its second part not until 1922), Leiner rejected the Kotsker emphasis on absolute truth and segregation from the wider community in favour of the approach of the Seer of Lublin. Leiner's departure from Kotsk in 1840 caused Menahem Mendel such pain and sorrow that he withdrew completely from public activity and lived in seclusion for the rest of his life.

Leiner's approach was completely different to that of the Kotsker Rebbe. Whereas the latter aspired to seek a permanent, absolute, and authoritative truth through the uncompromising study of Torah and halakhah, Leiner favoured autonomous freedom of judgement among various truths, in the spirit of the Seer of Lublin. In place of an approach that saw the word of God as 'engraved upon the tablets' (or as we would say, 'written in stone')—signifying one truth anchored in an unambiguous written tradition, definitive and obligatory, grounded in an absolute authority and serene certitude—he read 'freedom on the tablets', signifying the freedom to doubt and to reinterpret any holy tradition and every divine decree. Rejecting the notion of one authority and one truth, he championed the freedom to determine new standards beyond textual limits. Leiner believed that those endowed with inspiration should have the freedom of judgement to mould autonomous modes of worship and expand the human spirit through closeness to God.

Leiner insisted that there was no one unambiguous way to comprehend reality, no one way of understanding religious duty, reading biblical tradition, or serving God—no truth that is valid at all times and in every place. He advocated that adherence to accepted tradition and conventional forms should give way to varying perspectives dependent on the nature of the participants, the intention, circumstances of time and place, and the distinction between ultimate truth and appearances. In his view, man stands before a reality that contains an infinite number of meanings, but lacks a single definitive meaning. There is no assured point of departure or absolute truth, in so far as the divine essence is hidden from human comprehension. Its physical garb is no more than an illusion; human beings do not perceive the depth or variety inherent in the underlying divine authenticity, but only the superficial hue or appearance. To go beyond the superficial hue of manifest reality to its hidden depths, one must abandon the idea of a single truth valid for all times and all places. One must go beyond the overt meaning of Scripture, reject the accepted interpretation of reality, and question one's sense of concrete experience. Only in this way can one decipher the concealed divine will that is ever newly revealed in human consciousness, defining new horizons and new truths.

In *Mei hashilo'ah*, Leiner posits the deterministic assumption that everything is in the hands of Heaven, since the divine presence is the only reality.

Independent existence is an illusion; in truth, all actions are done according to the divine will. 'There is no being in the world except God', and 'God is in all actions . . . Without His will nothing can occur.'[20] 'All actions that you perform come from Him.'[21] 'All actions performed in the world seem to be those of flesh and blood, but thoughts seem to be the action of God: in these sections [of Genesis] God instructs us that the actions are His and the thoughts are from the human side . . . Performing the commandments or not is in the hands of God.'[22]

In this view, God is the direct agent in all human actions; man's apparent free choice is a mere illusion, as human will is predetermined by the divine will, hence all human actions are directed to a hidden divine purpose. Human actions, whether good or bad, are transformed into actions done by virtue of divine will and grace, in so far as 'all is in the hands of Heaven'. The corollary is that human beings have no certain truth; religious apprehension is mainly a process of elucidating the divine will and uncovering the truth it embodies. This reversal of assumptions concerning thought and action and the limits of human and divine responsibility seems to contrast human weakness, mortal nothingness, and intellectual limitations with God's omnipotence, omniscience, and certitude. This constitutes liberation from the conventional normative truths of time and place, obligating one to enquire perpetually into the meaning of the divine will beyond its manifest limits. Given the absolute nature of the divine will and the illusory nature of human action, uncertainty becomes a key feature of human life.

Another way of saying this is that man's essential doubt is the starting point for religious experience; for only through doubt can the apparent certitudes of the world be recognized as illusion. In this conception, absolute certitude can only be ascribed to the divine will. In a world that lacks autonomous substance, man can know only relative scepticism, changing truths, and broadening horizons because 'there is no being in the world except God'. In a world of illusion in which people have no ultimate control over their actions, there remains only freedom over one's spirituality, denial of the authority of flesh and blood, and alternative perspectives on the hidden divine truth (God's will) and the manifest divine truth (the overt sense of Torah and halakhah). The different divine wills are derived from one's mystical conception of the coincidence of opposites or the unity of opposing wills (expansion and withdrawal, ebb and flow, being and nothingness).

But the idea of a multiplicity of divine truths raises difficult questions: the established halakhah, publicly accessible, must stand in contrast to the hidden

---

[20] *Mei hashilo'aḥ*, vol. i, 'Shemini', 34.   [21] Ibid., 'Ha'azinu', 65.
[22] Ibid., 'Vayeshev', 14*a*.

divine will revealed esoterically to privileged charismatic individuals. If there are multiple divine truths, halakhah cannot be the unambiguous expression of God's will.

To summarize Leiner's notion: 'depth' reflects the divine perspective—the boundlessness, the coincidence of opposites, the multiplicity of wills, and divergence from appearances; 'hue' reflects the human perspective within the limits of time and place. Leiner also posits the existence of multiple divine wills. The manifest will corresponds to the simplistic interpretation (*pesher hadevarim*) of the Torah and its divine commandments; the hidden will corresponds to the deeper meaning (*omek hadevarim*), the 'root of life', and 'the utterance of God's mouth'. The manifest will corresponds to an external reality; because it is manifest, it is by definition unambiguous. The hidden will corresponds to an inner reality; because it is concealed it is open to interpretation through spiritual experience. It is the divine will as renewed in the present, heard through many voices and with a multiplicity of meanings. The dual nature of the divine will—manifestation and concealment—is reflected in the ambiguity of the Hebrew root *y-s-f*, meaning both 'to recur' and 'to come to an end'. The term is used in referring to the divine voice at Sinai: 'a great voice not *yasaf*',[23] which has been understood both as a great voice that does not recur (the manifest will); or as a voice that never ceases (the hidden will).[24]

Leiner distinguishes between inwardness and externality, root and hue, essence and garb, freedom and subjugation, not recurring and not ceasing. The tension is clear in his interpretation of the verse 'for man cannot live by bread alone but according to the utterance of God's mouth does man live'.[25] For Leiner, 'bread' represents the manifestation of God's will as expressed in the overt sense of the commandments, whereas 'the utterance of God's mouth' is the ever-renewed word of God, and it is by this that man must live. There is no one truth or single authority; rather, there is a multiplicity of divine wills, a multiplicity of perspectives, doubts, and variations. To limit oneself to the manifest divine will encapsulated in the 613 biblical commandments, to accept the established order and obedience to tradition within the limits of set authority, is to forgo the potential implicit in seeking out the daily renewal of God's limitless creativity. Challenging the nature of reality is the condition for deeper religious cognition and the discovery of truth. Leiner is vigorous in his condemnation of those for whom the manifest divine will is sufficient and who accept an authoritarian conservative interpretation of reality that leaves no room for doubt. Such serene certitude, he claims, is

---

[23] Deut. 5: 19.   [24] See BT *Sanhedrin* 17a.   [25] Deut. 8: 3.

not God's way: 'Jacob wished to live serenely, that is to say, he wished to avoid any act in order not to be affected by any doubt. But this is not God's will in this world.'[26]

Contrasting with this serene and obedient approach of unambiguous certitude—a path unchallenged by any doubt or contention, subtraction or addition, change or innovation—is the obstacle-strewn path of those who seek 'continuous revelation'. Such people wish to respond to the 'utterance of God's mouth', the concealed divine will that is perpetually renewed and requires autonomous discernment. This approach is exemplified in the biblical figure of Judah, who is always searching for timely divine instruction in the quest for inner truth, 'looking to God to show him the depth of truth in the matter'.[27] In order to overcome the surface of illusion in the concrete world, Judah enters dubious situations, acting against the halakhah when he attempts to deviate from the 'rote commandments of men':

This is the root of Judah's life, to look in all matters for the word of God and not to follow the rote commandments of men [Isa. 29: 13]. Even if he acted in a certain way yesterday, today he does not rely on himself, but only that God enlighten him anew with His will. This sometimes obliges one to perform an action against the halakhah, for 'It is time to act for God, they have transgressed Your Torah.'[28]

Responsiveness to God's word, according to this view, is manifested in the willingness to challenge accepted ways and to seek the inner truth through apprehension, insight, and deliberation. This requires rejection of rigid, absolutist interpretations in favour of an autonomous, enquiring position, and sensitivity to changing reality. This position, as formulated by Leiner in his homily on the verse 'for man cannot live on bread alone', as explained above, echoes the Seer of Lublin's distinction between 'awe' and 'love'. It differentiates between the unambiguous truth of the Torah as revealed at Sinai and the truth that is consistent with continuous revelation, according to which human beings re-establish the truth in every generation. In the latter view, Torah is conceived as an open cognitive framework. Contrasting Jacob—who followed a path of awe and serenity, unambiguous cognition, and the rote commandment of men rooted in the past—with Judah, who followed a path of doubt, open, changing cognition based on continuing revelation, and the overcoming of the norm in the name of the love of God related to present and future, Leiner clearly championed the latter:

When the human being conducts himself to avoid any doubt and preserve himself from any evil action, he is in a state of serenity. That is what God told him, that as long as one

---

[26] *Mei hashilo'ah*, vol. i, 'Vayeshev', 15*b*.   [27] Ibid.   [28] Ibid.

is in the body it is impossible to conduct oneself with so much precaution and awe, for God desires the person's actions, for in this world one must conduct oneself according to love and actions that are not so clear-cut.[29]

The proper way, according to Leiner, is to doubt, to question accepted authority, to reinterpret seemingly rigid Torah principles—in short, to deliberate and determine the will of God in changing circumstances and to search for new facets of comprehension and meaning.

The attempt to decipher the changing divine will and to fathom the underlying motives of human behaviour that deviate from the norm are portrayed as the quest for an inner truth, positing a redrawing of the limits of what is prohibited and what is permitted in response to a deeper understanding. It is associated with a readiness to go beyond the illusion of reality to reach a deeper and more complex truth—to perceive the 'depth' behind the 'hue', the expansion behind the contraction, the love behind the awe, and the changing inwardness behind the seemingly fixed externality. On this interpretation, the 613 commandments of the Torah as revealed at Sinai can only be part of the divine will, which by definition is ever renewed; the quest for truth requires doubt and questioning: 'It is through a person having doubt in Torah matters that he attains truth';[30] 'wherever the human being enters into doubt in worshipping God and in matters that require clarity . . . then he is greater than one who avoided doubts'.[31]

Through doubt one can approach an understanding of the true, deep will of God, beyond the halakhic system based on the 613 divine commandments: 'So that one will understand where the deep will of God inclines . . . and one looks to God to show the deep truth of the matter.'[32] At the level of halakhah, discussion revolved around 'sin for the sake of Heaven' or 'temporary suspension of the law'—the idea of abandoning the clear limits of the halakhic system for an alternative system based on the divine will being hidden. Doubt and the need to decide between the will of God revealed in the halakhah and the hidden divine will are associated in *Mei hashilo'ah* with transgressions and connected to the positing of autonomous norms and a readiness to deviate from halakhic norms, as exemplified by sins mentioned in the Bible. *Mei hashilo'ah* discusses this:

The word *bemo'ado* [at the appointed time or place; Num. 9: 13] indicates the place where God illuminates one's eyes. There it is allowed to act even against the principles of the Torah, as is written: 'It is time to act for God, they have transgressed Your Torah' (Ps. 119: 126).[33]

---

[29] Ibid. 14.   [30] Ibid., 'Beḥukotai', 44*b*.   [31] Ibid., 'Toledot', 10.
[32] Ibid., 'Beḥukotai', 44*b*.   [33] Ibid., vol. ii, 'Beha'alotekha', 28*b*.

When it is clear to a person that now is the time to act for God . . . then one must annul the principles of the Torah and only act on the basis of the insight that God gives the person.[34]

This situation sometimes obliges one to act against the halakhah for it is a time to act for God.[35]

A deterministic framework that claims that all is in the hands of Heaven introduces a new element into the discussion about sin. Leiner maintains that, since sinning is apparently done in conformity with God's will, the apparent sin is in reality a hidden *mitsvah*, an act of reparation in response to a divine intention, and therefore to be understood in a way that deviates from the plain sense of things; one must therefore determine the true intention behind the sin. Sins are presented as an individual moral protest, acts done out of deep religious insight that transcends the limits of time and place. Sin, according to Leiner, is relative and subjective. It relates to the agent and to personal inner intent, not to the action and its external interpretation. An action regarded as a sin according to the 'hue', or the divine will revealed in the past, may be seen as the fulfilment of a commandment according to the 'depth', or the divine will in the present or future; the greater the sin, the deeper the hidden divine intention. Biblical sins are therefore interpreted as having deep religious significance, for they are guided by God and express the depth of his intention. The disparity between the assessment of sin according to the overt divine will as embodied in halakhah, and the totally different evaluation according to the hidden will as deciphered by human consciousness (which judges from a novel perspective in changing circumstances), is very clear from Leiner's discussion in *Mei hashilo'aḥ* of the idolatry, sexual immorality, and murder associated with the biblical stories of Judah, David, Zimri, and Amaziah. Acts that tradition viewed, 'according to their hue', as severe sins are reinterpreted, 'according to their depth', as acts performed in response to the true divine will. Perhaps the outstanding example among many is that King David is the scion of the family of Judah despite the latter's involvement in sexual transgressions and murder:

For even though it appears that Perets [ancestor of David, see Ruth 4] acts against the halakhah, as we find with regard to the house of David, God testifies that this is because it is the time to act for God by transgressing the Torah and so, even though the sin of Er appears to be greater than that of Onan [Gen. 38] nevertheless his soul was greater in its depth than Onan's for he was the ancestor of the house of David [in so far as, from a mystical perspective, Judah's quasi-levirate son by Tamar counts as Er's], for the entire construction of the house of David is guided by God through acts which at the time appear to him to be sins, but [in retrospect] it was secretly ordained by God.[36]

---

[34] *Mei hashilo'aḥ*, vol. i, 'Ḥukat', 52*a*.   [35] Ibid. 'Vayeshev', 15*a*.   [36] Ibid. 16*a*.

Mei hashilo'ah emphasizes throughout how assessment of actions on the basis of the overt divine will embodied in the 613 commandments differs from that based on the hidden will 'secretly ordained by God'. The new freedom from the strictures of the traditional world fostered radical ways of thinking and the anarchistic belief that it is precisely actions that deviate from the norm—ideas that reflect autonomous judgement that breaks the bounds of tradition—that express deeper love and responsiveness to the divine will. On this view, acts that seem contrary to religious norms are in fact the articulation of a profound human understanding that goes beyond accepted limits in penetrating the depths of the divine will. The apparent sinner has thus in fact grasped the hidden divine will; its true intention is clear to him from the outset, and not only in retrospect as it is to others.

Leiner expounds this position by interpreting the Bible with the aid of dialectical categories. He posits the norm as the aspect of awe, contraction, overt meaning, and following the letter of the law, in contrast with the suspension of the norm in the aspect of love, breaking bounds, expansion, esotericism, and the quest for truth. The sinning Judah therefore embodies love, depth of insight, and readiness to contend with doubt; Jacob, Joseph, and Ephraim, who follow the commandments and flee from uncertainty, reflect serenity and conformity. According to Leiner, one must distinguish between commandments that are, in reality, hidden sin (Ephraim) and apparent transgressions that are the fulfilment of the hidden divine will and therefore the true commandment (Judah). In drawing the distinction between serene certitude and doubt, externality and inwardness, hue and depth, understanding God's will as revealed in the past and as revealed in the present, and between apparent meaning and the deeper divine intention, Leiner opens new territory for religious creativity.

The paradigmatic ability to penetrate the depths of the divine will and its concomitant of religious renewal are connected, in Leiner's thought, with attentiveness to the living divine voice that changes with time, beyond the inscribed voice set down in the past. This capacity is embodied in the activity of the tsadik, who binds it to freedom of thought and commitment to communal welfare. Whereas the Seer of Lublin emphasized the concrete social and religious manifestations of leadership by the tsadik, Leiner emphasized the supratemporal ideal of spiritual liberty. For Leiner, the role of the tsadik goes beyond community leadership in the concrete sense. Thus, the tsadik understands the deeper meaning of contemporary events. He distinguishes between apparent truth and depth, determines anew the limits of moral decisions, and sees beyond the hue of the revealed divine will to decipher its hidden depth. He embodies the ideal of freedom because it is he who interprets the divine will according to the circumstances of the time, and it is he who possesses the total freedom to determine contextually how best to serve God without consideration for accepted norms. His spiritual insights, derived from divine love, are deemed more relevant than traditional interpretations based on fear of sin; the interpretation of the inspired individual is more worthy than the legalistic approach of the traditional community and its institutions. For Leiner as for the Seer, devotion to God for the benefit of the community as a whole generates the freedom to reinterpret tradition, to give new meaning to sacred texts, and to decide among the fixed and variable manifestations of the divine will in mundane reality. The redemptive power embodied in the combination of refusal to accept the limits of time and space, humility in relationship to the higher worlds, and responsibility for the community's welfare is idealized in the figure of Moses, 'the man of God',[37] the most humble of men and the most exalted, who overcame the limits of time and space and led the people from slavery to freedom:

'She called his name Moses, because I drew him from the water' (Exod. 2: 10): For water lacks all hue, hinting at the simple will. This implies that our master Moses had no will or desire other than for the light of God. He had no personal interest regarding anything, for all his intention was the benefit of Israel . . . Moses had no intention and self-interest only for 'the Lord our God, the Lord is one', which was explicit for him at every moment. Therefore Moses our master was the truly free man, for if he had not been the truly free man he would not have been chosen from all Israel as the redeemer . . . He redeemed Israel because he was exalted in freedom.[38]

The hasidism of the Seer of Lublin and of Mordecai Leiner of Izbica embodied, each in its own way, an intense yearning for intellectual freedom. Both protested against the univocality of traditional reasoning, against the blind affirmation 'we will do and we will hear', and 'the rote commandment of men', and against the authority of accepted tradition. Both demanded recognition of a charismatic leadership that creates a new conceptual world by the power of mystical elevation. Both sought to expand the bounds of the traditional world and to break through its conceptual universe. Both presented a new image of God, stretched between past and present, between the manifest dimension and the hidden dimension, containing a set will and a changing will or a written voice, stemming from the past and embodied in the overt meaning of the text, and a renewed voice, the living spirit of God, embodied in an esoteric reading in the present.

This image of God as having a revealed will and a hidden will, a past voice and a present voice, generated the concept of a religious leader as one who

---

[37] Deut. 33: 1.   [38] *Beit ya'akov*, 'Shemot', 14*b*.

can respond to the divine duality. In this view, a religious leader must yearn for a deep understanding of the divine will. He must listen out for the divine voice renewing itself in the human consciousness. Aspiring to understand the written text containing the divine word, he must strive to break the yoke of tradition that precludes multi-dimensional interpretation and seek instead new insight by daring to doubt and to exercise his own judgement, directed to the general welfare. This constituted rejection of the conservative elements in religious life. It assumed that a leadership detached from narrow personal interests and acting in the name of an expansiveness fired by divine inspiration and religious enthusiasm to transcend boundaries and exercise freedom in the name of the love of God, yet ever conscious of its mission and public responsibility, could revive religious life for the benefit of the whole community and enable the quest for new truths. Religious renaissance and a new interpretation of the traditional world required reliance on a direct connection to the divine will in the present and not only on a mediating relationship grounded in the past. It required recognition of a variable, relative truth, not only a determinate, absolute truth concerning religious obligation anchored in the past. Critically, it required doubts and reservations, not only laws and commandments. Such ideas resonated among a wide circle of followers, but it also provoked hostile reactions.

When the first volume of *Mei hashilo'ah* was published in Vienna in 1860 by Leiner's grandson, Gershon Hanokh Leiner of Radzyn (himself a great halakhic scholar, renowned for having rediscovered the *tekhelet* dye that had been biblically ordained for *tsitsit*), he printed the following comment in large letters in his preface: 'Indeed I know that in several places the words will be hard on ears that have not heard and are unaccustomed to such ideas. Yet I collected them for the benefit of the initiated who know their value.'[39] This explanation did not make Leiner's ideas more acceptable; indeed, soon after the book was published it was publicly burned by hasidim who opposed them. As the scholar of Polish hasidism Aaron Ze'ev Aescoly has written: 'Hasidim of Kotsk attacked this book for the heretical thoughts in the spirit of Shabateanism which they found in it.'[40] None the less, the hasidism of Izbica-Radzyn continued: *Mei hashilo'ah* was supplemented by works written by the author's sons in continuation of their father's path: *Beit ya'akov* by his son Jacob Leiner and *Ne'ot deshe*, by his son Samuel Dov Asher Leiner. Leiner's other disciples, direct and indirect, included hasidic leaders of stature such as Judah Leib Eger and Tsadok Hakohen of Lublin.[41]

---

[39] On Gershon Hanokh Leiner see Magid, *Hasidism on the Margin*.

[40] Aescoly, *Hasidism in Poland* (Heb.), 116.

[41] See Brill, *Thinking God*; Magid, *Hasidism on the Margin*; Liver, 'Paradoxical Elements in the

Of the rigorous hasidim of Kotsk it was said, with some irony, that they sinned in public and performed *mitsvot* in fulfilment of the divine commandments surreptitiously; perhaps this was said of Izbica hasidim too. Their own approach would certainly have been that they were performing God's will because they were doing it with true intent; those who perform the divine commandments by rote, merely following the letter of the law as inscribed on the tablets, are actually falling short of God's will. Only by contemplating the depth of the divine will—listening and responding freely to the renewed divine voice, reinterpreting traditions and giving them new meaning—can one truly serve God.

Writings of R. Zadok Hakohen of Lublin' (Heb.); Elior, 'Changes in the Religious Thought of Polish Hasidism' (Heb.), 402–32.

TWELVE

Israel Ba'al Shem Tov and Jacob Frank
Hasidism and Shabateanism

> I have not attained the character of possessing a set opinion. For whatever I
> see, I see its opposite.
>
> Agnon, *Samukh venireh*, 251

M OVING towards the end of our discussion regarding the spiritual and
social characteristics of hasidism, let us now go back to early hasidism
and examine its relationship to the Shabatean world of the Frankist movement.[1] Like hasidism, this movement also developed in Podolia and Galicia
in the second third of the eighteenth century and caused profound change in
the Jewish world.

Both movements were revolutionary in their socio-religious character.
They arose at roughly the same time, and their founders, Israel Ba'al Shem
Tov and Jacob Frank, were born and lived in geographical proximity. They
had similar socio-cultural backgrounds, similar occupations, and great
charisma. Both had visionary inspiration that made them imaginative and creative. Both had the ability to communicate ideas through stories, and to win
followers by wonder-working; both were credited with magical powers, and
used their gifts to cure physical and psychic maladies, being designated
'masters of the Divine Name'. Both drew deeply on kabbalistic tradition to
illuminate the material world in the light of the sublime. Both were deeply
interested in their dreams and visions and both recounted them as autobiographical experiences, engaging their listeners and drawing them into their
circle of followers and disciples. Both had mystical experiences that led them
to new religious insights regarding the messianic era and inspired them to
propose a new conceptual world.[2] Neither teacher codified his doctrine,

---

[1] In the 18th century the followers of Jacob Frank were considered Shabateans; 'Frankist' was
a 19th-century designation. See Elior, 'Sefer divrei ha'adon' (Heb.), 482 n. 20.

[2] The Ba'al Shem Tov's experience of ascending to heaven in order to struggle against the tra-
vails of exile (represented by Satan) and to hasten redemption (as represented by asking the

though their innovations are to some extent preserved in letters and in spiritual handbooks compiled from their words by members of their respective circles. Yet despite their geographical, historical, cultural, spiritual, and socio-religious similarities, these two creative giants led their followers in very different directions.

The Ba'al Shem Tov's experience of closeness to God and contact with the higher worlds enabled him to establish new horizons for human apprehension. Through the power of mystical illumination, he revolutionized the conceptual underpinnings of religious thought on language, reinterpreting kabbalistic tradition to create a bridge that spanned the boundary between the divine and the human. While remaining within the orbit of traditional Jewish values, this reconceptualization necessarily led to the development of new patterns of social authority and responsibility and new social frameworks. Jacob Frank, by contrast, used his mystical inspiration to subvert kabbalistic tradition and eschatological expectations and to undermine the foundations of the traditional world. His nihilistic approach fostered anomie and anarchy.

Both men grew up in the eighteenth century in an area that was influenced by the mystical tradition and its multivalent symbols. It was a period in which Shabatean fervour forged new links between kabbalah, messianism, mysticism, anarchy, and nihilism.[3] Both men were inspired by the intensity of the kabbalistic corpus and a messianic vision that incorporated elements of the

---

messiah about the time of the redemption), is related in *Igeret hakodesh*, a letter he wrote to his brother-in-law, Gershon of Kutow. The text is translated into English in Jacobs (ed.), *Jewish Mystical Testimonies*, 148–55, and in Rosman, *The Founder of Hasidism*, 106–8. Jacob Frank's numerous promises to his followers concerning the redemption, viz. that all his actions were concerned with transforming exile into redemption, are preserved in his autobiography *Divrei ha'adon*.

[3] On the anarchy and nihilism that marked the growth of Shabateanism see the testimony of Thomas Coenen, an eyewitness to the consolidation of the movement in Smyrna, whose *Ydele verwachtinge der Joden getoont in den persoon van Sabethai Zevi* (Vain Hopes of the Jews Revealed in the figure of Shabetai Tsevi) was published in Amsterdam in 1669. Coenen was a priest appointed by the Calvinist Church of the Netherlands to the Dutch merchants in Smyrna, where he worked from July 1662 to 1668. His chronicle is the most reliable source on Shabateanism from its inception. See Scholem, *Sabbatai Ṣevi*, 105–11, 139–50, and index s.v. Coenen and Kaplan's introduction to *Ydele verwachtinge der Joden*, 16–18; on the bibliographical history of the chronicle see ibid. 21. For the intellectual background to Shabatean thought in the 18th century, see Scholem, 'Redemption through Sin', *Studies and Sources on the History of Shabateanism* (Heb.), and *Sabbatai Ṣevi*; see also Heilperin (ed.), *The Jewish Community in Poland* (Heb.); Scholem, *Studies on Shabateanism* (Heb.); Perlmutter, *Jonathan Eybeschuetz* (Heb.); *Hakhronikah*, ed. Levine; Liebes, *The Secret of Shabatean Faith* (Heb.); *Divrei ha'adon by Jacob Frank*, ed. Elior; and Elior (ed.), *The Dream and its Interpretation* (Heb.).

ancient *heikhalot* and *merkavah* mysticism.[4] The traditions on which they drew discuss pre-historic beginnings and the meta-historic end, as well as the mutuality of the manifest and the hidden. They also consider the esoteric image of God as interpreted mythologically in terms of creation and destruction, holiness and impurity, unification and separation, and combination and dissolution. Kabbalah deals with the mystery of emanation and creation in the hidden world and the mystery of exile and redemption in the revealed world. It discusses effusion and contraction, freedom and subjugation, the divine and the satanic, the overt sign and the occult signified, and deals with the limits of insight and knowledge and what lies beyond them. Kabbalistic texts thus consider the divine potential for causing chaos and destruction as well as for creating life. They convey ecstatic inspiration, conceptual depth, nihilistic relativism, and spiritual and social creativity. The mythical and magical dimensions in the mystical tradition nourish the sublime, sacred, and expansive, but also the grotesque, profane, and constraining.

The Ba'al Shem Tov and Jacob Frank were both influenced by kabbalah in their ideas of how manifest reality relates to exile and concealed reality to redemption, and likewise in their conceptions of the relationship between God and man. They were influenced by the same literary sources and ideological background but with very different consequences, and they came to represent totally different aspects of the dialectical coincidence of opposites implicit in kabbalistic tradition.

*

The Ba'al Shem Tov was born in Okop, Podolia, at the beginning of the eighteenth century; Jacob Frank was born in Korolowka, Podolia, in the second decade of the century.[5] Both were thus born in a geographical area

---

[4] The major concern of *heikhalot* and *merkavah* literature, written after the destruction of the Temple in 70 CE, is to describe the attributes of the celestial sanctuaries and the divine chariot throne, and the eternal divine worship of the angels who serve it. The liturgy sung by the angels was recited by mystics who were known as 'Descenders of the Chariot'. This literature is collected in Hebrew and Aramaic in Schäfer (ed.), *Synopse zur Hekhalot Literatur*; parts are available in English: see Alexander, 'The Hebrew Apocalypse of Enoch'. On *heikhalot* literature see Scholem, *Major Trends*, 40–79; Elior, *The Three Temples*, 232–65.

[5] Frank's birth date is variously reported as 1712, 1720, and 1726; evidence connected with writs of excommunication points to either of the first two as most likely, though the most frequently cited date is 1726. Concerning his birthplace there are also conflicting versions: Shmuel Agnon, one of the fathers of Hebrew literature and well versed in the Jewish history of Podolia and eastern Galicia, asserts that Frank was born in the Korolowka neighbourhood in his own home town of Buczacz (*The City and the Fullness Thereof* (Heb.), 214), rather than in Korolowka in Podolia (Kraushar, *Frank and his Congregation*, 47).

marked by the effects of Shabateanism: Podolia was ruled by the Ottoman Turks from 1672 to 1699, and Shabateanism was then rife in the Ottoman empire. The Jews, who enjoyed equal rights in the Ottoman empire both in theory and in practice, maintained commercial contact with their brethren: Jews from Podolia traded with Turkey and the Balkans, both strongholds of Shabateanism, and members of Shabatean circles in Smyrna, Salonika, Istanbul, and Adrianople passed through Podolia to and from Galicia and Poland. Both the Frankist movement and the hasidic movement thus developed in an area very much exposed to the influence of kabbalah-inspired Shabateanism.[6]

Shabateanism was a major source of conflict in the Jewish world of the early eighteenth century. Among the events that left their mark on the Jewish community was the apostasy of the believers in Shabetai Tsevi (1626–76), known in Turkish as Donmeh,[7] in Salonika under the leadership of Barukhyah Russo (1677–1720). The excommunication issued against them in 1714 by the rabbinical court of Constantinople was well known throughout the Jewish world but was not effective. As the author of *Beshreibung fun shabatai zvi*, Leib ben Ozer of Amsterdam, wrote in 1718, 'There are a great number of believers in Shabetai Tsevi in Salonika studying kabbalah and engaged in every evil transgression.'[8] Shabatean teachings were not restricted to the Salonika community; testimonies from various Shabatean circles in Podolia indicate that they were circulating there from 1722.[9] The polemic of Moses Hagiz (1671–1750) against Nehemiah Hayon (1650–1730) in the second and third decades of the eighteenth century, culminating in Hayon's excommunication in 1713 and again in 1726 and in the publication of numerous books about the dispute, was well known in the wider Jewish community.[10] In 1725 came the first of many accusations of Shabateanism levelled against Jonathan Eybeschuetz (1695–1764), rabbi of Prague, following the publication of *Va'avo hayom el ha'ayin*, which Shabateans and some of his disciples attributed to him; serious allegations, excommunication, and

[6] For historical background, see Balaban, *On the History of the Frankist Movement* (Heb.); Brawer, *Galicia and its Jews* (Heb.), 197–275; Heilperin, *Records of the Council of the Four Lands* (Heb.); Gelber, 'History of the Jews of Brody' (Heb.); and Weinryb, *The Jews of Poland*, 236–61.

[7] 'Turncoat' or 'apostate'; they themselves used the Hebrew term *ma'aminim*, 'believers'. See *EJ* vi. 148–52, s.v. 'Doenmeh'; *Shirot vetishbahot*.

[8] *Sipur ma'asei shabetai tsevi*, 126, 189–90.

[9] See Scholem, 'Barukhyah, Head of the Shabateans in Salonika' (Heb.), 343, 375–6; Agnon, *The City and the Fullness Thereof* (Heb.), 213–15.

[10] See Carlebach, *The Pursuit of Heresy*, 8–10 (the whole book is about the polemic between Moses Hagiz and Nehemiah Hyon). See also *Shever poshe'im* by Moses Hagiz, against Hyon, Abraham Cardozo, and Solomon Ayalon.

rabbinical court decrees followed.[11] *Ḥemdat yamim*, a book published anonymously in 1731 and which gained great popularity, was by 1732 regarded as a dangerous Shabatean text. At the same time the Italian scholar Moses Hayim Luzzatto (1707–47) was persecuted on account on his mystical works *Adir bamarom* and *Zohar tinyana* (literally, 'second Zohar'). His claim that they were inspired by heavenly mentors led him to be accused of Shabateanism, and in 1730 the rabbis of Brody excommunicated him. Forced to leave Italy, he sought refuge in Frankfurt, but in 1735 his books were interred in the Frankfurt cemetery. He continued to Amsterdam before leaving for Acre in Palestine in 1743.[12]

Controversy over Judah Leib Prossnitz, the Shabatean mentor of Jonathan Eybeschuetz, and the prolonged campaign of Jacob Emden (1697–1776) against the latter in the 1750s further increased the spread of polemical publications directed against Shabateans, as individuals and as a group. They were excommunicated repeatedly by communities throughout the Jewish world; indeed, many documents of the Va'ad Arba Ha'aratsot pertain to the anti-Shabatean polemics of the era. The intensity of the storm aroused by suspicions and accusations of Shabateanism is clear not only from the works of Eybeschuetz, Emden, Hagiz, and Hayon, but also from the journals, letters, and memoirs of their contemporaries—Moses Hayim Luzzatto, Leib ben Ozer, sexton of the Amsterdam congregation and author of *Sipur ma'asei shabetai tsevi* ('An Account of the Doings of Shabetai Tsevi'), Dov of Bolechow, author of *Divrei binah* ('Words of Wisdom'), the storyteller Abraham of Shargorod, and various travellers. All had much to say on the matter.

The Shabatean crisis climaxed in 1759 when Jacob Frank and hundreds of his followers underwent mass baptism in Lvov.[13] This development vindicated those rabbis who had argued that Frank and his Shabatean followers were not to be considered Jewish.[14] But the events that culminated in the

[11] See Perlmutter, *Jonathan Eybeschuetz* (Heb.). On persecution of Shabateans, see Carlebach, *The Pursuit of Heresy*; Schacter, 'Rabbi Jacob Emden'; id., 'Motivations for Radical Anti-Shabateanism'; Liebes, *The Secret of Shabatean Faith* (Heb.); Oron, 'The Book *Gehalei esh*' (Heb.).

[12] *Igerot ramḥal*, in Ginzburg, *R. Moses Hayim Luzzatto and his Contemporaries*, 18–40, 257–76, 283–91, 325–30, 409–16.

[13] Until its annexation by the Ottomans in 1672, Podolia was part of Lvov province. On the baptism in Lvov see *Hakhronikah*, ed. Levine, §48; Kraushar, *Frank and his Congregation* (Heb.), i. 190–1; Brawer, *Galicia and its Jews* (Heb.), 267. Dov Ber Birkental (1723–1805) describes in his *Memories*, ed. Vishnitzer written in the late 18th century, his participation in the public debates that preceded the conversion.

[14] According to Emden in *Sefer shimush*, 82*b*; Balaban, *On the History of the Frankist Movement* (Heb.), ii. 269, and hasidic tradition, on which see below.

public conversion of 1759 had started three years previously, in 1756; once the Shabateans illicit behaviour had been exposed, the Jewish communal authorities had persecuted and humiliated them, and worse. Thus, revelations of orgies and other wild behaviour by Frank's followers in Lanzkron, Podolia, under the influence of Donmeh practices in Salonika, led to accusations and persecution of suspected Shabateans and bans of excommunication against Jacob Frank. Public disputations between Frankists and rabbis in 1756/7 in Kamieniec-Podolski, the capital of Podolia, also had a major impact. Deprecating the Talmud as falsehood and superstition, the Frankists, who wanted to take revenge on the rabbis who had persecuted them, confirmed the veracity of Christian blood libels; ecclesiastical support for their position led to public burnings of the Talmud in Kamieniec, Lvov, Brody, Zolkiew, and other Jewish communities in eastern Galicia and Podolia. The Shabateans, with major concentrations at this time in Busk, Rogatyn, Nadworna, and Podhitza in Podolia, sought further recognition and protection from Church and state from the accusations brought against them by Jews. They notified the Church authorities that about a thousand men, led by Jacob Frank himself, would be baptized, and demanded the right to separate existence as Christians with a Jewish identity. Their demands included the right to marry exclusively among themselves; to observe both Saturday and Sunday as the sabbath; to abstain from eating pork; to retain traditional Jewish dress, including sidelocks and beards; to retain their Jewish names together with their new Christian names; and to possess works of kabbalah.[15] They also demanded a distinct area of settlement in eastern Galicia where they could keep their separate identity and traditional habits. The demand to retain classic Jewish signs of identity even after conversion indicates the Frankists' conflict between their inner world and the external world, between the reality of Jewish exile and the desire for redemption and freedom to live according to a new world order that had started with Shabetai Tsevi. They sought to express their spiritual freedom by embracing Christianity in a very superficial way while still regarding themselves as Jews but along anomic, anarchistic Shabatean lines. Their demands, which were intended to secure the shelter of the Church against Jewish excommunication and persecution, but which lacked the depth of true religious intention, were published by the Church in 1759 and distributed widely, causing huge consternation among Jews and Christians alike, but they were ultimately rejected: baptism had to be unconditional in order to merit the protection of the Church.[16] In the

---

[15] Balaban, *On the History of the Frankist Movement* (Heb.), ii. 206–7.

[16] See Kraushar, *Frank and his Congregation* (Heb.), 133–5, 190–1. See also Balaban, *On the History of the Frankist Movement* (Heb.), ii. 276–9; Elior, 'Sefer divrei ha'adon' (Heb.), 547;

autumn of 1759 Frank and hundreds of his followers converted to Christianity in public ceremonies in Lvov and Warsaw.

These dramatic events, which took place in the public arena (about thirty rabbis, led by Hayim Cohen Rapaport of Lvov, participated in the Lvov disputation in the summer and autumn of 1759), challenged the equanimity of the Jewish population in Podolia and Galicia. Many joined Shabatean circles. Among them were Hayim Malakh and Jacob Vilna, who went on to disseminate the radical Shabatean doctrines emanating from the circle of Barukhyah Russo and Samuel Primo. Many others, already influenced by the personalities and teachings of Shabetai Tsevi, Nathan of Gaza, Abraham Cardozo, and the circle that produced *Ḥemdat yamim* in Salonika, were further affected by the personalities and publications of the circle of Jonathan Eybeschuetz, and by Eybeschuetz's son Wolf, who in 1760 announced himself as a Shabatean prophet, converted to Christianity, and lived in Dresden as the head of an influential group of Jewish Christians.[17] In this way the Shabatean movement blurred the external boundaries of Jewish identity and also undermined the internal unity of the Jewish community.

From investigations conducted by the rabbinic court in Satanow, affirmed by the Va'ad Arba Ha'aratsot in 1756, and partly documented in the books of Jacob Emden, we learn the scope of Shabatean activities in Podolia. The investigations revealed that because the Shabateans believed that Shabetai Tsevi was the messiah and that the messianic era had therefore begun (as noted above, they in fact called themselves *ma'aminim*, 'believers'), they rejected the Torah—which they called the Torah of Creation, or the Torah of the Tree of Knowledge—on the grounds that its laws governing the permitted and forbidden were relevant only to the period of exile, which had ended with the advent of the messiah. They sought instead to live according to the Zoharic doctrine of an eschatological Torah of the Tree of Life, or Torah of Emanation—a Torah for the messianic era, when the categories of permitted and forbidden would lose their relevance; since only good would prevail, eternal life would be the legacy of all, and there would be no death and no evil. People would live according to the Torah of the Tree of Life and would be transformed into angels; the biblical commandments would have no relevance in this mystical, messianic new world. Many of these ideas appear to have been a reaction to the hardships of exile: the ardent desire for liberation inspired far-reaching changes in religious thought and practice. The concepts

Hakhronikah, ed. Levine, sects. 48, 60–1; *Divrei ha'adon*, §903. On the meaning of conversion in the historical context of 18th-century Poland see Teter, 'Jewish Conversions to Catholicism'.

[17] Liebes, *The Secret of Shabatean Faith* (Heb.), 77–102. Cf. Schacter, 'Motivations for Radical Anti-Shabateanism'.

they adopted had a broad theoretical basis in kabbalistic literature, starting with *Ra'aya mehemna* and *Tikunei zohar* from the Middle Ages and continuing in the sixteenth century with the introduction to Hayim Vital's *Ets ḥayim*, which attempted to redefine the relationship between halakhah and kabbalah. But only in Shabateanism was the Torah of the Tree of Life treated as a Torah for the present. The religious anarchy espoused by Shabatean messianism called for a teleological 'sanctification of sin' and created an antinomianism totally antithetical to the foundations of Jewish tradition.

The Shabatean doctrines disseminated in Podolia in the early eighteenth century gained broad acceptance. Almost certainly, the popularity of the nihilistic and anarchistic Frankist ideas that promised a different kind of world was connected to the hardships of Jewish life in Podolia and Galicia at that period. Quite apart from the economic suffering that accompanied the wars and disorder of the times, Jews faced opposition from the Church and hatred on the part of the population; they were accosted with blood libels[18] and subject to oppressive edicts and terrible persecutions, antisemitic literature, and deprivation of every human right—a truly deplorable situation.[19] This raises the question of whether powerlessness to change external circumstances encourages people to seek relief in the infinite significance and hope of messianic belief.

The 1750s found both the Ba'al Shem Tov and Jacob Frank active in Brody, Satanow, Kamieniec, Jazlowitz, Kosow, and Miedzibhoz in Poldolia.[20] Evidence for this is to be found in *Shivḥei habesht* and in Jacob Frank's teachings as they have come down to us in such works as *Divrei ha'adon* and *Hakhronikah*.[21] As we have seen, the hasidim of the Ba'al Shem Tov were themselves suspected of Shabateanism. From the 1770s on they were persecuted and excommunicated for this reason, even though their outlook and way

---

[18] Thirty-two blood libels were recorded in the 18th century in the areas where Frankism was gaining ground, and 2,000 young Jewish women were baptized between 1730 and 1820 (Balaban, *On the History of the Frankist Movement* (Heb.), i. 92). The phrase 'blood libel'—the accusation that Jews ritually murdered Christians in order to obtain blood for religious rites—recurs in different contexts throughout European history but does not, so far as I am aware, appear in any English dictionary. It is one aspect of the demonization of Jews in literature, in trials, and in public debates and ceremonies which characterized the period. See e.g. Guldon and Wijaczka, 'The Accusation of Ritual Murder in Poland'; Hundert, *Jews in Poland–Lithuania in the Eighteenth Century*, 72–6.

[19] This is described and documented in detail in Balaban, *On the History of the Frankist Movement* (Heb.), Brawer, *Galicia and its Jews* (Heb.), and Hundert, *Jews in Poland–Lithuania in the Eighteenth Century*, 72–5.

[20] See Gelber, 'History of the Jews of Brody' (Heb.).

[21] On *Divrei ha'adon*, see Shmeruk, 'The Book *Divrei ha'adon*' (Heb.).

of life were very different from those of the Shabateans. The error is easily explained by the proximity of time, place, and sources of inspiration. The traditional communal leadership feared any divergent organization, and any attempt to replace the established ritual practices of Ashkenaz with kabbalistic liturgies and rites. Hasidim felt that the latter offered a new spiritual intensity, which by giving access to a world beyond the world of concrete reality offered freedom from the constraints of subjugation and exile; but the rabbis opposed it as a sign of rebellion against communal authority. All those claiming kabbalistic inspiration were opposed as sectarians and apostates, whatever they called themselves; but in fact hasidism and Shabateanism were vastly different in their ideas and goals and in their attitude towards the traditional world.[22]

Several hasidic legends reflect the complex relationship between Shabateanism and hasidism. One tells how the Ba'al Shem Tov died in 1760 of a broken heart because the circumstances that led to the Frankist apostasy of 1759 caused him great grief. Nahman of Bratslav, the Ba'al Shem Tov's great-grandson, wrote: 'They say in the name of the Ba'al Shem Tov that he suffered two perforations in his heart because of the Shabetai Tsevi affair and that is why he passed away.'[23] The precise context lends itself to several interpretations of the cause of his death: whether it was 'sorrow and pain', or an attempt to make reparation in the higher worlds for Frank's apostasy. In any event, various traditions connect the Ba'al Shem Tov's death with events pertaining to Shabateans and Frankists. *Shivḥei habesht* discusses a variety of interactions between Shabateans and hasidim in the Ba'al Shem Tov's lifetime. It emphasizes that the apostasy did not occur on the initiative of the Shabateans but of those rabbis who shamed them and wished to exclude them from the Jewish people:

The aforementioned wicked sect all apostatized because they were treated with scorn and great contempt . . . They converted out of shame, and because of those who apostatized. I heard from our rabbi that the Ba'al Shem Tov said that the Shekhinah wails and says: as long as the limb is connected [to the body] there is hope for a remedy; but when it is amputated there is no remedy for ever; for every Jew is a limb of the Shekhinah.[24]

---

[22] On the connection between hasidism and Shabateanism, see Elior, 'R. Nathan Adler and the Frankfurt Pietists' and 'Hasidism: Historical Continuity'; on the allegations of Shabateanism levelled at the hasidim see Wilensky, *Hasidim and Mitnagedim* (Heb.), i. 62, 66 n. 29, 67 n. 32, 261, 304; ii. 45–6 104–5, 141–3, 151, 178–9. For historical and literary background to the period, see Agnon, 'The Banished One' (Heb.). On contact between hasidism and Shabateanism, see Piekarz, *The Rise of Hasidism* (Heb.).

[23] *Likutei moharan*, i, §207.   [24] *Shivḥei habesht*, ed. Rubinstein, 107–8.

Of all the members of that generation whose words have survived, the Ba'al Shem Tov is the only one to have expressed grief at events that led to the apostasy of fellow Jews, 'limbs of the Shekhinah' despite their sin. A later hasidic tradition likewise stresses the responsibility of the community and its rabbis in precipitating the apostasy from fear of the growth of Shabateanism. This tradition also emphasizes the Ba'al Shem Tov's explicit opposition to this process and the enormity of the tragedy that caused the Shekhinah so much grief:

That cursed sect in their great wickedness totally abandoned the Jewish people and vio-lated the entire Torah deliberately and defiled Israel, for many souls were trapped in their net of impurity. For that reason the holy rabbi R. Hayim Cohen [Rapaport of Lvov] forced them to leave the religion completely. Nevertheless our holy master the divine R. Israel Ba'al Shem Tov saw, when his soul ascended above, that the Shekhinah wails over them and lamented, saying: so long as a limb is attached at least there is hope; now it is severed completely.[25]

There is an earlier hasidic tradition about the complex relationship between Shabateanism and hasidism. It is expressed in a story that reflects the attraction and the repulsion, or the similarity and the difference, between their mystical leaders. It relates to a dream that the Ba'al Shem Tov had about Shabetai Tsevi and addresses the transitions of identity associated with conversion:[26]

The Ba'al Shem Tov also related that Shabetai Tsevi came to him and sought rectifica-tion [*tikun*] and he said . . . that *tikun* is to become bound up together soul and spirit. So he [the Ba'al Shem Tov] began to connect himself to him—carefully, for he was afraid, for he [Shabetai Tsevi] was a great evildoer.[27] Once the Ba'al Shem Tov was asleep and Shabetai Tsevi, may his name be obliterated, came to the Ba'al Shem Tov in his sleep and tempted him to apostatize, God forbid, and he threw him down with a mighty throw until he fell into the deepest She'ol.[28] The Ba'al Shem Tov saw where he was, and real-ized that he was on the same tablet [meaning a table or a place of apostasy and tempta-

---

[25] *Heikhal haberakhah*, 'Ki tavo', 28: 57.

[26] The text that follows is from *Shivhei habesht*, ed. Rubinstein, 133–4. The citation includes additions based on the Yiddish Korets version and the Lubavitch manuscript of *Shivhei habesht* and scholarly references cited there. Cf. the manuscript version in Mondshine's facsimile edition, p. 98.

[27] The Yiddish text adds: 'If one wants to effect rectification, it is necessary to examine one's place, to determine in which deep husk one is found, and he [the Ba'al Shem Tov] did not want to enter such a place of danger.'

[28] The text is not clear as to who threw whom: Abraham Rubinstein, Joseph Weiss, and Ben-Zion Dinur maintain that it was the Ba'al Shem Tov who did the throwing, but the Yiddish ver-sion states explicitly that it was Shabetai Tsevi. From studying the Hebrew and Yiddish, Yehudah Liebes and I have inferred that it was indeed Shabetai Tsevi who threw the Ba'al Shem Tov.

tion to convert] as Jesus. The Ba'al Shem Tov recounted that he [Shabetai Tsevi] had a holy spark, and the Impure Side trapped him.[29] It was learned from the Ba'al Shem Tov how this fall occurred as a result of a great spirit and anger.

The relationship between hasidim and Shabateans continued to be complex after the Ba'al Shem Tov's death in 1760 because the actions of the Shabatean apostates led by Jacob Frank continued to affect the attitude towards hasidim. It can be assumed that the persecution of hasidim by the rabbinic and communal establishments from the 1770s on was directly linked to the intensification of fear regarding the spread of Shabateanism through Podolia and Galicia under Frank's leadership.[30]

As outlined in Chapter 7, in 1760 Frank was imprisoned in Czestochowa because incriminating testimony by members of his circle had raised doubts about the sincerity of his apostasy. Even while he was in prison, Frank's devotees visited him and conveyed proclamations and letters to the outside world. From the moment he was released in 1772, and indeed for some time before, he disseminated epistles throughout Podolia and Galicia calling on Jews to convert. Frank's followers wrote:

When he left Czestochowa in late 1772 he sent us, the undersigned, to several towns, including Lublin, Lvov, and Brody, on a mission from him, to proclaim to all fearers of God, that they may know, that a time will come when all Jews will be compelled to apostatize. It is an edict from God Himself, and may take whatever fashion it may be. Whoever will faithfully enter the shelter of faith of the house of the God of Jacob [Frank], the God of Jacob will help, in order not to be lost.[31]

It was in the same year that the hasidim were first excommunicated, and this is unlikely to have been mere coincidence. The first writ of excommunication, issued in 1772 in the name of Elijah of Vilna (the Vilna Gaon), states explicitly that 'the sect of the hasidim is saturated with the heresy [epikoresut] of Shabetai Tsevi'.[32] Most likely, the renewal of Frankist activity heightened communal tensions; the circulation of his calls for apostasy engendered a sharp reaction to any manifestation of kabbalah, hasidism, or Shabateanism. The hasidim, who regarded themselves as faithful Jews, rejected any connection

---

[29] A Lubavitch manuscript has a different version: 'He had a spark of the messiah but was trapped by the Impure Side', meaning that he converted to Islam as a result of the victory of the evil side over the holy side.

[30] On the question of the relationship between Shabateanism and hasidism and a survey of different scholarly views, see Elior, 'Hasidism: Historical Continuity'.

[31] Quoted in Brawer, *Galicia and its Jews* (Heb.), 272. For up-to-date scholarship on Shabateanism and Frankism, see Elior (ed.), *The Dream and its Interpretation* (Heb.), i. 551–80.

[32] *Shever poshe'im*, quoted in Wilensky *Hasidim and Mitnagedim* (Heb.), ii. 96.

to Shabateanism,[33] but for the rabbinic establishment there was no clear demarcation: both were called *ḥasidim* ('pious ones') by their contemporaries. In the eyes of the communal leadership, anyone who modified the accepted Ashkenazi rite by introducing Lurianic practices, occupied themselves with kabbalistic studies without authorization from the community, or disregarded communal authority and participated in independent prayer groups, was to be excommunicated.

These strictures affected hasidim as well as Shabateans, despite the fact that the former identified as faithful Jews committed to the traditional world, albeit with some modifications of ritual. They concentrated on uncovering the divine essence of material reality through devotion to God and contemplation of him in order to redeem the Shekhinah and elevate the divine sparks to their source. In the hasidic view, thought, consciousness, and language link the human world to the divine world; in so far as they are the manifestation of the divine spirit, they link man to God and expand the bounds that limit man in this world. The Shabatean ethos of Jacob Frank was quite different. For Shabateans, the revealed world is devoid of all meaning; the element that connects it to the divine world is hidden from ordinary human beings, a secret revealed only to Shabetai Tsevi and Jacob Frank. Moreover, if daily life is to be lived according to a conceptual world that pertains to messianic reality, then nothing is forbidden and everything is permitted. If the real world is meaningless, then concepts of commandment and sin are meaningless.

Jacob Frank and the Ba'al Shem Tov were clearly charismatic individuals, following Max Weber's definition.[34] In the religious context one can add to the extraordinary qualities in this definition that a charismatic individual radiates a feeling of immediate contact with higher worlds and acts on the basis of knowledge that is not revealed to others. By virtue of this he engenders highly significant changes in the world of thought and the world of action; he may break existing laws, establish new ones, and reinterpret existing traditions. Both Jacob Frank and the Ba'al Shem Tov, endowed with mystical inspiration and charisma, revived elements of kabbalistic tradition and its messianic themes. Their intentions, however, were totally different.

Frank's autobiographical composition *Divrei ha'adon*, narrated by him but written down by his followers, presents him as a fearless individual with hidden power—a claim that resonated precisely because of the Jews' tendency to fearfulness as a minority community living in exile. Claiming to be the sole

---

[33] See Wilensky, *Hasidim and Mitnagedim* (Heb.), ii. 178–9; further allegations that hasidism was a form of Shabateanism can be found in the writings of its opponents collected by Wilensky: see ibid., i. 62, 66, 67, 261, 304 and ii. 45, 46, 104, 141, 143, 151, and 178–9.

[34] See Ch. 1 n. 1 and Ch. 10 nn. 6 and 8 above.

repository of true kabbalistic powers, he convinced his followers of the existence of terrifying mystical and mythological beings that he alone could see
and control; the price of his protection was total submission. In his passion to
overthrow the world order based on the laws and values governed by the Tree
of Knowledge and its standards of good and evil, Frank posited an order governed by the Tree of Life—a world beyond the constraints of life and death,
forbidden and permitted, good and evil, and accessible only to his believers.[35]

The Ba'al Shem Tov, by contrast, focused his new order on the all-
embracing divine reality that animates the universe and illuminates it with
the light of *ḥesed* (mercy) and greatness, binding together the totality of
revealed elements in a hidden unity. For him the visible world was inseparable from the divine spirit that animates it, and accordingly he required his
followers to seek at all times the divine infinity lying beyond the limits of corporeality. He expressed in a variety of ways the idea that the visible world,
detached from its divine source, is an illusion, the product of limited understanding; the only genuine Being is God.

From the perception of reality as God-suffused, of the entire universe as
one unifying Being rather than an amalgam of independent particulars, came
the idea that every human being can perceive God and have access to him at
all times and in every place and every way. Attaining this status requires a
sense of detachment from the manifest world and concentration of thought
on the truth of reality from the divine vantage point. It is not dependent on
esoteric knowledge, but rather on a conscious focusing on the elements
common to the divine spirit and the human spirit. These are articulated in
language—in words themselves, and in lucidity of thought. The infinity of
language—perpetually preserving, perpetually creative—is the element common to all and hidden from no one; in the consciousness of the Ba'al Shem
Tov, it became the bridge between God and man. In his own words, Being
draws on the continuous flow of the letters of divine speech that are the root
cause of existence: 'in each letter there are worlds, souls, and divinity'; each
person comprehends this world and has access to the higher worlds as far as
his thoughts permit. In this way the human being, whose creative spirit and
formative thought is grounded in words, becomes a partner in the divine
process of creation that constantly takes place through the Holy Tongue.
Human language constitutes a window onto the realm of the divine. In order
to facilitate concentration on the ubiquity of the divine presence, the Ba'al

---

[35] See Doktór, 'Jakub Frank'; the text is available in Polish in Frank, *Księga słów Pańskich*, ed.
Doktór. An interim edition of the Hebrew translation by Fania Scholem, *Divrei ha'adon*, was
published in 1997; a partial English translation is available in *The Sayings of Yakov Frank: A
Selection*, trans. H. Lenowitz (Berkeley, 1978).

Shem Tov sought to devote himself to the superior worlds; accommodating the vicissitudes that man perceives in the material world required adoption of divine perspective. The consequence of conceiving God's glory as 'filling the whole universe' was to posit a link between the human spirit and the divine and help man overcome his physical limitations.

Jacob Frank's vision, by contrast, took his followers to a hidden place, a mythological world where they would be assured an eternal life of plenty so long as they followed his teachings unquestioningly. During the transition to this assured imaginary reality, he insisted that his followers should segregate themselves from the rest of society and reject the traditional way of life, abandoning the Torah and enslaving themselves to his whims, visions, and demands. This is the story told in *Divrei ha'adon*, *Hakhronikah*, and other Frankist documents.[36]

The Ba'al Shem Tov did not cut his followers off from the traditional world. He did not demand secrecy, blind obedience, or submissiveness, and he did not offer his followers a future beyond the limits of human comprehension. Instead he sought to illuminate existence in this world in the light of the divine spirit, which is apparent to all who want to see it and dispels the enigma of being. In the reality he posited, the state of human being is enlightened by the all-embracing divine being, which he conceptualized as the abundant effusion of *hesed*, divine joy, and sanctity. To parallel this all-encompassing divine immanence, he sought to establish a social order offering 'comradely love' to those he termed 'my men of precious quality'. These groups evolved into hasidic communities—the 'collective' of Bratslav hasidism, the 'men of our peace' of Habad hasidism, the 'beloved comrades' or 'holy communities' of other hasidic groups. His drive to establish communities reflected an important intellectual insight: the world exists only through man's ability to see it and reveal its divine nature. Verbal images of divine encompassing therefore become the foundation of human brotherhood.

The collective emotion of religious brotherhood—the sense of belonging and partnership, mutual responsibility for the community as a group and as individuals, responsibility for a way of life that is at once physical and exalted—ebbed and flowed in different periods, affecting the spread and vitality of hasidism. As with any historical phenomenon, reality did not always match the vision. However, the Ba'al Shem Tov and his successors consistently sought to make tangible the presence of the divine infinity in the material world. They tried to demonstrate the reflection of the sublime in everyday life and to minimize the pettiness that dominates human life through a preoccupation with materialism. They saw their task on earth as

---

[36] See Elior, 'Sefer divrei ha'adon' (Heb.); Scholem, 'Redemption through Sin'.

being to open 'the window of the word' to reveal the spiritual foundations of the material world and apply the divine dialectic to human thought. They strove to understand the hidden essence of the world beneath its apparent form, to explicate the divine coincidence of opposites in relation to the human mind, and to uncover the spiritual unity of material multiplicity. Through the infinity of consciousness and the infinity of language they were able to embody spiritual freedom and bridge the disparity between abstract and concrete.

When applied to the social reality of the hasidic community, the kabbalistic vocabulary of effusion and *ḥesed*, love and devotion, emanation and elevation of sparks, unification and connectedness, tsadik and Shekhinah—concepts that in the earlier mystical tradition had referred to the divine world and its enigmas—became concepts that moulded social reality. From hasidic writings it is evident that some of the concepts took on new significance in consequence of this process. In particular, ideas involving asceticism, selflessness, and submission—ideas associated with increasing the spirituality of that which is corporeal, or transforming being into nothingness—came to be applied to the tsadik, while the ideas involving the continual flow of the divine abundance—overflow and *ḥesed*, emanation and drawing down, or transforming nothingness into being—came to be understood in the context of improving the welfare of the community.

Frank applied the duality of the divine dialectic and the conceptual richness of kabbalistic terminology to himself alone. He presented himself as a divine figure uniting opposites, and arrogated to himself the divine power, infinity, and freedom. His followers were completely subjugated to him, a socially isolated group subject to abasement and alienation in an atmosphere of secrecy, sinfulness, reproof, dashed expectations, betrayal, punishment, and guilt. He imposed a new Shabatean order of nihilistic messianic and antinomian vision, based on the incarnation of divinity in a flesh-and-blood messiah who transcended the limits of life and death. Isolation from the traditional community rendered his believers dependent on his leadership and the inspiration of his vision, in which overt, palpable experience was meaningless and only the hidden and promised had value.

The Ba'al Shem Tov tried to draw the parallel between the divine dialectic and human consciousness. Just as the divine spirit emanates and withdraws, expands and contracts, ebbs and flows, so the human spirit experiences vicissitudes of spirituality and physicality, expansiveness and pettiness. His social ethos, according to some traditions, tended to egalitarianism (as implied by his application of the term 'my precious people' to 'all human beings'), and was directed to broad public dissemination of his teachings rather than secrecy and limited social access: his grandson Moses Hayim Ephraim of Sudylkow reported in his name that 'every person in every moment upon entering the heavenly shrine of love with great cleaving and sanctifying God's name is achieving the divine unity'.[37] Other disciples of the Ba'al Shem Tov report that he said that 'all the members of the community have to be like saints in order to do all their deeds with *devekut* to God';[38] 'every person is surrounded by the externality of this world but when he is ascending then he is divested of corporeality';[39] 'It is well known that [every] person from Israel is a part of the divine being in actuality and can unite himself with God with no partition'.[40] The Ba'al Shem Tov sought to bring people closer through the promise of paternal and fraternal protection in this world, following the notion that 'His [i.e. God's] glory fills the entire earth' accords dignity to the entire community blessed through the tsadik, as later noted explicitly by his disciples: 'The tsadik always has to beg mercy on Israel and on all the existential aspects of the world since this is the divine will of the creator.'[41] The grandson of the Ba'al Shem Tov wrote in the name of his grandfather: '[the tsadik] has to integrate with all creatures and has to connect himself with all the souls as is well known from my grandfather of blessed memory'.[42] As we have seen, Jacob Joseph of Polonnoye drew a distinction between *anshei homer* and *anshei ru'ah* (men of matter and men of spirit), but the absence of this distinction in other hasidic traditions suggests that it was Jacob Joseph's rather than his master's.

The Ba'al Shem Tov described himself as 'a man who lives beyond nature', attentive to the Shekhinah, the 'world of speech', that spoke to him. However, the hasidic ethos did not focus on the Besht's figure but rather on the divine elements that were revealed to him through his mystical experiences, which he communicated to his followers. In *Shivhei habesht*, in the writings of the Maggid of Mezhirech, in the literature of Habad and that of Polish hasidism, it is clear that the divine 'world of speech' can address anyone, and the divine voice is audible to anyone who listens for it. Moreover, every individual should be aware of the divine presence at all times and try to understand the mystical unity of being and nothingness, revealed and concealed, the practical and the sublime, the overt sense and its interpretation. Man should strive for the intellectual and spiritual expansiveness of the

[37] *Degel mahaneh efrayim*, 'Lekh lekha', 12.
[38] Ze'ev Wolf of Zhitomir: *Or hame'ir*, 'Kedoshim', 136a.
[39] Elimelekh of Lyzhansk: *No'am elimelekh*, 'Lekh lekha', 5b.
[40] Menahem Mendel of Vitebsk: *Peri ha'arets*, 'Vayeshev', 22.
[41] Jacob Isaac of Lublin: *Zot zikaron*, 24.
[42] Ephraim of Sudylkow: *Degel mahaneh efrayim*, 'Shelah lekha', 73b.

divine perspective, to go beyond himself by perpetual attentiveness to the divine voice ever renewed in the human mind in order to permit speech and actions that transcend apparent constraints. Those who are unable or unwilling to attain this level may rely on the tsadik, as their emissary in this world and in the higher worlds, to act for them.

The Ba'al Shem Tov described himself ascending to the Garden of Eden, to the realm of the Tree of Life, and conversing with the messiah who promises him that redemption will be nigh when his 'fountains flow outward'[43] through public teaching of the Torah he learned from him. The Ba'al Shem Tov identified himself with traditional leaders: Moses, 'the man of God'; Simon bar Yohai, traditionally regarded as the author of the Zohar; Joseph Karo, whose mystical vision is revealed in *Magid meisharim*; Isaac Luria, as depicted in the introduction to *Ets ḥayim* and *Shivḥei ha'ari*; and Ahijah the Shilonite, as described in the Midrash and in the Zohar. He internalized the ideas found in these works and revived their voice through his person. When he speaks of himself, his connection to the mystical tradition and to the messianic perspective is clear, and likewise his self-perception as both the agent of the community and an emissary of the higher worlds. Traditions about the Ba'al Shem Tov also tend to blur the boundaries between the revealed and the esoteric, between the human and the divine, between the word written explicitly in the past and the word implicitly expressed in the present. He taught his hasidim to examine what is manifest in the light of the hidden and to decipher the duality of existence: 'My master, of blessed memory explained that all concerns of this world have an inner purpose.'[44]

Jacob Frank also focused on duality, claiming to discern the essence and its opposite in every state of affairs, but his overall perspective was very different. He described himself in *Divrei ha'adon* as a serpent-messiah (based on the numerological equivalence of *naḥash* (serpent) and *mashiaḥ*) who kills and gives life, smites and engenders. He further identified himself with the biblical twins Jacob and Esau. Jacob, blessed by his father Isaac as a result of his deceit, fled and struggled, was crafty and tormented, but his future was assured; Esau, demeaned and disinherited as a result of his brother's deceit, lived by his sword, an enemy and powerful avenger who represents the force of the cursed and rejected who have nothing to lose. Jacob Frank took all the stories about Jacob the biblical patriarch as referring to him directly and guiding his path, and all the traditions relating to Jacob's twin brother Esau as directing his messianic activities; accordingly, he called the transition from life in exile to a life of redemption under his leadership 'the way of Esau'. He

---

[43] Prov. 5: 16. *Igeret hakodesh*, trans. in Jacobs, *Jewish Mystical Testimonies*, 150–1.

[44] *Toledot ya'akov yosef*, 'Emor', 395.

likewise identified with traditions about Shabetai Tsevi (whom he depicts as a woman dressed as a man, suggesting an androgynous parallel between Shabetai Tsevi and the Shekhinah as presented in the Zohar); with the antinomian Barukhyah Russo, who led the Shabateans in Salonika; and with biblical figures who are imprisoned or implicated in sin and deceit, rejection and insult, sexual licentiousness, plots, pretence, and disguise. Having abandoned all constraints of culture, religion, and tradition, he was more shameless, guiltless, and fearless than any other Jewish historical figure. He spoke openly about himself, his violent and criminal history in the overt world, and his messianic self-image of perversion in the hidden world.

The fascinating portrait that emerges from *Hakhronikah* and *Divrei ha'adon* reflects a duality, an androgynous identity of power and helplessness, masculinity and femininity, ignorance and esoteric wisdom, shackled prisoner and triumphant regent, hovering between revealed and concealed worlds. A violent streak in his personality yearned to shatter social systems and introduce militaristic rule and institutionalized leadership. There are frequent references in his discourse to disorder and anarchy, and calls for obedience; his followers seem to have been too attached to their traditional upbringing and insufficiently responsive to his anarchistic and antinomian demands. His protean personality takes on new identities, religions, and roles, and combines them in a mythical-mystical duality: the sacred serpent meting out life and death, and the messiah who transcends the limits of life and death. This supra-temporal figure mediates between hidden reality and manifest reality by destroying the established order so that a new reality can emerge in the context of pretence and duplicity. Through mystical language and behaviour that defies rational explanation, he attempts to show how an action that is insignificant when understood from the perspective of the Tree of Knowledge is of great significance when interpreted in the context of the Tree of Life. Frank was the spokesman of anomie, and the embodiment of anarchy, wilfully nullifying the foundations of the world of the Tree of Knowledge with its differentiation between good and evil, permitted and prohibited, commandment and transgression. Making no distinction between spiritual vision and the material world, he called for the abrogation of law and abandonment of the yoke of the commandments: 'All religions, all laws and all books until now, have died'; 'we must honour our master . . . by breaking all laws and religion'.[45]

The Ba'al Shem Tov, like earlier mystics, typically blurred the distinctions between divine and human, reality and imagination, revealed and

---

[45] *Divrei ha'adon*, §219.

concealed. But the mixing of spheres that he envisaged—the dismantling of conventional conceptual structures and the construction of new ones— pertained to the world of thought and inspiration, apprehension and imagination, intention and exegesis, not the realm of practice. Hasidism expanded the domain of spiritual understanding and altered individual consciousness. It presented new categories for comprehending the world through the ability to transcend the self and gain awareness of the nature of the divine through *bitul hayesh* and *devekut*. It showed the value of questioning the nature of the world and the potential for dialectical reversal, but it did not entirely abandon the norms of communal life. The changes it did propose were inspired by Lurianic custom and the kabbalistic tradition; they were made with the intent of elevating standards of performance and sanctifying the encounter with higher worlds, not with the aim of throwing off the yoke of the divine commandments and breaking the law in the mundane world.[46] On the contrary: when the Ba'al Shem Tov said that '*mitsvah* [divine commandment] is related to *tsavta* [Aramaic for togetherness], implying that in obeying divine commandments one achieves togetherness with the divine light',[47] or that 'the individual must connect himself and his thought perpetually to the Creator and thus Kudsha Berikh Hu [the *sefirah* of Tiferet] and the Shekhinah [*sefirah* of Malkhut] and all the worlds are bound together and unified',[48] he bestowed new significance on the religious act.

In contrast with the group involvement in devotion to God that characterized hasidism, Frankism focused on the figure of the leader. Jacob Frank was an unrestrained anarchist who declared openly his freedom from all norms and taught his followers that laws were irrelevant. The absence of law and order among his followers created a vacuum that Frank filled with his own personality. With the abandonment of accepted boundaries and common symbols, he alone became the source of divine authority and the eternal power that commands obedience and submission. He instituted public rituals that gave concrete form to concepts deriving from the kabbalistic tradition. Images found in sacred texts, poems, and legends—images derived from the realms of dream, vision, madness, and kabbalistic myths concerning divine processes (including sexual conjugation among the *sefirot*)—were implemented in a carnival of the grotesque in total contravention of the existing order. In this way, kabbalistic concepts underwent a mystical and cultic ritualization and became the basis for nihilistic behaviour. Hasidic tradition explicitly and obliquely connects the preoccupation with kabbalah with

---

[46] See Elior, 'R. Nathan Adler and the Frankfurt Pietists'.
[47] *Ba'al shem tov al hatorah*, ii. 27.   [48] *Degel maḥaneh efrayim*, 12.

the Shabatean–Frankist breakdown that ensued. Rabbi Tsevi Hirsch of Zhidachov (d. 1831) writes:

I heard from my teacher [the Seer of Lublin] who said about those disciples regarding the affair when the sect caused desecration of God's Name during the time of R. David Segal [late seventeenth century] that this happened because they wanted to attain the vision of Elijah and prophecy and the holy spirit through unifications of names. But they did not resolve their character traits and did not submit their materiality, so that they did not merit it. They concentrated on unifications without purifying their matter and imagined for themselves the highest forms beneath the divine chariot. Thus thoughts of adultery overcame them, may God preserve us. And that is how it happened. So far is what my teacher said. He also said, in the name of the Ba'al Shem Tov, that fools learned this wisdom without power or intelligence or reverence, and that is why they made ideas corporeal, and that is how they left the community of Israel.[49]

Rabbi Tsadok Hakohen of Lublin wrote:

I . . . saw in a printed book by a saintly person a discussion of the sect of Shabetai Tsevi, may the name of the wicked be effaced: what happened to them is the result of their occupation with kabbalah while their hearts were full of worldly lust, and they made the ideas corporeal, so that when they saw phrases about conjugation, embracing and kissing and the like, they fell into an adulterous lust, may God preserve us, until they were exceedingly wicked.[50]

Shabateanism replaced religious norms with a behavioural system derived from a celestial or messianic existence, an era of redemption in which concepts of commandment and sin were inapplicable. This new reality could not be verified independently or empirically because only the charismatic ability of its standard-bearer made it palpable; according to the new messianic tradition, he alone was the link between the hidden and the revealed.

Jacob Frank established a reality among his followers that completely overturned the existing order. Believing that the messianic epoch had already arrived, he introduced models of behaviour that were quite inconsistent with Torah law. He made concrete the messianic idea expressed in the words of the prophet 'For a Torah shall emerge from me',[51] a verse rendered by *Leviticus Rabbah* 13: 3 as 'For a new Torah shall emerge from Me', and founded an order grounded in a divine law stemming from kabbalistic literature in its Shabatean interpretation. Sexual relations that were forbidden by Torah law as incestuous were permitted. He encouraged his followers to respond to his

---

[49] *Sur mera va'aseh tov*, 30a (Lublin, 1912 edn., p. 55); an English edition of this text has been edited by Louis Jacobs: *Turn Aside from Evil and Do Good: An Introduciton and a Way to the Tree of Life* (London, 1995).

[50] *Sefer hazikhronot*, 64. On R. Tsadok see Liver, 'Paradoxical Elements in the Writings of R. Zadok Hakohen of Lublin'; Brill, *Thinking God*.   [51] Isa. 51: 4.

demands in this area by quoting the mystical adages 'incestuous relations are the King's sceptre' and 'there is no incestuous [inhibition] above'.[52] He thus annulled biblical prohibitions and established a reality devoid of shame, guilt, or fear. Laws and norms, except for those of his own invention, were declared meaningless. His followers, educated in the norms of the traditional world, appear to have acquiesced unwillingly; he frequently had to reassure them that in the world of the Tree of Life they would be free from the sway of death. But the price to be paid for the promised partnership in eternity was absolute submission to Frank on earth. In Frankist parable and ritual the ordinary man is helplessly blind; Frank alone is omniscient, seeing beyond the limits of time and place, witness to the existence of another reality to which the limits of life and death, subjugation and redemption, forbidden and permitted, do not apply.

The Ba'al Shem Tov's teaching also ties the human being to the divine being through various links that blur the distinction between them. This is evident from his statements regarding the elevation of divine sparks, from his assertions that 'prayer is conjugation with the Shekhinah' and that the 'world of speech' speaks through man; and from his teaching about 'the tsadik [as] the foundation of the world' and about the human being as 'a ladder set up on the earth and the top of it reached to heaven, and the angels of God ascending and descending on it '.[53] It is likewise evident in the unifications, intentions, and devotions, in the conduct of 'the spiritual man who is above nature', and in the totality of kabbalistic concepts that the Ba'al Shem Tov makes accessible to each person. The substantial broadening of the realm of religious worship is phrased as follows: 'The primary occupation of Torah and prayer is that one should cleave to the spiritual inwardness of the infinite light within the letters of the Torah.'[54] This formulation derives from the assumption that God is omnipresent, ubiquitous in every utterance and thought, from which one may arrive at the obligation of devotion to God at all times and in every way. This intense focus on the divine element present in every word, letter, and event, frees man from this-worldly limits and endows him with intellectual and imaginative freedom. Correspondingly, it emancipates him from subjugation to other people.

Shabateanism claimed to speak in the name of the freedom embodied in redemption and in the messianic idea. Believers, however, soon found themselves subjugated to an anarchistic and nihilistic messianic figure who imposed a tyrannical regime of submission, segregation, duplicity, and secrecy, reducing

---

[52] See Elior, 'Sefer divrei ha'adon' (Heb.), 521–8.

[53] *Toledot ya'akov yosef*, 'Lekh lekha', 50; cf. *Ben porat yosef*, 42a.

[54] *Toledot ya'akov yosef*, 89.

their freedom in every sphere. Hasidism, by contrast, aimed to expand the limits of the human spirit. It determined that 'the human being is set on earth and his head reaches the heavens'.[55] It declared that man must know one great principle: 'there is no curtain between a human being and his God'.[56] It affirmed with respect to all people that, 'where a person's thoughts are, that is where he is totally present';[57] that, 'according to a human being's thoughts, so there are worlds above him placed upon him. If his thought is holy and spiritual, so are the worlds above him';[58] and that, 'according to the refinement of a person's thought so the worlds rest upon him, and so things happen to him in his sight and hearing'.[59]

Hasidism sought to illuminate the physical world in the light of the unity of the infinite divine and human spirit, and to include all people in this unity through thought, speech, and language. By choosing this point of departure, which illuminates the human world with the light of the divine and reshapes the limits of finite corporeal existence in the light of the infinite divine reality, hasidism became committed to projecting the divine attributes on to the human world. Effusion and emanation, freedom, infinity, wisdom and intelligence, spiritual liberty, the dialectic of nothingness and being, the infinity of thought and speech implicit in the language of creation, together with loving kindness and mercy, righteousness and truth, brotherhood and providence—all of which were linked to divine processes and their kabbalistic interpretations—were reinterpreted in ways that unified the divine and the human. Combination and separation, love and fear, effusion and contraction, nothingness and being, the infinite and the finite were all to be considered part of the dialectical structure unifying the divine and the human. And transcendence of natural limits is perpetuated through the powers of thought, spirituality, and creativity.

[55] *Toledot ya'akov yosef*, 'Tetsaveh', 239.

[56] Ibid., 'Bereshit', 22.

[57] Ibid., 'Ḥayei sarah', 69.

[58] *Ben porat yosef*, 'Vayetse', 56*b*.

[59] *Degel maḥaneh efrayim*, 'Ekev', 24.

THIRTEEN

Scholarship on Hasidism
Changing Perspectives

> All beauty and majesty may be found wherever there is a combination of two
> opposing elements.
> *Seder hatefilot,* 19a

THE study of hasidism touches upon the traditional world and the modern era. It must be concerned with kabbalah and messianism, with charismatic leadership and with the broad dissemination of new mystical ideas and new social frameworks. It must likewise be concerned with the opposition that hasidism faced, whether from the champions of Enlightenment, as represented by the Haskalah movement, or from the supporters of the traditionalist establishment, the mitnagedim. Given this broad context, developing an understanding of the hasidic movement requires a variety of critical perspectives and methods of investigation. No one scholarly approach can cover all aspects of hasidic history as reflected in the hundreds of works of hasidic literature that in turn reflect the conceptual approaches of different hasidic groups over three centuries. The purpose of this chapter is to set out the main scholarly approaches that have been adopted.

In fact, the scholarly study of hasidism has undergone several stages since its beginnings in the late nineteenth century. Scholars' viewpoints have been considerably influenced by their historical circumstances and cultural and social environment. There is nothing remarkable about this, in so far as it is a commonplace of historiography that the historian's cultural and ideological orientation can significantly influence the perspective of investigation, but the phenomenon is even more pronounced with a movement of such longevity. To set the scene, therefore, I shall begin by briefly characterizing the various historiographical schools and their theoretical approaches; I will then discuss the major schools in more detail.

The early maskilim such as Judah Leib Miesis, Isaac Levinsohn, and Joseph Perl, who were the first to engage in the study of hasidism, were negative towards it because they were influenced by mitnagedic writings.[1] They

---

[1] For examples of these writings see *Kinat ha'emet* by Miesis, *Beit yehudah* by Levinsohn, and *Ueber das Wesen der Sekte Chassidim* by Perl.

contrasted the mystical, 'benighted' Judaism, represented by kabbalah, Shabateanism, and hasidism, with rational, 'enlightened' Judaism, starting with Maimonides and continuing through the mitnagedim and down to the Haskalah. Somewhat later, scholars such as Eliezer Zweifel, author of *Peace on Israel* (*Shalom al yisra'el*, 1868), refuted mitnagedic criticisms of hasidic practices as unwarranted innovations by using hasidic sources to identify their origins in kabbalistic literature. In keeping with the spirit of the times, scholars such as Ilya Orshanski and Pesach Marek saw hasidism as a revolutionary movement, emancipating the Jewish masses.[2] But the works of all these scholars pale into insignificance compared to the major studies undertaken in the late nineteenth and early twentieth centuries by the school that developed around the German Jewish historian Heinrich (Tsevi) Graetz and the Russian David Kahana (Kogan). Both were hostile to hasidism, and their influence is considered in more detail below. Russian Jewish historian Simon Dubnow likewise had a major influence; he was the first to study hasidism in a more systematic and scholarly way by accumulating and analysing historical, literary, and archival material. Thanks to this approach, hasidism began to be seen as an evolving totality, changing through history. Other European Jewish scholars had different agendas. The Romantic school, whose major exponent was Martin Buber, saw hasidism as expressing a new dialogue between God and man and bringing about a way of life that engendered community. The socialist–Marxist school, represented by Raphael Mahler, interpreted hasidism in the context of the class struggle.

As the centre of gravity of Jewish scholarship began to shift away from Europe and towards Jerusalem, the study of hasidism began to be influenced by new conceptions of Jewish nationhood and new attitudes to the study of Judaism as a religion. The nationalist school of Jewish history that developed in Jerusalem around such scholars as Ben-Zion Dinur, Jacob Katz, Shmuel Ettinger, and Chone Shmeruk saw hasidism in the context of Jewish history as a whole and took an interest in the social background to its development. They were therefore concerned to establish its relationship to the wider world of Ashkenazi Jewry and to analyse the nature of its leadership compared to that of the traditional world.

Other scholars were less interested in the social origins of hasidism than in its mystical roots. They attempted to understand the distinctiveness of hasidism in relation to kabbalistic tradition and its role in the spiritual processes of continuity and change. This mystical school, also based in

---

[2] See e.g. Orshanski, *Yevrei u Rossii*; Marek, 'Krizis yevreiskovo samoupravliennie i khasidism'.

Jerusalem, included such scholars as Gershom Scholem, Rivka Schatz-Uffenheimer, Joseph Weiss, Isaiah Tishby, and Joseph Dan.

Recent decades have seen a critical re-examination of the historical, social, and ideological assumptions of earlier scholarship and the integration of some of the different approaches. Many of this generation of scholars are students, successors, and critics of the two Jerusalem schools. Active today in Israel and around the world, they study hasidism from a variety of new angles. They have generally refrained from writing comprehensive histories but have focused instead on questioning the validity of previous historiographical assumptions regarding particular facets of hasidism, based on the study of historical documents, archival data, and hasidic literature.

*

The first scholarly study of hasidism was the work of the German Jewish scholar Heinrich Graetz (1817–91). Working in the cultural milieu of the Haskalah, he emphasized Judaism's ethical, philosophical, and universal values; hasidism was viewed with hostility because it failed to conform to the image of Judaism that enlightened European Jewry sought to portray. He dubbed hasidim 'obscurantists', 'rebels against the light',[3] and 'benighted'. David Kahana, his Russian-born contemporary (1838–1915), author of the Hebrew volume *History of Kabbalists, Shabateans, and Hasidim*, likewise regarded hasidism as mystical, segregated, benighted, insufficiently rational— in short, as distinctly 'non-Western'. The titles he chose for his books on hasidism and mysticism are a clear indication of his attitude: *Avnei ofel*, 'Stones of Darkness' (from Job 28: 3) and *Avnei tohu*, 'Stones of Vacuity' (from Isaiah 24: 11).

The first studies of hasidim were thus undertaken by maskilim who had been influenced by the mitnagedic viewpoint which saw hasidism as undermining traditional Jewish society. Their scholarship described hasidism as seen by its opponents rather than in its own terms, as presented in its own literature, hence the erroneous impression, which is prevalent down to the present day, that hasidism was a popular, unlearned movement. This type of judgemental position, which rates a cultural phenomenon in terms of a preferred primary value and a dominant religious-social norm instead of in its own terms, is unacceptable by contemporary scholarly standards.

As I have already shown, the difference between hasidim and mitnagedim lay not in intellectual background or social status but rather in the acceptance

---

[3] See Job 24: 13.

or otherwise of mystical ideas. In the hasidic world-view, the divine presence
is manifest and accessible to all through the figure of the tsadik. In the traditional world-view there is a hierarchical order, based on halakhic categories,
which determines relative closeness to the sacred with reference to social
standing and intellectual attainment. In consequence of these different world-
views, the emergence of hasidism led to conflict over the basis of authority
and the emergence of new frameworks for religious worship. The hasidic–
mitnagedic polemic of the times indicates clearly that the contemporary intellectual elite was divided in its allegiance.

The profound religious world that emerges from the study of hasidic writings—thousands upon thousands of pages—offers unambiguous evidence
that accusations of ignorance are without foundation. On the contrary:
hasidism was a highly articulate intellectual and spiritual movement that
advocated equanimity regarding the material world in a desire to overcome
the limits of physical existence and become one with God. Deriving mystical
inspiration both from this equanimity and from their contemplative closeness
to divine infinity, the hasidic leaders became alternative sources of authority.
Their ability to attract followers on account of their charisma implicitly and
explicitly undermined the traditional sources of authority and the existing
hierarchy.

The negative image of hasidism among Jewish historians living in pre-war
eastern Europe derived in part from their tendency to depict early hasidism
on the basis of its contemporary manifestations. This point of departure does
not satisfy the standards of historical criticism, which presumes that every
phenomenon changes with time, that one cannot infer earlier developments
from later ones or depict early stages on the basis of the later. Perhaps the
true pioneer in the scholarly study of hasidism in this respect was Simon
Dubnow (1860–1941).[4] Certainly he laid the foundations for scholarship
based on documents rather than impressions; but while significant portions of
his archival work remain valid, his descriptions are not always accurate and
his evaluations are debatable. Moreover, he often interpreted archival and
bibliographical material in the light of maskilic hostility to hasidic practices.
None the less, the factual basis of his work made its contribution significant
in its day, and the documentary evidence he amassed is still considered to be
of value.

In the 1920s Martin Buber (1878–1965) gave a new direction to hasidic
scholarship when he characterized the hasidic religious temperament as
expressing a struggle to preserve concreteness that is lived as the indubitable

---

[4] See Dubnow, *History of Hasidism* (Heb.).

place of the encounter between the human and the divine, and attempted to account for the vitality and spiritual character of the movement in terms of this factor. He considered the telling of hasidic stories to be an attempt by teachers of great charisma to facilitate the encounter with the divine.[5] But, in striving to understand hasidism with the tools of religious philosophy, Buber ignored the historical circumstances in which it had arisen and concentrated instead on its spiritual distinctiveness, which he defined as 'mysticism transformed into ethos'. His views were very influential, and even those who disagreed with him for ignoring the historical circumstances of hasidism recognized the importance of his contribution. Buber's book *In the Orchard of Hasidism*,[6] in which he attempted to define the distinctiveness of hasidism as a spiritual movement and the significance of its social vitality, and the various studies in which he tried to indicate the dialogic element in hasidic thought, were unquestionably a major contribution towards an understanding of the mystical nature of hasidism.

Gershom Scholem (1897–1982) dealt with hasidism as part of the history of Jewish mysticism.[7] Seeking to present its spiritual relationship to previous currents, he analysed their continuity and the differences between them. Likewise he wished to clarify disputed historical questions regarding the Ba'al Shem Tov as the founder of hasidism and to identify his main ideas. He argued that hasidism had neutralized or abandoned the messianic tendencies that had been central to its kabbalistic and Shabatean predecessors, replacing the yearning for national redemption with a personal objective of rectification (*tikun*) of the cosmic balance and mystical devotion to God (*devekut*). For Scholem this was the heart of hasidic teaching: an intimate and persistent connection to God, meaning a connection to the divine element embodied in the Torah through the inner sense of the letters.[8]

Scholem and Buber debated which sources were most important for the study of hasidism. Scholem, who strove to integrate an understanding of the spiritual phenomena and the circumstances of their historical emergence, preferred the homiletic literature as articulating the theoretical innovations of hasidism and locating it in the continuum of historical and intellectual evolution. Buber, who wished to understand the significance of religious renewal dependent on charisma and its narrative expression, preferred the legends of the hasidic tales with their inspiring stories of charismatic leadership and the vibrant reality of the hasidic community.[9]

---

[5] See Urban, *Aesthetics of Renewal*.

[6] *Befardes haḥasidut.*   [7] Scholem, *Major Trends in Jewish Mysticism*, ch. 10.

[8] *Scholem, 'Devekut*, or Communion with God'.

[9] See Buber, *The Hidden Light* (Heb.), introduction; id., *Tales of the Hasidim*, introduction.

Ben-Zion Dinur (1884–1973), like other historians of his generation (Gershom Scholem, Isaac Baer (1888–1980), and Jacob Katz (1904–98)), was influenced by the Zionist culture of Jewish national renaissance. This group of scholars attempted to account for the persistence of the Jewish people through two thousand years of exile by emphasizing the continual yearning for redemption in frameworks that went beyond those provided by the traditional world. Their work was unquestionably influenced by the experience of national renewal, by questions of exile and redemption, and by a concern with the relationship between conservative and innovative factors in Jewish history. Dinur provided a detailed description of the spiritual and social background to the rise of hasidism, seeking out the hidden factors that motivated the movement. He concluded that hasidism was a movement of social opposition and messianic ideology, and explained the failure of the historical record to confirm its messianic nature by the need for secrecy prompted by the Shabatean crisis.[10] Isaiah Tishby (1908–92) continued along the same path, arguing against Scholem's claim that hasidism had neutralized the messianic element. This question became a central focus of debate in scholarship on hasidism, despite the fact that the messianic idea does not play a major role in hasidic literature.[11]

Another line of enquiry influenced by contemporary ideology was the attempt to study hasidism from a sociological perspective, presenting it in the context of power relations and class struggle. Simon Dubnow was the first to suggest that hasidism was a response to socio-economic distress, a development that he termed 'history answering the needs of the generation'. Ben-Zion Dinur likewise linked the emergence of hasidism with the difficulties facing Polish Jewry in all areas, and focused on its oppositional character. It was Raphael Mahler (1899–1977), however, who first presented the hasidic movement as populist religion and as a social revolution connected to class struggle.[12] He treated hasidism as a practical reflection of 'the hard living conditions of the Jewish petit bourgeois masses'. His thesis has been disproved by the findings of more recent historical research, which indicates that the socio-economic conditions in which hasidism arose did not differ substantially from those of the preceding period. Similarly, the sociological theory of hasidism as an oppositional movement is not supported by the documentary evidence. Jacob Katz presented a critical examination of such socio-economic positions, noting that one must distinguish between conditions that facilitate the spread of a phenomenon and conditions that make it necessary. His book

---

[10] Dinur, 'The Origins of Hasidism'.   [11] See Tishby, 'The Messianic Idea'.
[12] See Mahler, *Hasidism and the Jewish Enlightenment*.

Tradition and Crisis (first published in 1958) deals with how the displacement of the traditional leadership by the charismatic leaders of hasidism led to the breakdown of the boundaries of the traditional world. He observed, however, that although hasidism arose in conditions of crisis (the crisis of Shabateanism and the crisis of leadership), the distinctive nature of hasidism cannot be attributed to the crises from which it emerged.

The rise of hasidism was caused neither by Shabateanism nor by the disintegration of the community structure; at most they facilitated its spread. Shmuel Ettinger (1919–88) added to this critique by noting that social affairs are marginal in hasidic teaching.[13] Chone Shmeruk (1921–97) and Israel Heilperin (1910–71), comparing hasidic social activity to that of contemporary non-hasidic leadership, noted the common denominators and differences. Yeshayahu Shahar (1935–77), comparing how hasidic and non-hasidic literature reflect social attitudes, found sharper social criticism and greater social awareness in the latter; the hasidic sources in fact have little discussion of social issues.[14]

The historical school in general criticized the socio-economic explanations of Dubnow and Dinur. Jacob Katz, Israel Heilperin, and Shmuel Ettinger all ascribed significance to the novelty implicit in hasidic leadership, though each emphasized different aspects. Jacob Katz focused on the subversive elements of hasidism, and how the charismatic leadership of the tsadik had undermined the foundations of the traditional world. Shmuel Ettinger argued against this position, rejecting the claim that the hasidic leadership had had a disintegrative effect on Jewish society. He saw the distinctiveness of the system of leadership by the tsadik in that it accepted the legitimacy of the society from which it had arisen, despite establishing separate frameworks. He pointed to the sense of shared public responsibility and the channels of co-operation between hasidic leaders and the establishment, despite their differences regarding the source of authority. Israel Heilperin similarly disagreed with the view of hasidism as subversive: comparing ordinances promulgated by tsadikim with those of their traditional contemporaries, he demonstrated that the former did not actually deviate from the accepted communal regulations of the period.

In contrast to the position that saw hasidism as a movement of opposition with a clear sense of social purpose, others saw it as a movement of mystical inspiration, spiritual innovation, and religious awakening. Starting in the

---

[13] Ettinger, 'Hasidic Leadership'.

[14] See Shmeruk, 'The Social Significance of Hasidic Ritual Slaughter' (Heb.); id., 'Hasidism and the Kehilla'; Heilperin (ed.), *The Jewish Community in Poland*; Shahar, *Criticism of Society and Leadership*.

1940s, scholars of kabbalistic thought and hasidism such as Gershom Scholem, Isaiah Tishby, Joseph Weiss (1918–69), Rivka Schatz-Uffenheimer (1927–92), and Joseph Dan (b. 1935) sought in their own way to portray the spiritual distinctiveness of hasidism and its relationship to the kabbalistic sources. Scholem analysed the relationship of hasidism to Lurianic kabbalah and Shabateanism, describing the points where hasidism continued the path of its predecessors and the crucial points of divergence—the neutralization of the messianic position and the emphasis on *devekut* as a substitute for the messianic idea. Tishby linked hasidism with the thought of the messianic kabbalist Moses Hayim Luzzatto and disputed Scholem's thesis concerning the neutralization of messianic elements. Weiss depicted the rise of hasidism in relation to the oppositional conception and to Shabateanism, and strove to produce spiritual portraits of some of hasidism's primary figures. He proposed alternative models in the evolution of hasidism, which he called 'mystical hasidism' and 'faith hasidism', and discussed the religious conceptions that they entail. Schatz-Uffenheimer described the mystical world of hasidic thought emerging from the school of the Maggid of Mezhirech, with its extreme quietism requiring isolation from physical experience and worldly concerns. She also studied the conflict between the traditional normative values and the new spiritual values, attributing importance to the spiritual authority of hasidism and the spiritual autonomy that arose in some of its currents. Tishby and Dan discussed the intellectual evolution of hasidism in relation to kabbalistic tradition, and also devoted much attention to Habad hasidism and Bratslav hasidism.

Contemporary scholars of hasidic thought have returned to assessing the role of the kabbalistic conceptual system that inspired hasidism and its relationship to the social vicissitudes of hasidism. The great majority share the recognition that kabbalah and mystical inspiration are weighty factors in the rise and spread of the movement. Some, however, have placed greater emphasis on the breadth of the kabbalistic background needed in order to understand the fundamental formative concepts of hasidic consciousness and the religious and social transformation they effected. The current scholarly discourse is shaped by new attempts to evaluate the stages in the spread of hasidism in relation to Shabateanism, in relation to hasidism's distinctive social frameworks and their theoretical sources, and with regard to links between its kabbalistic background and social innovations. Current studies are characterized by the attempt to understand hasidism from its own perspective, in the historical context from which it emerged and developed, while enquiring into the complex relationships among the historical, spiritual, religious, and social circumstances within which it operated.

Much of the scholarship in the field is still only available in Hebrew, although several works are already available in English. A volume edited by Gershon David Hundert and entitled *Essential Papers on Hasidism*, published in 1991, was the first anthology to offer translations of significant scholarly research on hasidism originally published in Hebrew; other anthologies followed, as detailed below. A number of monographs were also published in translation, including works by Martin Buber, Simon Dubnow, Ben-Zion Dinur, Shmuel Ettinger, Raphael Mahler, Gershom Scholem, and Mordecai Wilensky.

Scholarly investigation continues to expand in new directions. Studies published since the 1970s by students of the aforementioned scholars and by students of east European Jewish history have been devoted to the distinctive spirituality of different hasidic groups, new scholarly trends in dealing with hasidic historiography, the special problems of hasidic bibliography, and the typical literary models of hasidism. Studies of the spiritual distinctiveness of the Ba'al Shem Tov and the historical background to his activity stand along-side investigations of the historical and narrative elements in *Shivḥei habesht* that elucidate historical issues connected with the social circumstances in which hasidism arose and took root in ever-widening circles. To these can be added new studies on the hasidic tale, and clarification of the circumstances surrounding polemics within the hasidic world. New scholarly investigations of the relations between hasidim and mitnagedim, hasidim and Shabateans, hasidim and Frankists, and hasidim and maskilim likewise deepen our under-standing of the hasidic network.

Much of this recent work has been published in scholarly anthologies, and not all of it is yet available in English. The pioneering Hebrew volume *Tsadikim and Men of Action: Studies in Polish Hasidism*, published in 1994 and dedicated to the memory of Shmuel Ettinger, includes fifteen essays, a detailed index, and an incisive bibliographical essay.[15] *Hasidism Reappraised*,[16] published in 1996 and dedicated to the memory of Joseph Weiss, contains thirty essays, a detailed index, and a comprehensive bibliography. *Kolot rabim* ('Many Voices'), a memorial volume for Rivka Schatz-Uffenheimer, also published in 1996,[17] includes seven essays on hasidism. All these works propose a broad scholarly perspective and present the range of views on hasidic history and thought as it has crystallized in the scholarship of recent decades. Many other books and articles, detailed in the bibliography to the present book, deal with different aspects of hasidism and represent the scholarly positions of the

[15] Edited by Rachel Elior, Israel Bartal, and Chone Shmeruk.
[16] Edited by Ada Rapoport-Albert.   [17] Edited by Rachel Elior and Joseph Dan.

1990s. In varying degrees they are influenced by insights developed in the wider world of scholarship in the latter half of the twentieth century regarding the relativity of perspectives, the weight to be assigned to work that reflects a particular angle on events, and the necessity for critical evaluation that takes into account multiple points of view.

As we have seen, since the 1970s the foundations of scholarship on hasidism have been re-examined. New approaches have been formulated, and there has been critical evaluation of what had already been achieved. Among articles surveying the state and prospects of scholarship on hasidism in the 1990s from a historical and critical perspective are Joseph Dan's 'Hasidism: The Third Century', Ada Rapoport-Albert's introduction to *Hasidism Reappraised*, and the chapters by Arthur Green and Moshe Idel in the latter volume. Assessments of the state of research in the 1980s are found in the works of Ze'ev Gries and Immanuel Etkes,[18] and in the introductions to academic works dealing with the investigation of hasidism.

The study of hasidism is one of the most vibrant and fruitful areas in Jewish studies. It reflects both the richness of the subject and the multiplicity of research perspectives that have been adopted over the years. New directions in recent decades have included hasidic leadership (Immanuel Etkes, Ada Rapoport-Albert); the authorship and dissemination of hasidic writings and a comprehensive description of one genre, the literature on *hanhagot*, or model pietistic behaviour (Ze'ev Gries); the historical and social significance of economic data (Gershon Hundert, Moshe Rosman); the doctrine of Bratslav hasidism (Arthur Green, Yehuda Liebes, Shaul Magid, Tzvi Mark, Mendel Piekarz); the spiritual world of Habad hasidism (Rachel Elior, Naftali Loewenthal, Moshe Hallamish); historiographical criticism of Habad hagiography (Israel Bartal, Ada Rapoport-Albert); hasidic epistolary literature (Raya Haran, Nahum Karlinsky, Yehoshua Mondshine, Jacob Barnai); critical revision of early hasidism and new conceptions regarding the world of the Ba'al Shem Tov and his sources of inspiration (Rachel Elior, Immanuel Etkes, Karl Grözinger, Moshe Idel, Moshe Rosman); the place of *Shivḥei habesht* in hasidic historiography (Israel Bartal, Ze'ev Gries, Elhanan Reiner, Moshe Rosman); hasidic social institutions (David Assaf, Haviva Pedayah, Elhanan Reiner, Adam Teller); the relationship between kabbalah, Shabateanism, and hasidism (Rachel Elior, Moshe Idel, Yehuda Liebes); relations between hasidim and mitnagedim (Rachel Elior, Immanuel Etkes, Yehoshua Mondshine, Allan Nadler, Tamar Ross); the doctrine of the tsadik (Arthur Green, Ada Rapoport-Albert, Immanuel Etkes, David Assaf, Haviva

---

[18] See Gries, 'Hasidism: The Present State of Research'; Etkes, 'Research in Hasidism'.

Pedayah); the development of Polish hasidism from the Seer of Lublin to Mordecai Joseph of Izbica and his disciple Tsadok Hakohen (1823–1920) of Lublin (Allan Brill, Rachel Elior, Morris Faierstein, Yehuda Gellman, Shaul Magid); the significance of the hasidic story (Joseph Dan, Rivka Devir-Goldberg, Karl Grözinger, Gedaliah Nigal); and the relationship between hasidism and Haskalah (Shmuel Feiner, Marcin Wodziński). Joseph Dan, Arthur Green, and Mendel Piekarz, as well as Haviva Pedayah and Immanuel Etkes, have all worked on the relationship between the mystical and the social elements in hasidism; Gershon Greenberg has investigated messianic elements in twentieth-century hasidism in the context of the Holocaust; David Berger, Rachel Elior, Isaac Kraus, Aviezer Ravitzky, and Eliezer Schweid have examined messianic elements with respect to Habad.

In recent years, a new generation of scholars has contributed to a broader understanding and a more nuanced perception of hasidic spirituality and hasidic scholarship. Various dimensions of hasidic spirituality—concerning, for example, Barukh of Kusov, Ze'ev Wolf of Zhitomir, the teachings and the tales of Nahman of Bratslav, hasidic tales of the tsadikim, and the spiritual position of the students of the Maggid—have been studied respectively by Esther Liebes, Moshe Fogel, Tzvi Mark, Marianne Schleicher, Rivka Devir-Goldberg, and Ron Margolin. Martin Buber's hasidic anthologies have been examined by Martina Urban.

Unlike other historical subjects, hasidism is a continuing phenomenon, changing and evolving;[19] the study of the past can be enriched through the power of the present—as long as scholars are aware of the danger of interpreting the past with the eyes of the present and are careful in distinguishing periods, phenomena, and concepts.

---

[19] The last decade has seen the publication of three Hebrew anthologies devoted to scholarship on hasidism: *Meḥkarei ḥasidut* [Studies in Hasidism], ed. David Assaf, Joseph Dan, and Immanuel Etkes, Jerusalem Studies in Jewish Thought XV (Jerusalem, 1999), containing twelve new articles on various aspects of hasidism; *Bema'agalei ḥasidim* [Within Hasidic Circles], ed. Immanuel Etkes, David Assaf, Israel Bartal, and Elchanan Reiner (Jerusalem, 1999), a collection of fifteen new articles in memory of Mordecai Wilensky; and *Tsadik ve'edah* [Tsadik and Devotees], ed. David Assaf (Jerusalem 2001), a collection of twenty previously published, classic articles on historical and sociological aspects of hasidism.

FOURTEEN

Summary

> When one thinks about the superior world, one is in the superior world; for
> where a person's thoughts are, there the person is.
>
> *Tsava'at harivash*, 224

H ASIDISM has existed since the middle of the eighteenth century. As a
movement it is distinguished by the variety of its currents and the multiplicity of its manifestations. Its origins were associated with spiritual
awakening, mystical inspiration, and charismatic authority. These led in turn
to new forms of leadership, spiritual autonomy, and a highly articulated body
of literature presenting mystical conceptions, spiritual intentions, and social
goals—a great wealth of original intellectual ideas and spiritual creativity.
Over time, hasidism no doubt often diverged from the religious and social
ideals expressed in its literature, for example when exposed to the vicissitudes
of Jewish history. I allude to the behaviour of some hasidic leaders in the
Holocaust, when leaders saved their own skin and left their devoted followers
behind to be murdered (Belz is a well-known case),[1] and to the bitter quarrels
between the families of leading members of various dynasties over succession.[2] The response to hasidism within the Jewish community varied. Its
innovative conception of leadership, its conception of divine worship, and its
original social framework aroused support in some circles and hostility in
others. Hasidism saw itself as a movement of religious revival, operating in
the framework of the traditional world but searching for spiritual innovation,
changed consciousness, and a new conception of social responsibility. But its
opponents—mitnagedim, maskilim, and others who did not identify with
it—saw it quite differently.

One must beware of generalizations. Hasidism was not a monolithic movement, as is clear from the hundreds of hasidic texts and historical documents

---

[1] See e.g. Piekarz, *Ideological Trends* (Heb.); Schweid, *Between Destruction and Salvation*
(Heb.). Disputes on the behaviour of the leadership are recorded within the hasidic world as well
as in the scholarly community dealing with Holocaust studies. See the letters of Hasidei Belz cited
in Piekarz, *Ideological Trends*, 412–13.   [2] See Assaf, *The Regal Way*.

on the subject. One also needs to be aware of the circumstances of its growth, geographically as well as numerically. Each hasidic leader and each of the major hasidic groups developed an independent conceptual world with a distinct focus and emphasis. Yet despite the many sources, positions, and voices that are woven into the texture of hasidism, one can nevertheless identify several common strands. Let me, in conclusion, summarize them:

1. The uniqueness of the Ba'al Shem Tov derived from his power to revive the written kabbalistic tradition in the light of new revelations that blurred the boundaries between the human and the divine. He made the kabbalistic way of thought accessible to all and endowed it with new significance: hasidism was from its inception a movement of spiritual renewal and mystical awakening led by people gifted with charismatic inspiration. These innovations engendered the creation of new social frameworks appropriate to the way of life inspired by the emerging hasidic leadership.

2. The fact that hasidism has survived from the 1740s to our own times and flourished in different parts of the world suggests that its emergence is not dependent on particular social conditions. It has always functioned within the framework of traditional Jewish thought, respecting the traditional structure while adding new dimensions of religious consciousness and spirituality in keeping with the continued renewal of the mystical experience. These innovations aroused enthusiasm and devotion, but also criticism and suspicion. Hasidism has endured despite this tension.

3. The mystical blurring of boundaries between divine and human engendered a charismatic leadership model. The charismatic leader or tsadik relied on a legitimacy conferred by higher worlds. This enabled him to extend the limits of thought and action, and to assume physical and spiritual responsibility for his followers in return for their fervent support. In their devotion to him they sought his guidance in every aspect of their lives.

4. As charismatic leaders, tsadikim freely reinterpreted reality in the light of their relationship with higher worlds, and sought to bridge the gap between the revealed and the esoteric. They did so primarily through spiritual concepts such as selfless devotion to God, contemplation, divestment of corporeality, and transcendence of the self. Through contemplative meditation they aimed to overcome the limitations of physical being in order to become one with the divine. Such concepts, internalized in the consciousness of the individual, were inevitably not accessible to external critique; but although they were grounded in the personal autonomy of individual worship they brought about, directly and indirectly, far-reaching social changes.

5. Hasidism set up a new model of social responsibility. The tsadik's devotion to God gave him the ability to channel the divine bounty to his followers, enabling him to assume responsibility for them in return for their support and comradely love. The tsadik's followers thus formed an egalitarian community. Its members were bound to each other by mutual responsibility, and mutually elevated through their tsadik's devotion to God and connection to the supernal worlds.

6. Hasidism linked the mystical ascent to the higher worlds with social responsibility in the material universe and saw the significance of the physical world only in the divine animation that sustains it. In doing so, hasidism proposed a new relationship between the spiritual and the material. The perpetual transition from nothingness to being is reflected in the figure of the tsadik, who attaches himself to the higher worlds and channels spiritual and physical abundance to his followers.

7. Hasidism introduced radical innovations in its conceptions of God and man. Under the influence of kabbalistic tradition, it saw God as the unity of opposites: ebb and flow, being and nothingness, revelation and concealment, expansion and contraction, direct light and reflected light, encompassing all worlds and filling all worlds, hidden from man and yet ever present. In the hasidic conception, man is likewise seen as combining the finite and the infinite. The spiritual dimension is manifest in language and speech, and in man's transcendence of nature and the limits of sensory experience towards an apprehension of the higher worlds. In other words, God is manifest, omnipresent and sublime, in man's ability to think.

8. Human thought, infinite and creative, is perceived as breaching the boundaries between man and God. Human language, whose 'every letter contains worlds and souls and divinity', is likewise perceived as divine in its creative character, resembling the divine speech with which God created the world. The more hasidism ascended to the higher levels of the mystical spirit and expanded its conception of God, the more it expanded the conception of religion, deepened its conception of man, and recognized the boundlessness of human perceptual abilities. Expansion of the concept of the divine by perceiving everything as included in God broadened human spiritual autonomy and opened new channels for divine worship: 'With regard to any corporeal thing, let one consider how to elevate it and connect it to its source, for one can serve God through all things.'[3]

---

[3] *Tsava'at harivash*, p. 7, §20; *Keter shem tov*, p. 14a, §102 (Brooklyn 1981).

9. Hasidism created a conceptual world whose goal is to teach man to transcend the limits of being. It aimed to uncover the divine essence of physical reality, recognize the essential unity of opposites, and understand the commonality between the divine spirit and the human spirit. The preference for the inward-looking, personal relationship with the divine, in preference to the public ceremonial of divine worship, led hasidim to segregate themselves from traditional Jewish congregations and form new voluntary associations for prayer.

10. The purpose of divine worship, in the hasidic model, is mystical. It seeks to transcend the barrier between being and nothingness, renouncing the physical in favour of devotion to God. Through intense contemplative meditation, the physical self is left behind in order to allow connection and inclusion with the divine. Divine worship is thus based on a blurring of the boundaries between the heavenly and the mundane, on the closeness between the human spirit and the divine spirit deriving from the infinity of thought and the letters of the language. The tangible world should be rejected in favour of the abstract world of the spirit and loving devotion to God. The tension between dedication to abstract spiritual values and the demands of external reality is resolved in hasidism in the relationship between the tsadik and his congregation, each with its distinct role within the system.

11. The tsadik relies on charismatic authority and is considered to make concrete the divine being in this world. Transcending the barriers between the higher and the lower worlds, the tsadik acts as representative of his congregation towards God. Through his devotion to God he is able to channel God's bounty to them. The tsadik's ability to cross spiritual borders caused him to transcend social barriers too, linking him to his followers and linking his followers to each other. The mutual connection between the members of the hasidic community is known as *ahavat ḥaverim*, implying fraternal responsibility and comradely love. Their dependence on the tsadik introduced a new sense of mutual responsibility: 'when one sees a deficiency in another, one should feel the need to rectify personal faults'.[4] The idea of a fraternal community engendered an egalitarian outlook; the paternalistic responsibility for welfare promoted a belief in social justice. The religious innovations of hasidism had far-reaching social consequences.

12. In so far as hasidism views reality as relative in the light of the comprehensive divine presence—all is divine, all is illusion, and all worlds are merely imaginary when they are not apprehended in relation to the ever-sustaining divine light that preconditions their material manifestation—it generates

---

[4] *Ba'al shem tov al hatorah*, ii. 24.

acosmic, anarchist, paradoxical, and dialectical conceptions, and relativistic, sceptical, and pluralist outlooks.

13. Given its perception of infinite, limitless divine reality and of the living divine voice, perpetually re-heard in the consciousness of the tsadik (and through him in the hasidic community), hasidism espouses freedom of thought, freedom of interpretation, and freedom of leadership within human reality. It sees the world as encompassing dialectical opposites: love and fear, opacity and transparency, doubt and tranquillity. Yet there is always room for autonomous judgement, individual deliberation, liberty, independent insight, contradiction, and conundrum.

14. The dialectical nature of the hasidic conceptual system meant that it simultaneously conserved religious tradition and renewed religious consciousness. Both were seen as manifestations of the divine will. The traditional world of Torah and divine commandments introduces nothingness to the world of being, bringing spirituality into everyday life. Mystical worship elevates being to nothingness, emphasizing the spiritual essence that animates the world of action.

15. Hasidic thought ascribed a transformative power to God, to being, and to consciousness. It saw in everything a duality of meaning and a unity of opposites. True meaning lay beyond the simple aspect of things and the manifest face of reality. The social significance of this lay in the deep inner freedom of those who followed the hasidic path: regarding manifest reality as meaningless, they challenged the existing order and espoused new values.

16. The tension between commitment to the world of tradition and the desire for freedom from the domination of accepted frameworks determined, and determines, the character of the hasidic world. It remains within the limits of the norm while yearning to transform its meaning, and recognizes the potential of individuals to establish new bounds. All worlds are seen in the light of the vicissitudes of the divine, and all existence is understood in terms of processes of change and mutability. This is what explains the unique conceptual world of hasidism, the mystical awareness on which it is founded and its encompassing social significance.

Hasidism, in its ideal conception, offers a mystical approach to the great conundrums of the relationship between God and man, between the religious plane and the social plane. In its awareness of constant divine presence and the ever-renewed word of God, it takes upon itself the task of reading anew what is inscribed on the tablets and of redefining God, humanity, and the world in a profound spirit of freedom.

Glossary

aliyat haneshamah (lit. 'ascent of the soul') A state of mystical exaltation.

Atarah (lit. 'crown' or 'wreath') Another name for the Shekhinah.

atsilut (lit. 'emanation') The eternal process by which the divine source is omnipresently immanent in the world.

avodah begashmiyut (lit. 'worship through corporeality') The quest for the divine essence in the multi-faceted nature of material reality; viz., the expansion of religious worship to all areas of human life by according religious significance even to profane activities, by virtue of the thought that illuminates them and the intention that accompanies them.

ayin The infinite divine presence animating reality; the infinite divine endlessness.

ba'al shem A master of the divine name.

bitul hayesh (lit. 'negating being' or 'nullification of being') The transcendence of physical reality in order to uncover the divine element that animates it. In this ascent from being to nothingness the tsadik elevates not only himself but the souls of his followers: 'As the tsadik overcomes, raising himself to holiness, he elevates the entire world [his congregation] with him.'

derekh ḥasidut (lit. 'the path of piety'; pl. *darkhei ḥasidut*) The daily devotional practice derived from the mystical tradition. It entails withdrawal from this world, solitude, asceticism, a dedication to holiness, and an equanimity achieved by ignoring the world of the senses.

derush Homiletical literature.

devekut Total devotion to God to the extent of renouncing the realities of the material world and transcending one's own self in order to enter the domain of nothingness and achieve true communion with the divine through higher levels of spiritual apprehension.

devekut ba'otiyot A form of concentrated contemplation of the letters of the Hebrew alphabet that allows the transformative divine power and the transformative human power to amalgamate, and lets the ebb and flow of divine animation coalesce with human thought.

Ein Sof The Infinite, or Divine Endlessness.

gadlut Greatness of spirit, in the context of distancing oneself from the world and coming closer to God. Cf. **katnut**

gashmiyut Materialism.

hafshatat hagashmiyut (lit. 'stripping away of corporeality', 'divestment of materialism') A process that expresses the desire of the divine soul to transcend corporeality by means of prayer and contemplation and uncover the divine
element that animates it; stripping away the material husks so as to reveal the
divine core.

hafshatat hamahshavah (lit. 'stripping away of thought') A route to transcend
corporeality.

hamshakhah (lit. 'drawing down') Transformation of the divine nothingness into
being, for example by performing the divine commandments of the Torah.
When a tsadik performs the descent from nothingness to being, he draws down
abundance into the material world for his community.

hanhagot Specific hasidic practices; also published compilations of hasidic practice.

hasid (lit. 'a pious person') A person who acts with special kindness (*hesed*) towards
others, or one who, in the name of love of God and imitating his ways, is punctilious in observing religious commandments; also one who follows the teaching
and leadership of another person, both literally and figuratively.

hasidei ashkenaz A term used in the twelfth and thirteenth centuries with
reference to ascetics who were punctilious in the performance of the divine
commandments of the Torah.

hesed (lit. 'divine grace') An expression of celestial abundance.

hevlei mashiah (lit. 'birthpangs of the messiah') A concept that allows Jewish
suffering to be seen as a stage in the transition from exile to redemption.

hishtavut (lit. 'equanimity') An ascetic state in which all values and concepts relating to concrete existence are to be regarded as meaningless.

histalekut (lit. 'withdrawal') The practice of withdrawal from worldly concerns.

hitbonenut (lit. 'contemplation') Meditation on the spiritual vitality that underlies
physical manifestations in order to see in every thing 'its supreme root and
source'.

hitkalelut (lit. 'self-inclusion') Inclusion in the divine.

hitkasherut vehitkalelut (lit. 'affiliation and absorption') The ongoing intimate
relationship within the hasidic community—ties of affection, fraternity, and
mutual responsibility—which derives from the tsadik's status as the metaphysical link between the celestial and the terrestrial.

hitlabeshut (lit. 'enrobing') The process of movement from nothingness to being
that constitutes 'creation'.

hitpa'alut Ecstasy.

hitpashetut (lit. 'expansion') A term that conveys ideas of expansion, infinity, nothingness, and abstraction; the infinite expansion that is beyond apprehension; a

power that is creative and life-giving in a manner that transcends all delimitation, confinement, or form.

ḥokhmat ha'emet (lit. 'the wisdom of Truth') A synonym for kabbalah, the theoretical speculative background of mystical teaching.

katnut Pettiness or small-mindedness in the context of distancing oneself from the world and coming closer to God, in contrast to the expansive vistas of *gadlut*.

kavanah (lit. 'intent'; pl. *kavanot*) A meditation of mystical intent; the performance of ritual with *kavanah* became a hallmark of the hasidic identity.

kelipot The material 'husks' entrapping the sparks of holiness of the Shekhinah and thereby concealing the divine core of the manifest world.

Kudsha Berikh Hu (Aramaic) The masculine aspect of the deity in kabbalistic literature and prayer, also referred to as 'Tiferet' or 'the King'.

levush (lit. 'garb') External appearance or concrete form; divine infinity can be perceived only when contracted into a finite form.

magid (lit. 'one who relates') In hasidic circles, a popular (and often itinerant) preacher and storyteller. In kabbalistic terminology, an angel or supernatural spirit who conveys messages to those worthy of such insights.

mesirut nefesh (lit. 'conveying of [one's] soul') Transcendence of being by abandonment of one's soul to God.

mirmah dekedushah (lit. 'deceit of holiness', or 'holy sin') The Shabatean concept of sin as a way of deceiving the powers of evil. In this view, apostasy was not a cardinal sin but rather a subterfuge undertaken for the sake of the holy mission of redeeming the soul of the messiah in order to confuse the forces of evil concealing this spark of divinity in the husks of the *kelipah*. See also *mitsvah haba'ah ba'aveirah*

mitnagedim (lit. 'opponents' or 'dissenters') Used in different ways at different times; since the eighteenth century the term has come to be used to describe the opponents of hasidism from within the traditional Orthodox community.

mitsvah haba'ah ba'aveirah (lit. 'merit that comes through sin') A meritorious state achieved through a forbidden act in transgression of religious rules. See also *mirmah dekedushah*

nefesh behemit (lit. 'bestial soul') The bestial soul (also known as the 'eye of the flesh') seeks descent into the material world, to convert the spiritual into the physical in an attempt to distance itself from its source.

nefesh elohit (lit. 'divine soul') The divine soul strives to elevate everything to the spiritual level, to strip away materiality to reveal the divine element underlying the concrete manifestation.

nitsotsot 'Sparks of holiness' scattered through the universe in consequence of the breaking of the divine vessels when God contracted himself (a process known as *tsimtsum*) in order to make space for the world he was creating.

olam (lit. 'world') Homiletically, *olam* derives from *he'elem* ('concealment'); on this view, the world is but a concealment of the divine light that makes possible its manifestation. It is the concealed divine element that animates the revealed reality; the physical element is merely a material manifestation that allows the hidden divine reality to be perceived. *Olam* is also used to refer to the 'world' of the tsadik, in the sense of his hasidic followers.

ot (lit. 'letter', 'sign', or 'symbol') A marker that signifies an eternal meaning, as when one speaks of 'the sign of the covenant'. Hasidism attributes great importance to the letters of the Hebrew alphabet.

peruk (lit. 'breaking up', 'deconstruction') The transformative movement from the concrete to the abstract. Cf. *tseruf*

sefirah (pl. *sefirot*) A perceptible aspect or quality of the divine. The kabbalah of the late medieval period saw heaven and earth as linked through a system of divine *sefirot* that affect the earthly realm. They correspond to the spirit, soul, and divinity that cannot be grasped by man without a mediating, physical form to conceal their infinity.

Shekhinah The feminine aspect of the deity; also called Atarah (meaning 'crown' or 'wreath'), or Keneset Yisra'el.

sitra ahara (Aramaic; lit. 'the other side') In kabbalistic teaching, the 'side of satanic impurity' in the heavenly world; the embodiment of evil, impurity, exile, enslavement, chaos, and destruction.

sitra dekedusha The 'side of holiness' in the heavenly world; the embodiment of the yearning for good, the domain of sanctity, freedom, and harmonious order.

tikun (pl. *tikunim*) Rectification of the cosmic balance; mystical formulas aimed at restoring the divine order.

tsadik (lit. 'a righteous person') A charismatic leader whose legitimacy is conferred by higher worlds. The tsadik links the terrestial world of his followers with the supernal worlds, and channels the divine abundance to them.

tseruf (lit. 'combining') The transformative movement from the abstract to the concrete. Cf. *peruk*

tsimtsum (lit. 'contraction') The process by which God contracted himself in order to make space for the world he was creating; 'contraction' of the divine essence and its manifestation as finite being.

yihudim (lit. 'unifications') Mystical meditations aimed at restoring the ultimate unity of the divine purpose. *Yihudim* are permutations of letters, without meaning in themselves—names or mnemonics, devoid of semantic value, functioning in performative ritual language or in amulets and nostrums. The recitation of these 'words' dissolves language and consciousness; it is a process in which language is returned from a state of differentiated construction to one of undifferentiated deconstruction.

Bibliography

Kabbalistic and Hasidic Works

A classification and description of hasidic literature according to period and scholarly orientation can be found in the Scholem Collection of the National and University Library Jerusalem, catalogued in Joseph Dan, Esther Liebes, and Shmuel Reem (eds.), *Gershom Scholem's Library of Jewish Mysticism* [Sifriyat gershom shalom betorat hasod hayehudit], 2 vols. (Jerusalem, 1999).

Adir bamarom. Moses Hayim Luzzatto (Warsaw, 1886).

Avot derabi natan. Ed. S. Z. Schechter (Vienna, 1887).

Avodat halevi. Aaron Halevi of Starosielce (Lemberg, 1842; Warsaw, 1866; Jerusalem, 1972).

Ba'al shem tov al hatorah. Ed. Shimon Menahem Mendel Wodnik of Govartchov, 2 vols. (Łódź, 1938; repr. Jerusalem, 1975).

Beit ya'akov. Jacob Heilperin of Zwaniec, responsa (manuscript, *c.*1738).

Beit ya'akov. Jacob Leiner (Lublin, 1904).

Beit yehudah. Isaac Levinsohn (Vilna, 1838).

Beit yisra'el. Tsevi Hirsch Eichenstein of Zhidachov (Lemberg, 1834).

Ben porat yosef. Jacob Joseph of Polonnoye (Korets, 1781; repr. Jerusalem, 1971).

Boneh yerushalayim. Shneur Zalman of Lyady (Jerusalem, 1926).

Darkhei tsedek. Zekhariah Mendel of Jaroslaw (Lemberg, 1796; repr. Lublin, 1909).

Degel mahaneh efrayim. Moses Hayim Ephraim of Sudylkow (Korets, 1810; repr. Jerusalem, 1994).

Divrat shelomo. Solomon of Lutsk (Zolkiew, 1848; Jerusalem, 1955).

Divrei emet. Jacob Isaac Horowitz (the Seer of Lublin) (Zolkiew, 1830; Munkacs, 1942).

Divrei ha'adon by Jacob Frank [Divrei ha'adon leya'akov frank], trans. from the Polish by Fania Scholem, ed. Rachel Elior (interim edn., Jerusalem, 1997).

Divrei moshe. Moses ben Dan Shoam of Dolina (Polonnoye, 1801; Lemberg, 1887).

Dor yesharim. Hayim Simhah Leiner (Lublin, 1909; repr. Lvov, 1922).

Emek hamelekh. Naphtali ben Jacob Elhanan Bacharach (Amsterdam, 1648).

Ets hayim. Hayim Vital (Korets, 1784).

Galya raza. Anonymous (1543–53; Mohilev 1812); partial critical edn. of Bodleian MS Oppenheim 104, ed. Rachel Elior (Jerusalem, 1981).

Gahalei esh. Joseph Prager, 2 parts (New York, 1992); reproduction of MS Mic 108 Neubauer 2189 (1754/5), Bodleian Library, Oxford.

Hakhronikah: teudah letoledot ya'akov frank vetenuato. Anon. [written by a Frankist] (18th century); 1st published from Polish MS 2118, Lublin Public Library; ed. Hillel Levine (Jerusalem, 1984).

Hanhagot yesharot. Menahem Mendel of Przemysl (Leszcow, 1816).

Hayat hakaneh. Solomon Molcho (Amsterdam, 1658).

Hayei moharan. Nathan Sternhartz of Nemirov, 2 vols. (Lemberg, 1874; Jerusalem, 1947).

Hayim vahesed. Hayim Haikl of Amdur (Warsaw, 1891; repr. Jerusalem, 1975).

Heikhal haberakhah. Isaac Judah Yehiel (Isaac Eizik) Safrin of Komarno (Lemberg, 1869; repr. New York, n.d.).

Hemdat yamim. Anon. (Ismir, 1731; standard edn. Venice, 1763).

Hesed le'avraham. Abraham ben Dov Ber of Mezhirech ('the Angel') (Czernowitz, 1851; repr. Jerusalem, 1973).

Igeret aliyat haneshamah [*Igeret hakodesh*]. Letter from the Ba'al Shem Tov to Gershon of Kutow. First published as an appendix to Jacob Joseph of Polonnoye, *Ben porat yosef* (Korets, 1781); versions can be found in *Rabbi Israel Ba'al Shem Tov* (Heb.), ed. A. Kahana (Zhitomir, 1901), 99–101; *Shivhei habesht*, ed. Y. Mondshine (Jerusalem, 1982), 233–7.

Igeret hakodesh. See *Igeret aliyat haneshamah*

Igerot ba'al hatanya uvenei doro. Letters of Shneur Zalman of Lyady and his contemporaries, ed. David Zvi Hillman (Jerusalem, 1953).

Igerot kodesh. 'Holy epistles' by the Habad leaders Dov Baer (the 'Mitteler Rav'), by Menahem Mendel (author of *Tsemah tsedek*), and by Shneur Zalman of Lyady; ed. Dov Ber Levin (Brooklyn, 1980; 2nd edn., with appendices, Brooklyn, 1981).

Igerot kodesh: kuntres miluim, ed. Dov Ber Levin (Brooklyn, 1982); includes letters from Shneur Zalman of Lyady and Aaron Halevi of Starosielce. Published as an addendum to *Igerot kodesh*, ed. Dov Ber Levin (Brooklyn, 1980).

In Praise of the Ba'al Shem Tov. See *Shivhei habesht*

Kedushat levi. Levi Isaac of Berdichev (Slavuta, 1798; repr. Jerusalem, 1958).

Kehal hasidim. Michael Frumkin-Rudkinsohn (Warsaw, c.1860); see Dan, Liebes, and Reem (eds.), *Gershom Scholem's Library*, §10519.

Keter kehunah. Alexander Zederbaum (Odessa, 1897).

Keter shem tov. Sayings of the Besht, collected by Aaron ben Tsevi Hirsch Kohen of Opatow, 2 vols. (Zolkiew, 1784–5; Kehat edn., Brooklyn, 1981).

Keter torah. Pinhas of Polotsk (Shklov, 1788).

Kinat ha'emet. Judah Leib Miesis (Vienna, 1828); repr. in Y. Friedlander, *Hebrew Satire in Europe*, vol. iii (Ramat Gan, 1994).

Kol mevaser ve'omer: kovets ḥidushei torah. Hamelekh hamashiaḥ vehage'ulah hashelemah. M. Zelikson [Abraham Pariz-Slonim] ((?)Jerusalem, (?)1965).

Kuntres hahitpa'alut. Dov Ber Shneuri of Lubavitch (Königsberg, (?)1831); standard edn., with commentary, in Hillel of Paritch, *Likutei be'urim* (Warsaw, 1868); English edn. *Tract on Ecstasy*, trans. Louis Jacobs (London, 1963).

Kutonet pasim. Jacob Joseph of Polonnoye (Lemberg, 1866); ed. G. Nigal (Jerusalem, 1985).

Leḥishat saraf. Moses Hagiz (Hanau, 1726); on the Hayoun controversy.

Likutei moharan. Nahman of Bratslav (Ostrog, 1806).

Likutei torah. Shneur Zalman of Lyady (Zhitomir, 1848; Vilna, 1904).

Likutim yekarim. Anthology (Lemberg, 1792, repr. 1850; repr. Jerusalem, 1974).

Luḥot ha'edut. Jonathan Eybeschuetz (Altona, 1755).

Ma'amrei admor hazaken haketsarim. Shneur Zalman of Lyady (Brooklyn, 1986).

Magid devarav leya'akov. Dov Baer of Mezhirech (Korets, 1781); ed. Rivka Schatz-Uffenheimer (Jerusalem, 1976).

Magid meisharim. Joseph Karo (Lublin, 1646; repr. Jerusalem, 1960; new edn., with translations from Aramaic to Hebrew, ed. Yehiel Bar Lev, Petah Tikva, 1990).

Maor vashemesh. Kalonymus Kalman Halevi Epstein (Breslau, 1842; repr. New York, 1958).

Megilat sefer. Jacob Emden, ed. Abraham Bick from a manuscript in the Bodleian Library, Oxford (Jerusalem, 1979; Brooklyn, 1988).

Megilat setarim. Isaac Judah Yehiel (Isaac Eizik) Safrin of Komarno; ed. N. Ben-Menachem (Jerusalem, 1944); ed. Morris Faierstein, in *Jewish Mystical Autobiographies: Book of Visions and Book of Secrets* (New York, 1999); new edn. (Komarno, 2001).

Mei hashilo'aḥ. Mordecai Joseph Leiner of Izbica, 2 vols. (vol. i: Vienna, 1860; vol. ii: Lublin, 1922); English edn.: *Living Waters. The Mei hashilo'aḥ: A Commentary on the Torah*, ed. and trans. B. P. Edwards (Northvale, NJ, 2001).

Me'irat einayim. Nathan Neta Hacohen of Kalbiel, in *Ba'al shem tov al hatorah*, ed. Wodnik.

Me'or einayim. Menahem Nahum of Chernobyl (Slavuta, 1798; Jerusalem, 1960).

Merkevet hamishneh. Solomon of Chelm (part 1: Frankfurt am Oder, 1751; parts 2 and 3, Salonika, 1782; repr. New York, 1948; part 3, repr. Jerusalem, 1953).

Mesilat yesharim. Moses Hayim Luzzatto (Amsterdam, 1740).

Mishmeret hakodesh. Moses of Satanow (Zolkiew, 1746).

Mitpahat sefarim. Jacob Emden (Altona, 1768).

Nagid umetsaveh. Jacob Tsemah (Amsterdam, 1712; new edn. New York, 1986).

Nahman of Bratslav: The Tales, ed. and trans. Arnold Band (New York, 1978).

Nefesh hahayim. Hayim of Volozhin (Vilna, 1824; Benei Berak, 1989).

Ne'ot deshe. Samuel Dov Asher Leiner of Boskowitz (Piotrków, 1908).

Netiv mitsvoteikha. Isaac Judah Yehiel (Isaac Eizik) Safrin of Komarno (introduction to id., *Otsar hahayim*, Lemberg, 1858).

No'am elimelekh. Elimelekh of Lyzhansk (Lemberg, 1788; repr. Jerusalem, 1952); ed. Gedaliah Nigal (Jerusalem, 1978).

Noda biyehudah. Ezekiel Landau; 2 parts (Prague, 1776, 1811).

Notser hesed. Isaac Judah Yehiel (Isaac Eizik) Safrin of Komarno (Lemberg, 1856).

Or ha'emet. Dov Ber of Mezhirech (Husiatyn, 1889).

Or hame'ir. Ze'ev Wolf of Zhitomir (Korets, 1798; Warsaw, 1883; Jerusalem, 1968).

Or lashamayim. Meir of Stobnitsa (Apta and Lemberg, 1850).

Or torah. Dov Ber of Mezhirech (Korets, 1804).

Or yakar. Moses Cordovero; 1st published (in part) (Jerusalem, 1940); full edn., ed. M. Elbaum, 22 vols. (Jerusalem, 1962–95).

Orah lahayim. Abraham Hayim ben Gedalia of Zlotchow (Zolkiew, 1817).

Otsar gan eden haganuz. Abraham Abulafia. Oxford MS 1580; reproduced in Scholem, *The Kabbalah of Sefer hatemunah* (Heb.), 193–5.

Otsar hahayim. Isaac Judah Yehiel (Isaac Eizik) Safrin of Komarno (Lemberg, 1858).

Oz le'elohim. Nehemiah Hayon (Salonika, 1713); there is also a Berlin 1713 edn. which includes Shabetai Tsevi's *Raza demehemnuta.*

Pardes rimonim. Moses Cordovero (Kraków, 1592).

Peri ha'arets. Menahem Mendel of Vitebsk (Zhitomir 1814; repr. Jerusalem, 1978).

Peri tsadik. Zadok Hacohen of Lublin (Lublin, 1934).

Pirkei derabi eliezer (Venice, 1544); with exposition by R. David Luria (Warsaw, 1852).

Reshit hokhmah. Elijah de Vidas (Venice, 1579).

Seder hatefilot. Shneur Zalman of Lyady (Shklov, 1803).

Sefer gerushin. Moses Cordovero (Venice, 1602).

Sefer habahir. Anonymous, ?12th century or earlier. (Amsterdam, 1631); ed. Reuven Margaliot (Jerusalem, 1951); ed. Daniel Abrams (Los Angeles, 1994); English trans. Aryeh Kaplan (Northvale, 1995).

Sefer hafla'ah. Pinhas Horowitz, 3 parts (Offenbach, 1787, 1801; Ostrog, 1824).

Sefer haheziyonot. Hayim Vital (1609–12); autograph manuscript ed. Aaron Ze'ev Aescoly (Jerusalem, 1954); ed. Morris Faierstein, in *Jewish Mystical Autobiographies: Book of Visions and Book of Secrets* (New York, 1999); new Hebrew edn. by Morris Faierstein (Jerusalem, 2005).

Sefer hamefo'ar. Solomon Molcho (Salonika, 1529).

Sefer hameshiv. Sixteenth-century manuscript (Sefunot). British Library MS Or. Add. 27002. Published in part in an article by Gershom Scholem, 'The Maggid of R. Joseph Taitazak and the Revelations Ascribed to Him' [Hamagid shel r. yosef taitazak vehagiluyim hameyuhasim lo], *Sefunot*, 11 (1971–8), 69–112, and in part by Moshe Idel in 'Studies in the Method of the Author of *Sefer hameshiv*' [Iyunim beshitato shel ba'al 'Sefer hameshiv'], *Sefunot*, 17/2 (1983), 185–266.

Sefer haredim. Eliezer Azikri (Venice, 1601).

Sefer hatsoref. Joshua Heshel Tsoref (unpublished manuscript).

Sefer hazikhronot. Tsadok Hakohen of Lublin. Published as *Kuntres sefer hazikhronot: tsadok ben ya'akov melublin* (Lublin, 1913; repr. Benei Berak 1967; Jerusalem, 2001).

Sefer hitabekut. Jacob Emden (Altona, 1762).

Sefer shimush. Jacob Emden (Altona, 1758–62; repr. Jerusalem, 1975).

Sefer toledot ha'ari. Ed. Meir Benayahu (Jerusalem, 1967).

Sefer yetsirah. Anonymous. (Mantua, 1562; repr. Jerusalem, 1965). English trans.: *Sefer Yetzira: The Book of Creation*, ed. Aryeh Kaplan (York Beach, Maine, 1997).

Sha'ar hakavanot. Hayim Vital. The sixth of eight 'gates' or volumes constituting *Shemonah she'arim*, one of the major editions of Lurianic kabbalah (Jerusalem, 1987).

Sha'arei ha'avodah. Aaron Halevi of Starosielce (Shklov, 1821; repr. Jerusalem, 1970).

Sha'arei hayihud veha'emunah. Aaron Halevi of Starosielce (Shklov, 1820; repr. Jerusalem, 1989).

Sha'arei orah. Joseph b. Abraham Gikatilla (written before 1293; Mantua, 1561; repr. Jerusalem, 1960).

Shemuah tovah. Levi Isaac of Berdichev (Warsaw, 1888), printed in some later editions of *Kedushat levi*.

Shenei hame'orot. Samuel of Kaminka (Kishinev, 1896).

Shenei luḥot haberit. Isaiah Horowitz, 2 vols. (Amsterdam, 1649; Jerusalem, 1993).

Shever poshe'im. David of Makow (1714); ed. P. Turberg (New York, 1940); published in M. Wilensky, *Hasidim and Mitnagedim: On the History of their Polemics, 1772–1815* (Heb.) (Jerusalem, 1970), ii. 53–188.

Shever poshe'im. Moses Hagiz (Amsterdam, 1714).

Shevirat luḥot aven. Jacob Emden (Altona, 1756).

Shirot vetishbaḥot shel hashabeta'im. Collection of 18th-century Shabatean poems, originally written in Ladino; trans. Moshe Atias, ed. Gershom Scholem, introduction on the Donmeh by Isaac ben Zvi (Tel Aviv, 1947).

Shivḥei ha'ari. Solomon Dresnitz: letters written from Safed, 1607–9, on Lurianic hagiography; first printed in Joseph Delmedigo, *Ta'alumot ḥokhmah*, 2 vols. (Basle, 1629, 1631), vol. i.

Shivḥei habesht. Ed. Israel Jaffe (Kapust, 1814); ed. B. Mintz (Jerusalem, 1969); facsimile edn., ed. Y. Mondshine (Jerusalem, 1982); annotated edn., ed. A. Rubinstein (Jerusalem, 1992). English edn., *In Praise of the Baal Shem Tov*, ed. and trans. D. Ben-Amos and J. R. Mintz (Bloomington, 1970). Yiddish edn., Korets, 1814. *Die Geschichten vom Ba'al Schem Tov, Schivche ha-Besht*, ed. Karl E. Grözinger (Wiesbaden, 1997), vol. i, Hebrew–German, introd. Rachel Elior; vol. ii, Yiddish–German.

Shulḥan arukh shel ha'ari. By Jacob Tsemah ben Hayim and disciples of Isaac Luria (Safed, 1587; Jerusalem, 1961).

Sipur ma'asei shabetai tsevi. Leib ben Ozer of Amsterdam (Amsterdam, 1711–18); trans. Z. Shazar (Jerusalem, 1978).

Sod yakhin uvoaz. Meir Margalyot [Margulies] (Ostrog, 1794).

Sur mera va'aseh tov: hakdamah vaderekh le'ets haḥayim. Tsevi Hirsch of Zhidachov (Munkacs, 1901; Lublin, 1912); English edn.: *Turn Aside from Evil and Do Good: An Introduction and Way to the Tree of Life*, ed. and trans. Louis Jacobs (London, 1995).

Ta'alumot ḥokhmah. Joseph Delmedigo, 2 vols. (Basle, 1629, 1631).

Tanya: likutei amarim. Shneur Zalman of Lyady (Slavuta, 1797; repr. Kefar Habad, 1980); English edn. *Likutei amarim—Tanya*, ed. and trans. N. Mindel (pt. I), N. Mangel (pt. II), Z. Posner (pts. III and V), and J. I. Schochet (pt. IV) (London, 1973).

Teshuot ḥen by Gedaliah of Luniets (Berdichev, 1816).

Toledot ya'akov yosef. Jacob Joseph of Polonnoye (Korets, 1780; repr. Jerusalem, 1973).

Tomer devorah. Moses Cordovero (Venice, 1589); English edn.: Louis Jacobs, *The Palm Tree of Deborah* (1960).

Torah or. Shneur Zalman of Lyady (1836; Vilna, 1899; Brooklyn, 1978).

Torat emet. Judah Leib Eger, 3 vols. (Lublin, 1889–90).

Tsava'at harivash vehanhagot yesharot. Found among the papers of Isaiah, rabbi of Janov, who witnessed and listened to the Ba'al Shem Tov and Dov Baer the Maggid of Mezhirech (Zolkiew, 1793); Kehat edn.: *Otsar ḥasidim* (Brooklyn, 1975); English trans.: *Tzava'at harivash: The Testament of R. Israel Baal Shem Tov*, trans. Jacob Immanuel Schochet (Brooklyn, 1998).

Tsofenat pa'ane'aḥ. Jacob Joseph of Polonnoye (Korets, 1782); ed. Gedaliah Nigal (Jerusalem, 1989).

Va'avo hayom el ha'ayin. Attributed to Jonathan Eybeschuetz (manuscript, 1724); *Hasefer va'avo hayom el ha'ayin: shayekhuto lerabi yehonatan eibeshuts ve'erko lehavanat hamaḥloket bein rav yehonatan veharav ya'akov emden*, ed. Moshe Perlmuter (Tel Aviv, 1947).

Yeven metsulah. Nathan Neta Hanover (Venice, 1653).

Yosher divrei emet. Meshulam Feivush Heller of Zbarazh; first published as part of *Likutei yekarim* (Lemberg, 1792; 1905; repr. Jerusalem, 1966).

Zemir aritsim. Attributed to David of Makow (Aleksnitz, 1772); repr. in M. Wilensky, *Hasidim and Mitnagedim: On the History of their Polemics, 1772–1815* (Heb.) (Jerusalem, 1970), i. 15–26.

Zerizuta de'avraham. Abraham Heller (Lemberg, 1900; Brooklyn, 1990).

Zikhron yosef. Joseph Steinhardt of Fuerth (Fuerth, 1773; Jerusalem, 1969).

Zikhron zot. Jacob Isaac Horowitz (the Seer of Lublin) (Warsaw, 1869; Munkacs, 1942, repr. Ashdod, 2003).

Zikhronot reb dov meboleḥov. Dov Ber of Bolechow (1723–1805); ed. Mark Vishnitzer (Jerusalem, 1922); Yiddish trans. (Berlin, 1922; repr. Jerusalem, 1972).

Zohar ḥai. Isaac Judah Yehiel (Isaac Eizik) Safrin of Komarno, 4 vols. (Przemysl and Lemberg, 1875–81).

Zohar tinyana. Moses Hayim Luzzatto; ed. Yosef Avivi (Jerusalem, 1997).

Zot torat hakenaot. David of Makow (Makow, 18th century); manuscript first printed in M. Wilensky, 'The Polemic of R. David of Makow', 147–56.

Zot torat hakenaot. Jacob Emden; polemic against Shabateanism (Amsterdam, 1752). new edn.: Jacob Emden, *Sifrei pulmus*, 2 vols. (Ashdod, 1998).

Zot zikaron. Jacob Isaac Horowitz (the Seer of Lublin) (Lemberg, 1851; Munkacs, 1942).

Secondary Literature

AESCOLY, AARON ZE'EV, *Hasidism in Poland* [Haḥasidut bepolin], 2nd edn. (Jerusalem, 1998); first published in Israel Heilperin (ed.), *The Jewish Community in Poland* [Beit yisra'el bepolin] (Jerusalem, 1954), ii. 86–141; repr. in *Haḥasidut bepolin*, introd. David Assaf (Jerusalem, 1999).

—— *Jewish Messianic Movements* (Jerusalem, 1987).

AGNON, S. Y., 'The Banished One' [Hanidaḥ], in id., *These and Those* [Elu va'elu] (Jerusalem and Tel Aviv, 1974), 9–56.

—— *The City and the Fullness Thereof* [Ir umelo'ah] (Tel Aviv, 1973).

—— *Near and Apparent* [Samukh venireh] (Tel Aviv, 1971).

ALEXANDER, P. S., 'The Hebrew Apocalypse of Enoch', in J. H. Charlesworth (ed.), *The Old Testament Pseudepigrapha*, 2 vols. (Garden City, NY, 1983–5), i. 223–315.

ASSAF, DAVID, 'My Small and Ugly World: The Confessions of R. Isaac Nahum Twersky of Shpykiv' (Heb.), *Alpayim*, 14 (1997), 49–79.

—— 'Polish Hasidism in the Nineteenth Century: The State of Research and a Bibliographical Survey' (Heb.), in R. Elior, I. Bartal, and C. Shmeruk (eds.), *Tsadikim and Men of Action: Studies in Polish Hasidism* [Tsadikim ve'anshei ma'aseh: meḥkarim beḥasidut polin] (Jerusalem, 1994), 357–79.

—— *The Regal Way: The Life and Times of R. Israel of Ruzhin and his Place in the History of Hasidism*, trans. David Louvish (Stanford, Calif., 2002).

—— (ed. and trans). *What I Have Seen: The Memories of Yechezkel Kotik* [Mah shera'iti: zikhronotav shel yeḥezkel kotik] (Tel Aviv, 1998).

BAER, ISAAC, *Exile* [Galut], trans. from the German by Israel Eldad (Jerusalem, 1980).

BALABAN, MEIR, *On the History of the Frankist Movement* [Letoledot hatenuah hafrankistit], 2 vols. (Tel Aviv, 1934).

BAND, ARNOLD, *Nostalgia and Nightmare: A Study of the Fiction of S. Y. Agnon* (Berkeley, Calif., 1968).

—— 'The Politics of Scripture: The Hasidic Tale', in id., *Studies in Modern Jewish Literature* (Philadelphia, 2004), 109–28.

BARNAI, JACOB (ed.), *Hasidic Letters from the Land of Israel: From the Second Half of the Eighteenth Century and the Early Nineteenth Century* [Igerot ḥasidim me'erets yisra'el: min hamaḥatsit hasheniyah shel hame'ah ha-18 umereshit hame'ah ha-19] (Jerusalem, 1980).

—— 'The Historiography of the Hasidic Immigration to Erets Yisrael', in Ada Rapoport-Albert (ed.), *Hasidism Reappraised* (London, 1996), 376–88.

BARNES, D., 'Charisma and Religious Leadership: An Historical Analysis', *Journal for the Scientific Study of Religion*, 17 (1978), 1–15.

BARTAL, ISRAEL, 'Maskilic Criticism of Economic Aspects of Hasidism' (Heb.), in M. Ben-Sasson (ed.), *Religion and Economics: Mutual Relations. Festschrift for Jacob Katz's Ninetieth Birthday* [Dat vekalkalah: yaḥasei gomelin. Shai leya'akov kats bimelot lo tishe'im shanah] (Jerusalem, 1995), 375–85.

—— 'The Imprint of Haskalah Literature on the Historiography of Hasidism', in Ada Rapoport-Albert (ed.), *Hasidism Reappraised* (London, 1996), 367–75.

—— 'Shimon the Heretic: A Chapter of Orthodox Historiography' (Heb.), in I. Bartal, E. Mendelsohn, and H. Turniansky (eds.), *Studies in Jewish Culture in Honour of Chone Shmeruk* [Keminhag ashkenaz upolin: sefer yovel leḥone shmeruk] (Jerusalem, 1993), 243–68.

BAT-MIRIAM, YOCHEVED, *Meraḥok* (Tel Aviv, 1932; repr. 1985).

BERGER, DAVID, *The Rebbe, the Messiah, and the Scandal of Orthodox Indifference* (Oxford, 2001).

BIALIK, HAYIM NAHMAN, 'Language Closing and Disclosing', trans. Yael Lotan, *Ariel: A Quarterly of Arts and Letters in Israel*, 50 (1979), 106–14; repr. in J. Dan (ed.), *The Heart and the Fountain: An Anthology of Jewish Mystical Experience* (Oxford, 2002), 255–61.

BRAWER, ABRAHAM JACOB, *Galicia and its Jews* [Galitsiyah viyehudeiha: meḥkarim betoledot galitsiyah bame'ah hashemoneh-esreh] (Jerusalem, 1965).

BRILL, ALLAN, *Thinking God: The Mysticism of R. Zadok of Lublin* (New York and Jersey City, 2002).

BUBER, MARTIN, 'The Beginnings of Hasidism', in id., *Mamre: Essays in Religion* (Westport, Conn. 1946), 149–80.

—— 'Foundations of Hasidism' (Heb.), in I. Heilperin (ed.), *The Jewish Community in Poland* [Beit yisra'el bepolin], vol. ii (Jerusalem, 1954).

—— *Gog umagog: megilat hayamim* (Tel Aviv, 1967).

—— *Hasidism*, trans. C. and M. Witton-Davies (New York, 1948).

—— *Hasidism and Modern Man*, ed. and trans. Maurice Friedman (New York, 1958).

—— *The Hidden Light* [Or haganuz] (Jerusalem and Tel Aviv, 1946; 2nd edn. 1957).

—— *Befardes haḥasidut* [In the Orchard of Hasidism] (Jerusalem and Tel Aviv, 1945; repr. 1979); English trans. in 2 vols.: vol. i, *Hasidism and Modern Man* (1958); vol. ii, *The Origin and Meaning of Hasidism*, ed. and trans. Maurice Friedman (New York, 1960).

—— *Man's Way According to Hasidic Teaching* [Darko shel adam al pi torat haḥasidut] (Jerusalem, 1957).

BUBER, MARTIN, *Martin Buber's Ten Rungs: Collected Hasidic Sayings* (Secaucus, NJ, 1995).

—— 'My Way to Hasidism', in G. D. Hundert (ed.), *Essential Papers on Hasidism: Origins to Present* (New York, 1991), 499–510.

—— *Tales of the Hasidim*, 2 vols. (New York, 1962, 1972).

CARLEBACH, ELISHEVA, *The Pursuit of Heresy: Rabbi Moshe Hagiz and the Sabbatian Controversies* (New York, 1990).

COENEN, THOMAS, *Ydele verwachtinge der Joden getoont in den persoon van Sabethai Zevi Haren laetsten vermeynden Messias* [Vain Hopes of the Jews Revealed in the Figure of Shabetai Tsevi] (Amsterdam, 1669); Hebrew trans. *Tsipiyot shav shel hayehudim kefi shehitgalu bidemuto shel shabetai tsevi* by Arthur Lagawien Efraim Shmueli, introd. and notes Yosef Kaplan (Jerusalem, 1998).

DAN, JOSEPH, 'A Bow to Frumkinian Hasidism', *Modern Judaism*, 11 (1991), 175–93; first published in Hebrew, *Yediyot aharonot* (26 Sept. and 5 Oct. 1984).

—— *The Early Kabbalah*, trans. Ronald Kiener (New York, 1986).

—— *The Hasidic Story* [Hasipur hahasidi] (Jerusalem, 1975).

—— 'Hasidism' (Heb.), *Encyclopaedia Hebraica*, supplementary vol. iii (Jerusalem, 1995), 412–19.

—— 'Hasidism: The Third Century', in Ada Rapoport-Albert (ed.), *Hasidism Reappraised* (London, 1996), 415–26.

—— *Jewish Mysticism*, vol. ii: *The Middle Ages* (Northvale, 1998).

—— 'On the History of the Praise Literature' (Heb.), *Jerusalem Studies in Jewish Folklore*, 1 (1981), 82–100.

—— *On Holiness: Religion, Ethics and Mysticism in Judaism and Other Religions* [Al hakedushah: dat, musar, umistikah bayahadut uvedatot aherot] (Jerusalem, 1997).

—— *The Teachings of Hasidism* (New York, 1983).

—— ESTHER LIEBES, and SHMUEL REEM (eds.), *Gershom Scholem's Library of Jewish Mysticism* [Sifriyat gershom shalom betorat hasod hayehudit], catalogue, 2 vols. (Jerusalem, 1999).

DEVIR-GOLDBERG, RIVKA, *The Tsadik and the Palace of Leviathan: A Study of Hasidic Tales Told by Tsadikim* [Hatsadik hahasidi ve'armon haleviyatan: iyun besipurei ma'asiyot mipi tsadikim] (Tel Aviv, 2003).

DINUR, BEN-ZION, *At the Turn of the Generations* [Bemifneh hadorot] (Jerusalem, 1955; 2nd edn. 1972).

—— 'The Origins of Hasidism and its Social and Messianic Foundations', in Gershon Hundert (ed.), *Essential Papers on Hasidism: Origins to Present* (New

York, 1991), 159–208; revised and abridged English trans. by Eli Lederhändler of 'Early Hasidism and its Social and Messianic Foundations' (Heb.), in Dinur, *At the Turn of the Generations*, 83–227.

DOKTÓR, JAN, 'Jakub Frank: A Jewish Hieresiarch and his Messianic Doctrine', *Acta Poloniae Historica*, 76 (1997), 53–74.

—— (ed.), *Ksiega słów Panskich: Esoteryczne syklady Jakuba Franka*, 2 vols. (Warsaw, 1997).

DRESNER, S. (ed.), *The Circle of the Baal Shem Tov: Studies in Hasidism* (Chicago, 1985; rev. edn. New York, 1998).

—— *The Zaddik: The Doctrine of the Zaddik According to the Writings of Rabbi Yaakov Yosef of Polnoy* (New York, 1974).

DUBNOW, SIMON, 'The Beginnings: The Baal Shem Tov (Besht) and the Center in Podolia', trans. Eli Lederhändler from Dubnow, *History of Hasidism*, 41–75, in G. D. Hundert (ed.), *Essential Papers on Hasidism: Origins to Present* (New York, 1991), 25–57.

—— *History of Hasidism* [Toledot hahasidut], 3rd edn. (Tel Aviv, 1967).

ELIADE, MIRCEA, *Shamanism* (Princeton, NJ, 1974).

ELIOR, RACHEL, 'Between Divestment of Corporeality and the Love of Corporeality: The Polarity of Spiritual Conception and Social Reality in Hasidic Reality' (Heb.), in I. Bartal, E. Mendelsohn, and H. Turniansky (eds.), *Studies in Jewish Culture in Honour of Chone Shmeruk* [Keminhag ashkenaz upolin: sefer yovel lehone shmeruk] (Jerusalem, 1993), 209–42.

—— 'Between *Yesh* and *Ayin*: The Doctrine of the Zaddik in the Works of Rabbi Jacob Isaac, the Seer of Lublin', in Ada Rapoport-Albert and Steven J. Zipperstein (eds.), *Jewish History: Essays in Honor of Chimen Abramsky* (London, 1988), 393–455.

—— 'Breaking the Boundaries of Time and Space in Kabbalistic Apocalypticism', in A. L. Baumgarten (ed.), *Apocalyptic Time* (Leiden, 2000), 187–97.

—— 'Changes in the Religious Thought of Polish Hasidism: Fear and Love and Depth and Coloration' (Heb.), *Tarbits*, 62 (1993), 381–432.

—— 'Der Baal Schem Tov, zwischen Mägie und Mystik', in K. E. Grözinger (ed.), *Die Geschichten vom Ba'al Schem Tov. Schivche ha-Bescht* (Wiesbaden, 1997), pp. xxxv–lvi.

—— 'Different Faces of Freedom: Studies in Jewish Mysticism' (Heb.), *Alpayim*, 15 (1997), 109–19; forthcoming in English in an expanded edition to be published by the Littman Library as *Jewish Mysticism: The Infinite Expression of Freedom*.

—— 'The Dispute over the Habad Legacy' (Heb.), *Tarbits*, 49 (1980), 166–86.

ELIOR, RACHEL, 'The Doctrine of Transmigration in *Galya Raza*', in L. Fine (ed.), *Essential Papers on Kabbalah* (New York, 1995), 243–69.

—— 'Exile and Redemption in Jewish Mystical Thought', *Studies in Spirituality*, 14 (2004), 1–15.

—— 'Habad: The Contemplative Ascent to God', in A. Green (ed.), *Jewish Spirituality, 2: From the Sixteenth-Century Revival to the Present* (New York, 1987), 157–205.

—— 'Hasidism', *Routledge Encyclopedia of Philosophy*, ed. E. Craig (London, 1998), 242–5.

—— 'Hasidism: Historical Continuity and Spiritual Change', in P. Schäfer and J. Dan (eds.), *Gershom Scholem's Major Trends in Jewish Mysticism: Fifty Years After*, proceedings of the sixth international conference on the history of Jewish mysticism (Tübingen, 1993), 303–23.

—— *Jewish Mysticism: The Infinite Expression of Freedom* (Oxford, forthcoming).

—— 'The Lubavitch Messianic Resurgence: The Historical and Mystical Background 1939–1996', in P. Schäfer and M. Cohen (eds.), *Toward the Millennium: Messianic Expectations from the Bible to Waco* (Leiden, 1998), 383–408.

—— 'Messianic Expectations and Spiritualization of Religious Life in the 16th Century', in D. B. Ruderman (ed.), *Essential Papers on Jewish Culture in Renaissance and Baroque Italy* (New York, 1992), 283–98.

—— 'The Metaphorical Relationship Between God and Man and the Continuity of Visionary Reality in Lurianic Kabbalah' (Heb.), in R. Elior and Y. Liebes (eds.), *Lurianic Kabbalah* [Kabalat ha'ari] (Jerusalem, 1992), 47–57 [= *Jerusalem Studies in Jewish Thought*, 10].

—— 'The Minsk Debate' (Heb.), *Jerusalem Studies in Jewish Thought*, 1/4 (1982), 179–235.

—— 'The Paradigms of *Yesh* and *Ayin* in Hasidic Thought', in Ada Rapoport-Albert (ed.), *Hasidism Reappraised* (London, 1996), 168–79.

—— *The Paradoxical Ascent to God: The Kabbalistic Theosophy of Habad Hasidism*, trans. J. M. Green (Albany, NY, 1993).

—— 'R. Joseph Karo and R. Israel Ba'al Shem Tov: Mystical Metamorphosis, Kabbalistic Inspiration, and Spiritual Internalization' (Heb.), *Tarbits*, 65/4 (1996), 671–708.

—— 'R. Nathan Adler and the Frankfurt Pietists: Pietist Groups in Eastern and Central Europe During the Eighteenth Century', in K. E. Grözinger (ed.), *Jüdische Kultur in Frankfurt am Main, von den Anfangen bis zur Gegenwart* (Wiesbaden, 1997), 135–77.

—— 'Sefer divrei ha'adon' (Heb.), in ead. (ed.), *The Dream and its Interpretation*, i. 471–548.

—— *Theosophy in the Second Generation of Habad Hasidism* [Torat ha'elohut bador hasheni shel ḥasidut ḥabad] (Jerusalem, 1982).

—— *The Three Temples: On the Emergence of Jewish Mysticism* (Oxford, 2004).

—— ' "The World Is Filled with His Glory" and "All Men": Spiritual Renewal and Social Change in Early Hasidism' (Heb.), in M. Hallamish (ed.), *Alei shefer: Studies in Jewish Thought in Honor of Alexander Shafran* [Alei shefer: meḥkarim besifrut hehagut hayehudit, mugashim le'aleksander shafran] (Ramat Gan, 1990), 29–40.

—— (ed.), *The Dream and its Interpretation: The Shabatean Movement and its Aftermath—Messianism, Shabateanism, and Frankism* [Haḥalom veshivro: hatenuah hashabeta'it usheluḥoteiha—meshiḥiyut, shabeta'ut, ufrankism], 2 vols. (Jerusalem, 2001) [= *Jerusalem Studies in Jewish Thought*, 16–17].

—— ISRAEL BARTAL, and CHONE SHMERUK (eds.), *Tsadikim and Men of Action: Studies in Polish Hasidism* [Tsadikim ve'anshei ma'aseh: meḥkarim beḥasidut polin] (Jerusalem, 1994).

—— and JOSEPH DAN (eds.), *Rivka Schatz-Uffenheimer Memorial Volume* [Kolot rabim: sefer hazikaron lerivkah shats-ufenheimer] (Jerusalem, 1996) [= *Jerusalem Studies in Jewish Thought*, 12 and 13].

Encyclopaedia Hebraica [Entsiklopediyah ivrit], 34 vols. (Jerusalem, 1949–81).

Encyclopaedia Judaica (Jerusalem, 1974).

ETKES, IMMANUEL, *The Besht: Magician, Mystic, and Leader*, trans. Saadya Sternberg (Waltham, Mass., 2005).

—— 'The Besht as Mystic and Harbinger of Divine Worship' (Heb.), *Tsiyon*, 61 (1996), 443–6.

—— *The Early Hasidic Movement* [Tenuat haḥasidut bereshitah] (Tel Aviv, 1998).

—— *The Gaon of Vilna: The Man and his Image* [Yaḥid bedoro: hagaon mivilna, demut vedimui] (Jerusalem, 1998).

—— 'Hasidism as a Movement: The First Stage', in B. Safran (ed.), *Hasidism: Continuity or Innovation?* (Cambridge, Mass., 1988), 1–26.

—— ' "The Historical Besht": Reconstruction or Deconstruction?', *Polin*, 12 (1999), 297–306.

—— 'The Methods and Achievements of R. Hayim of Volozhin as a Mitnagedic Response to Hasidism' [Shitato ufe'alo shel r. ḥayim mevolozhin keteguvat haḥevrah hamitnagedit laḥasidut], *Proceedings of the American Academy of Jewish Research*, 38–9 (1972), 1–45.

ETKES, IMMANUEL, 'Research in Hasidism: Trends and Directions' (Heb.), *Mada'ei hayahadut*, 31 (1991), 5–21.

ETTINGER, SHMUEL, 'Hasidic Leadership in its Formation', in A. Rubinstein (ed.), *Essays on Hasidic Teaching and History* [Perakim betorat hahasidut uvetoledoteiha] (Jerusalem, 1978), 227–40.

—— 'The Hasidic Movement: Reality and Ideals', in G. D. Hundert (ed.), *Essential Papers on Hasidism: Origins to Present* (New York, 1991), 226–43.

FAIERSTEIN, MORRIS, *All Is in the Hands of Heaven: The Teachings of Rabbi Mordecai Joseph Leiner of Izbica* (New York and Hoboken, NJ, 1989).

—— (trans.), *Jewish Mystical Autobiographies: Book of Visions and Book of Secrets* (New York, 1999).

FEINER, SHMUEL, *Haskalah and History: The Emergence of a Modern Jewish Historical Consciousness*, trans. Chaya Naor and Sondra Silverston (London, 2001).

—— 'The Turning-Point in the Evaluation of Hasidism: Eliezer Zweifel and the Moderate Haskalah in Russia' (Heb.), *Tsiyon*, 51 (1986), 167–210.

—— and DAVID SORKIN (eds.), *New Perspectives on the Haskalah* (Oxford, 2001).

FERZIGER, ADAM S., *Exclusion and Hierarchy: Orthodoxy, Non-Observance and the Emergence of Modern Jewish Identity* (Philadelphia, 2005).

FINE, LAWRENCE, *Physician of the Soul, Healer of the Cosmos: Isaac Luria and his Kabbalistic Fellowship* (Stanford, Calif., 2003).

—— 'Pietistic Customs from Safed', in id. (ed.), *Judaism in Practice* (Princeton, 2001), 375–85.

—— *Safed Spirituality: Rules of Mystical Piety, the Beginning of Wisdom* (New York, 1984).

FOGEL, MOSHE, 'The Shabatean Character of *Hemdat yamim*: A Re-examination' (Heb.), in R. Elior (ed.), *The Dream and its Interpretation: The Shabatean Movement and its Aftermath—Messianism, Shabateanism, and Frankism* [Hahalom veshivro: hatenuah hashabeta'it usheluhoteiha—meshihiyut, shabeta'ut, ufrankism] (Jerusalem, 2001), i. 365–422.

—— 'Ze'ev Wolf of Zhitomir' (Heb.), Ph.D. diss., Hebrew University of Jerusalem, 2006.

FRIEDBERG, HAYIM DOV, *The History of Hebrew Print in Poland* [Toledot hadefus ha'ivri bepolaniyah] (Tel Aviv, 1950).

GELBER, NATHAN MICHAEL, 'History of the Jews of Brody 1584–1943' [Toledot yehudei brodi], in Yehuda Leib Hacohen Maimon (ed.), *Major Jewish Towns*, vi: *Brody* [Arim ve'imahot beyisra'el: brodi] (Jerusalem, 1955), 106–15.

GELLMAN, JEROME, *The Fear, the Trembling, and the Fire: Kierkegaard and Hasidic Masters on the Binding of Isaac* (Lanham, Md., 1994).

GINZBURG, SHIMON, *The Life and Works of Moses Hayyim Luzzatto, Founder of Hebrew Literature* (1931; Westport, 1975).

—— (ed.), *R. Moses Hayim Luzzatto and his Contemporaries: An Anthology of Letters and Documents* [R. mosheh ḥayim lutsato ubenei doro: osef igerot ute'udot] (Tel Aviv, 1937).

GOLDISH, MATT, *The Sabbatean Prophets* (Cambridge, Mass., 2004).

GREEN, ARTHUR, 'Early Hasidism: Some Old/New Questions', in Ada Rapoport-Albert (ed.), *Hasidism Reappraised* (London, 1996), 441–6.

—— *Tormented Master: A Life of Rabbi Nahman of Bratslav* (New York, 1981).

—— 'Typologies of Leadership and the Hasidic Zaddiq', in id. (ed.), *Jewish Spirituality*, vol. ii (New York, 1987), 127–56.

—— 'The Zaddik as Axis Mundi', *Journal of the American Academy of Religion*, 45 (1997), 327–47.

GREENBERG, GERSHON, 'Redemption after the Holocaust According to Machane Israel-Lubavitch, 1940–1945', *Modern Judaism*, 12 (1992), 61–84.

GRIES, ZE'EV, *Book, Author, and Story in Early Hasidism: From Israel Ba'al Shem Tov to Menachem Mendel of Kotsk* [Sefer sofer vesipur bereshit haḥasidut: min habesht ve'ad menaḥem mendel mikotsk] (Tel Aviv, 1992).

—— *The Hanhagot Literature: Its History and Role in the Lives of the Followers of R. Israel Ba'al Shem Tov* [Sifrut hahanhagot: toledoteiha umekomah beḥayei ḥasidei rabi yisra'el ba'al shem tov] (Jerusalem, 1990).

—— 'Hasidism: The Present State of Research and Some Desirable Priorities', *Numen*, 34/1 (1987), 97–108; 34/2 (1987), 179–213.

GRÖZINGER, K. E. (ed.), *Die Geschichten vom Ba'al Schem Tov. Schivche ha-Bescht* (Wiesbaden, 1997).

GULDON, ZENON, and JACEK WIJACZKA, 'The Accusation of Ritual Murder in Poland, 1500–1800', *Polin*, 10 (1997), 99–140.

HALLAMISH, MOSHE, 'The Theological Teaching of R. Shneur Zalman of Lyady' [Mishnato ha'iyunit shel rabi shne'ur zalman miliadi], Ph.D. diss., Hebrew University of Jerusalem, 1976.

HARAN, RAYA, 'A Bundle of Letters and a Letter: On the Methods of Copying Hasidic Letters' (Heb.), *Tsiyon*, 56 (1991), 299–320.

—— 'Inner Ideological Conflicts in Late Eighteenth- and Early Nineteenth-Century Hasidism: The Causes of the Dispute Between R. Abraham of Kalisk and R. Shneur Zalman of Lyady' [Maḥlokot ide'ologiyot penim ḥasidiyot beshilhei hame'ah ha-18 vereshit hame'ah ha-19: hagoremim lamaḥloket bein rabi avra-ham mikalisk levein rabi shne'ur zalman miliadi], Ph.D. diss., Hebrew University of Jerusalem, 1993.

HARAN, RAYA, 'R. Abraham of Kalisk and R. Shneur Zalman of Lyady: A Broken Friendship' (Heb.), in R. Elior and Y. Dan (eds.), *Rivka Schatz-Uffenheimer Memorial Volume* [Kolot rabim: sefer hazikaron lerivkah shats-ufenheimer] (Jerusalem, 1996), 399–428.

—— '*Shivḥei harav*: The Question of Reliability of Hasidic Epistles from the Land of Israel', *Cathedra*, 55 (1990), 22–58.

—— 'The Teachings of R. Abraham of Kalisk: The Elite Path to Divine Attachment' (Heb.), *Tarbits*, 66 (1997), 517–41.

HEILPERIN, ISRAEL (ed.), *The Jewish Community in Poland* [Beit yisra'el bepolin] (Jerusalem, 1954).

—— *Records of the Council of the Four Lands*, i: *1580–1792* [Pinkas va'ad arba' arat-sot: 1580–1792], 2nd edn., ed. I. Bartal (Jerusalem, 1990).

HESCHEL, ABRAHAM JOSHUA, *A Passion for Truth* (New York, 1973).

—— 'R. Pinhas of Korets and the Magid of Mezhirech', in S. Dresner (ed.), *The Circle of the Baal Shem Tov: Studies in Hasidism* (Chicago, 1985).

HILLMAN, DAVID TSEVI, *Letters of the Author of the Tanya and his Generation* [Igerot ba'al hatanya uvenei doro] (Jerusalem, 1953).

HISDAI, YA'AKOV, 'The Beginnings of Hasidim and Mitnagedim in the Light of Homiletical Literature' [Reshit darkam shel haḥasidim vehamitnagedim le'or sifrut haderush] Ph.D. diss., Hebrew University of Jerusalem, 1984.

HUNDERT, GERSHON DAVID (ed.), *Essential Papers on Hasidism: Origins to Present* (New York, 1991).

—— *Jews in Poland–Lithuania in the Eighteenth Century: A Genealogy of Modernity* (Berkeley and Los Angeles, 2004).

—— 'Some Basic Characteristics of the Jewish Experience in Poland', *Polin*, 1 (1986), 28–34.

IDEL, MOSHE, *Hasidism: Between Ecstasy and Magic* (Albany, NY, 1995).

—— *Kabbalah: New Perspectives* (New Haven, 1988).

—— 'Perceptions of Kabbalah in the Second Half of the Eighteenth Century', *Jewish Thought and Philosophy* (1991), 55–114.

ISRAEL, JONATHAN, *European Jewry in the Age of Mercantilism, 1550–1750*, 3rd edn. (London, 1997).

JACOBS, LOUIS, *Hasidic Prayer* (London, 1993).

—— *Seeker of Unity: The Life and Works of Aaron of Starosselye* (London, 1966).

—— (ed.), *Jewish Mystical Testimonies* (New York, 1976).

JAMES, WILLIAM, *The Varieties of Religious Experience: A Study in Human Nature* (Edinburgh, 1902).

KAHANA, ABRAHAM, *Rabbi Israel Ba'al Shem Tov* [Rabi yisra'el ba'al shem tov] (Zhitomir, 1901).

KAHANA, DAVID, *History of the Kabbalists, Shabateans, and Hasidim* [Toledot hamekubalim hashabetayim vehaḥasidim] (Odessa 1913–14; Tel Aviv 1926–7).

KARLINSKY, NAHUM, 'The Beginnings of Orthodox Hasidic Historiography' (Heb.), *Tsiyon*, 63 (1998), 189–212.

—— *Counterhistory: Hasidic Letters from the Land of Israel, Text and Context* [Historiyah shekeneged: igerot ḥasidim me'erets yisra'el, hatekst vehakontekst] (Jerusalem, 1999).

KATZ, JACOB, *Halakhah and Kabbalah* [Halakhah vekabalah] (Jerusalem, 1983).

—— *Tradition and Crisis: Jewish Society at the the End of the Middle Ages*, trans. B. D. Cooperman (New York, 1993).

KATZ-STEIMAN, HAYA, *Early Hasidic Immigration to Eretz-Israel* [Reshitan shel aliyot ḥasidim] (Jerusalem, 1986).

KRASSEN, MILES, *Uniter of Heaven and Earth: Rabbi Meshullam Feibush Heller of Zbaraz and the Rise of Hasidism in Eastern Galicia* (Albany, NY, 1998).

KRAUSHAR, ALEXANDER, *Frank and his Congregation* [Frank ve'adato] (Warsaw, 1895): pt. I of *Frank I frankisci polscy 1726–1816* (Kraków, 1895), trans. into Hebrew by Nahum Sokolow.

LAMM, NORMAN, *The Religious Thought of Hasidism: Text and Commentary* (Hoboken, NJ, 1999).

—— *Torah lishmah: Torah for Torah's Sake in the Works of R. Hayyim of Volozhin and his Contemporaries* (New York, 1989).

LANGER, JIRI [Mordecai Georgo], *Nine Gates to the Chassidic Mysteries*, trans. Stephen Jolly (New York, 1976).

LIEBERMAN, H., 'On Legends and on Truth with Regard to Hasidic Printing' (Heb.), in id. (ed.) *Rachel's Tent* [Ohel raḥel], vol. iii (Brooklyn, 1984), 14–103

LIEBES, ESTHER, 'Love and Creativity in the Thought of R. Barukh of Kossow' [Ahavah veyetsirah behaguto shel r. barukh mikosuv], Ph.D. diss., Hebrew University of Jerusalem, 1997.

LIEBES, YEHUDA, *The Creative Mysteries of the Book of Creation* [Torat hayetsirah shel sefer yetsirah] (Tel Aviv, 2002).

LIEBES, YEHUDA, '*De Natura Dei*: On the Development of the Jewish Myth', in id., *Studies in Jewish Myth and Jewish Messianism*, trans. Batya Stern (Albany, NY, 1993), 1–64.

—— 'How the Zohar Was Written', trans. Stephanie Nakache, in id., *Studies in the Zohar* (Albany, NY, 1993), 85–138.

—— 'The Messiah of the Zohar: On R. Simeon bar Yohai as a Messianic Figure', trans. Arnold Schwarz, in id., *Studies in the Zohar* (Albany, NY, 1993), 1–84.

—— 'New Material on R. Israel Ba'al Shem Tov and Shabetai Tsevi' (Heb.), in id., *The Secret of Shabatean Faith*, 262–5.

—— *The Secret of Shabatean Faith: Collected Essays* [Sod ha'emunah hashabeta'it] (Jerusalem, 1995).

—— 'Zohar and Eros' (Heb.), *Alpayim*, 9 (1994), 67–119.

LIVER, AMIRAH, 'Paradoxical Elements in the Writings of R. Zadok Hakohen of Lublin' [Yesodot paradocsaliyim bekitvei rav tsadok milublin], MA thesis, Hebrew University of Jerusalem, 1993.

LOEWENTHAL, NAFTALI, *Communicating the Infinite: The Emergence of the Habad School* (Chicago, 1990).

McGINN, BERNARD, *The Foundations of Mysticism: Origins to the Fifth Century* (New York, 1991).

—— 'Selective Affinities: Reflections on Jewish and Christian Mystical Exegesis', in Rachel Elior and Peter Schäfer (eds.), *Creation and Re-creation in Jewish Thought: Festschrift in Honor of Joseph Dan on the Occasion of his Seventieth Birthday* (Tübingen, 2005), 85–102.

MAGID, SHAUL, *God's Voice from the Void: Old and New Essays on Rabbi Nahman of Bratslav* (New York, 2001).

—— *Hasidism on the Margin: Reconciliation, Antinomianism, and Messianism in Izbica/Radzin Hasidism* (Madison, Wis., 2003).

MAHLER, RAPHAEL, *Hasidism and the Jewish Enlightenment: Their Confrontation in Galicia and Poland in the First Half of the Nineteenth Century* (New York and Philadelphia, 1985).

MAIMON, SOLOMON, *Lebensgeschichte* [Autobiography], ed. R. P. Moritz, 2 vols. (Berlin, 1792–3); trans. J. Clark-Marray, introd. Michael Shapiro (Oxford, 1954; repr. Urbana, Ill, 2001).

—— 'On a Secret Society', in Gershon Hundert (ed.), *Essential Papers on Hasidism: Origins to Present* (New York, 1991), 11–24.

MAREK, PESACH, 'Krizis yevreiskovo samoupravliennie i khasidism', *Yevreiskaya starina*, 12 (1928), 263–303.

MARGOLIN, RON, *The Human Temple: Religious Interiorization and the Structuring of Inner Life in Early Hasidism* [Mikdash adam: hahafnamah hadatit ve'itsuv ḥayei hadat hapenimit bereshit haḥasidut] (Jerusalem, 2005).

MARK, TZVI, *Mystics and Madmen in the Works of Rabbi Nahman of Bratslav* [Mistikah veshigaon beyetsirot rabi naḥman mibratslav] (Tel Aviv, 2004).

MONDSHINE, YEHOSHUA, 'An Early Version of the Besht's Epistle on his Heavenly Ascent' [Nosaḥ kadum shel igeret aliyat haneshamah lehabesht], appendix 1 to *Shivḥei habesht*, ed. Y. Mondshine (Jerusalem, 1982), 229–37.

—— 'The Two Incarcerations of the Old Rebbe According to New Documents' [Shenei ma'asarav shel rabeinu hazaken le'or te'udot ḥadashot], *Kerem ḥabad*, 4/1 (1992), 17–108.

—— 'Three Letters' [Sheloshah mikhtavim], *Kerem ḥabad*, 4/1 (1992), 109–13.

NADLER, ALLAN, *The Faith of the Mithnagdim: Rabbinic Responses to Hasidic Rapture* (Baltimore, 1997).

NIGAL, GEDALIAH, *The Hasidic Narrative: History and Topics* [Hasiporet haḥasidit: toledoteiha umekoroteiha] (Jerusalem, 1981).

—— *Leader and Congregation* [Manhig ve'edah] (Jerusalem, 1962).

—— 'On the Book *Keter shem tov* and its Sources' (Heb.), *Sinai*, 79 (1976), 132–46.

—— *Teachings of R. Jacob Joseph of Polonnoye* [Torat ba'al hatoledot] (Jerusalem, 1974).

—— (ed.), *Tales of Holy Men* [Sipurei kedoshim] (Jerusalem, 1977).

ORON, MICHAL, 'The Book *Gaḥalei esh*: A Document for the Struggle against Shabateanism' [Sefer 'Gaḥalei esh': te'udah letoledot hama'avak beshabeta'ut], in Rachel Elior (ed.), *The Dream and its Interpretation: The Shabatean Movement and its Aftermath—Messianism, Shabateanism, and Frankism* [Haḥalom veshivro: hatenuah hashabeta'it usheluḥoteiha—meshiḥiyut, shabeta'ut, ufrankism] (Jerusalem, 2001), i. 73–92.

—— and HENYA HEIDENBERG, *From the Mystical World of R. Nahman of Bratslav* [Me'olamo hamisti shel rabi naḥman mibratslav] (Tel Aviv, 1986).

ORSHANSKI, ILYA, *Yevrei u Rossii: Russko zakonodatel'stvo o evreiakh* (St Petersburg, 1877).

PECHTER, MORDECHAI, 'The Concept of *Devekut* and its Depiction in the Homiletical and Hortatory Literature of the Safed Sages in the Sixteenth Century' (Heb.), *Jerusalem Studies in Jewish Thought*, 3 (1982), 51–121.

PEDAYAH, HAVIVA, 'On the Evolution of the Social, Religious, Economic Model in Hasidism: The Redemption, the Association, and the Pilgrimage' (Heb.), in M. Ben-Sasson (ed.), *Religion and Economics: Mutual Relations. Festschrift for*

Jacob Katz's Ninetieth Birthday [Dat vekalkalah: yahasei gomelin. Shai leya'akov kats bimelot lo tishe'im shanah] (Jerusalem, 1995), 311–73.

PERL, JOSEPH, *Ueber das Wesen der Sekte Chassidim* (1815), ed. A. Rubinstein (Jerusalem, 1977).

PERLMUTTER, MOSHE ARYEH, *Jonathan Eybeschuetz and his Relation to Shabateanism* [Yehonatan eibeshuts veyahaso lashabeta'ut] (Jerusalem, 1947).

PIEKARZ, MENDEL, *Between Ideology and Reality: Humility, Negation, Annihilation of Being, and Attachment in Early Hasidic Thought* [Bein ideologiyah lemetsiyut: anavah, ayin, bitul mimetsiyut, udevekut bemahashavtam shel roshei hahasidut] (Jerusalem, 1994).

—— *Bratslav Hasidism* [Hasidut bratslav] (Jerusalem, 1972).

—— 'Hasidism as a Socio-Religious Movement on the Evidence of *Devekut*', in A. Rapoport-Albert (ed.), *Hasidism Reappraised* (London, 1996), pp. 225–48.

—— *Ideological Trends in Hasidism in Poland during the Interwar Period and the Holocaust* [Hasidut polin: megamot ra'ayoniyot bein shetei hamilhamot ubegezerot 1940–45 (hasho'ah)] (Jerusalem, 1990).

—— *The Rise of Hasidism: Intellectual Trends in the Homiletical and Hortatory Literature* [Biyemei tsemihat hahasidut: megamot ra'ayoniyot besifrei derush umusar] (Jerusalem, 1978).

RABINOWITZ, TSEVI MEIR, *Between Przysucha and Lublin: Men and Approaches in Polish Hasidism* [Bein peshiskhah lelublin: ishim veshitot behasidut polin] (Jerusalem, 1997).

RABINOWITZ, ZE'EV, *Lithuanian Hasidism from its Beginnings to the Present Day*, trans. M. B. Dagut, foreword by Simon Dubnow (London, 1970).

RAPHAEL, YITZHAK, 'The Harson Geniza' (Heb.), *Sinai*, 81 (1977), 129–50.

RAPOPORT-ALBERT, ADA, 'God and the Zaddik as the Two Focal Points of Hasidic Worship', *History of Religion*, 18 (1979), 225–96.

—— 'Hagiography with Footnotes: Edifying Tales and the Writing of History in Hasidism', *Essays in Jewish Historiography, History and Theory*, 27 (1988), 119–59.

—— 'Hasidism after 1772: Structural Continuity and Change', in ead. (ed.), *Hasidism Reappraised* (London, 1996), 76–140.

—— (ed.), *Hasidism Reappraised* (London, 1996).

REINER, ELCHANAN, '*Shivhei habesht*: Transmission, Editing, Printing', in *Proceedings of the Eleventh World Congress for Jewish Studies* (Jerusalem, 1994), vol. ii, sect. 3, pp. 145–52.

—— 'Wealth, Social Status, and Torah Study: The *Kloyz* in Eastern European Jewish Society in the Seventeenth to Eighteenth Centuries' (Heb.), *Tsiyon*, 58 (1993), 286–328.

ROSMAN, MOSHE, *The Founder of Hasidism: A Quest for the Historical Ba'al Shem Tov* (Berkeley, 1996).

—— 'In Praise of the Baal Shem Tov: A User's Guide to the Editions of *Shivḥei habesht*', *Polin*, 10 (1997), 183–99.

—— 'Medzibhoz and R. Israel Ba'al Shem Tov' (Heb.), *Tsiyon*, 52 (1987), 177–89.

ROSS, TAMAR, 'Rav Hayim of Volozhin and Rav Shneur Zalman of Lyady: Two Interpretations of the Doctrine of *Tsimtsum*' (Heb.), *Jerusalem Studies in Jewish Thought*, 1/2 (1982), 158–69.

SCHACTER, JACOB JOSEPH, 'Motivations for Radical Anti-Shabateanism', in Rachel Elior (ed.), *The Dream and its Interpretation: The Shabatean Movement and its Aftermath—Messianism, Shabateanism, and Frankism* [Haḥalom veshivro: hatenuah hashabeta'it usheluḥoteiha—meshiḥiyut, shabeta'ut, ufrankism], 2 vols. (Jerusalem, 2001), ii. 31*–50* [English section].

—— 'Rabbi Jacob Emden: Life and Major Works', Ph.D. diss., Harvard University, Cambridge, Mass., 1998.

SCHÄFER, P. (ed.), *Synopse zur Hekhalot Literatur* (Tübingen, 1981).

SCHATZ-UFFENHEIMER, RIVKA, 'Anti-Spiritualism in Hasidism: Studies in the Doctrine of R. Shneur Zalman of Lyady' (Heb.), *Molad*, 20 (1962), 513–28.

—— *Hasidism as Mysticism: Quietistic Elements in Eighteenth-Century Hasidic Thought*, trans. Jonathan Chipman (Princeton, NJ, 1993).

—— 'Man's Relation to God and World in Buber's Rendering of the Hasidic Teaching', in P. A. Schilpp and M. Friedman (eds.), *The Philosophy of Martin Buber* (La Salle, Ill., 1967), 275–302.

—— 'On the Nature of the Tsadik in Hasidism: Studies in R. Elimelekh of Lyzhansk's Doctrine of the *Tsadik*' (Heb.), *Molad*, 18 (1960), 365–78.

—— 'Spiritual Autonomy and the Torah of Moses: Studies in the Teaching of Rabbi Mordechai Joseph of Izbica' (Heb.), *Molad*, 21 (1963–4), 554–61.

SCHECHTER, SOLOMON, *Studies in Judaism: Essays on Persons, Concepts and Movements of Thought in Jewish Tradition*, 3 vols. (Philadelphia, 1896–1924).

—— 'Safed in the Sixteenth Century', in id., *Studies in Judaism*, 2nd series (Philadelphia, 1908).

SCHLEICHER, MARIANNE, 'A Theology of Redemption: An Analysis of the Thirteen Tales in R. Nahman of Bratslav's *Sippurey Ma'asiyot*', Ph.D. diss., Arhus University, Denmark, 2002.

SCHOLEM, GERSHOM, 'Barukhyah, Head of the Shabateans in Salonika' [Barukhyah rosh hashabeta'im besaloniki], in Y. Liebes (ed.), *Gershom Scholem Researches in Sabbateanism* [Meḥkarei shabeta'ut] (Tel Aviv, 1991), 321–90.

—— 'Devekut or Communion with God', in id., *The Messianic Idea in Judaism*, 228–50; repr. in G. D. Hundert (ed.), *Essential Papers on Hasidism: Origins to Present* (New York, 1991), 275–98.

—— *Explications and Implications: Writings on Jewish Heritage and Renaissance* [Devarim bego], ed. A. Shapira (Tel Aviv, 1975).

—— 'The Historical Image of R. Israel Ba'al Shem Tov' (Heb.), in id., *Explications and Implications*, 287–324.

—— *Kabbalah* (Jerusalem, 1974).

—— *The Kabbalah of Sefer hatemunah and Abraham Abulafia* [Hakabalah shel sefer hatemunah veshel avraham abulafia], ed. Joseph ben Shlomo (Jerusalem, 1965).

—— *Major Trends in Jewish Mysticism*, trans. George Lichtheim (New York, 1941).

—— 'Martin Buber's Interpretation of Hasidism', *Commentary*, 22 (1961), 305–16.

—— 'The Meaning of the Torah in Jewish Mysticism', in id., *On the Kabbalah and its Symbolism*, 32–86.

—— *The Messianic Idea in Judaism, and Other Essays on Jewish Spirituality* (New York, 1971).

—— *On the Kabbalah and its Symbolism*, trans. Ralph Mannheim (New York, 1965).

—— *Origins of the Kabbalah*, ed. R. J. Zevi Werblowsky, trans. Alan Arkush (Princeton, NJ, 1987).

—— 'Redemption through Sin', in id., *The Messianic Idea in Judaism*, 78–141.

—— 'Religious Authority and Mysticism', in id., *On the Kabbalah and its Symbolism*, 5–31.

—— 'The Shabatean Movement in Poland' (Heb.), in id., *Studies and Sources on the History of Shabateanism*, 68–140; first pub. in I. Heilperin (ed.), *The Jewish Community in Poland* [Beit yisra'el bepolin] (Jerusalem, 1954), 36–76.

—— *Sabbatai Ṣevi: The Mystical Messiah 1626–1676*, trans. R. J. Z. Werblowsky (Princeton, NJ, 1973).

—— *Studies in Shabateanism* [Meḥkerei shabeta'ut], ed. Y. Liebes (Tel Aviv, 1991).

—— *Studies and Sources on the History of Shabateanism and its Vicissitudes* [Meḥkarim umekorot letoledot hashabeta'ut vegilguleiha] (Jerusalem, 1974).

—— 'Tradition and New Creation in the Ritual of the Kabbalists', in id., *On the Kabbalah and its Symbolism*, 118–57.

—— 'The Tsaddik: The Righteous One', in id., *On the Mystical Shape of the Godhead: Basic Concepts in the Kabbalah*, trans. J. Neugroschel and J. Chipman (New York, 1991), 88–139.

—— 'Two Testimonies about Hasidic Groups and R. Israel Ba'al Shem Tov' (Heb.), *Tarbits*, 20 (1949), 228–41.

SCHWEID, ELIEZER, *Between Destruction and Salvation: Contemporaneous Reaction of Haredi Thought to the Holocaust* [Bein ḥurban leyeshuah: teguvot shel hagut ḥaredit lasho'ah bizemanah] (Tel Aviv, 1994).

SHAHAR, YESHAYAHU, *Criticism of Society and Leadership in the Musar and Drush Literature in Eighteenth-Century Poland* [Bikoret haḥevrah vehanhagat hatsibur besifrut hamusar vehaderush bepolin bame'ah ha-18] (Jerusalem, 1992).

SHILS, EDWARD, 'Charisma, Order and Status', *American Sociological Review*, 30 (1965), 199–213.

—— *The Constitution of Society* (Chicago, 1982).

SHMERUK, CHONE, 'The Book *Divrei ha'adon*: Its Variations from Yiddish to Polish' (Heb.), *Gal-Ed*, 14 (1995), 23–36.

—— *Essays on the History of Yiddish Literature* [Sifrut yidish: perakim letoledoteiha] (Tel Aviv, 1978).

—— 'Hasidism, the *Arendars*, and Farm Tenancy' (Heb.), *Tsiyon*, 35 (1970), 182–92.

—— 'Hasidism and the Kehilla', in Antony Polonsky et al. (eds.), *The Jews in Old Poland, 1000–1795* (London, 1993), 186–95.

—— 'The Social Significance of Hasidic Ritual Slaughter' (Heb.), *Tsiyon*, 20 (1955), 47–72.

SHOCHET, IMMANUEL, 'On Joy in Hasidism' (Heb.), *Tsiyon*, 16 (1951), 30–43.

SOLOVEITCHIK, HAYIM, 'Religious Law and Change: The Medieval Ashkenazic Example', *AJS Review*, 12 (1987), 205–21.

STACE, W. T., *Mysticism and Philosophy* (London, 1960).

TEITELBAUM, MORDECHAI, *The Rabbi of Lyady and the Habad Sect* [Harav miliadi umifleget ḥabad] (Warsaw, 1909).

TELLER, ADAM, 'Economic Activity of Polish Jewry from the Second Half of the Seventeenth Century to the Eighteenth Century' (Heb.), in *Kiyum vashever* (Jerusalem, 1997), 209–24.

—— 'The Shtetl as an Arena for Polish–Jewish Integration in the Eighteenth Century', *Polin*, 17 (2004), 24–40.

TETER, MAGDALENA, 'Jewish Conversions to Catholicism in the Polish–Lithuanian Commonwealth of the Seventeenth and Eighteenth Centuries', *Jewish History*, 17 (2003), 257–83.

TISHBY, ISAIAH, *The Doctrine of Evil and the Husks in Lurianic Kabbalah* [Torat hara vehakelipah bekabalat ha'ari] (Jerusalem, 1942; repr. 1984).

—— *Investigations into Kabbalah and its Offshoots: Studies and Sources* [Ḥikrei kabalah usheluḥoteiha: meḥkarim umekorot], 3 vols. (Jerusalem, 1982–93).

—— 'The Messianic Idea and Messianic Trends in the Rise of Hasidism' (Heb.), *Tsiyon*, 32 (1967), 1–45.

—— *The Wisdom of the Zohar: An Anthology of Texts*, trans. D. Goldstein, 3 vols. (Oxford, 1989).

TISHBY, ISAIAH, and YOSEF DAN, 'Hasidism' (Heb.), *Encyclopaedia Hebraica*, xvii (1965), 769–822.

TRUNK, YEHIEL YESHAIAH, *Poland: Memories and Pictures*, trans. E. Fleischer (Merhaviah, 1962).

TUCKER, R. C., 'The Theory of Charismatic Leadership', *Daedalus*, 97 (1968), 731–56.

URBAN, MARTINA, *Aesthetics of Renewal: Martin Buber's Representation of Hasidism at Kulturkritik* (Chicago, forthcoming).

—— 'The Hermeneutics of Renewal: A Study of the Hasidic Anthologies of Martin Buber, "Die Geschiten des Rabbi Nachman" (1906) and "Die Legende des Baalschem" (1908)', Ph.D. diss., Hebrew University of Jerusalem, 2003.

VISHNITZER, MARK (ed. and trans.), *The Memories of Ber of Bolechow* (London, 1922; repr. New York, 1973).

WEBER, MAX, *On Charisma and Institution Building: Selected Papers*, ed. S. N. Eisenstadt (Chicago, 1968).

—— *The Sociology of Religion*, trans. Ephraim Fischof (Boston, 1964).

—— *The Theory of Social and Economic Organization*, trans. A. M. Henderson and T. Parsons (New York, 1947).

WEINRYB, BERNARD, *The Jews of Poland: A Social and Economic History of the Jewish Community in Poland from 1100 to 1800* (Philadelphia, 1982).

WEISS, JOSEPH, 'A Circle of Pneumatics in Pre-Hasidism', *Journal of Jewish Studies*, 8 (1957), repr. in id., *Studies in East European Jewish Mysticism*, 27–42.

—— 'A Late Jewish Utopia of Religious Freedom', in id., *Studies in East European Jewish Mysticism*, 209–48.

—— 'Some Notes on the Social Background of Early Hasidism', in id., *Studies in East European Jewish Mysticism*, 3–26.

—— *Studies in Bratslav Hasidism* [Meḥkarim baḥasidut bratslav], ed. M. Piekarz (Jerusalem, 1975).

—— *Studies in East European Jewish Mysticism and Hasidism*, ed. David Goldstein (Oxford, 1985); pbk. edn., introd. Joseph Dan (London, 1997).

WERBLOWSKY, RAFAEL JEHUDA ZWI, *Joseph Karo: Lawyer and Mystic* (London, 1962).

WERTHEIM, AARON, *Laws and Customs in Hasidism*, trans. Shmuel Himelstein (1960; English edn. Hoboken, NJ, 1992).

—— 'Traditions and Customs in Hasidism', in G. D. Hundert (ed.), *Essential Papers on Hasidism: Origins to Present* (New York, 1991), 363–98.

WHITE, HAYDEN, *The Content of the Form: Narrative Discourse and Historical Representation* (Baltimore, 1987), 26–57.

WILENSKY, MORDECAI L., 'Hasidic–Mitnaggedic Polemics in the Jewish Communities of Eastern Europe: The Hostile Phase', in G. D. Hundert (ed.), *Essential Papers on Hasidism: Origins to Present* (New York, 1991), 244–71.

—— *Hasidic Settlement in Tiberias until the Death of R. Abraham of Kalisk, 1810* [Hayishuv haḥasidi biteveriyah ad petirato shel rabi avraham mikalisk, 5570] (Jerusalem, 1988).

—— *Hasidim and Mitnagedim: On the History of their Polemics, 1772–1815* [Ḥasidim umitnagedim: letoledot hapulmus shebeineihem bashanim 5532–5575], 2 vols. (Jerusalem, 1970; 2nd edn. Jerusalem, 1990).

—— 'The Polemic of Rabbi David of Makow against Hasidism', *Proceedings of the American Academy of Jewish Research*, 25 (1956), 137–56.

WILLNER, ANN RUTH, *The Spellbinders: Charismatic Political Leadership* (New Haven, 1984).

WINOGRAD, ISAIAH, *Thesaurus of the Hebrew Book: A List of Books Printed in Hebrew Letters from the Beginning of Hebrew Printing in 1469 to 1863* [Otsar hasefer ha'ivri: reshimat hasefarim shenidpesu beot ivrit mereshit hadefus ha'ivri beshenat 1469 ad shenat 1863] (Jerusalem, 1993–5).

WODZIŃSKI, MARCIN, *Haskalah and Hasidism in the Kingdom of Poland: A History of Conflict* (Oxford, 2005).

ZAK, BERAKHA, *Moses Cordovero's Gates of Kabbalah* [Besha'arei hakabalah shel mosheh kordovero] (Jerusalem, 1995).

ZEITLIN, HILLEL, *In the Orchard of Hasidism and Kabbalah* [Befardes haḥasidut vehakabalah] (Tel Aviv, 1976; 2nd edn. 1997).

ZINBERG, ISRAEL, *A History of Jewish Literature: Hasidism and Enlightenment 1780–1820*, trans. B. Martin (Cincinnati, 1976).

ZWEIFEL, ELIEZER TSEVI, *Peace on Israel* [Shalom al yisra'el], 4 vols. (Zhitomir 1868–73; repr. Jerusalem, 1976).

Index of Biblical References

Subject Index

Printed and bound by CPI Group (UK) Ltd, Croydon, CR0 4YY

13/04/2025

14656579-0002